MEMOIRS OF PRINCE VON BÜLOW

The World War and Germany's Collapse

1909-1919

MEMOIRS OF PRINCE VON BÜLOW

PRINCE BERNHARD VON BÜLOW

MEMOIRS OF
PRINCE
VON BÜLOW

·III·

The World War and Germany's
Collapse

1909–1919

Translated from the German by
GEOFFREY DUNLOP

ILLUSTRATED

BOSTON   1932
LITTLE, BROWN, AND COMPANY

CONTENTS

CHAPTER VI

CHAPTER VII

CHAPTER VIII

CHAPTER IX

CHAPTER XIV

CHAPTER XV

CHAPTER XVI

CHAPTER XVII

ILLUSTRATIONS

MEMOIRS OF PRINCE VON BÜLOW

The World War and Germany's Collapse

1909–1919

CHAPTER I

My Journey from Berlin to Hamburg (July 17, 1909) — Old Memories and Fresh Impressions — In Hamburg — The Hotel Atlantic — Herr Pfordte — Ballin's Plan for a Meeting between the Admirals Defeated by Bethmann's Opposition — By Steamer from Hamburg to Cuxhaven; Thence to Norderney — The Minister, Doctor Rosen — The Friendly Demonstrations on My Retirement — I Answer Letters and Addresses.[1]

I HAD said my farewells to the capital and now sat opposite my wife in the saloon car, transformed by the kindness of many friends into a bower of roses, carnations, and orchids, in her honour. No other city, in the days before 1914, was so lavish with her flowers as Berlin. The train bore us from Berlin to Hamburg.

My first emotion was one of thankfulness to God who, throughout an eventful, sometimes stormy decade, had permitted me to shield our land from harm, extend and consolidate her power, promote her well-being, and yet preserve in honour that peace of which, above all, we stood in need. I thanked my dear wife for her devotion. It had kept me fit to do my duty amid the nerve-racking activities of twelve strenuous years. I had often travelled on this line between Berlin and Hamburg, to Kiel, to make the Emperor a report, or, in his company, do honour to the royal sport of yachting, on board his fast yacht *The Meteor*, or the graceful *Iduna* of the Empress. Now, a retired Imperial Chancellor, retracing the same well-known route, memories of my boyhood came to life in me. I thought of my kind father who, when we travelled, had let slip no chance of adding to my knowledge of a countryside, or of extending my historical horizon. We passed through Spandau, the ancient residence of the first Hohenzollern electors, where, on November 1, 1539, Joachim II had taken the Sacrament *sub utraque*, and paved the way for the new doctrine through the whole March of Branden-

[1] These letters and addresses are given in the appendix to this volume.

burg by his act. There too stands the Juliusturm. It once concealed that Prussian "war treasure" which for so long held the popular fancy. But in the fiscal reforms that caused my downfall, the
sums in debate already far exceeded this "treasure", and the time
was yet to come when milliards far surpassing the millions of which
so much was made in those days were to be wrung from our
exhausted, martyred people. Kremmen, Fehrbellin, rose along the
sky line : Kremmen, where the men of the March did battle with
the men of Pomerania ; they who, in after years, were to fight so
stoutly side by side. Fehrbellin, the first great victory in the heroic
annals of Prussian Brandenburg. The spirit of our greatest Prussian poet, Heinrich von Kleist, hovers above this glorious country-
side. Wilsnack recalled to mind a deed of violence perpetrated by
one of my own ancestors. In 1383 the gallant knight, Hennecke
von Bülow, a valiant, nicknamed *"Grosse Tête"*, having retaken the
free cities Plau, Dömnitz, and Neustadt, set fire in barbarous fashion
to Wilsnack, in the course of a raid on the Bishop of Havel-
berg. Nor would he even spare the church in which the Blessed
Sacrament was exposed. The Host had remained unconsumed. It
bled, and the "Holy Blood of Wilsnack" became a famous place of
pilgrimage. "By the Holy Blood of Wilsnack" was a current form
of oath in the Middle Ages. The Bülows paid, by excommunica-
tion for three years, for the crime of this unworthy son. Since, in
the centuries leading up to the Reformation, my family gave five
exemplary bishops to the Church, four at Schwerin and one at Lebus,
I trust that this lapse of a single member has not left us with an
indelible stigma. And the criminal did not long survive his crime.
Our family chronicle relates how, shortly after the sack of Wilsnack,
"Grosse Tête" was borne away to hell, at the age of scarce thirty
years.

We passed the Düssin estate, the property, for many generations,
of my ancestors in the direct line. "Of nearly ninety estates," I
said to myself, "which the family has owned since the fourteenth
century in Mecklenburg, scarcely twenty remain in our possession.
How will it be a hundred years from now? And especially if the
central government is clumsy and short-sighted in its policy."

The train pulled up at Ludwigslust, which I had often visited as a boy, to pay my respects to many worthy uncles and aunts. I fancied myself back in the *Biedermeierzeit*, the age of Frederick William III, with its scent of lavender, its gold snuffboxes. How respectfully, in this city of the arts which a royal caprice called into being, I had admired the gilt drawing-rooms of the Schloss; the gardens, with their long avenues, the waterfall, with its broad double cascades. I could still distinctly remember the court chapel, together with its singular inscription: "*Magnus Dux Megapo-litanus, Magnus Peccator Magno Redemptori*", but could not recollect the name of the Grand Duke and great sinner.

The mausoleum at Friedrichsruh! On the many journeys I have taken from Berlin to Hamburg, I never saw it without being moved to serious thought. Nor had it ever stirred me more than on this 17th of July, 1909, on my way from office into retirement.

The unrest of my last exciting weeks of chancellorship had left me no time for a real talk with my wife. I could explain to her, now, my deeper reasons for resigning. No doubt my fiscal reforms would have gone through in the shape in which I first suggested them had the Emperor's latent hostility not encouraged the Centre to oppose me, the Conservatives to leave me in the lurch. William II, in contrast to his father and grandfather, had paid more heed to wounded vanity than to reasons of State, of political logic and prudence. My wife had known the Emperor as a boy. He had always shown himself most gracious to her and she still remained very attached to him. She encouraged my resolve to do nothing that could in any way prejudice the Crown. This decision was made easier by the fact that petty, selfish, and clumsy Conservative tactics had been, in no small measure, responsible for the non-acceptance of the Death Duties, the premature split in the *bloc* — and my resignation. My wife agreed that much might not have happened as it did had certain of our old friends been spared to stand at my side in the last, critical winter in office . . . friends who could understand me, who remained courageous and steadfast but who, meanwhile, had been called away by death. With Richthofen as Foreign State Secretary, so frivolous and slipshod a handling of the *Daily Telegraph* manuscript as Schön, Müller, and Klehmet had allowed themselves would not have been a possibility. Arenberg, with his energy and experience, could have made the Centre adopt a more reasonable attitude and would certainly have managed to prevent the intrigues of an Erzberger. Had Count Limburg-Stirum led the Conservatives he would never have overshot the mark, like Heydebrand, the narrow-minded dwarf, and his insignificant creature Westarp. Old Wilhelm von Kardorff, for many years in the confidence of the Bismarcks, a man of fire and of wide outlook, would have given me better support, as leader of the Empire Party, than his successor, the timid and muddle-headed Hatzfeldt-Trachenberg.

The towers of Hamburg came into view; the city with the distant view of the sea. At the station Ballin and Felix von Eckardt were awaiting us; a great crowd had gathered to give us welcome. We went, with these two friends, to the Hotel Atlantic, as usual. Little Pfordte received us at the door. He was one of the curiosities of Hamburg, as the mouse in the Marienkirche is a curiosity of Lübeck. Just as every apprentice who went to Lübeck was supposed to have had a look at the mouse, whoever, in the good old days, visited Hamburg, was told to make the acquaintance of Pfordte since, in this most gastronomic of German cities, he supremely represented the art to which Brillat-Savarin devotes his "Physiologie du Goût", and Karl Friedrich von Rumohr his "Spirit of the Culinary Muse." Of Pfordte, as of the dwarf Perkeo on the Heidelberg cask, in Scheffel's song, it could be said that, though great in wit he was small in inches. He had come as a penniless boy from Wittenberge, to finish his days in Hamburg as a high authority in his trade. He served us with a choice but brief repast which did full justice to his saying that "in Hamburg we dine, whereas, in other towns they eat." To clear myself of all suspicion of bragging, I must add that I lay no claim to being a gourmet. I eat, as a rule, whatever is set before me without really noticing it much. This, of course, Herr Pfordte could only deplore, though he kindly assured me that even my gastronomic deficiencies did not in the least detract from his deep admiration of my policy.

With my Hamburg friends I sat on until well after midnight, exchanging impressions, thoughts, and also, alas, anxieties. Ballin regretted most of all that I had been prevented from reaching an understanding, on the *tempo* of naval construction, with England. His resourceful brain was already at work on a new project. A meeting must be arranged during the summer in Switzerland — at Mürren or Engelberg — between the heads of the German and British navies, Tirpitz and Lord Fisher, at which they could strive for the friendly solution of their difficulties. Ballin, rightly I thought, proceeded on the assumption that Tirpitz, whose constant itch it was to dabble in politics, though not always with the happiest results, would be likely to show a more conciliatory spirit if he were given sole power to negotiate and not forced to confine himself to criticism. Ballin supposed that diplomatic laurels would also not displease the English admiral. In the summer of 1909 he did, in fact, use all his influence to win over the two sovereigns to his project. Edward VII approved his suggestions and promised to persuade Lord Fisher in this sense. When, on August 3, 1909, William II returned from his trip to the North, Ballin went to meet him at Swinemünde. The Emperor, whom Ballin could influence, and who always welcomed a fresh idea, especially if he considered it original, consented at once, and summoned Bethmann-Hollweg, who had also come to Swinemünde to meet him. But when Ballin developed his suggestion in the presence of the new Imperial Chancellor, the latter pulled a very long face, and answered sulkily, "I respectfully protest against this suggestion. I had considered as my particular province and the principal object of all my efforts, the establishment of confidential and really friendly relations with England. In Your Majesty's absence I have been studying the matter *au fond*, with all the documents. It is my especial field and I cannot allow it to be encroached upon." "Bethmann," concluded Ballin, in the account he gave me of the incident, when we met not long afterwards, "looked so ill-humoured that the Emperor, who cannot bear to have discontented faces about him, let the whole matter drop and said, when the Chancellor left, 'You saw how vexed he was. After all, I can't begin the Bethmann-Hollweg epoch with a row, now that the Bülow epoch has just ended with one.'"

Next morning we descended the Elbe on the splendid *Victoria-Louise*, one of the largest Hamburg-America liners. The excellent Ballin came with us as far as Cuxhaven. Via Altona we passed the Donnersburg, where the Imperial couple had stayed for the manœuvres of 1904, there to receive the news of the Crown Prince's betrothal; then on, past Oevelgönne, where old sea captains, sitting before their quaint little houses, spy out upon each passing ship, scour her from end to end through their telescopes, and sadly evoke sea memories. We passed the country house in which I was born, at Flottbek. It stands on the Flottbek "Chaussée" which, with reason, Detlev von Liliencron once called the most beautiful road in Germany. This poet, our neighbour and friend, had died, to our deep regret, at about the time of my resignation. The "Chaussée" was thronged with people, who greeted us with "Hoch" and "Hurrah." The finely pointed spire of the church of Nienstedten came into view — the church in which I was baptized, by a worthy old pastor of seventy, long since gone to his reward. He rests close by the gates of the churchyard in which I too shall sleep my last sleep. Baptizer and baptized will arise and stand face to face on the last great day of resurrection. We passed the picturesque old houses which jut out over the river at Blankenese, sometimes compared to Sorrento for its beauty and, after its fashion, no whit less beautiful in my eyes. Schulau, Wedel, Glückstadt drifted by; the Elbe grew ever broader, ever mightier. To the right Brunsbüttel, from which, ten years before, I had set out with the Imperial couple for England: to the left, Cuxhaven, and then, at last, the sea — *thalassa* — the eternal, which Xenophon's hoplites saluted on their return from the Euphrates, with shouts of triumph, from Paphlagonian heights; the sea which, in the words of Gerhart Hauptmann, the one true German poet of to-day, has tumbled for countless ages its blind water masses, sightless as the never-ending centuries.

At Cuxhaven we changed our boat. A small steamer took us on to Norderney. A slim volume, presented to me not long before by Rosen, the Councillor of Legation, had served as my reading on the journey: "The Maxims of Omar Kháyyám", that tent-maker, who made it his boast that he had woven the tents of philosophy rather than the homes of shepherd nomads. He lived at the dawn of the twelfth century, at Nishapur, in northeast Persia. Rosen, his German translator, had been one of my best colleagues at the Foreign Office. He was born in Jerusalem, where his father had been consul in Bismarck's time. From his boyhood up he had had a thorough knowledge of the East, had taught Persian and Hindustani in the University School of Oriental Languages in Berlin, and served as consul in Beyruth, Bagdad, and Teheran. For some years he had lived with Lord Dufferin, the English Ambassador at St. Petersburg, Constantinople, Rome, and Paris, Governor-general of Canada, and subsequent Viceroy of India. Rosen had accompanied him to India where, in contact with this distinguished statesman, he could extend and sharpen his political sense, and learn the art of ruling men. He had rendered me many services during my chancellorship: first, in 1905, as the head of a mission in Abyssinia, where he concluded a commercial treaty which proved of the greatest advantage to Germany; then in Paris, on the eve of the Algeciras conference, as negotiator with Rouvier, and finally as Minister at Tangier. He had translated the tent-maker's maxims in the saddle, as he journeyed here and there, up and down the caravan tracks of Persia. I may add that, after my time, he did further excellent service as a Minister, in Bucharest, Lisbon, and at the Hague. At Bucharest he enjoyed the particular favour of King Carol, who was delighted with his perfect manners, his wide culture, and intelligence. At Lisbon, that English annex, where he found himself *dépaysé* in 1914, he obtained all that was possible by temporizing. As Minister at the Hague he witnessed the Imperial flight to Holland and, in one of the most difficult situations for any Imperial representative, gave proof of great character and tact. His perfect French and equally perfect English, no less than his natural distinction and thorough knowledge of the world, made of him an excellent Foreign Minister. He obtained this post in the May of 1921, in the Wirth Cabinet, but could not long agree with his Chancellor. Here are the first quatrains found in Omar Kháyyám, which I had taken to read on the journey:

Und lebtest du dreihundert Jahr und drüber noch hinaus,
Aus dieser Karawanserei musst du einst doch hinaus.
Ob du ein stolzer König warst oder ob bettelarm
Das kommt an jenem letzten Tag aufs selbe doch hinaus.

Nimm an, dein Leben sei ganz nach Wunsch gewesen — was dann?
Und wenn das Lebensbuch nun ausgelesen — was dann?
Nimm an, du lebtest in Freuden hundert Jahr —
Nimm meinethalb an, es seien zweihundert gewesen — was dann? [1]

It was the same eternal truth to which Bismarck, as Minister to the Frankfurt Diet, gives another form, in a letter to his wife, whom he reassures concerning a painful incident : "At eleven, the actor says the curtain will fall; after nine o'clock everything will be over."

We arrived at Norderney on the afternoon of July 21st in brilliant sunshine. The whole island had turned out to greet us : both summer visitors and inhabitants cheered us a welcome at the landing stage. The burgomaster delivered a friendly speech. On resigning I had registered an oath never to make any more speeches; for the last twelve years I had been forced to make far too many.

Weil viel Reden ungesund,
Gab Natur uns einen Mund.
Mit dem einen Maule schon
Schwatzt zu viel der Erdensohn. [2]

But the plain, friendly words of the burgomaster, the cordial welcome of all the good sailors and fisher folk, moved me so much that I forswore myself. I thanked them all for their welcome and told

---

[1] And should'st thou live three hundred and more years — what then?
Nevertheless thou 'lt leave the caravanserai.
Wert a proud king or cringing beggar — what then?
On thy last day thou 'lt vanish beyond the door.

Say then thy life was all as thy desire,
Say thou had'st read to the last page of the book,
Say thou had'st lived a hundred years' delight,
For aught I care make it two hundred — what then?

[I can find no near equivalent in Fitzgerald. — Translator.]

[2] Too much talking makes you ill.
One mouth Nature gave us,
When she might have given two.
We talk too much to save us.

VILLA KLEIN-FLOTTBEK

The view from the study.   The Elbe in the background

them briefly that I saw in their kindness to me a part of the national idea which I had done my best to serve, truly and faithfully. The national idea, I continued, was personified in the Hohenzollern dynasty, which had pointed out its way to the German people, from the days of the Great Elector to the Great King, whom Norderney then already served, and from the Great King on, to our good old Emperor. Our present Sovereign, I added, also served the national idea, with a generous heart and the very best intentions. "For so long as Kaiser and Nation are at one, we can look out in confidence to the future." If here at Norderney, as elsewhere, my resignation could bring me such a harvest of sympathy, it must be because my sole and cherished aim had been the welfare of my country, the welfare of the State and of the dynasty, indissolubly linked to one another. Whatever served, whatever was a necessity to the nation, was equally a necessity to the Crown. This speech, like my previous interview with Eckardt, was made to prevent people's attributing my resignation to the Emperor, since that, in view of the November crisis, and of the many incidents which led up to it, would certainly have damaged the Crown and dynasty.

At Norderney I found a heap of letters and addresses. To answer them all was the work of my mornings for several weeks. It made my afternoons seem all the pleasanter, when I could go for long rides along the shore, could watch the waves, and dream, before the eternal ebb and flow, on the chances of human life, the lives of nations. If here I mention these addresses, it is not from any petty vanity or wish to insist on having been in the right. A normal man has grown beyond all that by the time he reaches the age of the psalmist: he has had too many chances of learning the truth of the saying: *Vanitas, vanitatum, vanitas.* I merely wish to point out that many patriots, many cultivated people in all circles, could judge my policy more clearly than purblind Conservative chiefs, more rightly than vindictive Centre leaders, and did not, as so frequently happens in Germany, adopt without thought or discussion the narrow, petty notions of their party.

CHAPTER II

The Political Situation when I Retired — Last Conversations with Beth-mann-Hollweg — Last Sitting of the Prussian State Ministry — Details of Bethmann's Taking Office.

I HAVE already said that I did not vacate the Chancellor's palace without some anxiety for the future. Why should forebodings, as a rule quite alien to my nature, have filled my mind as I left the *Hohenzollern*, when my resignation had been accomplished, or on saying farewell to Berlin a few days later? I have never been inclined to hypochondria. *Nil desperandum* is an ancient device of the Bülows. It was engraved on the official seal of my great-uncle and godfather, Karl von Bülow, a staunch and "die-hard" native of Altmecklenburg. As Vice Director of the Chancellery and Grand Ducal Chamberlain of Mecklenburg-Schwerin he had stoutly upheld the old constitution. With all his old-fashioned notions in politics he was a man of abounding freshness and energy. "Now's the time to hold on at all costs", was his attitude after every setback. Why had I felt so moved, so shaken almost, at receiving from some person unknown, on the night before I left Berlin, a melancholy poem by the dead poet, Ernst von Wildenbruch, composed soon after Bismarck's resignation, and which read as follows:

Wenn ich an Deutschland denke, tut mir die Seele weh,
Weil ich ringsum um Deutschland die vielen Feinde seh.
Mir ist zur Nacht die Ruhe des Schlafes dann zerstört,
Weil stets mein Ohr das Flüstern und böses Raunen hört,
Mit dem sie sich bereden zu Anschlag und zu Rat,
Um Deutschland zu verderben durch eine schwere Tat.
Dann kehren die Gedanken bei ferner Zukunft ein
Und fragen: Wird denn jemals das Deutschland nicht mehr sein?

Und wenn ich also denke, wird mir so weh, so schwer,
Wie wär die Welt, die reiche, alsdann so arm und leer ![1]

My fears did not concern the German people which, properly
guided and shown any high and noble ideal, has always in reserve
within itself the most abounding stores of strength and energy.
That had been fully shown by the elections of 1907. Nor was I
anxious for our army, the bravest, best disciplined in the world, the
army most capable of resistance, from the fine old Haeseler and the
gallant Bock von Polach, down to the last musketeer. My anxious
thoughts were all for the Kaiser, though, at the same time, I mistrusted my successor. William II was as incapable of determining
and controlling our peace-time policy, as of military leadership, if
ever it should come to war. That, in both these fields, he should so
have overrated his capacity was, alas, a further proof of his lack of
judgment. In a fit of arrogance he had said to Count Alfred
Waldersee — the Count himself had told me of the incident — when
relieving him of his post as Chief of the General Staff, to shelve him
then, as general in command at Altona, that he, the Emperor, had
no need of any Chief of Staff. In war he would make his own
decisions; would lead his army, as Frederick the Great had done
before him. For peace time all he needed was a secretary. In reality, even in peace time, not to mention any possible war, he stood in
utter need of a mentor, councillor, and friend; of a man who would
be continually at his post, who could understand how to deal with
him; of a representative who could always be trusted to see things
straight.

Was Bethmann-Hollweg the right choice? Partly because, a

---

[1] My soul thinks of my country, and mourns within my breast,
Since now, on all sides round her, I see the foemen pressed;
Then, in the night, I waken and cannot sleep again,
But I must lie and hearken to the one malicious strain
Of bitter, whispering voices, murmuring each to each
Telling of pacts and offers, in low and evil speech;
Ready to rise against us and strike a bitter blow,
Ready to strike my country and lay her children low.
That so my thoughts go striving to some far distant day
And I must ask: "Shall ever this Empire pass away?"
Till, as the thought assails me, my heart sinks down like lead,
And the bright earth, the splendid, stands empty, barren, dead.

few weeks previously, at our last talk on board the *Hohenzollern* I had advised the Emperor against him, I considered it doubly my duty to initiate him now, as fully as possible, into home and, above all, foreign affairs.   Loebell had never concealed from me the fact that Bethmann was mistrustful and inflamed against me.   Valentini had told my successor that I had shown no enthusiasm at his appointment.   I had sent a signed copy of my portrait with a few friendly words of dedication to every other Minister and State Secretary.   Why not to Bethmann?   Loebell, as he repeated all this, was holding a small photograph of myself.   He begged me to avoid misunderstandings which might be to the detriment of the State and, so as to ease from the outset any friction between myself and the ruffled, hypersensitive Bethmann, to sign it "To my welcome successor."   I did as this faithful colleague suggested and am very glad to think that I did so, since to-day my conscience is quite clear when I consider my relationship with Bethmann.

Loebell was the old and intimate friend of both Bethmann-Hollweg and Valentini: later he regretted bitterly the high opinions he had held of them.   The excellent Frau von Loebell told me in 1915 or 1916 that the thought of how he had constantly defended them and taken their part against myself had since caused her husband sleepless nights.   Here I may add that, in the end, Loebell and Bethmann became completely estranged.   In 1917, at the time of the July crisis, Loebell, then Prussian Minister of the Interior, advised the Kaiser to change his Chancellor, since Bethmann, both in foreign and home affairs, had proved himself entirely insufficient, and was, in any case, used up.   The change, he had said, must be made before the announcement of Prussian electoral reform, since one should not pour new wine into old bottles.   Bethmann mentions this in his heavy "Memoirs", where his tone towards Loebell is most unfriendly and aggrieved.

That peculiar, hypersensitive spirit which had always been a part of Bethmann's nature was revealed most clearly in the last conversation we had together, on the eve of my departure from Berlin, July 17, 1909.   My account of this will follow the rough notes which I jotted down almost at once.   In the first of these I began by showing the new Chancellor that our position in the world, to all appearances a brilliant one, was, in actual fact, much better in every way than it had been since Bismarck retired. But the uttermost prudence and circumspection were still as necessary as ever. Geographically our position was always perilous. The terrain which diplomacy must tread abounded in snares and pitfalls — was undermined even. I was convinced that war was not inevitable. For the twelve years in which I had held office we had avoided it with flying colours, and before me for almost three decades, in spite of an occasional crisis and several really serious incidents. Peace must, and could, be maintained. We had nothing at all to gain from war and everything to hope from peace, since time was working on our side. But we should have to go warily and skilfully. It was a question *de ne pas prêter le flanc*. Bethmann answered that I had won my best successes — Tangier and Bosnia — more by daring. With Tangier I had gained a mortgage on Morocco and, above all, brought down Delcassé, the craftiest and most dangerous of our adversaries. With my "gallant" handling of the Bosnian crisis, the finale of my political career, I had "scored" and "finished" in "really brilliant fashion." I countered with the very words I had previously used to the Emperor: "*Ne bis in idem!*" This was enough to make Bethmann feel a little hurt. He hoped, in a ruffled voice, that even he might one day score a success on the same terrain over which I had moved with such agility. At which I cited: "*Non cuivis homini contingit adire Corinthum.*"

This seemed a most unfortunate quotation. The worthy Doctor Schmidt of Neu-Strelitz, the head of the Carolineum grammar school there, had been perfectly right forty-five years before, in warning the fifth-form boy, Bernhard von Bülow, against too many quotations and adjuring him to the careful weeding out and further selection of those he used. This line from Horace's "Epistles" I had better have kept to myself. Bethmann, the *ex-alumnus*, nay "*primus omnium*" of Schulpforta, was only too susceptibly aware exactly what the quotation implied. Visibly ruffled, he digressed into copious protests that he knew he lacked special training as a diplomat. But he trusted that, with patience and hard work, these defects of training might be remedied. "I shall soon get the hang of foreign policy," he told me twice, with a kind of pathos.

I should not have considered it right to allow this talk with my successor to degenerate into personal dispute, and therefore kept it strictly academic. But I seized on the phrase "to get the hang of", and affirmed that it was quite impossible to "get the hang" of foreign policy overnight. An administrative official, transferred from Trarbach to Aurich, might reasonably hope to "get the hang" of the ins and outs of East Frisian peat-cutting, as quickly and successfully as, already, he had mastered the needs of a wine-producing country in Mosel. But foreign affairs were not a science and still less were they a branch of ethics. They were an art, in which success is not to be gained either by good intentions or diligence, but simply by the use of a special gift, presupposing *flair*, tact, and intuition. I added that I should always be most ready to give both advice and loyal support to a colleague of so many years' standing as Bethmann. Whenever, and in whatever circumstances, he considered it advisable to do so, he could come to me in the fullest confidence. He could be in no doubts of my patriotism, and since, from the bottom of my heart, I desired my country's fame and prosperity, security and prolonged well-being, I wished him too, in all sincerity, the best of good fortune while in office. He acknowledged this with a stiff, very dignified, little bow. I had glimpsed an abyss of thin-skinned self-esteem.

Nor did Bethmann, in actual fact, once ask me to advise, after retirement, on any situation confronting him. Never — literally never — either directly or indirectly, did he consult me : not even in the summer of 1914, when embarking on that disastrous series of steps begun by the ultimatum to Serbia, nor throughout the mortal crisis provoked by it. Not once during the whole World War did he ask what I thought of the position nor what I felt might be the possibilities of peace. The most he did was to make uneasy enquiries of where I lived and my associates. When he made his fatal decision to reëstablish Poland, he had not troubled to get my view of it, still less had he given me any chance of warning him against this crazy project, in the names of Frederick the Great and of Prince Bismarck. In this last, or rather penultimate talk on policy, before I laid aside my office, I refused to let his touchy ill humour prevent my advising caution with Russia, as gravely as I had already warned the Emperor. Russia was the key to the world position. For so long as we were at peace with Russia, neither France, nor in particular England, would dare attack us. And — apart from a clear and firm Prussian policy in the Eastern Marches — our relations with Russia would depend both on our handling of the Dardanelles question and on our skill in holding the balance even between Russian and Austrian interests in the Balkans. "Never forget that the Dardanelles are a red-hot cinder. Remember Prince Bismarck's example of how to deal with it in such a way as to prevent either Austria being overrun and sacrificed, or ourselves entangled in conflict with Russia by her government. Such conflict could have no good results." Thirteen years before poor Walter Rathenau cried "*Pace!*" at the Genoa Conference I left my successor, Bethmann, with the word "*Pax*" on my lips.

Another long interview followed in which we discussed relations with England. Remembering the sensitiveness which Bethmann had betrayed at our last talk I opened this second "conversation" with a direct and friendly appeal. I said to him, in the pleasantest tone, carefully avoiding any hint of instruction :

"My dear Bethmann, unlike myself, you did n't spend your best years abroad. You have never made a personal study of the position in Austria and France, in England, Italy, and Russia, in Hungary, Greece, and Roumania. With our administration, on the other hand, you are far better acquainted than I am. You are a brilliant jurist and, in spite of fairly hopeful beginnings, I never succeeded in becoming one. But, unlike myself, you did not grow up in a house of diplomats, and you have not been forced to knock about the world as I have. You are not in touch with almost every — I might say every — European sovereign and most European Ministers. Nor are you on terms of personal friendship with the leading statesmen in many countries. I have no desire to force myself upon you. I by no means yearn for political activity.

'*J'en ai pardessus la tête,*' and am delighted to be allowed to rest at last.   I am almost inclined to inscribe over the Villa Malta porticoes the lines which Lord Brougham, that famous English statesman, whom in other things I should not suggest as a model, set above the doors of his villa at Cannes:

> *Inveni portum, spes et fortuna valete!*
> *Sat me ludistis, ludite nunc alios.*

"But to you I can only repeat that I am always at your disposal in any contingency."

The cordial tone in which I spoke seemed to make some impression on Bethmann.   His face became more good-natured.

This second conversation developed along quite amicable lines. I advised him to achieve as soon as possible the agreement I had begun with England, on the *tempo* of naval construction.   He would find it far easier than I had done to collaborate with the Emperor in this matter.   He had still the attraction of novelty to his Sovereign, whereas, in the eyes of the All Highest, I had become a stale back number.   But he must not yield to the illusion that Anglo-German relationships were susceptible of being shifted overnight onto the plane of ungrudging, fully confident intimacy.   What could be gained was the certainty that the position with England would not get worse, that it would remain normal and correct.   To hope for anything better would be to ignore traditional English policy.   England had, for centuries, shown mistrust of any other Power in the ascendant, politically or even economically, and, in certain cases, she had been hostile.   Spain, Holland, France, and Russia, had all, one after another, had this experience.   Our unexampled economic rise, our position of great political strength, our lightning progress in commerce and industry in particular were to-day England's chief preoccupation, her subject of close attention and hard thought.   That did not of necessity mean that war with England was approaching.   Nothing need be considered as inevitable.   But we must see to it that relations with England did not grow worse, and this, with tact and foresight, could be managed. King Edward was not bellicose, although very inconvenient politi-

cally. He would deliver no surprise attack. Nor was he going to
live for ever. At our last meeting I had been struck by the look of
illness in his face, his thick neck, his heavy footsteps. His pre-
sumptive heir, the present Prince of Wales, was a very calm, phlegmatic gentleman, far easier to get on with than *Monsieur son père.*
We were already so formidable at sea that England would find it
inadvisable to pick any needless quarrel with us. But we must
never forget that, as the world stood, a serious European conflict might lead on to universal war, with all its incalculable
consequences.

" Any major conflict [I said to Bethmann] would mean that we
must fight for life or death. It would imply the most monstrous
stakes. We have nothing at all to gain from war. An attempt
to force the Danes, the Swiss, the Dutch, or the Belgians onto
our side is only conceivable to a madman. An extension of the
Empire towards Eastern Europe would be a not less dubious undertaking. We have far too many Poles within our frontiers as it is !
Don't let us force on naval construction. And especially not the
construction of battleships. That above all ! Please take to
heart the things I said to Tirpitz, in those last serious letters I
exchanged with him on the subject of too lopsided a naval policy,
a policy which can only concentrate on more and more new
armoured craft and dreadnoughts. I wrote to him most gravely
and emphatically. You will find all my warnings and suggestions,
reports and memoranda, in the archives. Already Bismarck, as
Tirpitz himself once told me, considered it wrong to concentrate
exclusively on the bigger types of armour-plated ship. It would
be far better if we developed our submarine strength — the U-boat.
And on the other hand, we should certainly see to it, with no misplaced haggling over pence, that our land armament is flawless;
that we surpass the French in this respect or, in any case, remain
quite level with them. France is, and remains, the disturbing factor in Europe. But in the end the French, for all their magnificent
patriotism, will find their three years' service hard to bear. On the
day when France decides to lay down this unnatural burden of

armament and perceives that she can never get beyond us, the
possibility of many years' peace will be to hand. Don't ever let
yourself be disturbed by stupid talk about our 'zigzag' policy.
When Odysseus steered his lucky course between Charybdis and
Scylla, no doubt all the grumblers on his ship reproached him, too,
with steering zigzag. No other policy is feasible unless we let it
come to preventive warfare, and such a course would be criminal,
since I can only repeat that time is on our side."

We parted on the best of terms. My successor even seemed to
have been mollified.

Next day I attended my last sitting at the Prussian Ministry of
State. I briefly reminded my hearers of the fact that twelve years
had passed since first I had been given a voice in the councils of the
Royal State Ministers, on that day when I was presented to the
Assembly by my honoured predecessor, Prince Hohenlohe. After
an all too brief probation of three years I had, for nine years, enjoyed the honour of presiding at the sittings of the Council. I had
no desire to adopt a tone which I disliked, the tone of exaggerated
praise. But, as a man who had travelled much, who had studied
many cities and many customs, I must express my very real conviction that few official bodies could boast such industry, such careful
sense of duty and varied knowledge, as the Royal Prussian Ministry of State. Great men had set their firm, clear seal on the Prussian official; such kings as Frederick II and Frederick William I;
such great statesmen as Stein, as Hardenberg, as Bismarck, the
founders of the Zollverein, as Motz and Maassen, whose spirit conceived the Berlin University, as Wilhelm von Humboldt, the founder
of Prussian education, the father of that Prussian schoolmaster
who won us the battle of Königgrätz, Altenstein. Last but not
least came the men whom we ourselves had known — Von der
Heydt and Miquel, Maybach and Budde, Botho Eulenburg, and
Robert Zedlitz. I concluded, more or less, as follows: "The best
of governments is in vain unless the foreign policy of a nation be
conducted firmly and adroitly, with prudence and courage; unless,
at home, the laws are built up from the premise expressed by Thiers,
that brilliant French statesman, in the words, '*Gouverner c'est pré-*

voir.' Such supreme direction of policy is the task of the Prussian Premier and German Imperial Chancellor." Warmly and sincerely I wished my successor all good fortune.

I had spoken, as I usually did, impromptu, and almost on a note of conversation. Bethmann replied in a long and careful speech, a polished speech, which gave almost overwhelming expression to the Council's regret at my retirement, their grateful admiration of my work. Next day he sent me the text of his oration. Some of his remarks had been curtailed, others omitted altogether. But the broad gist of his speech remained. I reproduce the following extracts:

I thank Your Highness, in the name of the Prussian State Ministry, most respectfully for the kind farewells you have just bidden us. We all still labour under the deep impression left on our minds by the latest political events, and await, with very real anxiety, the process of their further development. It fills us with particular regret that such incidents should have induced Your Highness to request, of His Imperial and Royal Majesty, your release from all the functions of office, including those of President of the Royal Prussian Ministry of State. We especially deplore that your retirement should not be entirely free from a feeling of all too justifiable bitterness. But Your Highness shares this misfortune with most, perhaps with all, great statesmen, and, just as in all matters of State and policy the sharp perception of Your Highness has ever discerned the broad decisive contour, so too, when your policy is remembered, the laurels you have reaped will be unfading — a reward of which none can ever deprive you. This little cloud will soon have been dispelled by the sun. The Royal Ministry of State is proud to have laboured under Your Highness in the joint performance of those great tasks which you brought to their successful conclusion. For Prussia I need only repeat the words — Canal Bill, Schools Act, Eastern Marches policy, Mining Regulations Act, Officials' Insurance — to indicate a few of those stages in the march of progress, some of which demanded a hard struggle, each of which will remain for ever associated with the name of Prince von Bülow. But, linked with these, came the series of your Imperial successes, all so many triumphs for Germany; in Colonial Policy; in the strengthening of our army and navy; in the laying down of new and surer foundations for German commercial relationships, social legislation, and, above all, foreign policy. Your Highness' official life has been all action. Few other statesmen have done so much. It was an act, and perhaps the most considerable — a triumph which only Your Highness' skill could have secured — which won over wide circles of our people, who till then had lived by political negation, to that positive and constructive share in the State which has broadened out the whole basis of German politics. These present commotions will soon have passed. The ruffled waves have brought much mud and slime to the surface, but the stream itself will flow quietly onwards. It is the note of all Your Highness' achievement that it was never concerned with the rewards and successes of the minute, but reckoned on, and will still be valid in, the future. Both history and public opinion will acknowledge it. We here do homage to it to-day. We thank Your Highness for the tasks you have performed for Kaiser and Empire, for King and Fatherland. We thank you for the true and steady friendship which shared and lightened our common toil. To our heartiest greetings we add the hope that our work together in the Royal Prussian Ministry of State will remain a bright spot in Your Highness' memory.

The Chancellor wrote to me next day:

MOST ESTEEMED PRINCE,

Your Highness desired some record of the words in which, at the Royal State Ministry, I tried to express our regret at your loss and thanks for all your achievement. In reconstructing my speech to send it to you I am again most painfully aware of a very inadequate attempt. I must therefore ask you to be indulgent. All that I said was deeply meant; much owed its inspiration to the moment. Here too I have not tried to polish.

I am thankful to say that the first spate of letters and despatches has been dealt with, so that now I am free to get to work. For me that is the only method of preserving stability and balance. I shall be most grateful if, some time hence, you will allow me to open a correspondence with you, so as to rectify certain impressions and conclusions. To-day I can only again repeat my thanks for all that Your Highness has done for me in the last few years. My most respectful greetings to the Princess, and please believe me, in constant and sincere esteem,

Your Highness' most devoted,

BETHMANN-HOLLWEG.

Were these protestations of heartfelt devotion, of profound respect, really genuine? I do not suppose this grateful letter concealed real double-dealing, real hypocrisy. But the future was to show Bethmann-Hollweg for the weak character he was, and spineless people can never be deeply grateful and never really sincere.

My successor's appointment to the chancellorship was not without its attendant omens. When finally it was announced that he succeeded me, I asked my wife to call on Frau von Bethmann and tell her that she would be most willing to place at her entire disposal her experience in the management of the Palace. Frau von Bethmann was an excellent woman. She had found it at first a little difficult to decide to give her hand to Theobald, whose origins were in every way so different, since she herself was a Pfuel, of the old junker family of the Mark — the family of which Theodore Fontane has so many pleasant things to relate in his charming "Wanderings in the Marches." Once married to Bethmann, however, she became his good and most affectionate wife, and their marriage was a very happy one. When my wife arrived in Frau von Bethmann's drawing-room, the latter exclaimed, with tears in her eyes, "This is simply a misfortune for my poor husband. I love my husband, and because I love him I wish he could have been spared this test. In spite of all his devotion to duty, his conscientiousness and scrupulousness, and so many other brilliant gifts — he is n't the man for such a position. He's always so undecided, so hesitating, so given to worrying over trifles, till, really at times, he does n't know what he's doing. Why, it's become quite a family joke. We often say, 'Father has changed his mind to-day three times,' or 'For three days now Father has been trying to make up his mind.'"

My wife found it really difficult to pacify and console Frau von Bethmann, who acted, during the years that still remained to her, as a very good influence on her husband.

CHAPTER III

After My Retirement: Schmoller, Oncken, Riezler, Philip Eulenburg.

THROUGH my whole term of office Professor Gustav Schmoller had supported me with unvarying sympathy and friendship. On August 7, 1909, I answered as follows from Norderney a letter in which he had cordially expressed his real grief at my retirement:

You touch on the three great questions which, as Chancellor, pre-occupied me most. In Foreign Policy it is indeed the task of our genera-tion to consolidate German security and obtain our independence on the seas, without entering, in the achievement of these aims, through a series of mutual misunderstandings, into any major conflict with England. To both our countries such a clash would of necessity be fateful, and ominous in the destiny of the world.

At home I saw as my chief task the gradual incorporation into the monarchist and nationalist body-politic of the fourth estate, after the fashion in which, a century ago, the third was invited to participate, to the general advantage of our people. Though in this most difficult branch of legislation we are, of course, still in the rudimentary stage, I venture to hope that these beginnings are rich in promise for the future; that our feet are already set upon a path which, now, we shall follow to the end. Finally, as our second great task in home policy, I see the work of national embankment, by the methods of German colonization, against the Polish deluge which threatens us. It is a duty handed down to us by our fathers, since here it is not merely a question of continuing the work of the Great King, but of the great German thirteenth-century colonists.

Schmoller's answer contained the following:

The political skies have continued to darken since your retirement. This is not felt merely by your friends and admirers. Admittedly Herr von Bethmann is a man of exceptional merit, with many capacities for statesmanship. Yet, though I have no wish to seem critical of his present attitude of reserve, I get the impression that, on the whole, he would make a better professor than Chancellor. He finds it painfully hard to surmount the *rationes dubitandi*. That vital gift of bold decision which can infect men's minds and sweep them along with it, seems to be altogether denied him. His wife once told me of the hours — even days — of painful effort which he gives to the preparation of a speech.

Professor Hermann Oncken, the biographer of Rudolf von Bennigsen, sent me an article he had published on the home situation in Germany. My answer contained the following corrections of various errors, current in Liberal circles, on the objectives of my policy at home :

I know that many Liberals have criticized my deliberate and reasoned support of our agricultural interest, — that consideration with which, in several measures, I handled the Conservative Party — in so far as it was possible to consider them ! — with due regard to the welfare of the nation as a whole. But my reasons for adopting such a course were not those of mere upbringing and tradition, *influence du milieu*, etc. They were solely due to the fact that, responsible as I was to the country, I felt it to be my bounden duty to safeguard the world status of our people, attained so late, and at the cost of such heavy efforts. Any hurried transition, made at the expense of her agriculture, to the conditions of a purely industrial, purely commercialized State would, in my opinion, mean to Germany what the shedding of her ballast might mean to a sailing ship, if the masts were raised and full sail hoisted. For so long as German Social-Democracy remains what it is, unluckily to-day, in the vast majority of its supporters — dogmatic, unpolitical, anti-national — so long as this dogmatism retains its grip over the minds of most workers in German industry, so long shall we be doubly in need of the counterweight of our peasant population. And while it still seems difficult for Liberals to set to work on practical politics, free of all subservience to theory, we cannot afford to loose that reserve fund of political energy and experience which Conservatives have at their command. On the whole, I feel I have given practical proof, both in office and by the fact of my resignation, of how useful and necessary to the State I deemed the collaboration of Liberals. Our future depends on our making the Liberals more political, the Conservatives less narrow-minded.

In relating our farewell audience at the "Green Hat" I have already said how William II — in his account of me to the Federal representatives — described as one of my worst lapses, as the mistake which had made our breach inevitable, a certain Foreign Office recommendation, sent in without my having been consulted, that the Councillor of Legation, Hermann Rath, should be promoted to a post of Resident Minister.   I may say, *en passant*, that the recompense would have been a very modest one.   The following letter from Herr vom Rath, who died soon after my retirement, received by a mutual friend and dated June 28, 1909, may serve to show this despised minor official as a far better judge of men and things than the people in whom His Majesty placed most confidence :

Since I live buried in the country I did not hear until to-day that the Chancellor has asked for his dismissal, and that the request is likely to be granted.   My satisfaction at his having taken such a step was enough at first to dispel even my fears of what may come of it.   Yet this latter anxiety is considerable.   Who is to inherit the confidence which Prince Bülow inspired in all his friends, or the respect he could induce in his enemies?   My satisfaction springs from the reflection that I have supported with my name and fullest conviction the home and foreign policies of a statesman who, to the end, remained consistent and sincere.   The Chancellor's attempt to modernize the Conservatives' outlook, and so keep the party at the helm, has come to grief on their own short-sighted policy of self-interest ; a policy which has rendered them odious to the great majority of our people, and not merely to the industrial masses. Bülow's methods of the last few years have still further reduced the number of "reds" by depriving the Socialists of their best slogans.   The line he took was sound, energetic, and constitutional.   The Democrats, during the *bloc* period, have renewed and become a moderate Liberal party.   They will now be forced into line with the extreme Left Wing, in opposition to the present majority in the Reichstag, while the National Liberals, so useful to the government as a whole, will in future be shelved and excluded from legislative action.

In the Press Bureau, in the days when I was still a Chancellor, there served a young official, Doctor Riezler, who attracted attention by his vivid admiration of myself.   I retired, and this boyish enthusiasm was promptly transferred to his new chief, though not until young Doctor Riezler had written very correctly to assure me

of his most respectful thanks for all my kindness during the years
in which he had been so lucky as to work as my subordinate and
"learn from" me.   The Empress Frederick, whose intellect was
enhanced by her sense of humour, loved a certain story of how one
day as she wandered amid the splendours of Windsor Castle, she
had come upon a housemaid in floods of tears.   She asked her what
was the matter.   Had her young man, her "sweetheart" jilted her?
The poor child had said, with a certain display of indignation : "Oh,
no ! It is not for love that I feel unhappy.   Thank God I can love
any man."   Doctor Riezler, too, was one of those eager people who
distribute their affections impartially.   He too could "love any
man" who dispensed from the cornucopia of promotions.   With
me, however, he forswore himself when, shortly before the outbreak of war, he published, under the pseudonym "Rüdorffer" his
"Characteristics of Modern World Policy", a book containing many
loveless strictures on my whole political method.   "Rüdorffer"
used my policy as the dark background which would throw into
more splendid relief the brilliant achievement of my successor.
Alas, he was so imprudent as to indulge in a prophetic strain on the
ripening fruits of Bethmann's wisdom — prophecies of which 1914
was soon to be the grisly denial.   It so happened that, in the second year of war, Riezler, at a Berlin dinner table, began talking to
a guest from Vienna who, as part of a general conversation on war
and pre-war political literature, began to observe that in Berlin
there had been some excellent books written on politics, as well as
some extremely stupid ones.   In connection with these last he at
once mentioned "Rüdorffer's" "Characteristics."   His neighbour
attempted a gentle nudge, which became a vigorous thrust in the
ribs, followed by a fierce jerk of the head at Riezler, who by now sat
crimson in the face, as his book was damned from A to Z.   At last
the Viennese asked, in all innocence: "But what has Herr Riezler
got to do with Rüdorffer's idiotic book?"   *Tableau*, as the French
express such moments !

In August, 1917, a very important Rhenish newspaper observed
with a certain justice, à propos of this "Rüdorffer" book, "This
book has its peculiar charm.   It foretells the developments of world-

policy precisely as they did not happen." In the war, under Bethmann-Hollweg, whose trusted collaborator he soon became, Riezler
played a most unfortunate rôle. Together with Hans Delbrück
he was among those advisers of the Chancellor who urged the resus-
citation of Poland, the most lamentable blunder we made after 1914.
By 1917 the following lines were going the rounds of Berlin :

> *Ein schöner Wahn schafft uns nicht Frieden,*
> *Der Hohlweg sperrt den Blick zum Horizont.*
> *Ihm ward durch einen Riez die Welt zu sehn beschieden,*
> *Doch hinter diesem Riez war alles leer.*[1]

Wahnschaffe was what is called a "fine-looking man." Bethmann-Hollweg had misled us into the "Hohlweg" (hollow way)
of the war, and Riezler — the crevice — was certainly empty. The
best thing about him was his wife, the charming daughter of
Liebermann, the painter. Naturally, on the fall of the Empire,
Riezler was quite as eager to be taken aboard the good ship "Republic" as he had been, at the time of my retirement, to cultivate
"les beaux yeux" of Bethmann. After the November Revolution
he at once urged the value of his services, as Chief of Cabinet, on
Ebert. The honest Ebert, however, did not find him sufficiently
industrious and had no confidence in his character. He very soon
showed him the door.

Among so many other proofs of real affection and recognition
which reached me after my retirement, the following, from Philip
Eulenburg, both stirred and filled me with melancholy. I had
tried, in so far as it was possible in the limits of my official position,
and with the kind help of Doctor Renvers, to make his situation
more endurable at the time of the action — taken very much
against my wishes, and in spite of all I could say to dissuade him
— which, later, led to his arrest on the evidence of a Starn-
berg fisherman. I had not set eyes on poor "Phili" since I caught
sight of his melancholy figure, standing at the back of the

---

[1] A "fine madness" (Wahnschaffe) will not make peace for us.
The ravine (hollow way; *i.e.* Hohlweg) blocks our view of the horizon.
He was destined to see the world through a crevice
But beyond that crevice there was only emptiness.

courtroom, at the hearing of my case against Brandt, the "author." Nor did he write till after my retirement :

MY DEAR BERNHARD,

I think I wrote to you — or if not I sent you word by Alfred — to say that you would not hear from me again for so long as you remained a Chancellor. I considered it my duty as your friend to do nothing to increase those difficulties — the result of a chain of horrible circumstances — which had begun to beset you in consequence of our old, a hundred times tested, affection. Nor, even to-day, should I be writing to you, had I not chanced on a paragraph in the paper, announcing that, within the next few days, you would be going to stay with Alfred in Berne. It filled me with a sudden, violent longing to be back again with my two dear friends, as in the old days. Then, since I had long owed Alfred a letter, I was impelled to add this to you, though without any object in doing so. But at least I shall be able to tell you a little of all that troubles me concerning you. I will do my best not to say a word about my own fate. You knew me well enough when I was happy — enough of my way of thinking and feeling; of my mother, my children and Augusta — to be well aware how things stand with me. I do not think you the kind of friend who would ever forget the ties between us. *Der Tag* is the only paper I ever look at. My present hatred of politics — it almost amounts to a disease — made me choose this non-political newspaper, so as to know more or less what is happening. We both have learned to read between the lines. So that therefore I could follow your course. I consider your retirement a disaster and have now the sense of being a passenger on a ship captained by a mummer, and whose first mate is really an Alpinist. Moreover, the captain fancies that "*le moment est venu*", to create new records by means of some "colossal" voyage, in spite of the disastrous failure of his last attempt at record-breaking. The moment is finally upon us which we both foretold with a certain terror. I don't grudge you your freedom; it may enable you to realize how one must feel when even the freedom for which he longed is denied him. Unless he is forced to do so, the captain will never have you back, though one day even that might happen. A certain Max Fürstenberg is the person chiefly responsible for the present turn of events, in so far as they affect yourself. I have sure information as to that, from a source in his erstwhile Fatherland, now grown narrower. Certainly the Conservatives were guilty of very great stupidity; but the real source of all the trouble lies elsewhere.   The hunt was already raised by certain people, suckled in the First Guards' Regiment.   All the same, I can't spare even you a reproach ; just as my grave was dug by Holstein because I never feared him enough (how often, since, have I not had cause to think of your warnings !) so Holstein, too, stoked up that engine which should eventually bear you out of office, because you were too afraid of him.   Nor can I repress another criticism.   It has always surprised me that a mind which knew the Germans so thoroughly should have chosen to work on so reasoned an assumption as the *bloc* policy.   Will Germany ever be ripe for such tactics?

You can imagine how, in letter after letter, people have done their best to persuade me to see in you the origin and source of all my misfortunes — all this disaster to me and mine.   Many people are really annoyed by the sight of a firm and constant loyalty which will allow nothing to shake it. Nor could my assurances convince them that you would be the last person likely — above all as far as *we* were concerned — to burden his conscience with the thought of having played false.   Only one thing seemed difficult to explain : the fact that neither the official, nor even the semi-official Press, cared to take up the cudgels on behalf of one of the highest German functionaries, and fight scandals and scandal-mongering newspapers. Surely the whole affair from the beginning had resolved itself into a question of power — Press or Government !   And the Press won.   Just as it won in the November days !   Never again will a government be able to recapture that lost terrain.   Harden sent 145 printed accusations into court against me.   Out of all these 145 — all of which were exposed for the lies they were — 2 were enough to ruin me.   Two wretched lies — out of all that 145, hatched by my equals, in spleen and envy of me, in order to send them to Harden !   Now I am sick to death, so sick that I have scarcely any hope of ever seeing the end of the trial which is certain to clear my name and reputation.   Surely, by the fact of this proportion — 143 to 2 — the official Press was well in the position to have taken up the gauntlet straight away.   But no — I have often had to think of your warning that I am one of the best hated people in Germany.   Well — my friends know if I ever deserved to be !   I don't allude to the stupid, monstrous slanders prepared, from the very outset, by the general's *camarilla* against me, and which, in the end, proved strong enough to tie your hands.   Do you really think such things would have been possible under Albedyll or the good old gentleman?   A horrible mixture of hatred, cowardice, envy, and short sight.   But enough of it all !   I can only assure you that my thoughts will go with you to Villa Malta, that my mind grows tranquil at the thought of your kind and charming wife. May nothing ever shadow her peace, and may my dear, kind Donna Laura enfold you in the bliss of her spirit! How the Princess will love arranging the Villa Malta, and how beautiful it will soon have become! If you feel you can manage to do so please write to me from Rome about your life there. I am a dead man. But surely, from time to time, we visit the dead in their graveyards. This long letter has cost me real fatigue and nervous exhaustion. But it has done me good to talk to you again, in the old way, after so long. Now I have said enough. . . .

As I read this letter, which contains, in spite of its occasional half-truths, some really deep and generous feeling, as well as some brilliant *aperçus*, there rose to the surface of my mind the thoughts which had besieged me two years previously, at the time of the hopeless Eulenburg scandal, of which I have given some account. Has the State the duty — has it even the right — I asked myself, to brand abnormal instincts with its infamy? This letter re-awakened all my pity for an old friend endowed by the gods with an unusually charming personality, many generous gifts, and the impulses of genuine nobility, along with this perilous inclination. When, at about that time, I received a petition, signed by a number of intellectuals, for the abrogation of Paragraph 175, I had consulted Doctor Renvers on the proper attitude of the State towards such problems. He answered, "As a doctor, I can only tell you that, from the purely scientific standpoint, what we class as 'unnatural vice' is no more 'pathological' than 'normal' impulse. Nor need I trouble to remind you that the ancients saw nothing more reprehensible in the Emperor Hadrian's delight with the melancholy beauty of Antinous than in Anthony's passion for Cleopatra. And yet, as a citizen, I protest against setting these two things on equal footing. If the stigma of unnatural vice is removed, the moral and physical health of our people will suffer for it." His answer confirmed my resolution to turn a deaf ear to all appeals for the abrogation of Paragraph 175. No doubt my own pronounced repugnance at anything in the least unnatural may also have impelled me to this decision. I answered Eulenburg:

DEAR PHILI,

Your letter, received in Berne, has given me much food for reflection. My feelings towards your dear mother, your splendid wife, are those of the deepest respect. I am heartily concerned for the future of your delightful children. For many years we lived on the closest terms of friendship. How could I, therefore, ever be indifferent to your misfortune? All I could do, within the limits of my duty as Chancellor, I did to prevent those deeply tragic events which, as a man, cut me also to the heart. I did whatever was in my power to make your position somewhat easier, and I earnestly hope that the affection of your nearest and dearest is a real consolation to you now; that you find true comfort in the thought that God's goodness and pity are stronger than all the pain of this wretched earth. A very heavy year lies behind me. From my boyhood up I have been in harness, and the last twelve years were a time of uninterrupted strain. Now I must have rest and the chance to recuperate. I have chosen to settle in Rome because its vast historical perspectives lead on the mind to philosophical thought and facilitate the study of history which, as you know, has always fascinated me. Rome is one mighty past, and so the city can hold herself aloof from to-day. I am reading a great deal. This summer I have managed to get through the whole six volumes of Gorce's "Histoire du Second Empire", and am now engaged on the even thicker volumes of Gregorovius' "History of Rome in the Middle Ages." I have also gone back to the ancients — Virgil, Sallust, and above all, Tacitus and Homer. I have always had a particular affection for the classics and here, in the land which formed their cradle, they become more living to me than ever.

Goethe once said that he had never really read the Iliad and Odyssey till he could read them on the shores of the Mediterranean. I can feel exactly as he did.

My mother-in-law is in her eightieth year. Her great age makes her very glad to have her daughter by her side for the short space of life which still remains to her. My wife is exhausted by the twelve years of restless, enervating activity inseparable from what is usually called "a leading position" in Berlin. She has no desire to go into society here. She too can find her peace and consolation for all our disappointments here on earth in such simple pleasures as music and gardening. It was very moving and delightful to see Alfred and his family again. . . .

May God protect and give you peace,

Your BERNHARD B.

It is scarcely surprising that many people should have judged Philip Eulenburg guilty since, in all the years until his death, from the breaking off, on grounds of his ill health, of the perjury proceedings against him, he could never summon up the courage to demand the reopening of his trial although, for this considerable period, he received many visitors at Schloss Liebenberg, all of whom found him fairly well, and most of them reported him to be in fairly good spirits. Personally I had only gradually brought myself to doubt his complete innocence, though my doubts, alas, seemed confirmed by the negative outcome of these proceedings.

As a footnote to the letter given above, I must add that " the first mate" whom Eulenburg derides as "an Alpinist", was the Foreign State Secretary, Herr von Schön, who had made himself of use to the princes, as their guide into the mountains at Berchtesgaden. That is the one sentence which Haller (in his life of Prince Philip zu Eulenburg-Hertefeld, p. 367) chooses to pick out of this long letter, the rest of which he utterly ignores, presumably because its note of gratitude would not harmonize with a very one-sided portrait. Prince Max Fürstenberg, the owner of Schloss Donaueschingen, who succeeded Philip in the confidence of the Emperor, may certainly have intrigued against me. He never found me sufficiently responsive to the often exaggerated claims and aspirations of his Austrian fatherland. The "generals' *camarilla*" — Generals Hülsen-Häseler, Kessel, and Plessen — could see in Philip only a degenerate, both because of his inclination towards spiritualism and marked love of intrigue. This made them insist all the more vigorously on his taking some action against Harden and so clearing himself of the charge of sexual perversion. The "envious equals" were two of Eulenburg's youthful bosom cronies, Count Bolko Hochberg and Prince Richard Dohna, who, as I previously mentioned, had turned against him, in the course of his intrigue against Hofrat Pierson.

This retrospective glance at the woes and tremors of poor "Phili" induces an obvious comparison, both of fate and abnormal inclination, with the tragedy of Oscar Wilde — the difference being that the poet was forced to undergo a rigorous punishment which the prince succeeded in escaping.   The Englishman, in compensation, ranks higher as an artist than the German.   "De Profundis" and "The Ballad of Reading Gaol", "The Picture of Dorian Grey", and "Salome", are on a far better creative level than "Songs of the Skalds" or "Rosenlieder."

CHAPTER IV

Some Character Studies à propos of My Retirement — Tschirschky — Schön — Kiderlen — Radowitz — Jagow — Monts — Flotow — Walter Rathenau, His Relationship to Kaiser and Republic.

DURING the good Emperor Frederick's last illness, as later, on the fall of Prince Bismarck, I had gained too complete an insight into the wretched lack of principle in most humans — especially those whom we dub "men of the world" — to be troubled, or even very surprised, by the sensation, now I had ceased to be Chancellor, of a sudden drop in the fervour of my warmest admirers, of those subordinates who had been heartiest in their honest expressions of personal loyalty. Tschirschky who, when I had him made ambassador, kept insisting with such generous frankness how much he prized my good opinion, who since had never let slip the chance of assuring me, to my face or in a letter, that his feeling for me "would never change", made prompt use of the Imperial visit to Vienna (in the May of 1909) to let the Kaiser know he had suffered "unutterably" at the time of the November crisis. William II had a streak of simplicity in his character which here again I wish to emphasize, since it reconciled us time after time. He himself related with real emotion this proof of the "rocklike" loyalty of the German Ambassador in Austria, and expressed his Imperial thanks by sending Tschirschky his photograph, expensively framed and inscribed with a gracious dedication. But never again did Tschirschky let me know he was alive.

I have already told how, as the Bosnian crisis drew to a head and the November storm began to lower, the Secretary of State, Von Schön, took to his bed. When the storm abated and the foreign crisis seemed finally overcome, he reappeared upon the scene. In days gone by he had kept assuring me of his warmest "most wholehearted" adherence, adding that he "would strain every nerve" to live up to the good opinion I had formed of him, since he well knew how much he owed to my influence and "kindly interest" in his work.   Now "*le baron de Schoen*" went off to the Kaiser to tell him of non-existent personal efforts he had made to overcome the Bosnian trouble.   Nor did he scruple in the least to censure me severely for the "spinelessness" of my attitude to the Parliament and people; my drastic — far too drastic — criticism, in November, 1908, of the gracious person of my Sovereign.   This last had made Schön feel so angry as to bring on a severe heart attack.   His Belgo-Parisian wife wrote off at once to Brussels and Paris to say that I was "*un homme fini*" and in Berlin announced in every diplomatic drawing-room that as "loyalists" she and her husband refused to have anything more to do with me.

Kiderlen wrote to me after my retirement:

MOST ESTEEMED PRINCE,

Now that these days of strife and excitement are over and the equally strenuous aftermath, during which Your Highness must have received so many deep expressions of sympathy — will you permit a subordinate, but none the less devoted admirer to affirm once more his real and unalterable feeling of deep esteem for yourself which no outward change could ever affect.   As a German, and even more as a Foreign Office official of long years' standing, I can only deplore Your Highness' withdrawal from the sphere of such successful activity.   I need scarcely labour this point, though I may add that I gained a sufficient personal insight into the heavy and responsible duties which Your Highness so successfully discharged to feel that you may even experience a certain relief as you look back in peace and tranquillity, free from the daily harassments of office, on all your brilliant achievements.   Your Highness, I am sure, will understand me if I add a wish that, even in future, you may remain in very close touch with Germany — both with our home and, above all, with our foreign situation — so that neither the Emperor nor the Fatherland need ever finally relinquish your experienced and invaluable counsel.   But my main purpose in writing this to Your Highness is to thank you, most honoured prince, and the princess whom I reverence so deeply, from the bottom of my heart for all the kind hospitality you showed me, and so to record the most respectful gratitude I have always felt for such a chief. Nor shall I ever cease to be grateful for the memory of this last winter, during the whole of which I was privileged to work under your immediate supervision.   I hope that Your Highnesses intend to spend some part of the winter or of next summer in Berlin, and that then, on leave, I may get the chance of giving you both my personal assurance of constant and unalterable gratitude.   For the moment this letter must suffice and the knowledge that I am always entirely yours.

With all good wishes for your health, and in the hope that you will convey my respects to the Princess, I remain, in the memory of an old and unchangeable esteem,

Your Highness' most devoted and obedient
KIDERLEN.

Yet even this profound and trusty loyalty, this deep and unshakable devotion, lasted no longer than was necessary.   Kiderlen's letters to Frau Kypke, published soon after his death, show how his opinion of me varied, till at last he relinquished me altogether, turning against me as soon as it seemed to him certain that I was finally out of favour with the All Highest.   I should like to add, without more ado, that this flight from fallen grandeur has been experienced by many a far better man.   What experience Bismarck must have had of it!   That greatest of Chancellors complained in his letters, but still more in conversation that, after his fall, he was avoided "as though I had been smitten with the plague", by former acquaintances and hangers-on and, most of all, by former subordinates.   "Many mongrels" would go far out of their ways to avoid having to walk down Unter den Linden where they might have to meet his eldest son, the once fêted and surrounded Count Herbert.

In the 'thirties of the last century, under the title "Dictionnaire des Girouettes" (weathercocks) there appeared a list of all the public men whose holiest convictions and so, of course, their friendships and connections, had changed since 1788.   It was a voluminous publication.

Yet, even among my subordinates, there were one or two pleasing exceptions.   The Ambassador von Radowitz, at one time my exacting superior and later a diligent and very useful subordinate, preserved his self-respect and wired as follows: "Will Your Highness allow me to express my deep esteem and gratitude for the unfailing kindness you have shown me. All good wishes for the future well-being both of Your Highness and the Princess."

Whoever retires from such a post as the chancellorship — a post which has given him absolute power over the hopes and future careers, the whole official weal and woe, of many less highly placed colleagues — must naturally expect all kinds of unfriendliness. *Homines sumus.* Yet some of the people with whom the service brought me into contact may certainly be said to have exceeded the normal measure of ingratitude which is only to be expected on such occasions. Their cases are not typical but instructive.

The most striking was that of Gottlieb Jagow. In the days when I was still an ambassador — it must have been in about 1895 — I received a letter from Hermann Jagow, a good old comrade in my regiment, who by then had long since laid aside his sword and beaten it into a ploughshare. He wrote that he had a younger brother whose health was poor and his means very inadequate but who, none the less, longed to be a diplomat. Could I make any use of him as attaché? Rome, with its milder climate and moderate scale of expenditure would be, the letter added, the fulfilment of Gottlieb Jagow's wildest dreams and hopes. I wrote off on the young man's behalf to the Foreign Office, saying that I should always be very glad to take him into the Embassy. Soon after this he reported at the Palazzo Caffarelli, where he was welcomed in the friendliest possible fashion, and lived for two whole years as a son of the house. I should be tempted here to quote the apostrophe in Schiller which the Friedländer addresses to Max Piccolomini :

> Think how they led you through the winter camp
> Into my tent at Prague, a tender boy

had there not been such an immense physical difference between Gottlieb Jagow's puny stature and that of the swashbuckling knight-at-arms who, with lifted sabre, fluttering plume, and hair streaming in the breeze, forces his way into the Swedish encampment outside Neustadt, eager for death. As Secretary of State and later Chancellor, I still kept a fatherly eye on Jagow. I only had him assigned to such cheap and salubrious posts as he requested — Hamburg,

Munich, and later Rome again, as third, second, and first secretary. In 1906, after my fainting fit in the Reichstag, Gottlieb was transferred to the Foreign Office, which wanted to find out how much my little protégé really knew. While I was convalescent, he came to see me, to tell me how his delicate health was beginning to give way under the strain of the sedentary life and heavy work required in the political department. Moreover, he was longing to be a Minister. I obtained for him the pleasant little sinecure of German Minister to Luxemburg, from where he would often run across to Brussels to remind me of his continued existence through my step-daughter's husband, Count Wallwitz, then Minister to the Belgian Court. Count Monts left Rome, aware that he had made himself impossible there, both to Italians and the German colony, and I suggested Jagow as his successor. I have already admitted stupid mistakes in some of my judgments of other people. To have suggested Jagow for Rome was one of the worst. "What," asked the astonished William II, "do you really want to send that little squirt out into the world as an ambassador?" In my own defence, however, I may say that Jagow's long stay in Rome had made him well acquainted with the terrain there, that in 1909 we were on the best of terms with Italy, and that Monts had been so grossly tactless and managed to create so much ill feeling that a modest and pacific successor such as Gottlieb Jagow seemed desirable. Gottlieb brimmed over with delight when he heard of such undreamed-of promotion — from Luxemburg to the Palazzo Caffarelli! I had given him the glad tidings before a little dinner to which we invited him. When dinner was over he approached me timidly in the library and began in a voice that gulped with emotion, "Your Highness, I'm not much of a speaker" — this was undoubtedly true of him, and he showed it all too clearly four years later when, under Bethmann, he became a Secretary of State. In 1909, however, he continued, "But I really must try and tell Your Highness how grateful I am and how loyal I shall always be to you. I might even say my *love* for Your Highness will never cease as long as I live." I replied, "You've been long enough in Rome to know the position there. I think you'll do your job very well and clear up some of the mess that Monts has left. As for the rest, you come of a very good family and so I hope you 'll behave yourself accordingly." Alas, even that hope was vain ! A few days later Jagow wrote to my wife :

MOST ESTEEMED PRINCESS,

To-day I received the order which definitely confirms my appointment. It is very delightful to find oneself at the summit of a career, and my heart is full of gratitude and joy ! I cannot tell you how happy and thankful I feel. May I ask you to convey my very deep and sincere thanks to the Prince. I do not want to burden him with a letter, since I know that his time is already far too occupied. This heavy winter must have made quite superhuman demands on his resistance. I only hope I shall succeed in justifying his confidence. Donna Laura, I am glad to say, seems from her letters, to be in the best of health. For all her eighty years she has kept the fresh alertness of twenty. It is wonderful to think that I shall be seeing her again so soon, and certainly I will do whatever I can for her. I am also very glad to have to tell you that I have better news from Italy of Flotow. His letters from Berlin were all so terribly hopeless and depressed. The change of air seems really to have done him good. With deepest gratitude I remain,

Your Highness' ever devoted
JAGOW.

After my retirement Jagow, who meanwhile had moved to Rome, wrote again to my wife, on July 14, 1909 :

MOST ESTEEMED PRINCESS,

Perhaps I really ought to congratulate you, now that the die is definitely cast, on having escaped your Berlin treadmill; but any event so serious for the Fatherland as the Chancellor's relinquishment of our policy moves me too deeply for that, and fills me with too many sad and anxious thoughts. Apart from my personal regret at the loss of such an honoured chief, my feeling as a German makes me ask myself : How will the ship of state be able to do without such a helmsman ? And you yourself, I imagine, will not leave the old Palace in the Wilhelmstrasse, which you made into such a charming home, without at least some regret. The long years for which you have lived in it have brought you many joys and successes, as well as a heavy burden of duties, and the memory of it all will be linked with the thought of such pleasant, happy hours created and shared with many guests. I myself was so often permitted to enter your happy circle that, to-day, I must thank you for that also, as I do again with all my heart, as well as for all the many other kindnesses you have shown me. May I beg you to give the Prince my deepest and most heartfelt thanks, together with my great regret at a loss for which we all must suffer. He has shown me immeasurable kindness from the day when, fourteen years ago, I first came to Rome as attaché till this moment when, thanks to him, I find myself in such a splendid post. I shall never forget my debt to him. One small consolation for these events is the pleasant thought of seeing you again, in the Eternal City, next winter. All Rome is as delighted as I am.

With the deepest, most grateful esteem for yourself and the Prince, believe me, honoured Princess,

Always your obedient
JAGOW.

But, alas, all the fervid assurances so feelingly expressed by Gottlieb Jagow did not stand being put to the test in the winter 1914–1915. He had been willing enough to take my hand when it could raise him from very modest beginnings to the high rank of ambassador. Once risen, in the all-decisive hour, he easily denied the gratitude of which he had been so eager to assure me. I regret it more for his sake than mine, since I have learned to seek my consolations in a basic and liberating contempt; but certainly I regret it for the Fatherland which suffered, as I presently shall prove, the most grievous harm through Jagow's behaviour when they had made of him a Secretary of State.

He had a bosom friend of his own age, Johannes von Flotow. *Arcades ambo.* They had been at school together at the Ritterakademie in Brandenburg, on the Havel. Both had been members of feudal students' corps — Jagow of the Bonn-*Borussen*, Flotow of the Saxo-*Borussen* at Heidelberg. They had entered diplomacy together, were both equally sickly, and equally nervous about their health. Both were somewhat quiet and shy in manner, although in reality they were pushful, in the word's most offensive sense. The sentimental affection uniting them was that of the "glorious youths" the Nisus and Euryalus, to whom Virgil has erected a monument :

Fortunati ambo. Si quid mea carmina possunt
Nulla dies unquam memori vos eximet aevo,
Dum domus Æneae Capitoli immobile saxum
Accolet, imperiumque pater Romanus habebit.

To be sure Jagow and Flotow were not by any means so good-looking as these two young heroes of the Æneid. Both, when at the age of nearly fifty they bowed their necks under the chaste yoke of Hymen, took mates almost equally mature. Jagow led a virgin of forty-one to the altar, Flotow a widow of forty-nine. Jagow, as my Chief of Department, through the last months I was in office, often sorely tried my patience and put to the severest tests that urbanity for which I am so celebrated and with which I have so often been reproached, because he was determined to lose no time and ensconce himself, before my retirement, in some kind of ministerial post. With this in view he made the most convulsive efforts to scare first one and then another Minister from his perch, and so alight on it himself. At first he kept an eye on Munich, then occupied by Carl von Schlözer. Schlözer was a nephew of the brilliant Ambassador to Washington and Minister to the Vatican, Kurd von Schlözer, well known for his historical monograph on the relations between Frederick the Great and Catherine II, and for his history of the German Baltic Province, more famous still for his charming "Roman Letters", and most of all for unswerving loyalty to Bismarck, as whose inconvenient subordinate he had once served in St. Petersburg, to become in the end a most useful diplomatic instrument, and to whom he remained true after his fall. His nephew, Carl, also published a very delightful book, the humoresque "Aus Dur und Moll." Like his uncle he was very witty. After getting engaged in Cairo to a charming lady from the Rhineland, he announced it to me with the words: "You see, I too have won my battle of the Pyramids." On my retirement he sent me his particular thanks for having protected him against the poisoned "flea bites" (*e.g.* Floh-flea) of "Floh-tow." When Flotow perceived that Munich was not coming his way, he turned his yearning gaze on Karlsruhe, the Baden *Residenz*, less splendid than Munich, and yet not a bad little post. This led to a scene which might have been taken from a farce. The Prussian Minister in Karlsruhe, Herr von Eisendecher, who had worked there for a quarter of a century, felt it officially incumbent on him to lodge a formal enquiry with the Foreign Office whether it intended to keep him longer as His Prussian Majesty's representative to the Court of Baden. He believed that he could assure his superiors that official circles in Baden, and in particular the Grand Duchess Louise, desired him to retain his post. When Flotow received this letter, to deal with it as my personal representative, he sent me word that the Minister in Karlsruhe was asking to be put on the retired list. He, Flotow, would be more than delighted to be given a chance of the post. He added that the climate of Karlsruhe, a mixture of Alpine freshness and the warmth of the Rhenish plateau, would be ideal for his very delicate health. I answered that if, to my deep regret, Eisendecher really did want to retire, I should have to give the matter serious thought before I could appoint his successor. Soon after this, on private business, Eisendecher came to Berlin. We had asked him to dine, but I was unable to be present, since a heavy chill had laid me low, and the good Renvers packed me off to bed to sweat it out as quickly as possible in order that I might be able to speak in the Reichstag. When Eisendecher arrived at the Chancellor's Palace with his wife, the Princess was struck with the glum look on their faces. The cause of this was soon apparent. Eisendecher had received a wire from Flotow, acting as my Chief of Department, to say that his resignation had been received and would go through the proper official channels. My wife went in to me at once to explain the matter, and I sent her back with word to Eisendecher that I had not the slightest intention of suggesting his recall to the Emperor. I should be delighted to learn that he was willing to continue his valuable service at Karlsruhe. She gave that excellent Minister my message, to his great relief, and the equal disappointment of Flotow, who also happened to be dining with us, and who said to her in a venomous whisper, "This will mean my death." In the short time left him till my retirement he made several further frantic efforts to obtain, first Copenhagen and finally even the modest Oldenburg. Having missed the last, he left Berlin.

When, a few days before leaving Berlin for good, I sent for him in order to clear up some minor, outstanding official matters, I was given that answer received by Schiller's "Queen Elizabeth" in reply to her command, sent by Lord Kent: "Let Leicester come." But Kent replies: "He craves your pardon. He is shipped to France."

A mere Chancellery servant brought me my message to the effect that Herr von Flotow had just left Berlin for Norderney. He went to escape the farewell celebrations in my honour. Nor, when I followed him to Norderney, was he part of the crowd which welcomed me on the landing stage, though most of our other acquaintance there had gathered, even the Regierungspräsident of Aurich, Prince Carl Ratibor (he later became an excellent Upper President of Westphalia) who had come across from the mainland on purpose to be present at my arrival. But Flotow appeared that night at dinner and then on one pretext after another stayed with us for nearly a week. Later I was to learn in Berlin that he had remained for the special purpose of sending a daily report, on my habits and attitude, to the capital. To be sure, there was not much for him to write except that in the mornings I stayed in the house and went out riding every afternoon. He became very excited, however, when a deputation of six hundred Civil servants from Wilhelmshaven appeared in Norderney with an address, assuring me of their loyalty and appreciation, and could not even manage to calm down when I thanked these worthy fellows in a cordial, but entirely non-political speech, assuring them that I, as an old Civil servant, well knew how much our country owes its officials. In Flotow's view it was "not altogether correct" for a retired Minister of State to receive addresses and ovations.

When Flotow at last had ceased to haunt our villa, returning to Berlin to continue his pursuit of a sinecure, there appeared our first really welcome visitor to Norderney after my retirement. This was Walter Rathenau, a man of very unusual gifts, and certainly not without a peculiar distinction of spirit, who now seemed even more interesting than he might have done had I not just been enduring Flotow. I had made Rathenau's acquaintance two years pre-

viously, through Bernhard Dernburg, the recently appointed Chief
of the Colonial Section of our Foreign Office, who asked me whether
I would be willing to receive his best friend, Doctor Walter Rathenau. I answered that it would give me real pleasure to meet the
son of so esteemed a personality as the General Director of the
A.E.G.(General Electric Company), and that already I had heard
how gifted he was. On the following afternoon I was sitting out
on the terrace of the Chancellor's Palace, a favourite resting place
in summer, since the door of my study opened out of it, when,
escorted by one of my footmen, Walter Rathenau first came into my
presence. At that time he was scarcely forty, though he looked
older. Immaculate. A most winning personality. His movement, as he approached, was faultless; the kind of entrance one
associates with a *jeune premier* of the Théâtre Français — Delauney
or Guitry — in a play by Victorien Sardou or Émile Augier, come
to ask the heavy father for the hand of the daughter he adores.

"Your Highness," he began, in a mellow voice, laying his right
hand on his heart, "before you do me the honour of receiving me, I
feel there is something I ought to tell you; or perhaps I had better
say, confess." A little pause and then, in the most mellifluous voice,
"Your Highness, I am a Jew."

I replied that I did not think I had given grounds for any accusations of prejudice, especially not of anti-Semitic prejudice. "From
Prince Bülow," Rathenau rejoined, with another ceremonious inclination, "that is the answer I expected."

He remained for quite a long time and we had a most stimulating
talk, *de omni re scibili*, to be followed by many others like it, in Berlin, Norderney, and Rome. Walter Rathenau soon became our welcome guest. He was always brilliant, possessed a most unusual
faculty of absorbing and adapting any subject, was, above all, unusually versatile. Italy still remembers her Giovanni Pico della
Mirandola, who flourished in the first spring of the Renaissance.
Pico spoke with equal fluency Latin and Greek, Hebrew, Chaldean,
and Arabic. He strove to wed philosophy to religion, to reconcile
Plato with Aristotle, and laid down the premises of his thought in a
polemic of ninety-nine theses, the famous and dreaded "*Conclu-*

siones philosophicae, cabbalisticae, et theologicae." Rathenau was
not quite so many-sided, yet he could talk with equal ease and delight of Philo of Alexandria, the Hebrew-Hellenist philosopher whose
spirit seemed akin to his; of the latest *coup de bourse* of the Bleich-
röders; of a new technical discovery or a picture by his cousin,
Max Liebermann. I do not deny that Rathenau may have been
too many-sided. On the whole his father, the founder and director
of the A.E.G., made a deeper, more lasting impression than the
son, whom he himself is said to have described as "a tree which
had put forth less fruit than blossom." In politics at least Walter
Rathenau lacked the sober judgment, the objectivity, the quiet
and reasoned balance which are essential, and was, above all, not
sufficiently matter of fact. Nor do I feel he would ever have made
a statesman. He had personal knowledge of England, Italy, and
France. Yet, in spite of it, he often made mistakes and would
waver between an excess of impulsive optimism and the black exaggeration of despair. This also applied to personal relationships,
especially those with other Israelites. I have known him both the
closest friend and bitter enemy of Maximilian Harden.

When first we met he was a great admirer of Bernhard Dernburg, who had introduced us. But, on his return from a trip they
had taken together through our African Colonies, Rathenau seemed
never able to still his itch to pour out scorn on the Colonial Minister
who, in torrid jungles, had worn a frock coat and over it the red and
white striped ribbon of the Zanzibar "Order of the Shining Star."
Dernburg, on his side, kept assuring whoever could be got to listen
that Rathenau's continual posturings, his never-ending praise of
himself, had made him impossible to all the other members of the
party. Treitschke, in Volume IV of his German History, declares
that, when Heine quarrelled with Börne, all the worst stinks of the
Ghetto were released in great swathes over Germany — and certainly there was no scent of roses when Rathenau got to grips with
Bernhard Dernburg. The chief complaint which Rathenau's intimates seemed to make against him was that of his inordinate vanity.
I cannot endorse it, since I had not enough personal experience. All
I can say is that, personally, I was never worried by this much cen-

sured failing of Rathenau's, since I found it so extremely naïve. Albert Ballin, who had known him from his boyhood, and very much respected his brilliant gifts, loved a story of how Walter Rathenau had once said to him, "Since this world was created there have only been three really great men, and, curiously enough, they were all Jews — Moses, Jesus, and — I scarcely like to mention the third." *Se non è vero è ben trovato.*

It is not to be denied that Walter Rathenau was very ambitious and very subjective; too ambitious and far too subjective to have made a good diplomatic instrument, much less leader. Soon after he had been so horribly murdered, Haniel, his Secretary of State, who was always devoted to his Chief, told me that, in his opinion, Rathenau's political reputation had been saved by his early death. He would soon have mismanaged the Foreign Office. For all his gifts he had been too restless, too individualistic, far too unstable: had had a fresh idea every day, but followed none to its conclusion and could never allow a project to mature. Above all, he had seen events and people in much too personal a light.

Though I feel I should defend Walter Rathenau against this oft-repeated charge of vanity — since I found Doctor Hugo Preuss, the author of the Weimar Constitution, whose acquaintance I was later to make, far vainer, with less reason for being so — I will admit that he was inclined to pose, that at times he could be really affected, and was often far too *maniéré*. I do not know what truth there is in the story which Ballin and Dernburg loved to tell of him, that, while his father lay at the last gasp, Walter learned his speech for the funeral which he then proceeded to run through in front of the looking glass, carefully rehearsing in advance each effect he intended to use at the grave. The speech, which later he sent me, bound in morocco, was, I may add, a very beautiful one. But it is certain that Walter Rathenau did not possess that naturalness of manner proper to not merely our greatest Germans, to such men as the Emperor William I, the Emperor Frederick, Bismarck, Moltke, and Roon, Helmholtz and Mommsen, but to lesser lights — to Windthorst and Bennigsen, Menzel and Ulrich Wilamowitz-Möllendorf, Maybach, Budde, Schmoller, Miquel, Lenbach, Liebermann, Göben,

Schlieffen, Hindenburg, Walter Loë, and Häseler — and which makes so pleasant a factor in personality.

When, in the spring of 1922, I returned from Rome to Berlin, Rathenau, then at the Foreign Office, called on me at the Hotel Bristol. The purpose of his call was a proof of his real delicacy of feeling. At the time of paying his court to the Chancellor, Wirth, he had said, in some speech or article, that he considered Wirth by far the most notable of the last eight or ten German Chancellors. Maximilian Harden, who had once been Rathenau's bosom friend but turned against him as soon as he rose to be a Minister, had demanded maliciously, in the *Zukunft*, whether Rathenau really considered Joseph Wirth, who so far had done nothing at all, during the short time in which he had held office, more notable than Prince von Bülow. Rathenau seemed most anxious to assure me that he had never meant anything so tactless. I laughed and soon put him at his ease, and we had a long and very friendly talk, during which he recalled a remark he had made in the autumn of 1914, as we stood together at the windows of my suite in the Adlon. He had pointed at the Brandenburger Tor, and said: "Can a monarch of such arresting personality, so charming and human as a man, so utterly inadequate as a ruler, as the Emperor William II — with an impossible Chancellor like Bethmann and a frivolous Chief of Staff like Falkenhayn, ever expect a triumphal return through that arch? If he gets it, history will have no meaning."

Now he pointed again through the window of the Hotel Bristol, at the crowd on Unter den Linden, and added: "If I went down now on to the middle avenue of the Linden and shouted — 'Cheers for the good old days! Cheers for Bismarck! Cheers for Kaiser and Fatherland! Cheers for our old and glorious Prussian army!' — I should possibly be arrested at once. But the men, apart from a few down-and-outs, would be deeply moved by what I shouted, and the women would all blow me kisses. Suppose I were to shout: 'Long live the Republic!' Every one would begin to laugh. To Germans the word 'Republic' sounds Philistine; there's something prosaic, almost ridiculous, about it."

Walter Rathenau possessed, in unusual measure, that gift of being able to laugh at oneself which I have often met in educated Jews. One day we were discussing the editor of a certain Democratic Berlin newspaper with a very extensive circulation. He fully agreed with all my praises of this editor's style and reputation for sincerity. When I added that it seemed to me a pity that the party limitations of such a publicist should so often make his thought seem monotonous, and so arouse the longing to contradict him, Rathenau replied: "You're perfectly right. Do you know what would happen to me if I were forced to read only that paper for long?" I shrugged, and Walter said, with a subtle smile, "I should find myself becoming anti-Semitic." The *mot* was worthy of a Heine.

The last sight I had of Walter Rathenau was at a garden party, which I attended with my wife, held in the garden I knew so well, of the villa of the Secretary of State. He seemed overjoyed at our having come and thanked us again and again. There, for the last time, I shook hands with him. The news of his death, soon afterwards, came as a very painful shock. Ten years before this tragic finish of a life that had promised so much — ignorant, then, of all the sorrows the immediate future held in store — we had gone for a long walk together along the shore of the North Sea. Rathenau had talked to me of his work, while I, in return, had confided many personal and political memories. He was the first who seemed to be really eager to have me begin to write my memoirs. Alas, many things were to happen before I could settle down to the task. At the end of August, 1909, I received from him the following lines:

Many and most respectful thanks for the honour of Your Highness' letter. I feel that I have touched my highest distinction in the esteem and confidence which you place in me. An official act could only externalize the honour, it would have no power to increase it. Life has given me the great happiness of sometimes being able to serve others. But the happiness of accepting kindnesses — the more freely and gratefully, the less I have managed to deserve them — is something which I have learnt from Your Highness. That day on which you first received me as a friend was the beginning, for me, of a new epoch. When I think of the delightful cordiality with which, for the last two years, you and the

Princess have welcomed me — of all that you have done to cheer my solitude — and remember the evenings in the Wilhelmstrasse, our talks, and the pleasant days at Norderney, I find myself assailed by a new emotion, almost painfully aware of an obstinate hope that one day, perhaps, I may be able to show Your Highness my gratitude with something more effective than mere words.

On a very different plane from the above, may I, without incurring the suspicion of that personality in politics which I have heard you criticize so often, devote some space to a curious observation on the decisions of His Excellency, von Valentini.   I do not consider it a mere accident that Herr von Valentini should have ignored the second of my African expeditions. A certain channel of information, whose source I am still unable to locate, though I imagine it not far from the Colonial Office, has spilt the following drops of explanation.   Your Highness had approached the Emperor on behalf of certain other gentlemen — among them Privy Councillor Witting — as well as of my insignificant self.   The All Highest did not accede to your suggestions.   But Herr von Valentini seems to insinuate, in the letter which Your Highness was so kind as to show me, in the strictest confidence, that this statement of the matter is incorrect, in so far, at least, as I am concerned.   Is it conceivable that certain other informations were collected from His Excellency Dernburg, who thus got to hear of other names?   And might he not have answered in such a manner that my two African expeditions fused into one, by the method which jurists define as "continued felony"?

Your Highness will forgive this *intermezzo*, which mere curiosity made me insert, and let me return to the serious theme of this letter.   I was very delighted, at Norderney, to notice how well Your Highness seemed, and your kind letter confirms my impression.   I feel doubly honoured and delighted that the Princess should so graciously have remembered me; that she even joins you in suggesting that I visit you in Rome in the near future. The energy and good health I brought back with me have been sorely taxed these last few days, and did not prove themselves sufficient to keep me over yesterday in Berlin.   I went away into the country.   At the time when both the mass of the people and those who form our popular opinion were equally decisive in their rejection of "the greatest man of the century", I, who had nothing but admiration for the Count's patient effort and self-sacrifice, was already in the happy position, with my colleagues of the Studiengesellschaft, of being able to protect his life work. But, as an engineer, I find myself unable to share in the riotous acclama-

DR. WALTER RATHENAU

tions of the assembled populace of Berlin — and even more in the kind of hysteria which now tries to put into the shade the achievement of such great poets and thinkers as Germany could produce in Bismarck's day; or indeed under any of her great statesmen.

With deepest respect,

Your Highness' ever devoted

WALTER RATHENAU.

The tart little sentence concerning "the greatest man of the century" and all the acclamations he received, naturally referred to Count Zeppelin. Such phrases sprang from a certain inclination to petty jealousy which sometimes rather disturbed Rathenau's friends. His difference with Von Valentini, which he mentions near the beginning of his letter, concerned, as had my previous letter to him, the decoration which, shortly before my retirement, I had striven to secure for Rathenau. In the previous year, by direct application to His Majesty, I had procured him the *Kronenorden* (second class). This Order, with the pretty blue ribbon on which it is worn round the neck, had pleased Walter very much. I had hoped, before finally going out of office, to give my friend the added satisfaction of receiving the Star of the *Kronenorden*, that decoration nicknamed by young officers the *Sternickel*, since he set great store by such outward marks of distinction. But neither His Majesty nor Valentini would agree to this.

Finally I must reproduce a letter received from Rathenau by my wife, towards the end of 1909 :

MOST ESTEEMED PRINCESS,

At last the near approach of Christmas with all its attendant New Year festivities gives me the chance of sending you and the Prince these few words of devotion and respect. I am delighted to learn that you have found both peace and good health in the City of classic memories. We in the North, on the other hand, feel much the poorer by your absence. All the zest has gone out of politics. We must trust that they are in the best of hands, though that feeling of abundant vitality which can alone give richness and strength to any work of life or art, is absent from them. Caution and reserve, the careful husbanding of our forces, have replaced that freedom of method which made of policy an art : yet such qualities, in themselves very admirable, tending in quieter times to foster the growth of a nation, and be generally beneficial in their effects, make a strange contrast to-day with the mighty inner expansion of the country, the tremendous pressure which our ripened strength produces from without.   So that once again, policy and government seem threatening to become the poorest, least autonomous, part of the nation, and the private citizen tends again to lose all interest in them, and turns to his profession for an outlet.   Politics apart, I cannot tell you how much I miss both you and the Prince, nor with what emotions I look back on these last years. Those last delightful days together in Norderney seemed to give me the impression that His Highness had based a complete equanimity on the sovereign freedom of his thought.   I seem unable to free myself from a less dispassionate view of events.   May I beg Your Highness to assure him of my most respectful devotion?

CHAPTER V

William II's Attitude towards Me after Retirement — The "Press Stunts" — Schiemann — A Talk on the Subject of My Retirement between the Emperor William II and Count Friedrich Vitzthum-Lichtenwalde — The Aspersions in the "Märkische Volkszeitung" — A Letter to Bethmann — He Replies from Linderhof — Wahnschaffe, the Head of the Imperial Chancellery, in Norderney — Exchange of Letters between Myself and Bodo von dem Knesebeck on the Events of November, 1908.

I T was inevitable that certain ugly traits in the character of William II should affect me the instant I had retired. For twelve whole years I had been forced repeatedly to make observations which augured no good to me personally, once the political bond had been removed. In spite of all my Sovereign's protestations — and at times they had been really overwhelming — I had, therefore, entertained no illusions, no hopes of gratitude, or even of better treatment at his hands than he had meted out to each of my predecessors — and, most of all, to the greatest.

But there were certain limits which I had decided must not be overstepped.

William II, as I never can sufficiently insist, could be amiability itself with any one whom he happened to like for the moment, and for as long as he continued to do so. *"Comme l'Empereur est bon garçon,"* a pleasant and clever Frenchman once remarked to me when we had spent the day together on board the *Meteor* at Kiel, in company with the Kaiser, Prince Henry, and several of the admirals. And certainly William II could be *"bon garçon"* — *très bon garçon*, until he became exactly the reverse; till "nerves" and ill temper took possession of him, or he fell a victim to his arrogance, that Nemesis of the autocratic monarch, checked by no solid system of restraints.

In 1909, for as long as I was still in personal touch with him, he never really lost all self-control, but managed to preserve a certain discretion, in the interests of the State, and his own dignity. In the days of the November crisis he had doubtless given free rein to his tongue, in private talks with such people as Theodor Schiemann, Hans Oppersdorff, Eckardstein, and Eugen Röder, to whom he had said many spiteful and very inexact things about me. Previously, even, he had chafed under such a discouraging mentor. But not until our definite breach did he fling discretion to the winds. All the rancour which had simmered since the November days, rancour whose deepest source lay in his chagrin at my having seen him cut so poor a figure, could at last be given its full vent.

Professor Schiemann, whom he commanded to accompany him on his North Sea trip, was given his own, entirely inaccurate version of the November crisis and asked to publish it in the *Kreuzzeitung*, of whose staff the professor was a member. At about the same time Röder, the Master of Ceremonies, importuned the deputy, Erzberger, to sing the same refrain in the *Märkische Volkszeitung*. When, six years later, we met in Rome, Erzberger himself admitted to me — though he put it a little less bluntly and with many expressions of regret — that Röder had given him a hint that he would be serving the Centre Party's interests and would, at the same time, do himself a good turn with the Emperor, by assisting the All Highest to spread "the truth about the November crisis." So that therefore that same Matthias Erzberger, stigmatized in 1906 in innumerable marginal notes, as "arch-liar", "toad" — "Jesuit" even — was called in, three years later, as special witness for His Majesty.

But, before my sincerest efforts to shroud in a decent oblivion such slips and failings of the Crown as brought on the November hurricane had been threatened by the *Kreuzzeitung* slanders and those of Erzberger's party newspaper, I received a letter from my good old friend Count Friedrich Vitzthum, the Chief Court Chamberlain of Saxony and President of the first Saxon Chamber, which threw a pronounced and violent light on the Emperor's mood since my retirement. This letter (September 25, 1909) contained the following:

To-day I want to tell you in strictest confidence, of a talk I had on the 20th, in the ancient and historical *Kapellensaal* of the Albrechtsburg in Meissen with His Majesty. The Saxon Minister, Beck, one of your deepest admirers, who stood a few steps away from us all the time, and must therefore have caught something of what we said, patted me on the shoulder when it was over with the friendly words, *"Nibelungen troth!"* I hope that you also will approve of me when I tell you that my friendship for yourself made me go perhaps further than was necessary. Throughout the Emperor's reception I had purposely been keeping in the background, so that he did not notice me until we all sat down to table, because then I happened to sit just opposite him. He began to chaff me at once, in his usual hearty, cordial manner. He drank my health at dessert and, the moment the meal came to an end, he made straight for me — halfway down the room, although I had done nothing to catch his attention — and shook me by the hand with the words: "We have n't seen each other since Bernhard retired." While he lit his cigarette at my cigar I answered: "No, Your Majesty. But I 've been stopping for a fortnight with Bernhard at Norderney." "Oh — and how did you find him?" "As well as possible, Your Majesty. We went for a ride every day and I was surprised to see what a firm seat he still has." "Oh — and otherwise how did he seem?" "Your Majesty knows I'm one of Bernhard's closest friends. I should n't dare to give you my impressions freely if Your Majesty had n't asked me directly. I found Bernhard very alert mentally. But he seemed most hurt at hearing all Your Majesty has been saying about him." "It was n't easy to part from Bernhard. But he betrayed me at the time of the November crisis. We stood shoulder to shoulder, and he ought never to have admitted in the Reichstag that he considered my behaviour unconstitutional. He ought to have said that he 'd known and authorized everything." "I can't judge of that, Your Majesty; but I know Your Majesty will forgive me if I say you have never been more popular than at present . . . and that might not have been the case if Bernhard had taken a different line. I can assure you that he did what he thought was right, in the interests of Your Majesty and the dynasty, and that Your Majesty has had no more loyal servant than Bernhard. Surely Your Majesty's present popularity is a proof that Bernhard did the right thing?" "Yes, certainly. The people shout for me everywhere. They are on my side all over Germany. It 's because Germans are so anxious to show me that they can see what bitter injustice I 've had to suffer." "Excuse me,

Your Majesty, if I tell you that Bernhard's whole attitude did a great
deal to cause this swing-over. All this success speaks in his favour. And
now it hurts him very much to hear Your Majesty say that at the time, he
let himself be influenced by Harden. I know for a fact that Bernhard
has never spoken to Harden — never met him; never even seen him.
From first to last Harden attacked him and attacks him still, although he
has resigned." "That may be so, but, in that case he was influenced
indirectly by Holstein. For the last six months Holstein had had Bernhard entirely under his thumb. It was Holstein who really governed
Germany." "Your Majesty may perhaps recollect that I have always
detested Holstein, and that, in former years, I deplored his influence at
the Foreign Office. But on Bernhard he had no such influence, as Your
Majesty seems to believe. Bernhard has often told me that he continued to see Holstein after his fall for two reasons: first, because Holstein knew too much and, if he were roused, might publish it, to the
detriment of the State; and, second, because, as I 'm sure Your Majesty
will appreciate better than any one, it would not have been 'the act of a
gentleman'¹ to ignore a man whom one had known for thirty or forty
years simply because he fell from power." "Bernhard had ceased to be
the same. He 'd grown so forgetful, ever since that fainting fit in the
Reichstag. Among other things he seems to forget that I had discussed
the whole *Daily Telegraph* interview beforehand with him at Norderney:
that he himself had helped me to correct my plan of campaign, and
revised my letter to my grandmother." "Your Majesty, I 've never
noticed that he was forgetful. The other day Bernhard seemed more
brilliant and full of life than ever." "Oh, yes, in conversation perhaps.
But when we discussed affairs he often seemed not to know what we 'd
been talking about the day before." "As to that, of course, I can't say —
but if that really is so — if, as Your Majesty believes, that really was the
result of his unlucky fainting fit in the Reichstag, surely Your Majesty
would consider it all the more reason for judging Bernhard leniently now."
"Well, so I did for a time. Otherwise we should have parted at once.
That was why I let it go on for so long. But when I asked the Conservatives how they could bring themselves to oppose the government, they
said to me that they could n't support a Chancellor who had let me down
in the way that Bernhard did."

Here the king interrupted us, since it was time to go and see the illuminations. But the Emperor kept talking to me excitedly; trying — it is

¹ "Gentleman-like" in the original.

the only expression to use — to justify himself, till the king came back a second time, when the Emperor broke off, rather unwillingly, and followed him. I should add, in justice, that he had not been in the least unapproachable. He listened quite quietly to every word I said and never once seemed annoyed when I contradicted him. All the other people present, among them the Minister, Metzsch, had been watching this long talk with the greatest interest. I had looked so serious and spoken with so much insistence that they must have seen, at once, it was n't a joke. Unluckily I do not possess your wonderful memory, which came in for so much criticism, so that you must content yourself with such rough outlines as I can remember of what passed between us. The Emperor, who had been in the best of tempers all that day, became noticeably serious on the boat from which we watched the illuminations. He stood there wrapped in his cloak and did n't say another word to me. Valentini, with whom I had a few words about our talk, said to me, "We are all most grateful to you. Every one has been doing his best to rid the Emperor's mind of these illusions. And as to Prince Bülow's memory, that was nothing but a silly, stale bit of gossip. No one else has such a memory as Prince Bülow. Naturally we 're doing all we can to prevent these mistaken opinions from spreading. But you must wait till the Prince comes to Berlin for the little Princesses' confirmation. He 'll meet the Emperor and everything is certain to be arranged." That was the end of our talk on this memorable day. It was n't so easy to keep one's end up with the Emperor, who always tries to overwhelm you with arguments. But I stuck to my point, and if the king had n't come along to separate us, our talk would probably have lasted a long time. I had many other things on the tip of my tongue to say to him. In any case, I feel I can say with justice that I showed him I was n't going to give in and was determined "to have my way." I hope it will have had this result — that, in future H.M. will become more moderate in expression and will do you rather more justice than he has in the last few weeks.

To this letter from my friend Vitzthum I may add that I never met Harden until after I had resigned the chancellorship. I met him — unless my memory is deceiving me — in the autumn of 1911, at Felix von Eckardt's house in Hamburg. Harden had always attacked me sharply, till at last we met and reached an understanding on various points. It is ridiculous to suggest that in the November crisis he influenced me, or I him. It is well known that Harden was not easy to influence; nor should I have allowed myself to be guided by any publicist, and certainly not by Harden who, quite apart from his violent antagonism to me personally, was politically on an entirely different plane. Certainly Harden was on the best of terms with Holstein, just as he was with Walter Rathenau, and with Baron Alfred von Berger, who at the time directed the *Deutsches Schauspielhaus*, and they were both good friends of mine. I made what use I could of this indirect connection with Harden for the sole purpose of inducing a less violent tone in his criticism of William II throughout the November crisis — just as I had previously tried to suspend this writer's attacks on Philip Eulenburg. It was very characteristic of the Emperor that, soon after this long talk with Count Friedrich Vitzthum, he should have bestowed on him the Order of the Black Eagle, to every one's amazement, since the Count had done nothing to deserve it and was not on the list of possible recipients.

The *Kreuzzeitung* and *Märkische Volkszeitung* articles containing the Imperial version of the November crisis, were both, more or less, a restatement of the things His Majesty had said to me at our interview of March 11, 1909, and which then I contradicted with so much energy. Even to-day I cannot be quite certain whether William II, in making such extraordinary affirmations, consciously invented or was the mere victim of autosuggestion. His vanity perhaps — his obsessive itch to be in the right — caused him, first to say a thing he knew to be false, and then go on repeating it so often that, in the end, he himself began to believe it.

When first I read these lying "revelations" at Norderney, I rang up Schön, the Secretary of State, in Berlin, and demanded an official denial of such stale *réchauffés* of Court gossip many times contradicted. I added that it seemed to me my duty to say plainly that it was against the interests of truth, against those of the country — and, still more, those of His Majesty — to attempt to retrace my resignation to anything that had happened in the November crisis or to any personal difference with the Crown. Schön, in a voice whose embarrassment even the telephone betrayed, implored me not to answer in the Press, since such a polemic might gravely injure the dynasty. He was, he assured me, certain that the Chancellor, whom he was going to telephone at once, would be able to arrange things satisfactorily.

Whereupon I wrote off a long memorandum to my successor, very moderate in tone but equally definite in substance. It contained the following:

The Secretary of State at the Foreign Office will have announced to you that I consider it necessary to publish a definite, clear, unambiguous, official *démenti* of the base suggestions to which I have been exposed for some time past. These accusations spread against me are barefaced and senseless lies. It is untrue that I knew anything at all beforehand of the substance of the *Daily Telegraph* article. In the press of official business, and because I had placed confidence in subordinates, I omitted to read that significant manuscript myself, and was, a few weeks later, amazed and horrified when I saw it reproduced in a Wolff despatch. Wolff's published the interview spontaneously, without having sought my permission. Besides a number of harmless generalizations on the desirability of improvement in German relationships with England, the article contained an observation on the anti-English feeling prevalent in wide circles throughout Germany which, though in itself also relatively harmless, would better have been left unsaid by the Emperor. In addition to the above, it contained the following points, each of which was a cause of that sensation its publication produced all over the world, as well as of the German emotions aroused by it: (1) The affirmation that His Majesty the Emperor had prevented Russia and France from "humbling England to the dust." (2) His Majesty's assertion that he had drawn up a plan of campaign against the Boers, and that this plan had in many ways resembled the strategy employed by Lord Roberts. (3) The suggestion that our fleet was being constructed with some intention of its eventual use in the Pacific, *i.e.* against Japan.

I had no idea, before seeing the interview in print, that His Majesty had even intended to touch on any of these matters in England; far less had I declared myself in agreement with him, or endorsed such declarations as advisable. While still in office I constantly implored His Majesty to exercise caution and restraint in all his political pronouncements. I was forced to devote a considerable proportion of time and energy to repairing the damage already caused by his former slips and indiscretions.   Especially did I beg the Emperor to make no declaration in England which could not safely be repeated to the Russian, French, Japanese, or American governments.   I was, therefore, for no instant in doubt that such unusual statements on France and Russia could only be interpreted in England as an attempt to cut across the *rapprochement* into which Great Britain was entering with these Powers, and that hence the consequences to Germany could not fail to be the reverse of all we wished. The very fact of my having read the letter to Queen Victoria mentioned by His Majesty the Emperor, of my having known it to contain only academic and aphoristic remarks on strategy — of no practical value whatsoever for the conduct of any war in South Africa — should go to prove that I could never have advised the All Highest, in the sense of his statements on the Boer War.   Finally, as to Japan; I had warned the Emperor repeatedly to avoid arousing more resentment in that sensitive and mistrustful government than he had already aroused on many previous occasions ("Peoples of Europe defend your holiest possessions," "Yellow Peril" speeches, etc.).   I remember that two or three years ago I wired to keep back a letter from His Majesty to President Roosevelt, which had been for several days in the post because, when informed of its contents, these seemed to me to contain imprudent statements on Japan. I cannot remember, in any of my letters to His Majesty, at the time of his English visit in 1907, having made any reference whatsoever to the matters discussed by him in England.   I do not believe I ever did so. But this I can affirm most emphatically — that never, on these three aforesaid points, either in writing, by word of mouth, letter, or telegram, did I endorse — nor could I possibly have endorsed — such declarations with regard to them as were later reproduced in the *Daily Telegraph*.   It is asserted in the *Deutsche Tageszeitung* that His Majesty the Emperor has recently shown "a politician" letters received from me at that time, expressing my assent to all he said.   Let him show me those letters! They exist no more than does the mysterious "politician."   I knew as little in advance of these recent declarations of His Majesty as I had known in advance of his letter to Lord Tweedmouth, of his protest against the candidature of the American ambassador, Hill, of his telegram to the Prince of Lippe, of the Swinemünde telegram to the Prince Regent of Bavaria; of all his numerous other indiscretions, from the "Hun" speech in the summer of 1900 to the "Pessimist" speech at the 1906 manœuvres.

These attacks to which I am exposed contain many further inexactitudes.   It is untrue that in June last I went to Kiel in the hope that His

Majesty might refuse my application to resign. On the contrary, I was fully determined, in view of the Reichstag situation, to stand firmly by my request to go out of office.

One further point I must insist upon, while neglecting many minor details — the assertion made in the *Kreuzzeitung*, that for long I had only enjoyed the "official" confidence of the Emperor, and that even this I had found it impossible to retain. His Majesty twice refused my resignation and, in doing so, emphasized his confidence. At the end of a most detailed audience, which he graciously accorded me last March, he again assured me, in the strongest, most cordial terms, of his absolute and unshakeable trust in me. Again and again His Majesty has addressed me in public; he has visited me and commanded me to Potsdam: in Berlin, Wiesbaden, Potsdam, etc., he has sought me out in the most affable and condescending fashion. On the day when we took our final leave of him, he invited my wife and myself to come to Potsdam for the birthday of Her Majesty the Empress. On repeated occasions (my birthday — May 3d; the eve of his departure for the meeting with the Emperor of Russia; and even on the rejection of my Death Duties) I have been honoured with Imperial telegrams, worded most unambiguously and cordially, in a way that could leave me in no doubt of his wish that I should continue to be his Chancellor. At Kiel, when I applied for my dismissal, he discussed with me in the friendliest possible manner both the foreign and domestic situations and the nomination of my successor. In what light will His Majesty appear if all this was nothing but pretence? Now that I have retired I only ask to be spared all unnecessary publicity — to be left to myself, to lead a life of peaceful independence. Yet I feel I have a right to demand the contradiction of such low slanders as would asperse the honour of a man who, with some success, and in circumstances of exceptional difficulty, was for twelve years Minister and Chancellor. Where shall we be if these stories are allowed to go on circulating; if, in the end, I find it impossible to keep silence, if, perhaps, a legal action becomes necessary, and the statements which I am forced to make on oath are opposed to what seem like Imperial declarations? Let the *Reichsanzeiger* be prepared to publish a firm and clear denial; let His Majesty consent to see me in the second half of next October; and, since then I proceed to Rome, the whole miserable business will be at an end. But, for such a *démenti* to be effective, it must state, without any beating about the bush, that the suggestions made in the *Märkische Volkszeitung*, and since embellished in many other semi-official newspapers, are inaccurate on every point, both as regards the *Daily Telegraph* article and my personal relations with the Emperor.

I have no doubt that you, my honoured friend, who worked at my side through all the difficult struggles of last winter, will make every effort, in the interests of dynasty and Fatherland, to avoid any further misunderstandings.

The above reached my successor at Linderhof, a little rococo *schloss* set in the Bavarian Alps, whither the Prince Regent of Bavaria had invited him to shoot a stag. There too were Privy Councillor von Flotow, who had found it a very easy matter to slip into the new Chancellor's good graces, and Captain Schwartzkoppen, my ex-adjutant, who served in the same capacity under Bethmann. Schwartzkoppen was one of the most trustworthy people with whom I have ever had to deal — honourable through and through. He told me afterwards that Bethmann had at first seemed really upset by my letter. His instant reactions had been as follows: every word I had written to him was true: he had worked at my side in the November crisis: he entirely approved my attitude. It was his duty — not merely as Chancellor, his duty as an honourable man — to speak his mind on the subject to the Emperor and implore His Majesty's permission to publish my *démenti* in the *Reichsanzeiger*. The honest Schwartzkoppen was delighted at this decent behaviour of his chief, and said so, modestly but bluntly. Not so Flotow, who, with a face of horror, asked the new Chancellor if he wanted to have to retire at the end of his third month in office. Anything like direct and open championship would be bound to entail an instant breach with the Emperor or, at the very least, would poison at their source all future relationships with His Majesty. It was the Chancellor's duty to devote his energies to the country, which had welcomed his appointment with delight and already was beginning to place its trust in him. At the end of certain hesitations, Bethmann set his foot on this road. He declared himself fully aware that to retain his responsible post was the first and most sacred of his duties. And it certainly looked as though he could only hope to stay in office if he "humoured" His Majesty on this subject.

So that Bethmann-Hollweg, according to the undoubtedly true

account of an honest and forthright witness, appears to have behaved in this instance as he did on the invasion of Belgium, on the extension of submarine warfare, and many another serious decision. He made up his mind, in obedience to Flotow's suggestions, not to answer my letter in writing, but to send Privy Councillor Wahnschaffe, the Head of the Imperial Chancellery, to Norderney, to beg me to put up no public defence against these semi-official slanders, which were, as Herr von Bethmann, of course, well knew, directly or indirectly inspired by His Majesty. Wahnschaffe soon arrived in Norderney. This official, I am sorry to say, was later to incur just censure for all his trepidations during the World War on the Polish question, and his attitude towards the Emperor's abdication. But I am bound to admit that, in this instance, he discharged a commission from his chief in a very proper and loyal manner. He told me frankly that he felt the demands excessive which he would have to make on my fealty and patriotic spirit. But he was persuaded that I, as a good Prussian, would show myself equal to every sacrifice to the Fatherland and Imperial House . . . that I would renounce any public *démenti* or any threat of legal proceedings. My abnegation seemed highly to gratify Bethmann, who had meanwhile returned to Berlin. He wrote me at once the following, somewhat tortuous epistle :

MOST ESTEEMED PRINCE,

Wahnschaffe has just been informing me of the result of his mission to Your Highness. First, I am very gratified indeed to learn from him that Your Highness is not dissatisfied with the verbal answer you have received to your letter of the 28th inst. I had never for a moment been in doubt that those very grave considerations which I felt it to be my duty to lay before you, in connection with any eventual public step Your Highness might feel called upon to take, either in the Press or in a law court, were the merest reflection of that spirit of loyalty and devotion with which you yourself are so imbued. Will Your Highness be equally assured that your demand for the speediest possible termination of a matter as prejudicial to yourself as it is to both Fatherland and dynasty is a standpoint I heartily endorse? Though lately I have done my very best, as I hope not entirely unsuccessfully, to muzzle a considerable part of the Press, and have also tried to open the eyes of several leading politicians, I am in further complete agreement with Your Highness that the matter of your reception by His Majesty is one that must be decided forthwith. Yet this can only be done through a personal interview with the Emperor, and, for that, it will be essential to choose a moment when I do not appear to him importunate. Since His Majesty leaves Rominten early to-morrow, and will travel by his usual route to Hubertusstock, via Königsberg, Cadinen, Marienburg and Langfuhr, I must postpone the interview till Hubertusstock — that is to say until the 9th inst. Much as I deplore this postponement, especially in the interests of Your Highness, the first essential is to avoid imperilling the results of my audience by choosing the wrong moment to broach the subject. I hope this judgment of the exigencies of a difficult situation is one which Your Highness can endorse. Should I succeed in reaching the solution conformable with Your Highness' just demands it will give me immense satisfaction, both humanly and politically speaking. In this assurance, to which I add my most respectful greetings to the Princess,

I remain, ever respectfully,

Your Highness' very devoted
BETHMANN-HOLLWEG.

On October 11th there followed another letter from the new Chancellor:

MY MOST HONOURED PRINCE,

Yesterday I left Hubertusstock, where I had been received in audience by His Majesty. The Emperor is most grateful to Your Highness for all the reserve which you have exercised in face of these deplorable Press attacks, and will be very willing to receive Your Highness, as I suggested. His Majesty intends, in addition to a verbal invitation extended to yourself and the Princess for the birthday celebration of H.M. the Empress, to command you both — presumably between the 18th and 22d — to luncheon in the most intimate circle at Potsdam. It did not, unfortunately, seem possible to select an earlier date, in view of existing arrangements. But I venture to hope that, even in this form, the intentions of the All Highest will be consonant with Your Highness' wishes, especially if — with the express approbation of the Emperor — I at once call the attention of the Press to Your Highness' reception at Potsdam in the near future. Even prior to this, however, I would consider it an exceptional favour to be allowed a talk with Your Highness. I have certain communications which I feel had better be made verbally, regarding my impressions, etc., and which, as I hope, will convince you of my own very urgent desire to bring about the speedy and definite solution of this most unhappy situation.   May I request you to present my deepest respects to the Princess, and believe me

Always your devoted
BETHMANN-HOLLWEG.

In obedience to the law of his nature Bethmann made very timorous efforts to quash the slanders spread against me.   Yet, at least, that goodwill was not lacking on which, so Schopenhauer declares, the whole of our moral being depends.   Herr von Schön was extremely careful to avoid having to take a definite attitude.   At that time he was obsessed with the single wish to exchange the post of Foreign State Secretary, a post which made excessive demands on both his industry and capacities, for that of Ambassador in Paris, on which he and his wife cast longing eyes.   Prince Radolin, the Ambassador, however, did not seem in any way eager to vacate the Embassy in the Rue de Lille.   This obstinacy resulted in a struggle between himself and Schön which, *soit dit en passant*, was to lead to some fairly grave political consequences, under the slack leadership of Bethmann.   Each competitor kept assuring the French that he was the only man to have in Paris; the man who could best be relied on to influence Berlin to a more accommodating spirit towards French aspirations in Morocco.   Naturally this increased the arrogance and pretensions of the French, so that the fruits of my agreement with France, of February 9, 1909, began to be lost not long afterwards.

Hammann had written again on my last birthday, saying how much he wished my happiness, how he prayed that the Divine blessing might yield us a rich crop of fresh successes, in the interests of the German Empire.   A year of heavy toil lay behind me.   By the grace of God, I had managed to withstand the severest strain, in full possession of every physical, intellectual, and spiritual power.   He wished I might remain for ever thus — the same both humanly and in politics; the same in effort as in success.   Now he wrote

again, sharply criticizing the "stale, silly gossip" of Martin, adding
that "this spiteful tomfoolery of the *Märkische Volkszeitung*" would
have produced very little effect had it not been for the less directly
venomous *Kreuzzeitung*, which had accused me of ambiguous hypocrisy in dealing with the famous interview. Schiemann, during
a chance conversation, had told him that the *Kreuzzeitung* article
had been the All Highest's version of the affair. Later the *Kreuzzeitung's* editor seemed to realize all the harm he had done. These
wretched "disclosures", though they did no good to the Conservatives, had exposed the country and the Crown to the danger of fresh
"Kaiser debates" in the Reichstag, as well as having involved me
in a conflict which could only be deeply deplored. On the one hand
I possessed an historic name, the honour of which I had to defend;
on the other my whole loyalist past. He hoped that, secure in the
knowledge that from history I had nothing to fear, I would not
court the applause of Liberals. The saying that only the Liberals
can provide a man with a posthumous reputation must be taken
with a grain of salt. In Caprivi's case, for instance, it had proved
false. The Secretary of State had shown him my protest to the
Chancellor. Its clear disproval of the falsities of the present Press
campaign had robbed these of all historical value. The *mot* on
"posthumous reputation" was, I think, coined by the *Berliner
Tageblatt*. But his spiteful mention of poor Caprivi came ill from
the pen of Hammann who, on Bismarck's fall, began his career as
the devout hanger-on of the second Chancellor.

The following letter, from an old regimental comrade, Bodo von
dem Knesebeck, the Kaiserin's *Chamberlain de service* and deputy
Master of Ceremonies, was very welcome and greatly moved me.
As a member of Their Majesties' suite he had watched, and himself
taken part in, the whole November crisis at close quarters. Nor
did he write in answer to any letter of mine:

This repulsive exhibition in the Press, originating solely from the fact
that certain people are desperately anxious to get whitewashed, has disgusted me so that I feel really ill and sick at heart. What hurts me most
of all is the version, fostered in a certain quarter from which these attacks
get their support, of the whole business in November. It all leaves a most

unpleasant after-taste of political vulgarity on the one hand, and, on the other, to put it most mildly, of lack of intelligence. You know how I feel about all that, and how, for the last twenty years, I had watched the growth of discontents, leading at last to an outburst of primitive passion which had had, too often, to be repressed. If to-day all this has been altered, the thanks are in no small measure due to yourself — to your handling of the situation which arose in those days of conflict. I am still persuaded that, with people losing their heads as they did at the time, far extremer resolutions might have been taken had the Reichstag, in the natural drive of events, begun to lose confidence in its Chancellor. Parliament would have taken the matter in hand and appealed direct to the Crown, over the head of the First Imperial official. The Conservatives, who went further than any one in their criticisms, inspired by party motives, would have been forced to go along with the rest, in defence of their whole previous attitude. Who still remembers that, when you stood up on November 11th, to shoulder the sole responsibility, you had nothing and nobody behind you, to support your defence of the Crown? Not one of the parties! Not the Federal Council! Not a deputy! You were thrown entirely back on your own resources, and it was not so easy to master such a situation as it is, now that everything has blown over, to criticize it all from selfish motives. I do not know if any other statesman has had such a Reichstag to face. I doubt it. But there — I've said enough! You must keep your usual equanimity. At nights, when I can't get to sleep, these things keep running through my head, and so I had to send you this letter. Many greetings to the dear and honoured Princess.

Always beside you in my thoughts,

Yours

B. K.

My answer to this companion in arms with whom, in the great old days, I had fought shoulder to shoulder, when together we advanced on La Hallue:

These days have brought me many proofs of friendship, but none has been so welcome or shown such understanding as yours! When, almost a year ago, the bomb burst — a bomb which might have been packed with any explosive — my first and only thought was to rescue His Majesty the Emperor, and bring him safe behind the firing line. I had been overwhelmed with work, was absorbed in very grave and difficult tasks of both foreign and domestic policy. I trusted my subordinates (Schön, Stemrich, Müller, Klehmet) and therefore did not personally examine the *Daily Telegraph* manuscript. These subordinates, out of respect for Imperial pronouncements, in fear lest further emendations might make the business worse than it was already, and also, no doubt, because they themselves lacked perspicacity, let the thing go through as it stood. I used all this to take all responsibility on my shoulders, in an article, which you yourself have read, published in the *Neue Allgemeine Zeitung*, since I was the official responsible. I ruthlessly exposed myself and the Foreign Office in order to shield the Crown. The Press, in so far as I could control it, was also influenced in this sense. But there are floods which cannot be dammed up. There are situations which inevitably lead to the detonation of long-accumulated high-explosive. In spite of every effort I could make, Press, public opinion, the whole nation, swept aside, in a burst of anger, this formal assignment of culpable negligence to the Foreign Office and insisted on asking the one question: Did His Majesty really talk like that?

And, if he did, then how are we to hinder any future repetition of such contingencies? For twenty years too many things had happened to arouse and embitter the widest circles. Faced as I was with this storm of anger, fraught with an elemental force, I still managed to keep my head, still directed all my efforts to this one object; to prevent the Crown's authority being lessened; so to act that, after such a storm, it might shine untarnished as before, as fair and glorious as ever, its radiance both here and abroad undimmed in the eyes of our German princes and people. For the Imperial Crown is the key and corner stone of our unity, security, and future.

But to achieve my end it was impossible to defend His Imperial Majesty in words, as previously I had defended him in the Lippe case, over the Swinemünde telegram, and in many similar instances. Nothing would have been gained had I done so. Nor could I stand up as a simple advocate. All attempts at denial and embellishment would have made things even worse than they were already. *Il fallait faire la part du feu.* In the Reichstag, therefore, I only rectified whatever was in the least amenable to justification. Above all, I managed to calm those Foreign Powers which had felt most indignant over the interview. I treated the whole affair with the seriousness with which it filled me also. Of His Majesty I begged that explanation which served to quieten, not only the Federal Council and State Ministry, whose members felt more roused

even than I, but the minds of all perceptive Germans, whose confidence
in the Monarchy I restored. This achieved, I could tell Her Majesty, the
Empress, that if His Majesty would only maintain six months' reserve
and permit himself no further indiscretions, the country would have
regained its inner peace. My further activities were as follows: I
advised His Majesty to be present, immediately after the crisis, at the
centenary dinner in the Berlin Rathaus, to show the world that, in spite
of all that had happened, he would be just as safe in the "Red House",
in the midst of democratic municipal councillors, as anywhere else between
the Niemen and the Meuse. I further saw to it that, on the Emperor's
fiftieth birthday, every German Prince rallied round him to attend the
celebrations. Then came the King of England's visit, which passed off
as smoothly and pleasantly as possible. Finally, in the domain of
Foreign Policy, I had managed, by the following spring, to secure for the
German Empire, and with that Empire for its Emperor, a position of such
strength and prestige at the end of the great diplomatic winter campaign,
as neither had known for twenty years. These last are the very words
used in the great English newspaper, never especially well disposed to
Germany. And a Russian diplomatist wrote in May: "It has unfortunately proved possible to reëstablish '*la suprêmatie allemande*' which had
been so happily lost since Bismarck's fall."

Moreover, throughout the whole country, the feeling has changed and
softened. Those small attempts made in the Reichstag to set parliamentary limitations on the Imperial prerogative came to nothing.
When, in May, at Frankfurt-on-the-Main, I attended the musical festival
and listened, at Their Majesties' side, to those eighteen thousand voices
raised in Wagner's "Emperor's Hymn" — one single note of boundless
acclamation in welcome of the Imperial pair — I could say to myself
that the promise I had given Her Majesty in November was now at its
complete fulfilment; that Crown and Emperor had weathered the
tempest unscathed!

That is the true state of affairs; the truth of history. I have ever
truly served His Majesty, and never more truly than in the November
days. In my twelve years of ministerial office I have done the Kaiser and
Empire many services, but nothing of what I did had more significance
than the work of my last six months as Chancellor. You can therefore
imagine what contempt these slanders in the Press arouse in me — this
miserable, staged indictment! But the contempt has gained the upper
hand over other feelings no less comprehensible — feelings of bitterness

and anger at so much petty baseness, such stupidity. I have been, from my youth up, a diplomat, and my father was a diplomat before me. I have served in turn as Minister, Ambassador, State Secretary, Imperial Chancellor. Yet, according to Conservative newspapers, I had not even the wit to see in advance how dangerous would be the effect abroad of the more controversial parts of the *Telegraph* interview. According to Herr Erzberger and the Clericals, I deliberately contrived a situation which would imperil the whole position of Germany, and which landed me, as Imperial Chancellor, in the tightest, most perilous corner in which any Minister could have found himself! No! I am not quite such a fool. Nor am I a knave. What a spectacle it would give the country if Court gossip and backstairs rumour were confronted with the irrefutable explanations I have just submitted to the Chancellor. What perfect food it would supply to the rumours of "*camarilla*" and "personal government." The parties are selfish to the core. The Centre and Conservative *bloc* is trying to refute the odium incurred by these negative results of an attempt to reform Imperial finances; nor do they care to seem to have to answer for my retirement. The Centre has no wish to show itself as merely revengeful, nor the Conservatives as that party which compelled a Chancellor deserving better treatment at the hands of vested interests and of agriculture to go out of office. That is why politicians are striving to unload this discredit on the Crown. Such are the motives behind the campaign of detraction which, you say, makes you sick at heart. I too have felt the need to express to you some of my feelings, who are bound to me by the ties of an old friendship, and whose letter showed so deep an understanding. We shall both be delighted to lunch with you *en route* for Rome, where we very much hope you will come and stay with us.

Ever your loyal friend,

BÜLOW.

CHAPTER VI

In Berlin — A Conversation with Bethmann (October, 1909) — Luncheon with Their Majesties at the Neues Palais — The Soirée for the Kaiserin's Birthday (October 22, 1909): My Last Meeting with William II before the World War — I go to Berne; My Brother Alfred — We Arrive in Rome; the Villa Malta — Its History — My First Walk Leads Me to the Capitol — My Life in Rome; Barrère — Von Loebell.

ON October 21st, we returned from Norderney to Berlin. Bethmann came hurrying at once to the Hotel Adlon, where we were staying, to thank me for not having begun a Press campaign, well aware how many German and foreign publicists would have been eager to offer me their services. His gratitude seemed even deeper that I had taken no politico-legal action against either Schiemann or Erzberger. Such a step could easily have resulted in incalculable consequences to the Emperor. "Your Highness," my successor added, with emphasis, "has done further immense service to Crown and country."

On the following day we had been commanded to lunch at the Neues Palais with Their Majesties. The Kaiser welcomed me as though we had parted the day before, with nothing unusual between us. But at luncheon his sole topic of conversation was Professor Dohrn's aquarium at Naples, which he kept adjuring me to visit. After the meal he went for a walk in the park, accompanied by two diplomatists, Herr von Mumm, our Ambassador in Japan, and Doctor Rosen, our Minister in Morocco, who had also been commanded to lunch with him.

He seemed to have forgotten my existence. This strange behaviour appeared to cause the Empress some embarrassment. She begged me, with touching cordiality, to sit beside her and look through an album of splendid photographs. As we sat examining these she said: "This morning the Emperor woke with such a head-

ache. He really must get a little air." In spite of the fact that
she was the same age as the Kaiser, there was something motherly
in her behaviour towards him.

We took our leave at the same time as Rosen and Mumm, who
informed me that William II had kept predicting, with more
imagination than reason, the outbreak of war in the near future
between America and Japan. For over twenty years His Majesty
had awaited such a war and seemed more than ever convinced that
its results would leave him master of the world. Both Mumm and
Rosen had striven, in vain, to oppose him.

That evening we returned to Potsdam. The soirée, held in honour of the Kaiserin's birthday, was very brilliant and lasted a considerable time. But His Majesty could not bring himself to address
me, though, in compensation, he began a long talk with my wife,
which lasted nearly an hour and a half. If, in July, on the evening
of our farewell dinner, he had honoured her with an address on
politics, this time he avoided all such matters and seemed most
eager to hear about the Villa Malta. Did my wife, he asked, intend
to arrange it as charmingly as she had furnished the Chancellor's
Palace? The Kaiser had a very high opinion of my wife's artistic
taste and sensibilities. On my retirement he said to Ballin, who
had soon passed on the remark to me : "I don't regret Bülow in the
least, but his wife will really be a loss. She could bring a kind of
cinquecento atmosphere into the drab prose of Berlin life." That
evening, in the Neues Palais, he also remarked, with a certain
acerbity, "No doubt you 'll be very glad to get rid of me. Both
you and Bernhard will have a far better time in Rome than I 'm ever
likely to get here."

The evening ended without my having received a word from
the Emperor, though Her Majesty had done her very best, by
marked and cordial attentions, to make up for the obvious coldness
of her spouse, and had several times begun long conversations with
us both.

I was not to see the Emperor again till five years later, in the
August of 1914, a few days after the bad advice of Jagow and Bethmann, in conjunction with his own vainglory, had blundered him

into the war which brought to earth our glorious, strong, and happy Empire. I must insist that neither his ingratitude nor his lack of even common politeness could, in the least, shake my loyalty to the dynasty, my love for Prussia and for Germany. I could always think of our good old Emperor William I — of the kind words he said to me at Frankfurt, at the time of my father's death. I could remember our dear Emperor Frederick and, had I felt the need of further comfort, should have received it when the daughter of William I, the Grand Duchess Louise of Baden, commanded me to the Niederländische Palais. She said to me then, with all the nobility, the dignity and gentleness of her nature: "I feel, as my father's daughter and brother's sister, that I must thank you for the many distinguished services which, for twelve years, you have rendered the Imperial House, Prussia, and Germany. I shall never forget them." She had far too much delicacy of feeling to allude directly to the differences between her nephew and myself. Not until the end of the audience, at the moment when I kissed her hand, did she add, with a slight stress on the pronoun: "I am not ungrateful."

A few days after this brilliant soirée, which the Kaiser gave in honour of the fifty-second birthday of his consort, I went on to Berne where, for many years, my brother Alfred had been our German representative. This visit did much to calm me. My brother was a deeply religious man. He considered my resignation as the event which would bring me happiness, as a grace for which I ought to thank God. "What doth it profit a man if he gain the whole world and suffer the loss of his soul?" And that man's soul is the most imperilled who is set in a place of high authority. My brother's absolute sincerity, his gentle and upright nature, had won him the esteem and love of the honest, plain-spoken Swiss. When relations between ourselves and Switzerland grew strained over the question of the Saint Gothard, a member of the Swiss Assembly advised the National Bund to accept the German *desiderata*, since the Minister, Von Bülow, was defending them. The Assembly knew Von Bülow as a just man and the friend of Switzerland. After Bismarck's death there were Germans who, under the influence of the Emperor, could sacrilegiously invoke the memory of that great-

est German Chancellor to assert that our foreign representatives
had no need to make themselves beloved — that, indeed, it was un-
desirable that they should be so.   Such people even went so far as
to criticize the American popularity of Baron Speck von Sternburg,
our able Ambassador to the States.   Far from courting greater
popularity, a German representative abroad should aim at making
himself feared.   Whatever he did he must "impose."   Yet Bismarck had affirmed, again and again, that perhaps the most essential
duty of any official in the Foreign Service is to inspire such sympathy and confidence that, in any case of strained relationships arising with his German fatherland, in the country to which he is
accredited, he may be able to serve as "bolster" and soften the inevitable shock.   An ambassador, Bismarck said, should be so popular
that, if his government makes a mistake, he can go on living on his
accumulated capital of friendships until the situation has improved.
Wilhelm von Humboldt suggested tact as the supreme law of diplomacy, while Talleyrand, never sentimental, left the saying: *"C'est
la bienveillance qui fait les grandes affaires."*

My brother received many Swiss.   One of them, a native of
Zürich, told me how, at home, he often met Bebel, whose daughter
was the wife of a Zürich doctor.   On hearing that I had resigned,
Bebel had remarked in his presence that, if he had not been so convinced an atheist, he would have felt that there was a special Providence watching over the German Socialist Party.   Bismarck, in
1890, had had ready a crushing measure against Socialism.   Though
Bebel felt the party could have withstood him, it would have been a
formidable blow.   Yet that had been the very moment chosen by
William II to show his great Chancellor the door.   He had deprived
himself of a statesman of genius and sown discord in the ranks of the
non-Socialists.   Sixteen years later, Prince von Bülow had attempted
another method of dealing with Socialism and one which might
have proved still more crushing, though, unlike old Bismarck, he
had not seemed ruthless and violent.   But he had driven in a wedge
between the Labour Party and the Liberal bourgeoisie as a whole.
His patriotic slogan at the elections had been telling enough to
capture many Socialists, so that the party sustained its worst defeat

in Germany. He had intended to use this parliamentary triumph
to steal what was left of Socialist thunder by a series of economic
reforms and spontaneous concessions to the spirit of twentieth-
century progress. And, in actual fact, thanks to the Bülow policy,
the attitude of the German people had grown less and less favourable
to Socialism, while, even within the party itself, the revisionists had
gained much ground. "And this is the moment when William II
sacks Bülow. Truly the good Lord God is kind to Socialists."

By the Saint Gothard, which once I had descended on foot, the
express bore us on into Italy. I saw Rome after an absence of twelve
years. Never had I been so deeply conscious of the salutary peace,
the eternal consolations of this city as now, when I had laid aside all
power, had left my Chancellery for ever, and, with it, every possibility of widely good and beneficent action. Yet, at the same time,
I found myself released from the many stings, disappointments, and
preoccupations of office. The Kaiser's wounded vanity; the petty
spite of the parties which I had opposed in the interests of the State;
Bethmann's jealous fear of losing his post — it was so acute
that when, during the War, I lived in the Hotel Adlon in Berlin, he
caused my every movement and acquaintanceship to be watched
by his own particular spies; all these had done me such ill service
that many people, since, have asserted that I was eaten up with the
desire to regain my post. To all such gossip I reply:

1. That had I received such a summons, I should, at any
moment, have been ready to resume the direction of affairs.

2. That I am convinced, in so far as I can judge the matter, that,
had I been recalled before the end of July, 1914, I could have prevented the outbreak of war. In any case, had I been consulted
before the ultimatum was handed to Serbia, I should have advised
against this piece of folly with all the urgent strength I might have
used to arouse a signalman whom I had found asleep at his post
at the moment when two expresses were due to cross. In 1914, no
matter how difficult the position, I should utterly have opposed any
Austrian military action against Serbia, unless previously authorized
by Germany, and until our government had proceeded to a full and
careful study of Serbia's answer.

3. Being neither fully informed of the inner meaning of events nor once asked to advise on the position, I could be of no possible assistance. My long experience of affairs has taught me that unless one is *au courant* of the whole of any political situation, it is possible to talk café politics, but never to give reasoned advice. The rumour of my having attempted to intrigue my way back into office is merely a very stupid piece of slander.

In Rome we settled down in the Villa Malta. The legacy which had come to us some years previously, from my mother's cousin, Wilhelm von Godeffroy, enabled me to purchase this villa. My great-grandfather, Martin Johann Jenisch, had had three daughters, of whom the eldest had married Wilhelm Rücker, my grandfather, the second Karl Godeffroy, the Hanseatic Minister in Berlin, whose forbears came to Hamburg from Geneva. The youngest became the wife of Count Wilhelm Redern, the Grand Chamberlain of Prussia, whom I have mentioned. She was a charming and most intelligent woman, distinguished in her body and her mind, full of the pride of Hamburg citizenship, and also very ready with her tongue. In Berlin, soon after her wedding, one of the princes asked her the silly question: "What is it your father deals in?" She parried at once with her answer: "Manners and intelligence."

Karl Godeffroy had only one son, Wilhelm, later to be raised to the Prussian nobility. He was what people love to call "a crank", though he did far more good in his life, and possessed a far finer spirit, than many of those whom we class as "men of the world." He was oddly stingy over trifles — would sometimes go to six or seven shops, in search of a new pair of boots until he had unearthed the cheapest pair. On his deathbed, even, he insisted on getting back his deposit on empty bottles, containers for the soda water he had drunk. Yet, at the same time, he would never hesitate at gifts of several hundred thousand marks, for any really fine and generous object. It was he who built the beautiful new church at Blankenese, who endowed the Church of St. Michael, in Hamburg, with its organ, one of the finest in Germany. Just before he died he sent for his bailiff and asked to be shown every claim to money he possessed. Since Godeffroy was very wealthy, he had been the constant object of begging letters.   Now he caused all his I.O.U.'s to be burnt in front of his eyes, and then took up the New Testament, with the words: "At last I can think only of God."   Soon after this he passed away.

He had left about twenty million marks, a considerable sum for those days, to various charitable objects.   Since my boyhood he had shown me the greatest kindness, as the eldest son of his eldest sister, and to this he later added a deep esteem, which expressed itself in the terms of his will.   He was a good Christian and a patriot.

Our purchase of the Villa Malta had fulfilled a wish of my wife's: personally I had seen it only once — on the night I dined there with Count Bobrinski, to whom, at that time, it had belonged.   But I placed the fullest possible confidence in my wife's judgment and taste.   Gregorovius' monograph on the Villa Malta, written in 1888, begins as follows: "This villa would certainly have merited to remain in the possession of Germany, since it holds many memories of our Fatherland.   For forty years it was the *Sans Souci* of the most art-loving of all German Sovereigns.   Here Ludwig of Bavaria held many courts, surrounded, not by order-bespangled diplomats, but by artists, full of talents and *joie de vivre*."   And Gregorovius continues: "The villa has most noble origins.   It is built on the site of the Gardens of Lucullus, and, under the Emperor Claudius, was the property of the Consul, Valerius Asiaticus, hounded to his death by Messalina, who coveted possession of his villa.   Tacitus records that her victim, as the faggots were being piled before his eyes, begged that his execution might be in another place, since he feared fumes from his pyre might damage the beloved trees of his garden.   And the villa gardens still contain magnificent trees — lemon and orange, three palms, pines and cypresses; ancient and splendid laurels.   I cannot, alas, conceal the fact that this villa sheltered some of the worst orgies of Messalina, nor that here she was assailed by avenging furies.   When Claudius gave the order for her death, his centurions found her stretched upon the earth, in her hand a dagger, which she had not the courage to use.   One of them administered her death blow.   Yet neither to the dreaded

Agrippina, nor to Nero, many of whose excesses had this same villa for their scene, did her tragic end serve as a warning. . . . Theodoric, king of the Ostrogoths, sacked the villa and removed its treasures to Ravenna. Belisarius made it his headquarters when he defended Rome against the Teutons. Classic Rome," concludes Gregorovius, "ends in the Gardens of Lucullus."

It needed Renaissance splendour to dissipate the barbarous fumes in which the Goths had enveloped the deserted villa. But, since the arts were born again, many magnificoes have dwelt in it — the Cardinals de Torres and Imperiali, Marini, and Acquaviva; the Bailli de Breteuil, that Ambassador from the Knights of Malta, who gave the villa its present name; Queen Casimira of Poland, the wife of Johann Sobieski; the Archduke Maximilian of Austria, a brother of the Emperor Joseph, Prince George von Strelitz, the brother of Queen Louise, and many another notability.

The garden was a perpetual delight to us, with its famous roses that climb to the summit of the terraces, and which earned the villa its other name, "*Villa delle rose*" — its beds of carnations, its water-lilies. I could understand what Mme. de Helvétius had intended, who said to Bonaparte, when, fresh from his conquest of Egypt, he came to visit her at Auteuil: "*Vous ne savez pas quel bonheur on peut trouver dans trois arpents de terre.*" In 1789 Goethe had planted in this garden the splendid palm tree which still grows there. Herder, who came with the Duchess Amelia on her journey from Weimar to Rome, there to be presented to Pius VI, under the title "*vescovo di Weimar*", had turned melancholy eyes on its lagetto. Fräulein von Göchhausen, that maid-of-honour who rescued the manuscript of the "Urfaust", wrote of him: "He who can find no happiness in Rome will never find his pleasure on earth." Goethe was less sorrowful than Herder. When King Ludwig of Bavaria wrote on March 28, 1829, to say he had bought the Villa Malta in Rome, the great poet turned joyously to Eckermann, to tell him how, from this villa, a whole panorama of Rome could be viewed; how no journey was too long for such a spectacle. And he sent his servant to fetch an engraving of Rome. "See here," he said to Eckermann, "Rome stretches away before your eyes. This hill is

of such a height that, at dawn and sunrise, you can see far away
beyond the city. Here is St. Peter's and here the Vatican. Truly
the king has chosen a magnificent place to dwell in." The great
name of Wilhelm von Humboldt is equally attached to Villa Malta.
He settled there in 1801, with his wife and children, among them that
little "Gabriele", later to become the wife of my great-uncle, Heinrich von Bülow, Prussian Minister to London and Foreign Minister,
who died in 1846. On December 9, 1802, Caroline von Humboldt
wrote to her friend, Charlotte von Schiller: "From the Villa Malta
we have a very noble view. Half Rome can be observed from its
windows, St. Peter's and the Lateran Hills, those great, rocky, isolated masses which limit the Roman horizon." When Von Humboldt was obliged to leave Rome which, surrounded by the fogs of
the north, he would often remember with regret, the Villa passed
to the "*Lucasbrüder*", Overbeck, Vogel, and Pforr. In 1827 it was
bought by the King of Bavaria, and, in 1829, he wrote, in his curious
style, to Goethe:

Delicious: to see in one's own flowery garden, rooted in free earth,
their heads raised to the free heaven, orange trees, glowing between dark
leaves. Having seen her, for twelve years I longed for Rome, and now
am as rejoiced at being with her as if I had met my mistress again. I am
at home! I can taste her delights without commotion. For this time
I have shaken off the chains of a Throne: here I live happily and in
private. With all the reverence which, as you know, I accord Germany's
greatest poet I remain,

> Herr Staatsminister,
> > that LUDWIG, who can appreciate your merit.

The modest little house in which the Bavarian king lived happily
for several winters now serves as gardener's lodge. Early in the
1870's Count Bobrinski built the new villa. This, although not
very large, is designed with real taste and intelligence. Here I
could settle down with my wife, who arranged our pictures, Gobelins,
carpets, and furniture, while I installed the greater part of our
library, begun with such passion by my father and which I had been
careful to complete, supplementing it with a number of rare edi-
tions. The great drawing-room of the villa contains a magnificent

fresco by Veronese — Phœbus, the radiant god of Song and Music, vying with Marsyas the flute player. This had been purchased in Venice by Count Bobrinski, in the 'sixties. For the hall I acquired another, by the cinquecento painter, Marcello Fogolino, a riotous "Triumph of Bacchus", with a very pleasantly tame lioness, surrounded by amoretti and tortoises. The most notable ornament of the hall is its marble chimneypiece, of German origin, also acquired by Bobrinski, who had found it in the Palazzo Altemps, on the Tiber. This palace had been built in the sixteenth century by Marcus Siticus, of the family of the Hohenems, of Vorarlberg. He had fought, as a good *condottiere*, against the Florentines and the Turks, but had exchanged his breastplate for the soutane, after having escaped death as by a miracle, in a coach accident, near San Pietro in Vincoli. He changed his German name of Hohenems to the Roman, Altemps (Alta-Ems). Before his accident he had had, by a beautiful Genoese, a son, who was the founder of his house. Marcus Siticus became nuncio to the Court of Vienna, was a Legate at the Council of Trent, and the fiery adversary of heretics. He lies buried in Rome, in the Blessed Sacrament Chapel of Santa Maria in Trastevere. Louis Pastor, in his "History of the Popes from the End of the Middle Ages", speaks of Cardinal Marcus Siticus, of the Villa Malta and its chimneypiece.

My first walk out into Rome led me to the summit of the Capitol, whence I could look down over the Forum, and, across the Forum, to the Palatine:

> And in yon fields below
> A thousand years of silenced factions sleep.

The sight, and this remembered line of Byron brought into my mind the reflection that soon time's wheel would have passed over Conservative and Clerical factions, over the flat and vulgar croakings of demagogic haters of thought and beauty. I remembered Chateaubriand, writing from Rome: *"Cette Rome, au milieu de laquelle je suis, devrait m'apprendre à mépriser la politique. Ici la liberté et la tyrannie ont également péri; je vois les ruines confondues de la république romaine et de l'empire de Tibère; qu'est ce aujourd'hui que tout cela dans la même poussière? Le capucin qui balaye en passant cette poussière avec sa robe, ne semble-t-il pas rendre plus sensible encore la vanité de tant de vanités?"*

I went to the Villa Mattei, the frequent destination of my walks with my friend Wilbrandt. There he would often quote these lines from Eichendorff:

> *Sie sangen von Marmorbildern,*
> *Von Gärten, die überm Gestein*
> *In dämmerenden Lauben verwildern,*
> *Palästen im Mondenschein.*
>
> *Wo die Mäschen am Fenster lauschen,*
> *Wenn der Lauten Klang erwacht,*
> *Und die Brunnen verschlafen rauschen*
> *In der prächtigen Sommernacht.*[1]

Eichendorff, whose sense of Italian beauty was so profound, never crossed the Alps, just as Schiller had never set eyes on the Lake of the Four Cantons, which he celebrates.

I would ride up the Gianicolo to the Sant' Onofrio cloister, and rein up at the ancient oak in the shadow of which Tasso sat, staring down on Rome with haggard eyes — Rome who conceals within her streets so many pomps and glories of the world, and, with them all, the sense of their inevitable decay:

> *Cadono le città, cadono i regni*
> *E l'uom, d'esser mortal, per chè si sdegni?*

[1] For they sang the marble beauties
  Amid dreaming thickets that lie
In the shadow of tangled alleys
  Where the stony pathways die.

And a palace gleams in the moonlight
  Its gardens run to seed
Though listening girls at the windows
  The throbbing lutes still heed.

Telling the ardours and languors
  Of the drowsy day's delight,
When muttering fountains answer
  The breath of a summer night.

I could ride on along the banks of Tiber, the river whose banks have seen more happenings than those of any river in the world, and which flows as gently to-day as ever it did in the days of Aeneas:

Leni fluit agmine Thybris.

Almost every morning I went out riding for two hours, often with Camille Barrère, the French Ambassador, who had been my friend for over thirty years, ever since the days when I lived in Paris. The War parted us, as it cut me off from two other Parisian friends, the brothers Paul and Jules Cambon. My favourite route was the one which Goethe loved so much, in the direction of Ponte Molle, and from there to the Acqua Acetosa. I was often reminded of this impression, which our greatest poet records: "It is really enough to drive a man out of his wits to contemplate the limpidity, variety, the vaporous transformations, the divine colouring of this landscape — and, above all, its distances." The air, the sunshine, the lizards darting in and out of the light, the cypresses, black against heaven — nothing of this has changed since Goethe's time. I could wander into all the museums, without a *Baedeker* or any prescribed and stereotyped notion of their beauties, spend hours in churches and galleries, and fully endorse the remark of my predecessor on the Pincian, the Byzantine Field Marshal, Belisarius, who had written to the brave Goth, Totila: "Of all the cities under the sun Rome is the greatest and most notable."

At last I had become a free man, knowing, with Socrates, that leisure is the most precious of our gifts ἡ σχολὴ κάλλιστον κτημάτων. That is a thing we Germans are slow to appreciate. Goethe complains that in the North, people consider any man an idler who does not toil and moil the whole day long. It was also pleasant to ride out to the Isola Farnese, towards that ground on which Veii once stood:

Altes Veji, auch du warst einstmals Fürstenbehausung,
Wo auf offenem Markt ragte der goldene Stuhl.
Jetzt tönt zwischen den Mauern die Flöte des schweifenden Hirten
Und dein Gräbergebiet wurde Ackergefild.[1]

[1] You, old Veii, were once the dwelling of princes
Where, on the open mart, glittered the law-giver's throne.
Now your streets are filled with the fluting of wandering shepherds
Over the graves of kings the goodman drives his plough.

VILLA MALTA IN ROME

As Propertius, even before the Christian era, had written on beholding that sad countryside.

I at last found time again for reading. From time to time, through many years of hard, exacting toil, I had remembered the melancholy saying of Ernst Dohm, a great wit, and the father of the *Kladderadatsch*. Dohm lay on his deathbed, and a friend came to ask how he felt. All Dohm would say was: "I'm annoyed when I think of the number of wonderful books I never got time to read."

But I, in Rome, undisturbed, could read through, from cover to cover, the whole of Mommsen's "Roman History", and the eight volumes of Gregorovius' "History of Rome in the Middle Ages." Thirty years after first dipping into them I could study the twelve volumes of Taine — "Les Origines de la France Contemporaine" — my perceptions sharpened by my own experience of power, more alert than before to seize the relationships of events, see the virtues and defects of the *homo sapiens*. I began to perceive how right had been my esteemed professor at Halle, in his insistence on that dictum of Goethe that, "in Rome we can read history otherwise than it is read anywhere else in the world: not, as we read it elsewhere, by trying to read slowly into its events, but as though a man were really at the heart of what he reads, since in Rome time is grouped around him, and he, in a sense, forms its centre."

I reread Byron and Goethe, Virgil and Horace, Livy and that Sallust whose gardens had been near the site of Villa Malta, and who therefore was, after a fashion, the tutelary spirit of my house. Since my boyhood I have been particularly fond of Sallust and this passage in Chapter II of the "Bellum Jugurthinum": "*Animus incorruptus, aeternus, rector humani generis, agit atque habet cuncta, neque ipse habetur.*" I had had the words engraved inside my watch case.

The attacks to which I was still subject at the hand of ex-Privy Councillor Martin, Eckardstein's trumpeter for the Loyalist League, which he directed — as well as those in many Conservative newspapers — had no power in them to shake my equanimity. Their insults and distortions of fact could not attain the measure of my contempt for them. But I regretted, for the sake of German agriculture, the absurd libels broadcast by the agrarian *Deutsche Tageszeitung*, and which continued long after I had resigned, though even these I felt no impulse to answer. Wahnschaffe, the Head of Bethmann's Chancellery, intervened on my behalf, on his own initiative, with the editor of the paper, Oertel — a man whose huge belly was invariably set off by a white waistcoat — and wrote to me then, that the latter, if only because of the stupid ingratitude they displayed, profoundly regretted the unchecked violence of expression of such Conservative contributors as Hahn.

One of my adherents, a very loyal, very intelligent one, was a retired officer of Dragoons, Herr von Huhn, for many years the Berlin correspondent of the *Kölnische Zeitung*. At the end of 1910 he pointed out to me that the silly accusations in Martin's book had just received a new lease of life, in the pious columns of the *Reichsbote*, and that in an unusually spiteful form. He added: "Your Highness, I imagine, is too far above such attacks to condescend to any kind of reply. Yet those who, for many years, could watch you at work, and so are able to form some kind of idea of the way in which things actually happened, are under no such restraint. For my part, I have felt it my duty to answer the gross falsifications of history contrived by the *Reichsbote*." The *Reichsbote*, that rigidly Evangelical organ, the favourite reading of the Kaiserin, and so of all her maids-of-honour, had attacked me fairly frequently, during my chancellorship. It considered me "too tender with Roman Catholics"; that is to say, it disliked my strictly neutral attitude. Like many another fanatic, its editor, old Pastor Engel, was honest. As soon as he became convinced — though not through any intervention of mine — that his accusations were really entirely groundless, he took them all back, most correctly, with a deep apology, published above his signature. I was glad of this for the worthy old man's own sake. The articles had left me quite indifferent. I could say, with Stendhal, my favourite French author after Montaigne: "*La vue qu'on a des hauteurs de Rome est faite pour changer en douce mélancolie la tristesse la plus colérique.*"

Herr von Huhn had also written, à propos of our domestic policy: "The situation in Germany has not improved since Your Highness' resignation. We are letting ourselves drift, in most alarming fashion, with the current, not knowing whither it will carry us. Your prophecy of a Philippi in the near future seems, I am sorry to say, more likely than ever to be fulfilled." Herr von Huhn, as a piece of strange news, added that, by order of His Majesty, there had been a kind of raid made on the Foreign Office, to lay hands on the letters and telegrams in which, so the Emperor asserted, I had been informed in advance of his extravagant sayings at Highcliffe. "Naturally nothing was discovered — and, where there is nothing, the Crown loses its rights."

Not long before my retirement my old and devoted colleague Loebell had, at my request, been appointed Oberpräsident of Brandenburg, a post for which everything fitted this son of the Marches. But, during the winter of 1908–1909, he had so over-worked himself, to serve me, that his health would not permit him to take up the post. He was forced to go into a sanatorium, in which he remained for some time. More than once he had gone to see Bethmann and point out that it was no more than his plain duty to oppose the organized slanders of the Press. Not only ought he to approach the Kaiser on the matter, but should himself make some public show of opposition. By speaking out in his predecessor's favour, he would consolidate his own popularity. But Bethmann was weak by nature and, as often happens in such cases, unable to be entirely true to anybody. Loebell never once succeeded in stirring him.

I consoled myself for all such petty vexations by remembering how Goethe had said of Platen that: "In a man of such great talent, it was unpardonable if, even in Rome, he could not forget the lamentable spite of German critics." Not that I wish in the least to compare myself to Platen, a great poet, but even I could feel that, in Rome, there were far better things to consider than annoyance with the trivial baseness which forms an essential part of all politics. Therefore, in so far as in me lay, I strove to acquire a little of Goethe's salve — the tranquil enjoyment of simplicity. With the help of Friedrich Noack, the excellent correspondent of the *Kölnische Zeitung*, I busied my thoughts with the

past and the history of the Villa Malta.   We discovered that one of
its inhabitants had been the Bernese, Karl Viktor von Bonstetten,
the *bailli* of Saanen and Nyon, a judge at Lugano, and who, as a
member of the Grand Council at Berne, did honour to his native
city.   He had preached eclecticism, as the disciple of Voltaire and
Jean Jacques; had been a most distinguished and witty stylist,
with an equal command of French and German.   Sainte-Beuve
devotes an interesting paper to him, in which he describes the "magnificent panorama" Bonstetten enjoyed from the windows of the
villa: "*De ce poste élevé il porta son invéstigation sur toutes les régions
de la cité, sur tous les cantons de l'Agro Romano, cette ceinture lugubre
et splendide qui l'entoure.*"   It was here, no doubt, that Bonstetten
wrote his chief work, "Le Voyage dans le Latium"; here, too, that
he made the acquaintance of the great Danish sculptor, Thorwaldsen.   At this period of his life Thorwaldsen lived in the Via Sistina,
in a house which still bears his commemorative plaque.   It stands
exactly opposite the terraces of the Villa Malta gardens.   When
Ludwig of Bavaria paced them, he could see straight down into the
sculptor's studio.   One fine day he walked in with a decoration
and proceeded to pin it on Thorwaldsen's breast, with the words:
"I decorate a soldier on the battlefield."   Thorwaldsen had
received his earliest laurels in 1802, in the Villa Malta, at the hands
of Friederike Brun.   When, on our arrival at the villa, I asked
Libianchi, our old Italian butler, to tell me who lived in the first-
floor flat of the house opposite the terraces, he answered, in rather a
solemn voice: "*Qui sta l'avvocato che fa i santi nel Vaticano.*"   He
meant, of course, that functionary of the Curia whose business it is
to plead against the *Advocatus diaboli*, in every process of canoniza-
tion.   I continued my questioning, and asked him who lived in the
flat above, and he said: "*Là sta un pazzo tedesco.*"

It turned out that the "*pazzo tedesco*" was my old school comrade
Bernhard Honig.   At the dear old Gymnasium in Halle his shyness
and conciliatory manner had earned him the nickname "sock-feet."
I sent word across, to ask if I might visit him.   He answered that,
though he had never felt anything but friendship for me, he begged
me to excuse his not receiving me.   I afterwards heard that, for

many years, he had lived in the Via Sistina through the summer
months — as a rule so torrid in the *"alma città di Roma"* — and
then gone back to winter in Germany. Rome did not please him
in the winter, because it is so crowded with foreigners. In summer
he could feel himself master of the *amoena Pincii spatia*, as the obe-
lisk on the Pincio describes them. He would water the flowers in
his loggia and listen to the songs of many birds, which he kept in
little gilt cages, while, during the freshest hours of the night, he
could always go for a ride in the Campagna. This way of living
pleased him so much that every visit seemed to him an intrusion.
I am tempted to believe that Honig was one of the few men I have
met who felt entirely satisfied with life.

If the Villa Malta has housed many distinguished guests — such
men as Humboldt and Bonstetten — it has also received an adventurer. Cagliostro came to it — the treasure seeker and master of
sleight-of-hand, "freemason", quack doctor, and disciple of the
Rosy Cross — the mystic and alchemist. In Rome they condemned
him to death. In Paris he had been locked in the Bastille, impli-
cated in the "affair of the necklace." Expelled by the Empress
Catherine from St. Petersburg, in Warsaw he persuaded the Poles
that he had discovered the elixir of youth. He announced himself
the Grand Master of Egyptian Masonry which, he declared, he had
himself resuscitated — was, in fine, one of the worst eighteenth-
century charlatans, in an age which produced so many, yet had the
honour of arousing Goethe's curiosity. In the Villa Malta he
organized an enthralling séance, very well described by the Frenchman, Marc Haven, in the interesting essay he devotes to this
chevalier d'industrie:

In May, 1789, in the Villa Malta, the summer residence of one of the
Maltese Knights, Cagliostro arranged a series of séances. In the presence
of the Ambassador of the Order, Bailli le Tonnelier de Breteuil, of the
French Ambassador, Cardinal de Bernis, of the Princess of Santa Croce
and Princess Rezzonico, with numerous other members of Roman society,
he caused the future to be foretold by a child, who stared into a carafe of
water. The child announced that, in the water, it could see a street,
crowded with people, all shouting, *"A bas le roi!"* and *"A Versailles!"*

At which Cagliostro exclaimed: "This child foretells the truth. In a little while Louis XVI will be dragged from his palace; the Bourbon Monarchy will fall; the Bastille will be razed to earth. Liberty will have triumphed over tyranny." "Oh," exclaimed the Cardinal de Bernis, "what a terrible prophecy for my king." "I much regret it," replied Cagliostro gravely, "but you will see — this prophecy will be realized." And the Cardinal, visibly perturbed, answered, "We shall see what we see."

Cagliostro's real name was Giuseppe Balsamo, and Palermo his native city. He died in prison, at Urbino, in the year 1795, having had the satisfaction of seeing the revolution come to pass, just as he had predicted it, to the terror of Cardinal de Bernis, Ambassador of His Most Christian Majesty.

CHAPTER VII

A Change in the Brussels Legation — Flotow's Intrigues against Wallwitz — My Correspondence with Bethmann — Bethmann's Reörientation of German Policy towards Belgium — Bismarck and Belgium in 1870 — Bethmann's Visit to Rome in March, 1910 — Frau von Flotow — The General Situation — The Reichstag Elections of 1912 — The Death of Edward VII — Herr von Kiderlen in Rome — Letters from Germany: Ernst Bassermann, Lichnowsky.

In the first weeks of January, 1910, I learned in Rome of an impending change in the Brussels Legation, news which not only vexed me personally, but caused me grave political apprehensions. My stepdaughter wrote that her husband, Count Nikolaus Wallwitz, for nine years German Minister in Belgium, where he had gained wide trust and popularity, had received a personal letter from the new Chancellor, suggesting that he should ask to be retired, since, for Brussels, another Minister was intended and no other post in the service seemed available. The reason given for such a step was the Imperial Government's decision to modify our Colonial policy. The Chancellor further requested Count Wallwitz to arrange his resignation in such a way as to make it seem a voluntary act, due solely to reasons of health. Wallwitz, who had thirty years' impeccable service behind him, behaved on this occasion like the patriot and gentleman he was. He left Brussels without a word of recrimination, even giving up the idea of a visit to his home in Saxony, for fear of arousing particularist hostility against the administration in Berlin. He did not return to Dresden till after he had spent some time in Wiesbaden.

After he had left Brussels I received the following letter from my successor:

MOST ESTEEMED PRINCE,

In view of the personal relationship between Your Highness and the Minister, Count Wallwitz, I feel it to be my duty to explain to you our motives for his forthcoming retirement. These will be entirely personal, and so confidential that I must beg you to divulge them to nobody.

Your Highness is perhaps aware that, for reasons of international policy, we have decided to change our attitude towards the Congo, in the sense of more energetic pressure on Belgium. Since the summer and autumn of last year, complaints had been received from the Colonial Ministry that Brussels was not giving enough support to the attitude we are now adopting. Our recent alteration of general policy met with such a reception in Brussels as would lead us to suppose the Minister there insufficiently in sympathy with this new attitude to Belgium. In these circumstances, demands were made in Berlin for a change of Minister in Brussels. These we laid before His Majesty, with the remark that it would no doubt be possible to find another post for Count Wallwitz. Personally I had thought of Madrid for him. But, and this is, of course, most confidential, my suggestion met with the categoric refusal of the Emperor, who demanded that Count Wallwitz be placed forthwith on the retired list and passed on him a derogatory remark. This naturally left us no choice. But I at once decided that his retirement must be effected in the most honourable manner, with every regard for the eminent merits of the Minister, who should himself be enabled to choose his moment for resigning. All this has been kept absolutely secret, and I should have hesitated to inform even Your Highness of it had I not been told that, from Brussels, you already have direct information.

Since the post, in any case, is vacant, you will, I am sure, approve my suggestion to His Majesty that Brussels be given to Herr von Flotow, who was for several years your collaborator. I think that you yourself once suggested that Flotow should be appointed to a post which would not make too heavy demands on his health.

May I beg Your Highness to accept my most sincere respects, and at the same time to present my kindest regards to Princess Bülow?

Your very obedient
V. BETHMANN-HOLLWEG.

Here is my reply :

All my thanks for the many kind things in your letter, received yesterday. The decision with regard to Wallwitz has naturally upset him and his family. Both his duties and the life he led there had made him very attached to Brussels, and he is moreover uneasy at the shock which he fears this decision may cause his mother, an old lady in her ninetieth year. As you may imagine, all this has been a blow to my wife, who has received some very sad letters from her daughter.

Before your letter reached me I had already written to Countess Wallwitz, begging both her and her husband to take it calmly. My advice need really never have been given, since they are self-controlled and well-bred people, who dislike demonstrations of any kind. I need scarcely say that I am aware that the interests of the service as a whole must determine all changes of appointment.

It is easily realized that I considered this shelving of Wallwitz as an act of personal hostility — more, as a piece of bad taste, since it was easy enough to see he had been sacrificed to make room for Flotow, whose ambitions had plagued me throughout my last year in office. Otherwise these bad manners did not affect me. But what did arouse my uneasiness in his letter (which had been composed by Flotow and was even written in his hand) was the announcement of "more energetic pressure" on Belgium, for "reasons of international policy." At first these words awakened only vague disquiet in me. Not till later did I really become certain that this sudden change of Minister in Brussels, with the modification it implied of our whole German attitude to Belgium, formed one of the grave contributory causes to the disaster of 1914.

Not long after this a very old friend, the Marchese San Giuliano, Italian Foreign Minister, disturbed me with a remark that Herr von Flotow, our new Minister in Brussels, appeared to pursue there *"une politique quelque peu mystérieuse."* He was for ever approaching the French and British Ministers, and seemed to consider it possible to make of Belgium and her Colonies another Poland; that is to say, a country to be divided up between Germany, England, and France. My anxiety was to become the gravest certainty when I read in the Belgian *Livre Gris* a report, dated April 2, 1914, from Baron Beyens, the Belgian Minister in Berlin, who had sent it in, four months before war was declared. In it he calls attention to the fact that Herr Solf, the State Secretary to the Colonial Office, had spontaneously suggested to the French chargé d'affaires and naval attaché a German-French understanding on the subject of the new railway lines planned by both countries in Africa. He further declares that Jules Cambon, the French Ambassador in Berlin, on his return from leave, had asked Herr von Jagow at the Foreign Office to inform him as to the purpose of these overtures on the part of our Colonial Ministry. Jagow had replied that, in his view, such a Franco-German *entente*, in which England too would be associated, might be a most advantageous step; to which Cambon answered that, in that case, Belgium must also be invited to a conference of the three Great Powers, since she herself was constructing new railways in the Congo. He even felt Brussels to be indicated as the proper city for such a conference, when all these matters could be arranged. Here is the end of the Belgian Minister's report:

Oh, non, répondit M. de Jagow, car c'est aux dépens de la Belgique que notre accord devrait se conclure. — Comment cela? — Ne trouvez-vous pas que le roi Léopold a placé sur les épaules de la Belgique un poids trop lourd? La Belgique n'est pas assez riche pour mettre en valeur ce vaste domaine. C'est une entreprise au-dessus de ses moyens financiers et de ses forces d'expansion. Elle sera obligée à y renoncer. L'ambassadeur trouva ce jugement tout à fait exagéré. M. de Jagow ne se tint pas pour battu. Il développa l'opinion que seules les grandes puissances sont en situation de coloniser. Le ministre des Affaires Etrangères de l'Empire Allemand dévoila même le fond de ses pensées en soutenant que les petits Etats ne pourraient plus mener, dans la transformation qui s'opérait en Europe au profit des nationalités les plus fortes, par suite du développement des forces économiques et des moyens de communication, l'existence indépendante dont ils avaient joui jusqu'à présent. Ils étaient destinés à disparaître ou à graviter dans l'orbite des grandes Puissances. L'Ambassadeur répondit que ces vues n'etaient pas du tout celles de la France, ni, autant qu'il pouvait le savoir, celles de l'Angleterre; qu'il persistait à penser que certains accords étaient nécessaires pour la mise en valeur de l'Afrique, mais que dans les conditions présentées par M. de Jagow, toute entente était impossible. Sur cette réponse M. de Jagow se hâta de dire qu'il n'avait exprimé que des idées toutes personelles, qu'il n'avait parlé qu'à titre privé et non en secrétaire d'Etat s'adressant à l'Ambassadeur de France. M. Cambon n'en attache pas moins une signification très sérieuse aux vues que M. de Jagow n'a pas craint de dévoiler dans cet entretien. Il a pensé qu'il était de notre intérêt de connaître les dispositions dont le dirigeant officiel de la politique Allemande est animé à l'égard des petits Etats et de leurs colonies. J'ai remercié l'Ambassadeur de sa communication absolument confidentielle. Vous en apprécierez certainement toute la gravité.

In the summer of 1870, when war had broken out between France and Germany, Prince Bismarck, who knew all the value of imponderabilia, hastened to enlist them in our service by revealing the French Government's plans against Belgian independence and neutrality, which the right of nations guaranteed. It was exactly the opposite forty years later, when the clumsy stupidity of our rulers gave our enemies every chance of arousing the public opinion of the world against our pacific, loyal people. I here repeat that this was mere stupidity — not malice. Those who, in 1914, had the direction of Germany's policy were neither cunning incendiaries nor ruthless swashbucklers — they were fools.

On the 3d of May, 1910, my first birthday out of office, my successor wrote me the following:

This third of May has awakened in me many personal and official memories. Allow me to present Your Highness, together with my gratitude and respect, my very best, most cordial wishes for the year on which you are now entering. In so splendid a city as Rome Your Highness will no doubt have become conscious of renewed and heightened vitality, fusing within itself a high seriousness and gentle serenity of spirit — as, in the gardens of Villa Malta, the laurel grows beside the rose bush. My memory of those delightful hours I was lucky enough to spend with you at Easter lies far too deep for me to be influenced by the political brawls of the last few weeks.

But this highly poetic comparison had not in it the magic to efface in me the painful impression already made by the feeble conduct of my successor — to call it by no other name — in the matter of the Brussels Legation. I may say, however, that I had received Herr von Bethmann very amiably when he visited Rome in 1910. I gave a dinner party in his honour, to which I invited many noted Italians, and praised my successor's talents and good intentions to the Foreign Minister, Marchese San Giuliano. Alas, without very much success! The keenly perceptive San Giuliano found Bethmann "*naïf et ennuyeux.*" And when, two years later, he paid his first visit to St. Petersburg, these were the identical epithets in which poor Bethmann was described: *naïf et ennuyeux.*

Bethmann had brought Flotow to Rome with him and they called together at Villa Malta. Flotow did his best to make good his treachery with a double dose of obsequiousness. After having tried in vain in Rome to give me some explanation of his conduct, he wrote from Brussels for my birthday:

MOST ESTEEMED PRINCE,

Will Your Highness accept my most respectful good wishes for your birthday, with the hope that, in the interest of the Fatherland, we long may be able to avail ourselves of Your Highness' vast range of experience, and be permitted to seek your aid and counsel? I very often think of Your Highness. My years in Berlin have left on me a deep impression, and I am fully conscious of all I gained politically by my close association with Prince von Bülow. Such contact did much to modify my whole conception of affairs; and, if, on his first taking office, I was able to do some service to my present chief, I know that this was solely the result of so good a political education. And my affection for Your Highness was very deep — deeper, perhaps, than you imagine. We were both aware that a cloud had come up between us, and the thought of it has caused me much suffering. But I hope all that is over now, since nothing remains in me but gratitude. That my career should have led me straight to Brussels is the last link in a chain of fatal circumstance, the thought of which still weighs upon my mind. Our hands were tied by an unexpected decision of the Emperor. My own wishes, as I think you know, would have led me along a very different road, and steps far more in accordance with them had already been taken with His Majesty. But which of us can break that chain of circumstance, stretching back to the beginning of time, to which his destiny has linked him! We all have to learn to bend our wills.

Let me conclude by simply saying how delighted I was to find Your Highness in such good health and spirits, and by asking you to give Princess von Bülow my most respectful greetings.

Your very devoted
FLOTOW.

The "cloud" between us was, of course, the result of Flotow's own intrigue, of which Count Wallwitz had been the victim. His suggestion that he had not really wanted to go to Brussels was an *impia et impudens fraus*. A few weeks after his appointment Flotow wrote to tell us that he was engaged to a Russian general's widow, Countess Marie Keller, née˗ Schahowskoy. In my description of Their Majesties' trip to Palestine I mentioned a Countess Mathilde Keller, a lady-in-waiting at the Prussian Court, and spoke of the Russian branch of the family, and of a general, Count Keller, who died a hero's death in the Russo-Japanese War. During a battle, he had gone to inspect a battery whose officers had taken cover in such a way as to be invisible to their men. For this the general reprimanded them and was given the excuse that they had no wish to expose themselves to certain death. Count Keller answered: "I'll show you how a Russian general dies!" — and remained on horseback beside the battery till an enemy shell came over and finished him. Flotow's married life with his widow was not a happy one. She was used to a man of strength and character, and treated poor Flotow without respect, even when he became Ambassador in Rome. During the war she divorced him and put announcements in all the Roman papers that now she would return to Russia, her country, and intended to resume the name of Keller. Her conduct may be excused by the fact that she had never really wanted to marry Flotow and accepted him *à contre cœur*. But Flotow had kept besieging her, not in the least dismayed by all her refusals. When her sister-in-law, Countess Kleinmichl, asked her how she could "ever have married that man," she declared with Russian *sans-gêne*: "*Je l'ai épousé pour me débarrasser de lui. Je m'ennuyais tant avec ses longues lettres dans lesquelles il demandait et redemandait ma main. Je me servirai de lui comme d'un intendant.*"

"When the purple robe falls the Doge goes with it," Verrina cries in Schiller's play, in fearful mockery of Fiesco, who has been cast into the sea. When Frau von Flotow left her second husband, he lost not only his wife's money but her beautiful villa in Cannes.

I have already told of my misgivings at the moment of handing over to my successor the political affairs of the Empire. Not that I was afraid of revolution. The 1907 election had clearly shown what vigorous forces of resistance to the selfish spirit of party politics, the doctrinaire insanity of Marxism, slumber within the soul of the German people. Nor, provided we could pursue a reasoned policy, without too many stupid mistakes, had we any real grounds for supposing that the peace of Europe would be disturbed. Though we, like Russia, England, above all France, had enemies of peace in our midst — personalities and groups whose sole object was to arouse international hostility — the current of pacific opinion was, almost everywhere, far stronger.

I was persuaded that if we showed goodwill to England in the matter of naval *tempo* she, on her side, could have no motive for provoking any world-wide calamity. Certainly we must be on our guard with Russia, and not seem in any way to oppose her aspirations in the Dardanelles, or arouse her suspicions by any imprudent gesture. Above all, in the Balkan Peninsula it would be necessary to keep a determined check on Austrian policy. The Dual Monarchy would have to be dissuaded from any act likely to run violently counter to secular Russian traditions. Nor must we ever lose sight of the fact that, should we be at war with France or Russia, England would not let slip such a chance of reducing to impotence the most powerful Continental State, who was also her worst economic rival. Nevertheless, in these conditions we could look forward tranquilly to the future. I repeat I never was oblivious of the dangers by which we were surrounded — of the enemies waiting their chance to spring — but I also had the deep conviction that, given the skill, the calm, the firmness indispensable, we could evade and confound these enemies.

My real uneasiness was born of my feeling that Bethmann was inadequate, of my knowledge that the Emperor was vain, with too high an opinion of himself. At home the *bloc* was shattered by the Conservatives and the defeat of my financial reforms. The consequence of so fatal a mistake, a result I had myself predicted, appeared with a kind of automatic precision. Every bye-election after my retirement showed a big increase in the Socialist vote.

Socialism, checked for six years in every part of the Empire, from East Prussia to the Palatinate, was alive again. The results of the 1912 Reichstag elections, on which Heydebrand and Westarp, his famulus, had embarked with scarcely conceivable illusions, while Bethmann looked on with folded arms, dismayed every clear-sighted patriot and encouraged our enemies abroad. An amusing Berlin comic paper, *The Ulk*, brought out a clever cartoon on these elections of January 12, 1912. A long and very wooden Bethmann-Hollweg stands reading his report to the Emperor. The report begins "110 Socialists." The Emperor, very depressed, and muffled in thick furs, sits on a bench. He has scribbled with his cane in the fresh snow — "Bülow." Did William II see what these elections meant? His usually Olympian approach to all major domestic problems makes me doubt it. But this big increase in Socialist votes, and deputies, constituted a serious menace to the future of the German nation. Of the ninety-six electoral areas recaptured in 1912 by the Socialists, sixty-six had been taken from them by the bourgeois parties in 1907. Of these twenty-nine had been Conservative and thirty-seven Liberal. The Liberal party was now reduced to the smallest number of seats it had ever occupied. In 1907 I had managed, for the first time in Germany, to get Liberals and Conservatives working together. After Bethmann's elections in 1912, Germany was given her first taste of the close coalition of all the Left Wing elements. In 1907 the Right had been the strongest group — with one hundred thirteen seats against one hundred six to the Liberals, one hundred five to the Centre, and only forty-three Socialist deputies. In 1912, one hundred ten returns made the Socialists the strongest single party in the Reichstag, against ninety Centre deputies, eighty-five Liberals, and only sixty-nine Conservatives of all shades. 1907 had been the worst defeat in the annals of the German Socialist party: 1912 was that party's greatest victory since there had been an Empire and a Reichstag.

The very real and grave significance of this result of the Bethmann-Hollweg régime and of the party tactics of Heydebrand and Westarp, was not clearly apparent until the war years, when the

fact that Socialists led the Reichstag amply explained that lamentable slackness of our domestic government, which forms so humiliat-
ing a contrast with the rule of other States in war time — with the
fierce energy of Lloyd George, Clemenceau, and the Italian Ministers. Hence, too, our fatal error of war policy, which Bethmann
and Jagow, from the start, directed towards the undermining of
Tsarism, in a vain and feeble hope of placating Socialists. The
stupid peace-feeler of December, 1916, the worse than naïve peace
resolution of July, 1917, the insensate reëstablishment of Poland,
even — may all, in the last analysis, be traced back to those fears
with which the strongest Reichstag party had succeeded in inspiring Bethmann-Hollweg.

The death of Edward VII, on May 6, 1910, was of the greatest
assistance to our foreign policy. I do not think he had really wanted
to fight us, as Skobelev and Boulanger had, in Bismarck's time, as
Delcassé and the English jingoes wanted to fight us when I was
Chancellor, and, later, the Grand Duke Nicholas and Poincaré.
But, inspired by hostility to his nephew, by his fear of our economic
rivalry, and the accelerated rhythm of our naval *tempo*, Edward VII
created difficulties, and, whenever he could, would put a spoke in
our wheel. For thirty years my personal relations had been excellent with this sovereign, at once so intelligent and, when he cared
to be, so charming.

Here is Queen Alexandra's answer to the wire I sent her on his
decease: "I am so deeply touched by your kind telegram of
sympathy at this time of my terrible bereavement."

The Agadir episode of 1911 was as deplorable as the 1912
election result. Like a damp squib, it startled, then amused the
world, and ended by making us look ridiculous. After the "leap"
of the *Panther* on Agadir there was a fanfare which, on Lloyd
George's speech, died down in the most inglorious *chamade*. A
few months later the Marchese San Giuliano said to me: "At the
moment when your Government gave way before Lloyd George's
brutal threat '*l'esprit nouveau*' was born in France — or rather
'*l'esprit belliqueux des Gaulois, qui dormait depuis 1871, et qui, en
1888 avait été refoulé par Bismarck, en 1905 par vous.*'"

Kiderlen-Wächter was responsible for the sending of the *Panther* to Agadir. In 1910 he had followed Schön as Secretary of State to the Foreign Office.

On his recall from Bucharest to Berlin many colleagues whom he met on the platform at Munich congratulated Kiderlen, and he answered: "Please don't congratulate me. I've been having a much better time on the banks of the Dimbowitza than I'm ever likely to get in Berlin. But at least you ought to be thankful at not having a great man like Schön as your chief any longer." To his death Kiderlen maintained that the fiasco begun by our sending the *Panther* to Agadir, and the failure of the ensuing negotiations, on Morocco and the Congo, with France, were solely due to William II, who, throughout this whole diplomatic campaign, veered from absurd threats and demands to utter discouragement and pessimism, leading on to unnecessary concessions. He added that, the moment he smelt powder, Bethmann had lost all self-control.

I last saw Kiderlen in Rome, in the January of 1912. He came to pay his respects to the King and Foreign Minister, neither of whom he had met before. He made a good impression on both. His evenings he spent with us at the Villa Malta. I thought he looked ill — his face had a worn and puffy look — and certainly he drank far too heavily. I advised moderation, but he answered that since he would not last long in any case, he was determined to deny himself nothing, but, in the beautiful words of Schiller, his countryman, would "savour all the lees of precious time."

On December 30, 1912, he died of a heart attack at Stuttgart, his native city, after having dined with Count Moy, the Bavarian Minister, and drunk six liqueur glasses of cognac, in spite of all the warnings of his host and even of the footman who served him. I shall always remember his last words to me as we said good night on the steps of the Villa Malta. I had wished him luck and added, "Drink less cognac, smoke a milder cigar, and don't be depressed; you'll pull through all right." He answered me: "Many thanks, Your Highness. But I'm only too well aware that, since you left us, both our home and foreign policy have been lamentable. How can you expect good policy from a —— and a weakling?"

In spite of all his faults, Kiderlen's death was a misfortune. He would never have pursued so stupid a policy as Jagow, his successor, initiated, with the full approbation of his chief.

I received many letters from Germany.   They all showed signs of grave dissatisfaction with Bethmann's government, and so of ever-increasing pessimism.   Even the winter after my resignation brought a front-page article in the *Berliner Tageblatt*, whose editor-in-chief, Theodor Wolff, had frequently attacked me while in office.   It was headed "An Open Letter to Prince von Bülow in Rome."   Here is an extract:

Though Your Highness lives in epicurean ease, you must sometimes still remember the Fatherland, and, faced with the ruins of the Forum, ask yourself what your successor is about.   "Alas," you probably exclaim, "I was reproached with being a frivolous *bon-vivant* — a 'man about town,' and, now, they have taken quite a different kind of Chancellor — a Chancellor innocent of the world, who knows only the seclusion of his study.   They all considered me superficial; yet now a captain is in charge of them, who might easily sink the ship.   Their joke against me was that all I ever brought them was flowers.   Perhaps a German weeping willow will make them regret my bouquets."

The article ended by declaring that I had been the dangerous enemy of Democracy, a difficult man, far more to be feared than "honest" Bethmann, who had "evoked the clattering skeleton of reaction in all its native hideousness and horror"; that Bethmann's every speech and act "gave forth a dank aroma of quietism, such a musty reek of seclusion, that doubtless Prince Bülow in Rome has to hasten from it to excavated statues in search of something more alive."   To-day the end of the article reads like a prophecy: "Herr von Bethmann-Hollweg will desert us when the vessel we placed in his hands lies shattered.   Or, to speak like Romans, we shall cast him from the Tarpeian rock, but without those Capitoline laurels which deck the forehead of Your Highness."

Soon after the Reichstag debate of November 9, 1911, Bethmann stood up to defend his hesitations over Morocco — his ordering of the *Panther* to Agadir and retreat before a brutal threat from England, leading on to the final disaster of the Congo Convention.   At the end of the debate, which had landed him in a definite defeat, Bassermann, in a letter to me, written from the Reichstag itself, summed up his impressions as follows: "All this palaver has resulted in so swingeing a government defeat as the Reichstag had never yet seen. I cannot remember so complete a crumpling up of both foreign and domestic policy." In the spring of 1912 he complained again: "Your Highness' prophecy is realized. Philippi is upon us! All is impotence and misery in the Wilhelmstrasse! Nothing goes right!"

And at Christmas in the same year: "A wretched and unfortunate policy. Nobody could govern more unskilfully. Philippi is bound to come. In the East the Polish danger keeps increasing. Half-measures are always the worst. . . . In the West the French mice have started to dance on all the tables."

Soon after this, in February, 1913: "Tripoli and the Balkan war are only the logical outcome of Agadir. At home a wooden, clumsy policy of temporization has reached its point of greatest rigidity. The same signatures — hesitation and muddlement — on everything."

In March, 1914, a few months before war was declared: "An impossible lack of method marks this government. 'To stick to his job' seems Bethmann's sole objective."

Bassermann had never entertained any illusions regarding my successors. As far back as June 23, 1909, on the eve of the rejection of the death duties, he had written to his wife — in a letter published after his decease: "What is to happen? Bethmann is a poor sort of creature — yet that weak, spineless figure may become Chancellor!" And from the Reichstag again, six months later, to his wife: "My opinion of Bethmann has not improved. He is a man who can get to grips with nothing — hesitant, timid, without decision or *entrain*, or the least real spark of talent in him, who is crushed and overwhelmed by any difficulty. What wretched poverty of ideas! What a contrast to Bülow! Yet into such feeble hands our tremendously vital country has fallen."

Nor did the Conservatives think better of him. Count Mirbach-Sorquitten, a staunch Conservative, wrote to me in the spring of 1912: "The present situation is discouraging. This, in a measure, is due to the statesman who directs our policy and seems always unable to choose between several courses. I have never liked the man, in spite of all my efforts to judge him impartially. He lacks any kind of 'go' or resolution."

At the end of 1912 I heard from Düsseldorf that Kirdorf, one of the biggest Rhenish industrialists, a man who, though he did not mince his words, was blessed with a very clear, decisive intellect, had declared that "if this goes on another three years Germany will have been landed in war or revolution." On December 30, 1912, I heard from a friend in Bethmann's Press Bureau. He closed as follows a melancholy account of the situation and state of public feeling in Berlin: "In such circumstances I, with many others, can only regret that Your Highness ever quitted the stage."

I was still more surprised at the opposition which even Harnack displayed to Bethmann's policy. This Court theologian, with his supple, alert opportunism, had nothing in him of the *atrox animus Catonis*. Nothing could have been further from Harnack's nature than an impulse to criticize powers that be. Whoever ruled, he turned to him his face, as the sunflower turns itself to the light. Yet even Harnack could write to me, on the signing of the Congo agreement, that this bargain, so unfavourable to Germany, had caused him "grave preoccupation." He added that it seemed to have been concluded in the hope that, now, the French would make friends with us. That was a most dangerous illusion, even if the strain were eased for the time being. Nothing had diminished the cause of conflict; it had, on the contrary, been intensified. "No god," said Harnack, "could eliminate our deepest cause of conflict with the French."

Adolf Wilbrandt, some months after my retirement, had written as follows in the January of 1910: "Our national inadequacy abroad continues as merrily as ever. But even in its domestic policy this new government gives an impression of trivial emptiness. Oh, for the glorious Bülow years!"

The historian Oncken wrote at the same time, with the present of a copy of his "History of the National-Liberal Party", and biography of its leader, Bennigsen. The detailed insight gained in writing it had, he said, made him perceive more clearly than ever how right I had been in saying, when I resigned, that our domestic future would depend on our making the Liberals more realistic, the Conservatives less narrow-minded. The whole course of events, domestic and foreign, in Prussia and the Empire, since my retirement, had begun to cause many citizens to think of Rome with longing.

The free-thinking professor and deputy, Schulze-Gaevernitz, regretted that, both as regards the Eastern Marches and his method of controlling Social Democrats, my successor should seem to lack my touch. Prince Lichnowsky, my ex-Chief of Department, wrote of Bethmann: "His candour and good intentions have won him friends. But he moves, rather than inspires them." Lichnowsky, who sighed for an embassy, was no outspoken critic of his new chief. The entirely independent Prince Hohenlohe-Oehringen also wrote: "Now you can sit at ease in your comfortable box in the world-theatre and watch the play after seemingly endless commotion. You will have the satisfaction of assuring yourself how rightly you once guided our policy, whereas, alas, we now see only uncertainty in the future."

Herr von Huhn, the Berlin correspondent of the *Kölnische Zeitung*, had written, even before the disastrous election, telling me how, in everything he handled, Bethmann could do nothing but procrastinate, and seemed to hope some miracle would save him. Nor was he taking any steps to prevent what looked like serious developments. The reason seemed his utter inability to become less bureaucratic and hidebound, in spite of his fund of philosophy and ethics. The All Highest cared very little for home affairs, since now he encountered far less opposition. That might not in itself have been a misfortune, except that things were simply taking their course, in the midst of a general disgruntlement. If, in Bismarck's day, people talked of "disgust with the Empire", it was now a case of "disgust with the government" — a "disgust" which gained ground every day. Germans had really lost their interest in politics. It was all too hidebound and hopeless.

Walter Rathenau wrote: "My private feelings need not be considered in connection with the loss Your Highness' resignation brought on us all. Yet private regrets are daily intensified by very real anxiety for our future. But at least such dismal reflections all lead me back to the hope that Your Highness will take it upon yourself to remain the adviser and 'faithful Eckart' of this people, whom you ruled so well for so many years."

I had managed, at last, through Loebell, to secure Walter Rathenau his decoration. He had fully earned, and been most anxious to receive it. In reference to this he wrote on January 15, 1910: "To-morrow I am commanded to the investiture and cannot doubt that this has some connection with Your Highness' efforts, last summer, on my behalf. This new distinction gives me most satisfaction as the proof of Your Highness' friendship and esteem. It is the very smallest part of all the kindness for which I owe you thanks from the depths of my heart. That for a whole two years you welcomed me as your friend, that you allowed me to live in personal touch with the sphere of your potent activities, the simplicity and charm of your home — these are the things which have earned my eternal gratitude, both to Your Highness and my deeply honoured Princess."

CHAPTER VIII

Adolf von Harnack's Visit to Rome — Harnack's Attitude to the Kaiser before and after the Revolution — Visit to Brandenburg-on-the-Havel in the Summer of 1913 — A Family Gathering at Doberan — My Commemoration Address at the Unveiling of the Monument to General von Bülow-Dennewitz — Congratulatory Letters — Count Roon — I Visit Fitger in Bremen.

WE were both overjoyed to welcome Walter Rathenau as our guest when he came for a fortnight to Rome. It was a real pleasure to wander among so many masterpieces with this stimulating and witty companion, who could inspire such divers trains of thought. I shall not easily forget the evening of April 21, 1910, when the whole Eternal City was illuminated for the Natalizio. Rathenau and I looked down from the loggia of the Villa Malta on a Rome glittering with lights, and could pass in review the many epochs of world history which here stand frozen into stone.

In the same year Adolf Harnack spent some weeks with us: a savant of the widest erudition, of subtle, I might say of Attic wit, which, however, his character did not equal. Heine once said that Atta Troll, the bear of the Pyrenees, had not had talent so much as character. In Adolf Harnack's case, this was reversed. Nobody else, excepting only Theodor Schiemann, could flatter the Emperor like Harnack. But Schiemann, the historian, flattered grossly; Harnack, the theologian, with subtle grace. Harnack's suppleness was that of the Greek rhetoricians and sophists, who betrayed and charmed the Persian satraps: he recalled the "Graeculi" of the Empire. I remember a dinner party, given in the Chancellor's Palace, to which I had invited the Emperor, and, at his command, his favourites, Harnack and Schiemann. After dinner Schiemann made his usual "bluff" attempt, saying that the German Emperor and King of Prussia need really only bear one title — "Supreme War Lord." That included them all and was the direct echo of

primitive ages, of the days of Chiefs of the Germani.   I cut short
this nonsense with the remark that I believed the old Germanic
chiefs had only been elected for a campaign, and that therefore I
considered we should do better by sticking to the hereditary monarchy.   Schiemann was annoyed and disconcerted.   Harnack,
however, stepped nimbly into the breach with the following: "Your
Majesty, I have something which I feel should be said in the presence
of Kaiser and Chancellor.   Since I've had the good fortune to have
a Prussian captain as my son-in-law, I've begun to see that
a Prussian officer knows more than all the professors put together."

William II, as candid and easily seduced as the most unsuspect-
ing village maiden, roared with laughter.   He slapped down his
strong right hand on his muscular thigh and shouted: "My God —
here's the first sensible professor I've ever met."

Harnack was the more dangerous favourite.   I am glad to say,
in this connection, that the Prussian captain whom Harnack had
mentioned went, like a brave man, to his death at the head of his
regiment soon after the beginning of the War, and that his widow,
or so I have been told, in her husband's old garrison, Torgau,
remained faithful to her husband's tradition even after the November revolution, when her father had conveniently changed his opinions.   Her brother, who before had been as ultra "loyalist" as
Harnack, forgot his loyalty overnight, and hurried to the Social
Democrats.   The witty Monseigneur Duchesne in Rome remarked
with justice on Harnack's desertion of the monarchy: "*M. Harnack a traité l'empereur d'Allemagne comme si celui-ci ne fût qu'un
simple Jatho.*"   Jatho, the pastor in Cologne, had been an enthusiastic devotee and hanger-on of Harnack.   But the master left his
disciple in the lurch, out of fear of the strictly orthodox Kaiserin
and her ladies, when he got into difficulties with the Consistorium.

Harnack had announced his visit in a letter containing the following: "A grey mist lies over Germany; but you have strayed
into the sunlight.   May its rays be ever warm and friendly, comforting you and bringing you fresh life.   I especially hope, even
to-day, that the German people may come more and more certainly
to realize what it owes to the guidance of Your Highness.   And I

certainly wish that the experience by which the lesson is acquired may not prove all too bitter."

But this same Harnack could never summon up the courage to contradict William II when he poured out accusations against me, though no one knew better than he how unjust and unfounded they all were. A time was even to come when this soft-spoken Court theologian praised to the Emperor the thorough knowledge and insight of Bethmann-Hollweg in contrast to the almost frivolous superficialities of Prince von Bülow.

Not long after Harnack's departure the Crown Prince and Princess appeared in Rome. The prince sent me word that, to his regret, he would be unable to visit me, since his father had strictly forbidden him to set foot inside the Villa Malta. I did not let this piece of bad manners disturb me. One day when Napoleon lost his temper with Talleyrand the latter made the dry remark: "*Quel malheur qu'un si grand homme soit si mal élevé.*" I had not the consolation of having been disappointed in a great man. But this, after all, was the same Sovereign who had suddenly shelved General von Leszczynski, one of our most capable officers, because, when he commanded an army corps at Altona, he had, on arrival at Friedrichsruh, paid a purely formal visit to Bismarck. A few years later Leszczynski retired to a small property which he had bought in the neighbourhood of Liebenberg, and Philip Eulenburg, the chief landowner in the district, who then still basked in the warmth of Imperial favours, succeeded, in half an hour, in procuring for his neighbour the Black Eagle. I met the Crown Prince on the evening of his arrival in Rome, at a dinner given in his honour by Queen Margherita. The sight of me obviously embarrassed him, but he greeted me with the calm and courtesy which in contrast to his Imperial father had earned him the esteem of the Courts of England and Russia, of the Emperor Francis Joseph and the Prince Regent Luitpold of Bavaria. His embarrassment visibly increased when the Queen asked him, at table, in my presence: "Have n't you seen the Villa Malta yet? Oh, but you must — you must go as soon as possible. It's so beautiful, and I'm sure you 'll be looking forward to a talk with Prince von Bülow."

Next day the Crown Princess Cecilie came to visit us. She said to us in her own charming fashion : "My husband has been forbidden to come and see you, but I'm disobedient, so I came." *"Fra bella e buona, non so qual fosse piu"*, as an old Italian sonnet has it. It might have been composed in her honour.

It seems to me, as I look back on the year 1913, that destiny wanted to give me a last sight of the force and splendour of pre-war Germany. At the beginning of June, we spent some very pleasant days at Brandenburg-on-the-Havel with our good friend Loebell. From there we visited the ruins of the Cistercian monastery at Lehnin, around which there hover so many legends. It once was called "the gate of heaven on the lake." We remembered the gloomy Vaticinium Lehninense, and so could enjoy all the better the radiance of the Havel itself, glorious in the June sunlight. A wise old saw, inscribed over the doors of the Rathaus, also pleased us :

> *So einer könut und sagen kann,*
> *Er hab es allen Recht gethan,*
> *So bitten wir diesen lieben Herrn*
> *Er wöll 'uns solche Kunst auch lehr'n.*[1]

This wisdom consoled me for the criticisms I had endured from each of the parties in turn. Jagow and Hammann, invited by Loebell from Berlin in my honour, could never stop gibing at Bethmann, the "Fabius Cunctator of the German Empire." They seemed to hope to please me by their gibes. But they were mistaken. They would have done far better if, instead of mocking Bethmann behind his back, they had tried to prevent his making mistakes — though, alas ! these mistakes were also theirs, since Hammann was Head of the Press Bureau and Jagow State Secretary for the Interior.

At Doberan, on June 19, 1913, I presided at a reunion dinner of Bülows. After the dinner, given in the Casino at the end of a very pleasant water party, I told them all how glad I was to be back in

---

[1] Whoever is able to say to us
"I 'm pleasin' everyone,"
We beg that honest gentleman
To show us how 't is done.

Germany : "Each year my heart leaps as I cross the Alps, and yet I can't feel altogether happy till I have passed the Main and come through the Thuringian forests, and North Germany lies spread out before my eyes — the long, straight, pale-grey roads, the broad acres and wide, flat spaces, the still lakes and pleasant beech copses, and far away on the horizon, the blue waters of the Baltic, over which our pleasant excursion has just taken us."

To the cousins, gathered around me, I related how, as a very young man, at the time when I was a lieutenant of hussars, I had drawn up a list of all the Bülows distinguished in the service of the State. I invited the younger members to do likewise — both so as to get to know our family history, and to be inspired to emulate the best of our kinsmen. "My father once told me," I continued, "that when he asked Prince Bismarck if he would care to have me in the Foreign Office — this happened more than forty years ago — he had felt it to be his duty to tell the Prince that already there were three Bülows in the service. First came my father, the Secretary of State for Foreign Affairs, then Privy Councillor Ernst von Bülow, and last, Otto von Bülow, for many years the old Emperor's travelling companion and, finally, Ambassador in Rome. So my father had asked Prince Bismarck whether four Bülows would not be too many, and the prince had answered : 'We can't ever have too many of them.' A few days later I had been attached to the Foreign Office, and so was introduced to the great man. I can see him yet, as though he were standing before me, with his bushy eyebrows and deep, impenetrable eyes. And he asked me, in the low, soft voice, which made such a singular contrast with his great height : 'Well, did you ever know a stupid Bülow?' I have always been frank. Our motto is '*Alle Bülowen ehrlich*',[1] and truth demanded that I should admit that certain Bülows have been — lesser lights. I therefore answered the prince : 'Yes, sir — I have known stupid Bülows, but not many of them.' He burst out laughing and told me of a certain Major Bülow, a frequent visitor at his father's, who had been a great *l'hombre* player, and very proud indeed of being a Bülow. This major could do

[1] All Bülows are honest.

nothing else but quote the opinion of the highly talented but very unlucky Dietrich Bülow on his brother, the victor of Dennewitz: 'Friedrich Wilhelm is my stupidest brother, and, in spite of it, the best officer in the army.' It is certainly not necessary for a young Bülow to make such a show of family pride as Dietrich, but the Bülows have as a family the duty of supplying the army and Civil Service with capable men. When my ancestor, Bernhard Joachim von Bülow, Marshal of the Court of Mecklenburg-Schwerin, appeared before Napoleon at Warsaw, at the head of a deputation from the States General of Mecklenburg, to demand the reëstablishment of the rightful sovereign whom the French had driven from his throne, his dignity so impressed the Emperor that he turned and said to his marshals: 'I have made you Marshals of France, but I could never make you gentlemen of Mecklenburg.' In an old family chronicle compiled by Paul von Bülow, our cousin's father, the Major General, Joachim, is described as follows: 'He was a perfect courtier, who at the same time had never lost the candour and sincerity of a gentleman. Such examples as this should be ever before the eyes of our family, an incentive to us all to do our duty.'"

I ended my speech by reminding them that the Bülows were proud of the fact that our family had given the army the most officers. And when, a year later, war broke out, a hundred direct descendants of the Knight Godofridus de Bülowe with whom, in 1239, our family chronicle begins, fought under the glorious white and black. Of this hundred a good third, thirty-two, gave their lives in the service of Emperor and country; even more were wounded, some very grievously. In the obituary which, after the War, I consecrated to the memory of these dead, I wrote as follows:

"Like many Bülows who had laid down their lives in former wars, these heroes died joyously for the fatherland, in the hope of an unclouded future and final triumph of their country. They are fortunate to have died for the German people without witnessing the collapse of the Empire. The memory of our gallant cousins will live on in the heart of every Bülow, and will be to future generations a living token of that spirit which once formed the glory of Prussia and Germany."

From Doberan we went on to Rehna. My ancestors before the Reformation had made many gifts and many endowments for requiems to the monastery of this little town. We climbed the hill-side beyond it, on which there still remains the barest ruins of an ancient castle of the Bülows. Most of the castle is no more, and the plough passes over it to-day. But the view from the hill on which we stood, out over the fruitful land around Lübeck and across to the bay of Neustadt, is a glorious one. When summer was at its height we passed some weeks on the beautiful estate of Friedrichstein in East Prussia with my old friend and comrade, Count August Dönhoff. From there on a visit to Schloss Preyl, to Countess Margareta Lehndorff, a daughter of the house of Kanitz, sung by Schenkendorf, and which gave Prussia so many distinguished men and women. Countess Lehndorff was the widow of our good old Kaiser's General Adjutant, Count Heinrich Lehndorff, an officer whom I had always respected. I also paid a visit to Königsberg, the former residence of the Grand Masters of the Teutonic Order, then of the Dukes of Prussia, the town where Prussia's kings had been crowned and where, after 1806, there began the reawakening of my country. In those days, while Frederick William III walked the Königsberg streets in his shabby coat, with all the simplicity which we see in his statue in the Tiergarten, where it faces that of Queen Louise, Stein and Hardenberg, Niebuhr and Wilhelm von Humboldt were silently preparing the rebirth, the rising and freeing of our people. It did my heart good to remember that the daughter of the noble Wilhelm von Humboldt, my great-aunt Gabriele-Bülow, had served at the Coronation of William I as first lady-in-waiting to the Empress Augusta. A Bülow had already been present at the crowning of the first Prussian king in the train of Queen Sophie Charlotte, the friend of Leibniz. This was Christina Antoinetta Bülow, *née* Krosigk Hohen-Erxleben, the wife of Wilhelm Dietrich von Bülow, a baron of the Empire, Grand Master of Ceremonies to the "philosophical queen", and first Chancellor of the Order of the Black Eagle. It goes without saying, since I am proud of my degree of doctor, *honoris causa*, of the University of Königsberg, the Collegium Albertinum, that I paid a visit to the tomb of the sage of Königsberg and read with emotion its inscription from the "Critique of Pure Reason": "The starry heavens above me, the moral imperative within." I should much have liked to visit the house in the Prinzessinstrasse which for twenty-one years had sheltered Kant, whose spirit destroyed the concepts and ideas of centuries, while his body never left its native town. But, the year before, the modest little house had been demolished to make way for a new building. One of my admirers presented me with a beautiful little pen portrait of Kant, and under the philosopher is a vignette of the house in which he lived. It hangs in my house at Flottbek.

On September 6, 1913, my wife and I were present at the unveiling of a monument at Dennewitz to General Friedrich Wilhelm von Bülow, for the centenary of the victory he had gained there. A deputation from the Infantry Regiment of Count Bülow von Dennewitz (6th Westphalians, No. 55) had come to the ceremony, to which from every corner of Brandenburg there had journeyed the men of the Marches, among them many veterans of our wars. The monument represents a militiaman of 1813, charging with the bayonet, while an officer at his side points to the enemy. The granite plinth presents a medallion to the victor of Dennewitz, under it this inscription from Ernst Moritz Arndt:

> *Auf, mutig drein, und nimmer bleich,*
> *Denn Gott ist allenthalben.*
> *Die Freiheit und das Himmelreich*
> *Gewinnen keine Halben.* [1]

On the further side of the plinth there is a bas-relief of charging Prussians, armed with bayonets and pikes, inscribed with the battle cry of the Landwehr, to which they went into action at Dennewitz: "Up and at 'em in the name of the Fatherland."

I had been asked to give the inaugural address. Having described the broad outlines of this battle, one of the rare days in history on which, contrary to Napoleon's axiom, God was on the side of

---

[1] Up and at 'em, never pale,
God is all about you.
Liberty and heaven
Are not for half-men.

the small battalions, I asked why Prussia, a hundred years before, had gained her victory.   My answer to this was the following:

Because the Prussian people had set victory, the liberation of their country, above riches, higher than all the passing goods of earth.   The generation of 1813 could see that material progress is not everything, that there are higher values than property.   Woe to the land whose wealth accumulates while the men who inhabit it decline.   The rising of 1813 was born of an ardent love of country, of holy rage against oppression, of implicit and manly trust in Our Lord, in "that God Who commanded iron to grow and would have no slaves."   The generation of 1813 triumphed by the knowledge in its heart that victories are not only to be gained by superior technique and numbers, but by the soul.   Such a feeling as this could nourish that heroic patriotism, could form that tragic resolution, which mark the men of 1813, and which Bismarck, our great Chancellor, inherited of them, who was born in the year of Waterloo, confirmed by Schleiermacher in the Church of Holy Trinity in Berlin, and who, with our good old Emperor, led on to its glorious conclusion the unfinished work of his predecessors.   In 1813 victory was on our banners, and so we could throw away our chains — because then one single thought had welded all classes in the nation, had made of it one single communion, setting the public good above all else, higher than the seeming good of individuals.   This unity dispelled the curse that had lain over the whole of German life, it subordinated all to the common weal.   That bitter saying of the greatest of German poets, that Germans are very worthy as individuals, but miserable when taken in the mass, had, in this case, proved itself a fallacy.   The men of 1813 sensed this truth: — that a country's well-being is not made up of the sum of its private interests, but of something which exceeds and dominates them.   What inspired Scharnhorst and Stein was their perception that the greatest possible number of citizens must be linked to the needs and interests of the State, so that the value to the State of the individual may correspond to his own perception of his citizenship, and so all Germans be linked together as essential parts of the national whole.   Yet this sentiment of general solidarity must include the necessary submission of individuals.   Only, on the one side unity, discipline and order on the other, will bring forth that national spirit, that public consciousness which, through every vicissitude of history, in spite of every blow of fate, can guarantee the persistence of a nation.

I established the fact that Dennewitz had been won by Prussians — that it had been a solely Prussian victory. "The men who fought and bled on this ground were sons of those Eastern Marches of which, in my first speech in the Reichstag, I said that they had set their indelible mark on our State, our army and our Civil Service. To have shaken off the strangers' yoke is, above all, the work of Prussia. We remind you of it, not as a boast, not to appease our pride, but because it is history. This little country, ruined and crushed to earth by Napoleon, a country of scarce five million inhabitants, set three hundred thousand men in the line. But more than this, it fought with the spirit of Stein and Scharnhorst, of Von Blücher and Yorck, of Von Kleist and Körner, of Arndt and Jahn, of Von Schleiermacher and Fichte, with the spirit which still animates those men whose portraits deck the memorial hall at Dennewitz, the spirit which showed Germany the way. And Germany can only keep that way for so long as she is guided by that spirit." And I concluded: "On the day after the battle the victor of Dennewitz wrote to his wife: 'If only we can make good this victory, we shall soon be the masters of all Germany.' The hope at that time remained unrealized. Another half-century had to pass before the advent of that great statesman, that prodigious man of destiny who, sustained by the confidence of his sovereign, directed our whole Prussian strength into the channel of German unity; the man who, with the perception of genius, chose the hour at which to cast into the balance in which empires are weighed the renovated strength of Prussia, the strength of the wise and energetic King William. That was the day of fulfilment, the day of realized hope and aspirations, the day of recompense for the sacrifice and pain of 1813. When in 1870 we heard again the call to arms, Treitschke, the prophet of the national idea, had every right to address the Royal Eagle:

> *Erfüllet sind die Zeiten,*
> *Wahrheit wird der Dichtung Traum.*
> *Deinen Fittich sollst du breiten*
> *Über Deutschlands fernsten Raum.*
> *Nimm der Staufer heil'ge Krone,*
> *Schwing den Flamberg der Ottone,*

Unseres Reiches Zier und Wehr:
Deutschland frei vom Fels zum Meer ! [1]

When those words of mine traced out the path of glory which, from Dennewitz and Sadowa, led us on to Sedan and to Versailles, I little thought that, in ten years, the President of the German Republic, Ebert, would be glorifying the convocation of the National Assembly in Frankfurt as one of the culminations of German history. The National Assembly at Frankfurt ! — that parliament which, from first to last, was a masterpiece of shortsightedness and ignorance, clumsiness and gossiping verbiage, equally a fiasco in speech and act. And Ebert passed in one stride from 1848 to the November revolution in 1918, which he had the assurance to present as the second great fulfilment of our history, without a word for the most venerated name in our annals, the name of the good old Emperor William, nor for the greatest of our statesmen, Prince Bismarck. I do not suppose that any other people would have endured such a travesty of its history. Ours will never heal, *can* never heal, unless it will remember its past, will think of it with reverence and pride. A nation without history, without tradition and reverence, is a nation without roots, a leaf in the wind. A people is only great through its history, its fidelity to its past, and the broad wisdom with which it can interpret its tradition. '*Je me sens patriote pour admirer à la fois Jeanne d'Arc et Voltaire,*' said Gambetta. And Napoleon declared : '*Je me sens solidaire de tous ceux qui ont gouverné la France avant moi, de Clovis jusqu'à Danton.*' In the last appeal he made to his electors, Giolitti, then eighty years old, pointed out the sæcular continuity which runs through the whole of Italian history, from the days of Rome on to the present ; and every Englishman is aware that the history of his country is one thing —

---

[1] The time is upon us,
The truth of poets is reality.
Thou shalt spread thy wings
Over the furthest corner of Germany.
Seize the holy Crown of the Hohenstaufens,
Brandish the blade of Otto,
Thou, the safeguard and jewel of our Empire !
Germany shall be free from rock to sea-coast !

the same from Alfred the Great to Cromwell, to Queen Victoria and King Edward."

My Dennewitz speech reconciled to me many old friends whom my *bloc* policy and death duties, as well as my suggested electoral reform in Prussia, had alienated. Count Waldemar Roon wrote as follows:

Your Highness must be so kind as to forgive me — I can't help myself — I must write to tell you how warmly I thank you for your magnificent Dennewitz speech. It came like a cooling draught in the arid desert of politics. Certainly Your Highness must have given new hope to thousands of patriots by it, and you therefore have no right to be surprised if you bring on yourself their warmest, most enthusiastic gratitude. Not only, as an old soldier, do I admire your really powerful, classic description, in so many direct and vivid strokes, of the strategy of that glorious battle — the manner in which you presented, in beautiful, gripping and, in the best sense of the word, popular language, the achievement of all who fought in it, from the hero who led them, down to the simplest private — but I was, if possible, even more heartened by the ethical and political lessons which you drew — lessons inspired by glowing patriotism, ripe wisdom and knowledge of life. May all — yes, all — Prussian and German patriots, especially these so-called leading statesmen, who certainly seem to have given up all attempt to lead, if leadership means action and initiative, and who hold the reins more slackly every day — not only hear, but lay to heart your warnings, so that at last they do their duty and show themselves men. And may the parties, with their vain, climbing leaders who, far from any genuine patriotism, seem ever more inclined to listen in shivering anxiety to the muddled, vain, and ridiculous suggestions of "the masses" or their insipid newspapers, at last pay some heed to your grave warnings and remember their national duty to the Fatherland.

The gallant Roon would not have been a German, and certainly not a German party man, if his letter, besides these words of wisdom, had not also contained a furious attack on another party — a party which, after all, was as much German as his own.

I want to lodge a definite protest, and in this I hope Your Highness will agree with me, against the pushing attitude of the Liberals who dare to call you their spokesman because once — and on one particular point — you happened to differ from the Conservatives. No! — whoever could make such a speech, and had his words forced out of him as you did by glowing love for his Prussian and German Fatherland, could never have anything in common with the spineless, watered-down Liberalism of to-day, and should not allow his name to be associated with it. Besides, no Liberal, since Treitschke closed his eyes, has ever been, or ever will be, capable of making such a speech as Prince Bülow's speech on the battle-field of Dennewitz. With the hope of your indulgence for the "parish politician" who had to speak out, and with many kind regards to the Princess, I have the honour of remaining,

Your Highness' most obedient, grateful,

Roon.

In the same year, 1913, so fateful in the story of East Prussia, Count Hans Kanitz was gathered to his fathers. He had been one of the best sons of the province — the descendant of a family which had taken a celebrated share in the rising of 1813. He was the master of Schloss Podangen, sung by Schenkendorf, where the vestal fires of selfless patriotism had been cherished through many gen-erations. After Kanitz's death Mirbach-Sorquitten wrote me as follows: "At one of the last talks we had together Kanitz and I discussed Bismarck's successors in the Chancellorship. Kanitz remarked: 'The best of them was Bülow,' and I found myself in full agreement with him."

From Dennewitz we went on to Bremen, where there lived one of my oldest friends, Fitger, the editor of the *Weser-Zeitung*. We were at loggerheads on almost every economic and political question, but none the less had long admired and respected each other.

Many things have happened since the day when, in my last Reichstag speech, I expressed the hope that our political tact might increase, so that at last we should have reached the point at which Germans do not consider their political opponents fools — or knaves. Now, after more than ten years — after a war and then a revolution — I ask myself still if we have made any progress in the matter. There remains a certain satisfaction in the feeling that I, at least, have endeavoured to clear my mind of such absurdities. Through the winter 1919–1920 I went for several pleasant walks with a Communist to whom I owe some interesting flashes of insight into the real Marxist mentality. *Au fond,* the majority Socialists are mere opportunistic, milk and water Marxians. Franz Mehring was perfectly right to dedicate his book on Karl Marx, a work of real value, brilliantly written, to the Communist, Clara Zetkin, the undoubted inheritor of the true Marxian spirit. One day, on one of these walks, my Communist friend, by way of a compliment, informed me that he was really glad to have got to know in me one of the few remaining representatives of pre-Communist mentality and culture and perhaps the last authentic "political *grand seigneur.*" Erzberger, Bauer, even the "elegant" Scheidemann, the "handsome" Wirth, had never given him that impression.

Between the excellent Fitger and myself discussions were never very serious, and not more serious now than they had ever been. He conceded me my Bismarck and my Treitschke; I willingly allowed him his Caprivi, whose memory he seemed touchingly to cherish, and his perverse and embittered Theodor Barth. Together we admired the monuments of the city of Bremen, whose wealthy, serious, energetic bourgeois have created many solid and beautiful things.

In Bremen I heard for the first time from Fitger the name of the Labour leader, Ebert, whom he described as an honest and "relatively reasonable" man — reasonable, that is to say, by contrast to the then deputy for Bremen who, if I am not mistaken, was called Henke. I was to meet Ebert five years later, at a fête in honour of the Reichstag, given at Uhlenhorst, outside Hamburg. He seemed a man of natural good sense and *savoir vivre.* At the end of yet another five years I met him again, at Aumühle, the residence of the Chancellor Cuno, and, after dinner, we engaged in a fairly long conversation on the whole distressful state of the country. More than ever I received the impression that this was a man of real ability, a genuine patriot. He converted me neither to Socialism nor the republic — that had not been the purpose of our talk. I shall never cease to consider it a crime and a blunder to have prepared the revolution in war time; nor do I think any better of the German revolution as such. I shall always maintain that our people is less adapted than any other to republican methods of government. But, having in the War beheld four Chancellors, each of whom proved an utter failure, beginning with Bethmann — having witnessed the flight of William II, the crash of the Empire founded by the genius of Bismarck and the wisdom of William I, I consider it a fortune in misfortune that the deluge washed up this man into the presidency. He at least could show that, in this our Germany, so lacking, alas, in all political sense, the working classes can still breed men of real worth, characters that earn every respect, and capable party leaders.

But let me return to the Bremen of 1913. Fitger, detached and logical, deplored the noisy reception just given by William II to King Constantine, his brother-in-law. Through the whole of my stay in Bremen my friend never tried to conceal from me the anxiety he felt at this fresh Imperial "improvisation." After my departure he wrote: "The reception in Berlin of the King of Greece has produced, in France and in Athens, the painful impression that might have been expected. Its final results will be the reverse of what was hoped. In Germany only the *Kölnische-Zeitung* attempts, very lamely, to justify it. Most of the papers are merciless in their criticism of this interlude. A new phase of personal intervention seems upon us."

Under the direction of Bethmann — or rather through lack of any direction by him — the inconsequence and incoherencies of the Emperor had by now assumed such proportions that Europe no longer took him seriously. He presented this same King Constantine, insulted and mocked by him in public, in 1897, at the time of his defeat in Thessaly, with that Prussian Marshal's baton wielded by Moltke and Roon, which the very heir apparent, Frederick William, and Prince Frederick Charles had only received as a reward for Wörth and Metz. In the winter of 1913–1914 a member of the Suite described as follows my successor's share in all this muddlement: "Poor Bethmann! People are giving him another three to four months at most. He looks very depressed, has family worries to contend with (his son had been mixed up in some very unsavoury business, had for the time being retired to a sanatorium, and was later to be given a post in South America by Ballin), and now is made to feel himself ridiculous.   His nerve seems to have gone completely.   H. M. treats him *du haut en bas*, but tolerates him because he gives way in everything."

CHAPTER IX

In the autumn of 1913 I broke my journey back to Rome in Montreux, where I remained for some little time as already I had done twice in the previous years. Lake Leman had always attracted me, ever since I was a student in Lausanne. I do not go so far as Nietzsche, who declared himself only happy in Swiss hotels, but I can well understand what Shelley and Byron, Rousseau and Voltaire, Gibbon and Dickens, Flaubert and Lamartine, the Dane Jacobsen and the Russian Turgeniev, all felt at the sight of Lake Leman. When I saw again the island of Salagnon, encircled with its gulls, the sacred birds of the lake, the green pastures of the Haute Savoie, the cold peace of the Dent du Midi — that whole panorama of Alps and waters which seems to give a foretaste of eternity, I was conscious of a complete moral harmony. I reminded my wife of Rousseau's words: *"Je n'ai besoin que d'un pré au bord du lac Léman, d'un ami fidèle, d'une femme aimable, d'une vache et d'une barque; quand j'aurai tout cela mon bonheur sera complet"* — and saying to myself that God had blessed me with a loving wife and faithful friends, that we had the money to buy ourselves a boat, a cow, and a meadow, I suggested that we should spend the winter in Montreux. But she would not listen. Rome was calling her.

I have always had in me the urge to strike, from time to time, a thorough balance with myself, if possible on long walks through beautiful country. This time I tramped all round Montreux; at times through almost Scandinavian pine forests, through chestnut and walnut copses which put me in mind of the South — at times through woods which recalled my own beloved country. Or I wandered up and down the narrow streets of little towns, which I knew of old, where the maize sheaves, just as in the old days, hung in serried rows under the roofs.   I walked up to the Dent de Jaman, to the Rocher de Naye and the Chamossaire, up which, forty-six years before, I had climbed as a student, and, fifteen years after that, as a young Counsellor of Embassy.   I could hear again the bells of Saint Saphorin.   In the midst of this magnificent country-side, as it were devised to make us forget our personal griefs, to give sensations of greatness and perpetuity, to soothe all discord from our souls, I could feel even more profoundly than I had in the train outside Berlin an emotion of thankfulness to God for the admirable mercy and loving kindness with which He had guided my feet through every vicissitude, snare, and tribulation of life.   His care of me had been that of which the good Moravians sing: at times I had not understood, but He had led me miraculously and mercifully:

> *Wie ein Adler sein Gefieder*
> *Über seine Jungen streckt,*
> *Also hat auch hin und wieder*
> *Mich des Höchsten Arm bedeckt,*
> *Gottes Engel, die er sendet*
> *Hat das Böse, so der Feind*
> *Anzurichten war gemeint,*
> *In die Ferne weg gewendet.*
> *Alles Ding währt seine Zeit*
> *Gottes Lieb' in Ewigkeit.*[1]

I knew God's goodness in having given me my wife, she who in all things understood, and in many completed me.   She, like my-self, had set peace of mind and quiet happiness above all the pass-

---

[1] As an eagle spreads his wings
Over his young
So, ever and anon,
His might has covered me.
God's angel, whom He sends
Has kept away the evil thing, the enemy,
His guard has been my preparation.
Each thing comes to pass in its own time
God's love is eternal.

ing goods of earth. She had built up a fair, harmonious home for me, a refuge for us both from the world which we saw, though we did not hate it, as from the hither side of a high wall, our peace untroubled by the deceptions, discords, and bitterness inseparable from political activity.

I looked back, too, on our silver wedding day in Rome, where we had kept it, nearly three years previously, on January 9, 1911. Pius X on this occasion had received us both in private audience. As we passed through the Papal apartments I had thought of Leo XIII, who, in these same rooms, I had seen not long before his death, and who made so lasting an impression on all who came in personal touch with him. Seldom have I encountered a human being whose spirit seemed so detached as this Pope's; he appeared to have transcended matter and, so to speak, re-absorbed it into himself. No taint of earth still clung about him. His robe was no paler than his cheeks, his great eyes glowed with the fire of genius. In the presence of Pius X all, even the non-Catholics, could feel themselves in the presence of a profoundly good, profoundly pious and humble man, in spite of his very real dignity. When, in 1879, on the eve of our departure for Berlin, my wife and I were received by Leo XIII, the venerable pontiff had allowed her to kneel and kiss his foot. He had comforted her then, with marvellous kindness, for her grief at leaving Rome and her mother. Her husband, he told her, had been called to an important post, in which he might do much good to the world and his country. Her duty, therefore, was to make his task as easy as she could, to help him, and go gaily to this new life. Leo XIII always showed my wife the greatest kindness. Shortly before his death he sent her his apostolic blessing, by the hand of Cardinal Kopp.

Piux X would not allow my wife to do the traditional homage and kiss his foot. With a charming smile he raised her up and held with us both a long conversation. I must here protest against the widespread rumour that Pius X in worldly matters, especially in his judgments of politics, was simple-minded, foolish even. In the long conversation with which he honoured me he touched on several questions of policy with sound good sense and even diplomatic acumen. His judgments on political personages, sovereigns, ministers, and deputies, were equally balanced and intelligent. And when, our audience done, he blessed my wife and told her kindly that he prayed God to take me too into His protection and follow me always with His grace, I felt as grateful to this noble old man as she did.

Adolf Wilbrandt, for thirty-five years our friend, had written to my wife for our silver wedding:

DEAREST DONNA MARIA,

My cousin Lisbeth Wendhausen, who is staying here too with my children and grandchildren, has just told me that January 9th is the great day — your silver wedding! Is she right? Is it the 9th? Twenty-five years since it happened, then! A whole twenty-five? — They must have wings.

Well, to think of all the things that have happened since, to you and your dear Chancellor — (he is still that to me). Family history and world history! A wonderful career his has been, up and up, till at last he reached the summit, and then an honourable, dignified, freely chosen end, an end which came as a loss to all of us, but still left us hopes and regrets.

And you have been the loyalty and poetry, the clear and happy music of his great life! One of the handsomest couples in German history. A wonderful mixture of Italian and German — perhaps the very best of all mixtures. Like golden double stars, you must stay for many years in the heavens.

I'm writing this in a hurry, so that it may reach you in time. I love you both from the bottom of my heart. Eternal friendship! Thanks! Joy — that you are alive —

I am,

ADOLF WILBRANDT.

To me Gustav Schmoller wrote as follows:

Twenty-five years of married happiness as the offset to a brilliant career! But you have earned them both, since the whole of these twenty-five years have passed in exacting, responsible labour for the Fatherland. Whoever has had the privilege, my dear Prince, of seeing fairly closely into the lives of yourself and the Princess, could as little doubt your mutual happiness as the fact that you were made for one another. It was only hard to choose which most to admire — the Princess's grace, talents, and charm, or your own wisdom and knowledge of how to handle men — the Olympian calm and joy of your personality. Could I have my dearest wish for Germany it would be that Prince Bülow come back again and rule us. But if I am to speak only for you, I wish you your own pure and untroubled happiness, at the side of such a wife as the Princess.

His praise of my wife I reproduce, since it is justified. This poet and scholar's tribute to myself I classed beneath the comforting dictum of old Ovid : "*Principibus placuisse viris non ultima laus est.*"

In my long tramps along Lake Leman — "clear, placid Leman", as Byron calls it, I was continually haunted by fears for the future of Germany, the land which I had served, body and soul, since the day, forty-three years ago, when I had set out for the wars as a young hussar. I forced myself in these solitary musings not to give way to the usual failing of retired politicians and diplomatists who come down to sit in the audience and find they want to criticize everything. I often remembered the *mot* of Schweinitz, an able ambassador under Bismarck, that *au fond* there are only two sorts of men, those in and those out of office. Everything pleases the ones : *tout est pour le mieux dans le meilleur des mondes possibles*; the others can only carp and assert that nothing is going right. But even when I had striven to be impersonal in examining the general situation, I still could not hide from myself the very gravest reasons for anxiety.

Our complete renunciation of Morocco, sealed by the Morocco Convention, represented a serious economic loss to Germany, whose trade with that country had scarcely been inferior to the French. For France it meant a considerable addition to her man power, which already was beginning to diminish. After all the world-wide sensation produced by our sending the *Panther* to Agadir, the wretched strip of Congo we had acquired by sweating blood and tears seemed certainly an inadequate compensation. And with it all we had exposed ourselves to the not unmerited reproach of having tried to profit by the distress of a country under our protectorate, to make money. In February, 1913, I had written to Bassermann :

The reasons which, in 1911, led us to abandon Morocco for Congo swamps have not proved themselves to have been justified : there has not been the promised amelioration of our relationship with France ; after all sorts of concessions, advances and offers of friendship, French public opinion is as hostile as it has ever been since 1871. This animosity expresses itself in formidable military efforts on a scale which, up to now, would have seemed impossible ; by the sending of Delcassé to St. Petersburg, which, though our official Press makes light of it, is considered as an omen by other countries. In these last years the French have grown much more self-confident, and this throws a shadow on Alsace-Lorraine.

More disquieting still were the modifications effected in the Balkan situation as the final result of the last wars. Their consequences might be disastrous unless our foreign policy were most skilful. When the news that Germany finally and definitely renounced Morocco reached the Consulta in Rome, the Marchese San Giuliano, the Foreign Minister — who himself later told me the story — took out his watch and noted down the date and the hour. He had then turned and said to his secretaries that now, though Rome till then had no wish for it, Italy would have to go to Tripoli. The Italian expedition into Tripoli also unleashed the troubles in the Balkans. On February 28, 1913, I analysed their origin and consequences in the following letter to Bassermann :

On the road which, from Agadir via Tripoli, has led us to the war in the Balkans we have, in two successive summers of crisis, suffered very grave material losses. Our whole situation has grown more precarious than before ; our prestige has suffered. It is very unfortunate that Vienna did not succeed in preventing this trouble in Eastern Europe, as she certainly might have done, considering the pacific character of most of the Balkan sovereigns. At the very least, before any declaration of hostilities, Austria should have given some clear ruling on the relationships of all the Balkan peoples.

I added that this deplorable turn of events was a consequence of the mis-valuation of effective forces in the Balkans.

Just as, in 1866, Napoleon III based his tactics on the presumed superiority of the Austrians over Prussia, until it needed Sadowa to dispel the last of his illusions, so too, on the eve of this Balkan war, Austria founded her attitude on the quite erroneous hypothesis of an easy victory for the Turks. This blindness, both of Berlin and Vienna, prevented any forceful intervention before the declaration of hostilities. The Turks were led to believe that nothing would be enough to alter the *status quo*. They were even egged on to fight, till their defeat showed all the error of these reckonings and also, alas, that the policy of the Triple Entente had been as superior to that of the Central Powers as the arms of the Balkan peoples to Turkish organization and strategy.

All that I felt dimly in those days I can express again quite clearly to-day. With a little more skill and foresight it should have been possible to prevent the war in the Balkans. A cold douche turned on Sofia would have been quite enough to stay King Ferdinand, a cautious and never aggressive monarch. A firmer tone in Constantinople would have forced the Turks to make the now necessary concessions. But we did nothing at all, neither in Belgrade nor yet in Athens; above all, nothing in Sofia, and the Turks were rather encouraged than dissuaded.

Kiderlen and Marshal von der Goltz fell into the same miscalculation on the military strength of the Osmanli —a proof that even the best specialists sometimes miss the wood for the trees. Kiderlen itched with impatience to see, as he himself expressed it, the good old Turks tan the hides of the Lower Danube sheepstealers. After manœuvres which took place at Kirkilisse, on the very same ground where, a year later, the Bulgarians crushed the Turkish army, Von der Goltz, that eminent strategist, declared that had it been a real battle, the Osmanli would have won the greatest victory in their history. The disappointment was therefore all the greater in Vienna, Budapest, and Berlin, when, in the March of 1913, the Bulgarians took Adrianople, where they captured twenty-nine pashas and threatened Constantinople itself. And soon, in Vienna and Budapest, disappointment had become anxiety, which grew at last into a fever when the victors of the first Balkan War quarrelled on the sharing of booty and the Serbs defeated the Bulgars with the aid of the Roumanians and the Greeks. I had therefore been all too correct in saying in my letter to Bassermann (February 28, 1913) that now, in the whole of Eastern Europe, the Austrian position had been modified — *funditus, et funditus in pejus.* The language used by Viennese and Budapest newspapers proved that there also this was felt, that agitation on both sides of the Leitha was increasing in the Dual Monarchy.

What I dreaded most of all was that Austria would aggravate an alarming situation by a policy of chicane towards Serbia. "Every possible mistake against Serbia is being made by Austrian pride," wrote Herr vom Rath, so versed in every Balkan problem. And he added: "Then there is this bamboozling of Roumania! Is the Triple Alliance gone into diplomatic bankruptcy? You who were once past master in the Balkan problem, and in your very just appreciation of Austrian and Russian policies, have now proved to be our prophet in these matters."

On December 30, 1912, I had written to Bassermann from Rome: "That very grave problem which Austria in the nineteenth century had to solve in Germany and Italy is now transferred for her to the East. Will Austria succeed with the Southern Slavs better than with the Italians and the Germans? Will she handle Serbia with more skill than she once handled Piedmont and Prussia? Pashitch is certainly no Cavour, and neither is he a Bismarck, any more than Serbia herself is comparable to Piedmont or Prussia; but who, sixty years ago, ever dreamed that Austria would be beaten? Will her *Divide et impera* enable her to keep the Serbs and Roumanians, the Greeks and Bulgarians, apart? It is by no means certain, since nothing could be done to hinder the formation of the Balkan League. It has come into being in spite of such deep-rooted antinomies as seemed to have rendered it impossible. It is very regrettable that the *status quo* should not have been preserved, since for us it was in every way better and far more propitious for our ally. We must also regret our vain efforts for Turkey."

I feared that, to regain lost ground in the Balkans, sacrificed by its own follies, the Hapsburg monarchy might be tempted to make use of the Pomeranian grenadier. My fears above all amounted to this: that the Emperor, should temptation present itself, led on by his own romantic generosity, the clumsy stupidity of Bethmann, and

the snobbish predilections of Jagow for feudal Austria, might get
us involved in war with Russia, and so with all the rest of the world.
"Clumsiness might transform our alliance with Austria into the
heaviest, most galling of fetters," the historian Schäfer wrote in
1912, in the preface to his "History of Modern Times." Nobody
was more conscious than I, who had guided my country's policy for
more than ten years, of the agony of not being allowed to advise on
situations which I knew, from long experience, to be dangerous, of
not being allowed any chance to give disinterested counsel to the
rulers. This torture is one to which Italian, French, and English
statesmen are not subject, since they, as parliamentarians, can
express their opinions freely and remain in continuous contact with
the powers that be. But the archaic organization of German government relegated our statesmen to the position of pensioned-off,
private individuals, and forced them to be silent and — I am thinking of my painful experience between 1914–1918 — to suffer. William II always took in very ill part any public expression of opinion
by an ex-Minister. This arose from his extravagant conception
of the rôle which a sovereign ought to play, even nowadays. Bismarck, fallen from power and in opposition, was in his eyes a rebel.
He often declared that the one thing which had pleased him
in Caprivi was that, after retirement, the latter never opened his
mouth. I do not remember any conversation in which the Emperor
asked an ex-Minister's advice — from time to time he may have
consulted Hollmann, but then only to rile Tirpitz, Hollmann's
successor, and in any case "little Hollmann" was more a buffoon
than anything else.

Through the whole five years, from my retirement until war
had been declared, anxious patriots, without my having stirred a
finger in the matter, kept expressing the hope that William II had
not decided to relinquish my advice for good and all. They did
their best to get His Majesty to change his attitude towards me, or,
if not that, to abstain from puerile discourtesy. Herr von Loebell,
my excellent Head of the Chancellery, had been appointed Minister
of the Interior. Both before and during the Great War and, above
all, in the critical days which led up to it, he kept begging

the Emperor to consult me. But always he encountered the same
conceited resistance from His Majesty. Ballin also did whatever
he could to get me recalled, or at least to keep me in touch with William II on all matters of foreign policy. He was convinced that,
before July 22d, and even before July 30, 1914, I might have saved
the situation. He felt equally sure that in 1916 I could have
found a way to negotiate with Russia, and could, in 1917, have come
to a reasonable understanding with England. But though they
were the closest friends, the Kaiser would not listen to Ballin. *Il
n'y a pas de pire sourd que celui qui ne veut pas entendre.*

Count August Eulenburg, as discerning as he was loyal, made
constant and tactful efforts to reconcile us. Once, in 1917, after
Bethmann's fall, at the end of a conversation with Ballin, H.M.
said to the Count: "You can go and tell my wife she'll have her
Bülow back." But, a few hours later, the intrigues of the German
Ambassador in Vienna, Count Botho Wedel, and of Gottfried
Hohenlohe, the Austrian Ambassador in Berlin — two minds and
but one single thought — had decided His Majesty to renounce me,
and Valentini managed to have Michaelis, the Undersecretary of
State, appointed as Bethmann's successor.

Five years previously, the clear-sighted Schmoller, in whom,
from that time on, the developments of our whole foreign policy
kept arousing all too justified trepidations, had made an effort to
reëstablish a normal relationship between His Majesty and myself.
He wrote to me in the summer of 1912 to tell me that his dearest
wish had always been to enlighten the Emperor, not for my sake
only, or even for the sake of the general good, but in William II's
own interest. How and when this could be managed he did not
know, since he himself had scarcely any official connections left.
But since Harnack enjoyed, at least once a week, the bliss of being
allowed to sun himself in the warmth of the Imperial rays, he had
sent him a short memorandum, with the request to pass it on to the
Sovereign. In a letter to me a few months later he admitted that
he had formed a wrong idea of his colleague Harnack, who, like Fal-
staff, evidently held discretion to be the better part of valour and
had not wanted to risk annoying his master. Schmoller enclosed

IMPERIAL MANŒUVRES

The Earl of Lonsdale, the Kaiser, Prince Max Egon zu Fürstenberg and the Austrian Military Attaché

the visiting card which, after a very long interval, he had received in answer to his letter :

Professor Dr. Adolf Harnack
Privy Councillor, General Director of the Royal Prussian Library
returns with many thanks the memorandum which you were kind enough to send him. This, though it has thrown no fresh light on the situation with which it deals, has by its clarity of statement, and the deep conviction it expresses, a real significance. It would be possible to transmit it to His Majesty, though certain deletions and emendations would have to be made. This does not, however, seem feasible for the moment, and I become with every day more persuaded that the proper intermediary in this would be, not Herr v. Valentini, whose official position constitutes too binding a restriction, but the present Chancellor himself.

I do not intend to lose sight of the matter.

With all esteem,
A. H.

"His Majesty's devil dodger", as the tall aide-de-camp, General Scholl, called Harnack, did not behave as did the Samaritan coming down from Jerusalem to Jericho, who rescued him that fell among thieves, who had beaten him and stripped him of his garments. Instead of pouring oil and wine, he followed the Levite who "went on his way." (Luke, x, 32.)

Yet, if William II remained deaf to the most disinterested counsel, justice obliges me to record that public opinion in Germany was not at that moment at all inclined to heed an ex-Chancellor's warnings. Nevertheless, my fears still haunted me. One of my oldest friends, a German lady married to a Frenchman, wrote to me from Paris that opinion there had completely changed since my retirement. "Millerand the Socialist," she added, "is doing his best to stir up French chauvinism everywhere. In any case it never really sleeps. The French have always adored '*le pantalon rouge.*'"

I was still more struck by a letter from old Geheimrat Mechler, who had directed the Central Bureau at the Foreign Office as faithfully under Bismarck, Caprivi, and Hohenlohe as under my own chancellorship. He had got on equally well with Herbert Bismarck and Holstein, Kiderlen, and Marshall. In his nearly fifty years of official life he had watched and experienced many things. This model official might have exclaimed with the chorus in "The Bride of Messina":

> *Die fremden Eroberer kommen und gehen,*
> *Wir gehorchen, aber wir bleiben stehen.*[1]

Geheimrat Mechler wrote as follows on New Year's Day, 1914: "It is really impossible to say whether the year of the ominous '13 has not brought more disappointments, ill luck, and sorrow than realized hopes and satisfaction. My personal observations make me fear that 1913 will have been fateful. At least, this seems to be the case in the history of every nation, in particular of our German Fatherland. I can only hope, as a good German, that next year will prove to have been better, and that 1914 may make good all that has been made evil by 1913."

In another letter to me old Mechler added: "Here in the north we have had a sudden fall of snow, unusually heavy and unexpected, followed by several days of equally unlooked-for warmth and sunshine, which has made the blossoms come along far too quickly. Frost nipped them all and laid them low, and now, for several days, it has been warm again. Neither politics nor Nature seem inclined to keep to their appointed courses, so times are equally bad for weather prophets and politicians. Could things ever be trusted to go as usual and history be always logical, I should suppose Your Highness tranquil on the world-situation. Since this, however, never is the case, I presume that you also feel some anxiety."

Back in Rome, via the Rhone and Simplon, I endeavoured to define my vague uneasiness by drawing up a detailed memorandum. How could I hope ever to have it read by the Emperor? I knew how William II disliked having to read even the shortest of *comptes rendus*. In 1890 he had scarcely troubled to glance through so important and historical a document as Bismarck's letter of resignation — and still less had he ever deigned to think about it. Should I not merely awaken his mistrust if I sent him the document direct?

---

[1] The foreign conquerors come and go,
We obey — but remain.

And Bethmann, alas, was not more likely to examine my suggestions without prejudice. That thin-skinned and pretentious Chancellor, full of a sense of his own superiority and very easy to offend, had allowed his two confrères, Jagow and Flotow, to persuade him that he would be making himself ridiculous if he adopted any line of policy suggested by the previous Chancellor. My whole education and career had brought me, through no merit of mine, many influential European connections. I was a better diplomat than Bethmann. He would simply be showing himself my "puppet" if ever he listened to my advice. Could he even be sure it would be sincerely given? Thus Jagow and Flotow, judging every one else by themselves, whispered in the ear of my successor. Who wants his successor to succeed? Even if the advice he gave were sound, Prince Bülow would be sure to take the credit for any eventual success, while attributing every setback in our policy to the clumsy methods by which his sage suggestions had been followed. Certain confidences of Loebell and Schwartzkoppen left me in no doubt that Bethmann-Hollweg, who, thanks to me, had been appointed Prussian Minister of the Interior, Imperial State Secretary for Home Affairs, Vice Chancellor and Vice President of the Prussian Council of Ministers, and who had, therefore, me to thank for his chancellorship, was a mass of petty jealousy and mistrust. In all his overemphatic protestations of undying gratitude and respect he had not once asked my advice in a concrete instance. There was nothing left but to attempt an indirect assault on the ears of Emperor and Chancellor.

I thought the matter over very carefully, and wrote briefly to Count August Eulenburg, the Head of the Imperial Household, whose subtle mind and balanced judgment were enhanced by real nobility of spirit and a patriotism that never flagged. I began by assuring the Count that my letter would remain a secret, that I had kept neither copy nor rough draft. I went on to say that I wanted nothing for myself. I had had my fill. Then I developed the following points:

Our retreat before the frown of Lloyd George, the unsatisfactory Congo Convention, had aroused all the latent pride of the French,

exciting their unslaked thirst for *revanche*. In any case of grave
complications arising between ourselves and Russia, France would
not again walk warily as she had in the winter of 1908–1909. This
was proved by her recent changes of personnel in certain important
government posts. In 1912 Poincaré had been made *Président du
Conseil* and head of the Foreign Affairs; in 1913 *"le bon Lorrain"*
was President of the French Republic, and Delcassé, scarcely three
months later, had gone as Ambassador to St. Petersburg. It was
therefore more necessary than ever to keep on the best of terms with
Russia. France was the one European country in which in certain
influential quarters (not in the people) it was justifiable to talk of
"war fever." The essential thing, however, was Russia's attitude.
The whole situation in the Balkans had altered to Germany's detriment, through wars which we had not managed to prevent. Turkey
and Bulgaria were defeated, the power and influence of Serbia and
Roumania had increased. All this was unpleasant for us and disquieting for Austria-Hungary. The essential thing was that the
latter should not give way to "nerves." It was a question of keeping a clear head and working to surmount the present difficulties,
which could not be expected to last for ever. No imprudent gestures, still less any provocative act ! I concluded with this couplet
of Goethe, a favourite piece of advice which I had often quoted to
the Emperor :

> Don't let yourself be caught to-day !
> You 've escaped a hundred times that way.

This saying may perhaps raise smiles from café politicians and
parlour strategists; it may seem most superficial to philosophers,
but, in practical politics, its value is continually being proved.

Eulenburg's answer to my letter, though very amiably expressed,
contained little to console me in its substance. He wrote that for
the moment His Majesty was in no mood to heed the very best-inten-
tioned warnings. The inspiring aftertaste of the jubilee celebrations in 1913, many moving proofs of loyalty, devotion, and gratitude
received by him and by his house on the occasion of his twenty-fifth
year on the throne; above all, his only daughter's marriage to the

heir of the Guelfs, at last reconciled, had all done much to increase His Majesty's *amour propre*. The moment when his daughter, led by the King of England and the Russian Tsar, had stepped to the altar, had seemed to him the culminating point of his whole reign and achievement, the visible sign that God was with him and with the Fatherland. Already General Plessen, the commandant at Imperial Headquarters and *général de service* of the Emperor, had written informing us of the joy which, once the engagement was concluded, filled all hearts in the palace at Berlin.

"Their Majesties are transported with delight, the august lovers radiant with happiness. The hand of God has wondrously guided us."

Joy was in Priam's Halls
Before the fall of that high city.

CHAPTER X

Bethmann-Hollweg's Policy from 1909–1914 — His Reticence with My-self on Politics — I Remain for These Five Years Eliminated — Lich-nowsky Appointed London Ambassador — The Opinions of Foreign States-men — Peter Carp Visits Rome — Krupenski and Sasonow's Instructions — Kokowzow and Kriwoschein in Rome — Sir Rennell Rodd, the British Ambassador — My Book "German Policy."

As already I have said so often, my successor never judged it necessary to give me the slightest information or ask me for a single piece of advice. Through the five years between my resignation and the outbreak of war in 1914 — *longum spatium aevi* — years full of changes and events which gave rise to many dangerous problems, Bethmann, so far as I was concerned, confined himself to platitude and commonplace, without once touching on any serious subject in my presence. The few observations on politics with which this suspicious Chancellor honoured me were made in a tone of pedantry and instruction, with an air of immense self-approbation. It was hard to repress a smile as one listened to the worthy Theobald enveloping the realities of life in involved, never-ending perorations, whose undertone was one of self-esteem. Even in intimate talks with one other person he seemed always to be lecturing on ethics to an audience eager to be improved. Our meetings were a series of monologues, though nothing of what he said to me in these days bore any trace of his future plaints after the final disaster of his foreign policy — his grieved attempts to prove to all the world that, in foreign affairs, he had inherited an impossible task. The thesis, later developed by his disciples, of my having caused the encirclement of Germany, was one he dared never lay before me. On the contrary, with me he was all optimism, full of fatuous confidence in himself.

In the few letters I received from him, letters in which he never failed to sign himself "your most devoted and ever-grateful", his observations were strictly academic.   In 1912, for instance, he wrote to tell me how much he regretted not to have been able to arrive at any adequate slogan for use in the general election.   "A majority composed of Liberals, Centre, and a few independent Conservatives is conceivable; but that would take us too far to the Left, so that the problem is still dangerous and insoluble."   The letter went on to say that he aimed at diminishing the task of the future assembly, and wished, above all, to keep it calm.   A clerical-conservative Chancellor was as impossible as one who favoured the Left.   Bismarck had declared that his task was to manœuvre his way among the parties and Bethmann intended to do as Bismarck.   It was certainly annoying, he added, not to be able to take an active part in the election and rally the parties with a cry.   But what was to be done !   Economic slogans were no use for winning an election ; such a programme never got discussed.   Ten years after all the recriminations of Left and Right, every one seemed satisfied with the Customs Tariff and Commercial Treaties of Von Bülow.   An anti-socialist battle cry, alas, would not be efficacious for the moment.   Hence, too, the ever-growing difficulty, not only for the parties, but for the government, of knowing what attitude to adopt towards Socialism.   Happily that party was so restless that its radical and revisionist elements no longer observed towards each other the most elementary rules of common politeness.   My successor proceeded to enlighten me on the foreign situation, of which, in a tone of joyous confidence, he gave me only the barest outlines.   "We make slow but steady progress with England."   "Nothing secret has occurred at the Foreign Office.   Sasonow's illness has delayed, without having jeopardized, the conclusion of the Potsdam conversations."   We should even achieve *rapprochement* with France, "provided the government there is strong enough."   On the whole this, as a rule so stolid Chancellor, showed all his Emperor's exuberance.

In the summer of 1913 I had met my namesake, Hans Adolf von Bülow, the Hamburg Minister.   For about a year, if the Chancellor were absent from Berlin, he had represented the Foreign Office with

the Emperor.   He was a man of great good sense and a useful diplomat, entirely devoted to Bethmann, who was always very kind to his
subordinates.   He confided that the present Chancellor had complained to him more than once that, personally, he could take no
pleasure in his function.   Bethmann was by nature sensitive and
always very upset by attacks in the Reichstag and press.   A malicious caricature was enough to bring on a sleepless night; he had
not the "rhinoceros hide" of Prince von Bülow.   The Emperor
was often ruder than any Chancellor should have allowed him to be.
"The only thing that keeps me in office is my feeling that I have
become indispensable to the peace of the world, and especially as
regards England.   Bismarck was a great man, but nobody really
had faith in him.   Your cousin, Prince Bülow, whom I respect so
much, was always very adroit and intelligent, but he too was not
really trusted.   I am trusted!   I have managed to gain the trust
of the whole of Europe, and that of England in particular; so that
now I feel it is my duty to remain, though at times it's most
disagreeable."

When Bethmann-Hollweg said all this to my namesake, we were
less than a year from the World War.   A terrible proof of the insufficiency of the fifth Imperial Chancellor of Germany, and yet a proof
that at least he was not perfidious, that he never had the slightest
intention of disturbing the peace of the world.   The man of the
Serbian ultimatum, who allowed Belgium to be invaded, was never
the wolf in sheep's clothing our enemies made him out to be.   He was
the sacrificial lamb who, in 1914, tried to assume the aspect of a wolf.

The "continuous progress" we made with England did not reach
the point of an understanding on the *tempo* of naval construction.
I had never managed, even before my fall from grace, to wring concessions on this out of the Emperor.   Bethmann might easily have
done so.   But unluckily my successor was so weak as to sacrifice
Paul Metternich in London to some narrow prejudice of Von Tirpitz
and the sudden whimsy of His Majesty.   One after the other,
Herr von Eisendecher, the Minister at Karlsruhe, Baron Wangenheim, the Minister at Athens, and Ferdinand Stumm, the former
Minister to Madrid, were considered for the London Embassy.

Finally it was decided to send Marschall from Constantinople to London. In spite of the Krüger telegram, which he had once approved and defended with emphasis in the Reichstag, he was welcomed there with that "good nature", a mixture of snobbery and benevolent curiosity, which the English reserve for all foreign celebrities — whether they come in the shape of an Italian tenor, a Parisian actress, an Indian nabob, or an European statesman of note. The ambitious Marschall hoped that London would be his last step before the Wilhelmstrasse. The Chancellor's Palace had formed the goal of his life. But, during a short stay in his native Baden, he suddenly died, like Kiderlen and Herbert Bismarck before him, the victim of Bacchus and overwork.

The Emperor next was inspired to send Prince Lichnowsky to London, although eight years before he had left the Service. The witty Mme. de Muchanow always said: "*Il faut demander au bon Dieu de ne pas exaucer nos prières,*" a thought the Greeks expressed more profoundly: "The gods, to punish, grant our wishes." Lichnowsky, who had served in Bucharest as Undersecretary of Legation at my orders and had been my Chief of Staff at the Foreign Office, was staying, in the autumn of 1912, in Hamburg, in the same hotel as myself, the "Atlantic", which, under Ballin's direction, with the aid of the gastronomic Pfordte, had become one of the best in the world. One night, as I was going to bed, Lichnowsky came rushing, full of delight, into my bedroom, shouting, "I've got it!" and brandishing an autograph letter from the Emperor. Its tenor was more or less the following: The Emperor had chosen Lichnowsky to be his representative in London. He must never forget that he owed his appointment to his Emperor, and not to the suggestions of the Foreign Office. The task which the All Highest imposed on him was to give good dinners in London, be seen at country houses and at race meetings, in brief be called "a jolly good fellow", and make himself thoroughly popular. He was to be the screen behind which His Imperial Majesty could finish building his fleet. This achieved, we should have world peace, the Emperor's life-long ideal. It should here be added in parenthesis that one could hardly imagine a more spontaneous declaration of the Kaiser's love of peace. William II was in the habit of unburdening his heart without reserve in letters to his personal friends.

When, next day, he reported at the Foreign Office, Lichnowsky was given a cold welcome there. Bethmann was appalled by this selection, for the difficult London embassy, of a diplomat who had not even directed a legation. Kiderlen affirmed that the new ambassador was "a baby", intellectually. This was an exaggeration, though the choice was certainly unwise. Lichnowsky had fine instincts, was honourable and generous through and through — what old Berlin would have called "a beautiful soul." At times he had flashes of inspiration. But first and foremost, he was an amateur and inclined to minimize the difficulties and dangers of his profession. He was never sufficiently conscious that, in politics, though ideas may be easy enough to harmonize, men and things present the real difficulty. Holstein, who liked Lichnowsky and protected him, used to say: "Dear old Lichnowsky always imagines that to gossip about a thing is the same as doing it." On the whole, Lichnowsky was a mere dabbler in politics rather than a political intellect; he was also inclined to be tactless and, more dangerously still, neurasthenic. It was essential that, in London especially, our Ambassador should be cool and self-controlled. Lichnowsky's five predecessors, Bernstorff, Münster, Hatzfeld, Metternich, and Marschall, had each his faults, but none was excitable like Lichnowsky. Count Lerchenfeld, the Bavarian Minister in Berlin, an intimate of the new Ambassador, said to me soon after his appointment: "Lichnowsky would never make a good captain in a squall. But, provided we have clear weather, he 'll be all right; and, thank God, the Chancellor keeps telling me that the English barometer is set fair."

Such was the general prognosis, and it seemed, on the whole, to be justified. If, in every European capital, but especially in Vienna and Berlin, policy, in the summer of 1914, had been more prudently directed — with more intelligence — Europe would, no doubt, never have stumbled into one of the worst catastrophes in all history. I think I have mentioned a remark made in November, 1913, by Professor Hans Delbrück, Bethmann's panegyrist and close friend.

"France," wrote Delbrück, "in her groundless apprehensions of Germany, had laid on herself the crushing burden of three years' military service. But this, in the last Eastern crisis, had not prevented France's realization of the common interests binding the two countries, above all in Greece, where Russia tried to assign to her a part which her every instinct made repugnant. Hence the present happy amelioration of Franco-German *rapports*. The growing friendliness which, for some time past, had entered our relations with England, would not be jeopardized by the continuance of our naval programme. There, too, amelioration was bound to come: at home and abroad antinomies were finding their adjustment."

On January 16, 1914, at the General Congress of Patriotic Societies held in Münich, the historian, Erich Marcks, concluded his speech in these terms: "If we take a general survey of the world we shall perceive that the clouds have grown less menacing. The difficult moments of our début on the stage of world politics are, we may be sure, at last behind us. The burden of crisis is being lightened. Germany has won more elbow room. We have succeeded in getting ourselves recognized as a naval power, just as once we got ourselves recognized on the continent."

On January 27, 1914, the last Imperial birthday before the war, Flotow, the Chancellor's favourite, delivered, in my presence, in Rome, an address to the German colony. He had carefully prepared and memorized it. Here is an extract: "The patriot who examines the international position to-day must feel entirely reassured by it. Thanks to the wisdom of Bethmann-Hollweg, and the skill of our State Secretary, Herr von Jagow, our position in the world is highly favourable. All the great powers are equally desirous of peace. All need peace. All look towards Germany and Germany's present diplomatic chiefs with full and cordial trust and esteem."

> Little know they
> Of hidden rocks
> Those sailors gay
> Who sail away.
> Of reefs and shoals
> And stormy weather. —
> Whose ship like an egg-shell, shall crumple together.

But the opinion of foreign politicians, even of those who meant us well, was not entirely in accord with such chronic outbursts in Germany of official and semi-official optimism. My old Bucharest friend, Peter Carp, came to see me in Rome in April, 1914. I motored him out to Hadrian's Villa on a delicious day in spring. As we wandered together about the Poikilé, where, eighteen centuries ago, Hadrian, the vain emperor, had loved to wander with his philosophers, Carp stood still and said to me with his usual abruptness: "You see in front of you the last friend of the Triple Alliance in Bucharest." Then, in a voice of calm anxiety, he explained his brusque and sudden outburst: "I, who had been for so long the German Minister in Bucharest, must know better than any one that Roumania had hoped, when she joined the Triple Alliance, that Germany would continue to be its dominant partner. Between Roumania and Austria, or rather between Roumania and the trans-Leithan half of the Monarchy, there had always been the gravest discord. Since I had resigned, both Italy and Roumania felt that the direction of the Alliance had passed to Vienna from Berlin. If war broke out, it was improbable that Roumania would follow the lead of Austria-Hungary.

"Whatever happens, I shall be faithful to Germany, faithful to the oath I took as a member of the Borussen Corps in Bonn: 'Borussia, I am yours from youth to age! This I swear before your colours; I swear it to the black and white flag.'[1] But on the day when things become critical, if the Alliance is directed from Vienna, as already seems to be the case, I shall be alone in my loyalty."

Some passing English and American globe-trotters stared in amazement at this energetic man with the white moustache, who spoke so loudly and made so many gestures. When, three years later, Roumania made her *volte-face*, Herr von Waldthausen, our Minister at Bucharest, a loyal and intelligent diplomat, told me how, in the winter 1913–1914, King Carol, with his usual suavity, but in a tone that could not be mistaken, had told him that the seat of the

[1] *Borussia, dir gehör' ich,*
Ob Jüngling oder Greis,
Zu Deiner Fahne schwör' ich,
Der Fahne schwarz und Weiss!

Triple Alliance was no longer, as formerly, Berlin. The balance had shifted to Vienna, and that, in any case of complications, would make it very difficult for his country to ally herself to the Central Powers. Herr von Waldthausen, as was his duty, informed Berlin of the King's declaration, only to receive the acid answer that the Triple Alliance, more than ever, was being directed by our government; it was in the hands of skilled and experienced statesmen, and this, so the Foreign Office hoped, had been our Minister's instant reply to the King — or, if not, he must repair his omission forthwith.

More, even, than by Carp's anxieties, I was stirred by a confidential statement made to me by my friend Krupenski, the Russian Ambassador in Rome, where I had met him first twenty years before, in the days when I was still Ambassador and he the First Secretary of his Embassy there. He was known all over Europe in diplomacy for his huge nose, deep voice, and impetuous gestures. For the rest, a thoroughly good fellow, Russian — old Russian even, to the backbone. Like most of his party anti-Austrian, yet never anti-German, and generally out of sympathy with "the decadent West." Yet this Austrophobe had married an Austrian, the good and charming daughter of a general, whom he had plagued into becoming a member of the Greek Orthodox Church, though that could not be achieved without some difficulty. Converts to the Russian Orthodox Communion, must, it is well known, be re-baptized, and, in Orthodox baptism the proselyte is plunged three times, naked, into holy water. When this had been done on the birth of the Grand Duchess Marie, Nicholas I, her father, asked his favourite, Prince Bariatinski, what impression the ceremony had made on him. The prince replied: "*J'ai été ravi, surtout parceque j'ai eu l'honneur de voir Son Altesse Impériale, Madame la Grande-Duchesse Marie Nikolajewna comme, malheureusement, je ne la reverrai plus.*"

Mme. Krupenski, at least, was allowed by the officiating pope to drape herself in a woollen garment which covered her from head to foot; but she did not escape her plunge into holy water. When, new-baptized, she told the other ladies of the Embassy how joyful she felt at having been converted to Orthodoxy, they all seemed very much surprised. It so happened that they were all Protestants from the Baltic province, who had not been in the least moved by the spectacle.

It was in April, 1914, that Krupenski called on me to read me a confidential letter just received from his Chief, Sasonow, the substance of which was that St. Petersburg had received information that Austria-Hungary was meditating an anti-Serbian *coup*. This had first been planned for the spring of 1913, but, on Italy's intervention, was postponed and the plan shelved for the time being. It was to be hoped that the project was now abandoned. In the present situation of Europe, any Austrian move against Serbia would be bound to endanger the general peace. Russia would definitely oppose a sudden anti-Serbian move by Austria. The present position was very different from that of the last Bosnian crisis (1908–1909), when Russia had still felt bound by a series of old conventions, made with the Hapsburgs, on the subject of an eventual annexation of occupied Herzegovina and Bosnia, as well as by the offers and suggestions made by Isvolski to Aehrenthal. Nothing to-day prevented Russia from extending her protection to the Serbs, whose religion and race were both her own. Moreover, in the last five years, the balance had shifted against the Central Powers. To sum up: it had been Prince von Bülow who then directed the course of German policy. His position in the world, and especially in Petersburg, had been more important than his successor's. He had possessed more skill and method than Herr von Bethmann. Krupenski had full authority, should a favourable chance arise of doing so, to set forth all the dangers to world peace of any rash anti-Serbian act by Austria. Krupenski added his own detailed assertion that, in the spring of 1913, the Dual Monarchy had indeed been planning an attack on the Serbs; that Italy alone had prevented it, though, on this occasion at least, she had happily been supported by Berlin. He begged me to warn my government, since he supposed that it still followed my advice. There I was obliged to disappoint him and had to admit that, in Berlin, my opinions were considered of no value, that nobody would be likely to listen to my summing up of any political situation. To this principle my successor Bethmann-Hollweg had held fast for almost five years. I urged Krupenski to get into touch with Flotow, and so with the Chancellor and the Foreign Office. Some few days later we met again. *"J'ai lu,"* he said to me, *"la lettre de mon chef à M. de Flotow; il a fait la moue quand je suis arrivé à la fin de la lettre de Sasonow. Il m'a dit qu'il lui était impossible de transmettre à Berlin une communication où l'on louait d'une manière fort exagérée le prince de Bülow au détriment de son successeur, tandis qu'en réalité M. de Bethmann était supérieur à M. de Bülow. Avec M. de Bethmann et M. de Jagou au gouvernail la politique allemande était dans les meilleurs mains possibles, et l'Europe, la Russie y comprise, en toute securité."*

It was not hard to understand why Flotow should not have wished to vex his chief and friend. Bethmann had just persuaded the Emperor, who at first would hear nothing of the proposal, to give Flotow the Roman Embassy, when Kiderlen's death made Jagow the Secretary of State at the Foreign Office. Both these selections were unfortunate, and this was very soon apparent. With a Chancellor who could keep him up to the mark, little Jagow might have made a tolerable assistant. As understudy to the timid and hesitating Bethmann, he doubled all his chief's faults and weakness. Flotow had already done very badly as German Minister in Brussels; still less was he capable of Italy, where petty intriguers are sooner unmasked than anywhere else.

In this same spring of 1914, I was visited by two old Russian friends — the ex-President of the Council and Minister of Finance, Kokowzow, and Kriwoschein, the Minister of Agriculture. The first, as he came to meet me, said to me with a malicious smile that he felt himself the innocent victim of Berlin policy. After a fairly long stay in Paris, where he had forced another loan out of the French, he had made a point of staying in Berlin, to show, *ad oculos*, that though Russia had made an alliance with France, and, as her ally, borrowed money from her, that did not in the least mean she intended any breach of good relationship with Germany. Every authority in Berlin had showered on him assurances of friendship, and these he had conveyed to his Sovereign. A few days later, back in St. Petersburg, he had met with a cold reception from the Tsar, who remarked in an irritated voice *"On vous a joué à Berlin."* And indeed, while he was gathering in Berlin his garland of friendship and esteem, our government had sent one of our best officers, General Liman von Sanders, to Constantinople, not as a mere instructor, but in full command of an army corps, stationed in the Dardanelles. It had been like stamping hard on a friend's pet corn. Nicholas II had relieved Kokowzow of his post, though it is true that this misfortune was also due to the intrigues of his predecessor, and erstwhile protector, Count Witte, who had now become his bitterest enemy. Kokowzow spoke of Witte with that *sans-gêne* so often a Russian characteristic: *"Ce bâtard d'un Waguemestre allemand et d'une Circassienne a fait le malheur de la Russie. A la fois grossier et faux, il a préparé la révolution, sans avoir la force de la dominer."* This, besides being excessive, was unjust. Though Witte may not have been born to become a constitutional Chancellor, he at least saw in time that autocracy was no longer possible in Russia, above all with a feeble Tsar like Nicholas II. Moreover, Witte was not a villain. His manners were very bad indeed. He was always rather inclined to brutality, often rustic, but never really malicious. His love for his Mathilde had something really simple and touching in it, no less than the pride with which he boasted that the daughter she had given him prior to their marriage had got for her husband *"un boyard, un véritable boyard, un noble de grande souche."* This was Kyrill Naryschkin, who, however, was more or less bankrupt.

Kokowzow did not believe that the Liman von Sanders incident was really due to our perfidy and malice. But evidently Berlin was in a state of unfortunate *désarroi*. The Russian Ambassador in Berlin had been informed by our Foreign Office that the Liman von Sanders' transfer had been arranged without their having been previously consulted. It was a personal order from the Emperor, given via the Military Cabinet. When the German Ambassador in St. Petersburg wrote home, describing the sensation produced in Russia by this incident, Bethmann and his collaborators pleaded extenuating circumstances. *They* had never been consulted. They would do their very uttermost in future to prevent such disagreeable occurrences, and General Liman himself should be instructed to observe

PRINCE MAX LICHNOWSKY
German Ambassador at London

the greatest caution. *"Le résultat final est que plusieurs pots ont été cassés, et qu'on a à St. Petersbourg l'impression qu'un grand désordre règne dans les sphères dirigeantes de Berlin."*

When, after the fall of Tsarism, the Russian archives could be examined, all the gravity of the blunder committed in this transfer of a German general to an active post in the Dardanelles was revealed. As soon as Poincaré had learned the emotion produced all over Russia by Liman von Sanders' mission, he assured Isvolski in Paris that France was fully resolved to stand back to back with her ally in the matter. Should anything aggravate the position, France would not flinch from the obligations her Russian alliance had imposed! Simultaneously M. Delcassé, then French Ambassador in St. Petersburg, assured Sasonow that Russia could count *"jusqu'au bout"* on French assistance in the Dardanelles. The French Republic would go to any lengths desired by the Tsar and by his government. When, *tant bien que mal*, the "Liman incident" had been closed, the Tsar informed Delcassé that Russia, at least in the South, had need of a maritime outlet; that recent German efforts to eliminate Russian influence in Turkey and close the Dardanelles to the Slavs might easily bring war between the Powers. He, the Tsar, only asked for peace, but refused to let himself be dragooned.

For many years the Dardanelles question had been the mainstay of Prince Bismarck in his efforts to keep contact with Russia. Even at the time of the Re-Insurance Treaty! For twelve years I had kept assuring Muraviev and Lambsdorff, Isvolski, and Count Osten-Sacken, the Grand Duke and Grand Duchess Vladimir, Fredericksz, the Minister to the Household, Count Witte, and, above all, Nicholas II himself, that I would remain in the Bismarck tradition and would never oppose Russia in the Straits. In my last conversations with Bethmann I had urgently called his attention to this question. The Dardanelles, I said, "are a red-hot iron." Till the very last day I was in power they had been my constant and earnest theme with the Emperor.

I must add that, even after this painful incident, Sasonow, the Russian Foreign Minister, advised against rupture with Germany.

Charles Rivet, the *Temps* correspondent in St. Petersburg, tells in
his book, "Le Dernier Romanof", that immediately the first emotion
had calmed, Sasonow forbade the Russian Press to attack Liman von
Sanders or the Kaiser, or to mention the affair in any exaggerated
terms.   Rivet's articles grew more violent in proportion, but Sasonow said to him, "*Quoique vous fassiez, vous ne nous brouillerez pas
avec l'Allemagne.*"   In his book Rivet adds: "*L'Allemagne s'est
chargée elle-même de prendre sur elle ce que redoutait tant cet excellent
M. Sasonow.   Tant mieux, disons nous, Français.*"   Kriwoschein
also informed me that, between Berlin and St. Petersburg, there had
recently been friction of all kinds.   When I asked if he considered
peace in danger he answered: "*A Dieu ne plaise !   Il y a de mauvais
éléments chez nous comme un peu partout.   Mais nous ne ferons certainement pas la folie d'attaquer ni l'Autriche, ni surtout l'Allemagne.
Une guerre entre les trois Empires serait, j'en suis convaincu, la fin de
trois grandes dynasties.*"

I passed on this reassuring answer to an old Russian lady of my
acquaintance, also in Rome for Holy Week, and she answered: "*Je
pense comme Kriwoscheim, et comme lui je forme des vœux ardents pour
le maintien de la paix.   Plus que cela, je crois au maintien de la paix.
Mais ce que je crains, c'est la révolution en Russie.   Avec un gouverne-
ment aussi faible et aussi inepte que celui que nous avons sous
Nicolas II en Russie, la révolution finira par triompher.*"

Had a policy as short-sighted as it was clumsy not ended by
landing us in war, it is probable that, within a short time, revolution
would have broken out in Russia, where it was ripe since the death
of Alexander III.   This would have averted any danger of a clash
between the two countries, since Russian revolutionaries wanted
no foreign complications.   Their one desire was to realize their
Marxist ideal.   All they asked was to be left in peace at home to
exterminate their Russian enemies.

In Rome we lived on terms of especial friendship with Sir Rennell Rodd, the English Ambassador, and his pleasant and very pretty
wife.   For the ninety-nine days' reign of the Emperor Frederick, Sir Rennell had lived in Berlin, as Secretary to the British
Embassy.   He had been in constant touch with the unhappy

Empress, at whose request he wrote in English a book on the deceased Emperor Frederick, whose nobility and chivalrous spirit he justly praises. This was enough to make him the victim of our Foreign Office, in particular Holstein, and one of the *bêtes noires* of William II. He was recalled; yet none the less, he remained very friendly to Germany. He had sent his eldest son to be educated, first at the Gymnasium in Hamburg, later to that of Weimar, that he might both know our economic expansion and soak himself in the Weimar spirit, since Weimar, to borrow a thought of Goethe, had the fate of Bethlehem, which began very small and ended great. When his schooldays came to an end and young Francis Rodd went on to Oxford, he took part there in the foundation of a club which received a subsidy from the Rhodes Fund, and whose object was to bring English undergraduates who wished to study the German language and literature into contact with German students at Oxford. These young men chose me the honorary president of their club. Sir Rennell told me that in the following summer the Anglo-German Club was intending to hold a big reception, at which a number of well-known English statesmen, who had Oxford degrees, were to be present. Would I, he asked, care to write an address to the Anglo-German Club for this occasion? I said that I should be more than delighted, and handed Sir Rennell an address which urged these young men to get to know each other, while remaining good Germans and good Englishmen. They must be assured that two such mighty peoples had every reason to live at peace and amity, working, each in his own way, to maintain the tranquillity of the world, and so the further progress of all mankind. By the time my letter should have been read to them these English and German undergraduates were facing each other in the trenches.

In the first months of 1913 a number of our German ruling classes, and among them many of my friends, had formed a group to bring out a "German Book" — a picture of our status in the world in the twenty-fifth year of the Emperor's reign, which also marked the glorious centenary of the rising of 1813 and the Battle of Leipzig. Among many other names concerned in this I may mention Friedrich Wilhelm von Loebell, Chief of the Imperial Chancellery during my last years in office, later Oberpräsident of Brandenburg and Minister of the Interior; Freiherr von Rheinbaben, former Minister of the Interior and Finance, Oberpräsident of the Rhenish Province; Count Schwerin-Löwitz, President of the Prussian House of Representatives; Doctor Körte, the Oberbürgermeister of Königsberg; and, finally, the economist Adolf Wagner.

The general editor of this work, which ran into three folio volumes, had gathered many brilliant collaborators. Professor Zorn of Bonn was to write on government and the State; Doctor Körte on self-government; Freiherr von Stengel, a professor of Munich University, on International Law; General von Bernhardi, one of our best strategists, on the Army; Herr von Lindequist, the ex-State Secretary to the Colonial Office, an expert on Colonial policy, on the Colonies; Adolf Wagner had taken as his province the relationships governing economic, social, and financial policy. Agricultural conditions were handled brilliantly by the able and moderate pen of Count von Schwerin-Löwitz, president of the Agricultural Council, and that of the somewhat subjective and impassioned but industrious and very gifted Freiherr von Wangenheim of Klein-Spiegel, the president of the Landowners' Association. Geheimrat Witting, president of the board of directors of the Berlin National Bank and ex-burgomaster of Posen, dealt with banking; Professor Zorn with the relationship of Church to State. The head pastor of St. Michaelis in Hamburg, Doctor Hunzinger, Professor of Divinity, a great preacher and distinguished theologian, had made a special study of Evangelism; that distinguished master of theology, Doctor Merkle, of Würzburg University, of Catholicism. Ulrich von Wilamowitz-Möllendorf, the son-in-law of Theodor Mommsen, and since his death our greatest living scholar, was to write on classical archæology, the Freiburg Professor, Below, on history, Professor Theobald Ziegler, on public life.

I had been asked to contribute the preface, which should only deal with German policy. "You must give us a lecture on German policy," one of the contributors had said to me, my colleague in the Upper House.

Naturally I was perfectly well aware of the limitations imposed by such an article. I should have been very tactless indeed to have taken advantage of the occasion to criticize my successor in any way, though I confess he was a very good target. But I should also have been lacking in patriotism had I, an ex-Imperial Chancellor, underlined, for all the malicious world to read me, the feebleness and error of our ways. I had no right to imitate Ham, the disrespectful son of Noah. My preface must scrupulously avoid whatever might shake the nation's confidence, or, even worse, arouse suspicions abroad. I have already said that, in Imperial Germany, a retired Minister was, in effect, excluded from further participation in politics, or, in any case, in active politics. Prince Bismarck had had this experience, and so had the excellent Posadowsky, even in republican Germany. The angry growls of the Titan of Friedrichs-ruh, all the flashes his dying genius still sent forth, did nothing to change the course of events. Nor was the active collaboration of Posadowsky as a deputy destined to prevent or better anything. Any opposition of my successor would have seemed, to William II, *lèse-majesté*. I had no fear of the *vultus instantis tyranni*, first because I was certain of myself, and secondly, because, at bottom, William II had nothing of the tyrant in his character. Yet, in spite of the exhortations of certain gossips, I was aware that the vast majority of Germans would never have understood such criticism, which they would certainly have set down to personal motives. I am perfectly willing to admit that this snuffing out of former Ministers was a grave defect in Imperial organization. It was one of the reasons which had impelled me, at the end of my political career, to believe that a swing towards Liberalism and progressive parliamentary methods was necessary.

In my preface, therefore, to this work, published by Reimar Hobbing under the title "Deutschland unter Kaiser Wilhelm II", I confined myself to the barest indication of certain points in our home and foreign policy. These points were extremely important and not well enough understood by our people, so lacking in political sense. I reminded them that France was irreconcilable. The ultimate goal of all her efforts would still, for many years to come, be the bringing into force of such conditions as might enable her to square accounts with Germany. I recalled the best definition I had ever heard of the French character, given by De Tocqueville, that great thinker, who had said more than fifty years previously of his nation — the most aggressive, militarist and chauvinistic in the world — *était apte à tout, mais n'excellait que dans la guerre*. I had no more illusions on the elastic power of recovery of this people, its ardent patriotism, ready to accept every sacrifice, than I had on its unbounded national pride, its hard, unsentimental will to dominate. As to England, I suggested that it would be just as imprudent to curry favour with her as to annoy her. I showed that we had come through the dangerous time which began with the laying down of our first battleship, and that henceforth England would not attack us provided our policy caused no breach with her.

For Italy, I recalled a saying of Bismarck's, that it was enough for him to see an Italian corporal with his flag and drum face west, not east. I added, "Everything else must depend on the form of any eventual European conflict; on the energy with which we can make our army serve our interests, on the diplomatic and military positions we take up. The full value of any alliance can never be determined until there is danger." The terrible summer months of 1914 have proved these last words only too fully justified.

Walter Rathenau, to whom I had also expressed such views, wired me as follows on receiving a copy of the book: "My heartiest thanks to Your Highness for your great work, which, together with Bismarck's *'Gedanken und Erinnerungen'*,[1] seems to me to express more completely than any other the whole essential spirit of German history."

Count Clemens Podewils, who, for five years, had assisted me as Bavarian Prime Minister in my efforts to build up our power and unity, wrote: "I have been reading with ever-growing enthusiasm this great publication of Your Highness, and shall study it again and again. Envy has never been my weakness, but in this case I have had to fight hard against it. In the end I could only say to myself 'It's ridiculous to be jealous of Goethe.'"

[1] " Thoughts and Memories."

But far more than such praise as the above, much of which I could only discount, since it came to me from personal friends, I was delighted at receiving the following from my dear old regiment, the King's Hussars, to which I had ordered a copy of the book to be delivered:

I beg Your Highness, in the name of myself and all my officers, to accept our most grateful, devoted thanks for your very kind letter of January 27th and the precious gift that came along with it. The work shall be set in the place of honour in our library. Though we ourselves should, in any case, always think with pride that we may call Your Highness one of us, it is good to know that future generations will have in this work a lasting monument, a reminder, ever before their eyes, of the fact that the name of Your Highness is connected with the regiment for all time. With my whole heart, on behalf of us all, I thank you for this wonderful proof of comradeship and attachment. May I add the hope that your feeling for the regiment will never change? With our deepest, most undying respect, I have the honour of signing myself

Your Highness' most obedient and devoted

JOBST HERMANN, Count Lippe.

(Lieutenant Colonel and Commandant,

H.I.M. King William I Hussars.)

During the War, in the spring of 1916, I published some reflections on German policy. My successor had not managed to keep the peace. I was therefore free to develop certain ideas, which three years before I should have suppressed. No patriot, however, in war time, has the right even to hint at any topic which might weaken his country's *morale* or lead her enemies to imagine that her strength is less than they had supposed it. On the objects of the War, I felt it my duty to follow exactly the lines laid down by our government. My book, "Deutsche Politik",[1] was translated into English, Italian, Spanish, and Russian. In 1916, one hundred fifty thousand copies of the German popular edition were sold.

[1] "German Policy."

CHAPTER XI

Berlin, June, 1914 — News of the Assassination of the Heir to the Austrian Throne — Conversations with Bethmann and the Emperor — Bethmann's Illusions.

At the beginning of June, 1914, I left Rome and came back to Berlin with my wife, *en route* for her "beloved island", Norderney, always one of her favourite dwelling places. It struck me as somewhat surprising that members of the Foreign Office staff and people in immediate touch with them should all have judged the world situation with an optimism which I could only feel to be exaggerated. On the late afternoon of Sunday, June 28th, we went to call on Frau von Lebbin, whom I had last seen six years previously in the flat where Holstein had lain dying. We had come to enquire for her, having heard that she had had a stroke, was paralysed and bedridden. We found her in a more than modest little room in the Uhlandstrasse, far from the Linden and the Hotel Adlon, where we were staying. Physically she was in a bad way, but this had not in any way impaired the old alertness of her mind. As we sat at her bedside the banker, Paul von Schwabach, whose family had for years been her close friends, rang up to say that the Archduke Francis Ferdinand and his wife had been assassinated at Sarajevo. Frau von Lebbin asked what I thought of this event and what I considered might be its political consequences. I told her that though, of course, from the moral standpoint, I considered it an abominable crime, its political consequences would depend on the way in which the matter was handled. It might either be a *débarras* or an *embarras*.

Most of the people whom I met in the next few days were inclined to consider the Sarajevo murder a *débarras*. Count Szögyényi, the Austrian Ambassador, a very loyal servant of the Habsburgs, the son of a Knight of the Golden Fleece, and himself

Chevalier of the Order, told me, when I expressed to him my sympathy, that though, as an Hungarian gentleman and a Christian, he could only deplore the fate of the Archduke and his noble wife, politically this elimination of the heir apparent seemed to him "a dispensation of Providence." The Archduke's violent nature, his hatred of the Magyars and blind predilection for the Czechs and Southern Slavs, together with his extreme clericalism, might have given rise to serious conflict, even perhaps to civil war. Abroad, his fanaticism, ungovernable temper, and obstinacy would have made of him an inconvenient ally. "*Requiescat in pace*," this Imperial and Royal Ambassador concluded unctuously.

From Kiel I heard that William II had received the news on board the *Meteor* as he sailed in the *Kieler Bucht*. At first it had upset him very much, since not long since he had stayed at Konopischt with the Archduke, admiring the famous roses and, after his custom, laying many plans for the future with this coming Emperor of Austria. But His Majesty was soon consoled — so soon, indeed, that his Suite had the greatest difficulty in making him give up the regatta — especially since, that year, he had every chance of winning the splendid prize he himself had offered.

All accounts from Vienna agreed that the profound animosity of the old Emperor Francis Joseph against his nephew and heir had come to the surface, in a way that seemed almost callous. With that hardness often seen in old people who have known much suffering all their lives, the Emperor had neglected nothing which might harm the memory of the Archduke, and especially of his morganatic wife, whom Francis Joseph had detested. Whereas the coffin of the Archduke had been borne on a splendid hearse, with gilt wheels and surmounted with the Archducal crown, the very simple coffin which contained his wife had nothing but a tiny coronet, and had followed on a very modest coach. Since the Archduke knew that his uncle would forbid the Duchess of Hohenberg's body to be laid in the Habsburg vault of the *Kapuzinerkirche* in Vienna, he had, as soon as they were married, built a chapel on the banks of the Danube, a few hours' journey from Vienna, where he might be laid beside the woman he loved. At the Emperor's order, the burial took place there during the night, in driving rain, and had been a spectacle recalling the most vivid scenes in the historical tragedies of Shakespeare.

Although the horrible murder was the work of a Serbian secret society with branches spread all over the country, many details go to prove that the Serbian Government had neither instigated nor desired it.   The Serbs were exhausted by two wars.   The most hot-headed among them might have paused at the thought of war with Austria-Hungary, so overwhelmingly superior, especially since, in her rear, Serbia had Bulgarians full of rancour, and knew that the Roumanians were untrustworthy.   The Archduke's open dislike of Hungarians had even gained him certain sympathies from the Southern Slavs.   Thus, at least, did Herr von Griesinger, our Minister in Belgrade, sum up the position, as did also the Belgrade correspondents of every important German newspaper.   This, too, if I am rightly informed, was the conclusion reached by the Austrian Hofrat, Wiesner, appointed by his government to investigate the crime in all its details.

One day, before our departure for Norderney, I met my successor in the Wilhelmstrasse.   I had just called at the Chancellor's Palace, where I had found that he was not at home.   Five years had slipped away since I gave my power into his hands.   He looked less harassed than I had expected.

He reminded me how, two years before, he had written to tell me he considered "pacification" his most essential task in home affairs.   Now this applied to foreign affairs still more.   It was not to be denied that the world's nerves were on edge, though really there was no valid reason for it.   To be sure, this murder was abominable, yet its political results would be to the good, since now the heads of the Russian Government, above all the Tsar, would turn from Serbia.   I said that I was not so sure of that.   In politics the Russians viewed things from a different moral angle.

We were passing the Hausministerium, in whose charming rooms I had first got to know Mimi Schleinitz, and Alexander Schleinitz, her husband, whom Bismarck had disliked so whole-heartedly, and later Prince Otto Stolberg, my honoured patron and friend; the rooms which house the President to-day. As we walked, I told my successor a story of Alexander I, that most idealistic of Russian autocrats, the sentimental and "tender" Tsar. The last ambassador to represent Napoleon at his Court, before the campaign of Russia, had been Savary, a general and the Duke of Rovigo. In certain rather delicate circumstances he had managed to retain the Tsar's confidence, thanks to his tact, good-nature and exceptional distinction of manner. War threatened and Savary was recalled. The Tsar embraced and shook hands with him. And when, in 1814, Alexander entered Paris with his allies, the Austrian Emperor, Francis I, and Frederick William III, King of Prussia, he sent for Savary at once. He received him very graciously indeed, enquiring, with gentle amiability, what post he at present occupied. The duke replied with a sigh that he had no post: he had fallen into disgrace with Louis XVIII. "Oh, leave that to me. I 'll soon put it right," reassured the autocrat of the Russias, and sent off for a close friend of Louis XVIII to beg him to inform his Sovereign that the Tsar was most anxious to see the Duke of Rovigo in a post befitting his talents and noble character. The Frenchman shrugged. "*Impossible, Sire! Le duc de Rovigo, alors Général Savary, a présidé à la cour martiale qui a condamné à mort le duc d'Enghien, cousin de Sa Majesté très-chrétienne.*" The Tsar was amazed. "*Comment! Il n'y a que cela! Et moi, qui dîne tous les jours avec Bennigsen et Onchacow, qui ont étranglé mon père.*"

The good Bethmann, who doubtless had ready his thesis of a localized Austro-Serbian conflict, looked really scared at my little story. I added that I had been told it after dinner, with a smile, by a Russian Grand Duke. "Thank heavens," Bethmann answered, "people are n't so cynical nowadays. I 'm certain that the Tsar and his councillors will heartily deplore and disapprove of this horrible Sarajevo crime, so that henceforth a moral abyss will separate Serbia from Russia. We, of course, shall quietly look on. What the world needs most is calming down."

A few days later we reached Norderney, where a new horse, the magnificent "Torero", awaited me. I resumed my usual rides, out to the lighthouse and around the island, and was astounded when

I read in the papers of the Austrian ultimatum to Serbia.   In Berlin nobody had so much as hinted at it.   From the very first instant, I could naturally see the full implication.   The papers, inspired by the Foreign Office, kept asserting that Austria had addressed this ultimatum *proprio motu;* that in Germany we had not known its tenor; that Austria was within her rights in any case; and that any conflict "could be localized", even an eventual war with Serbia. This hope seemed a singularly vain one.

But I still imagined we had reserved the right to examine Serbia's answer in detail and never dreamed that we had given Austria *carte blanche* for military action against the Serbs.   When, on July 25th, there came a telegram to say that Giesl, the Austrian Minister, had broken off relations at once, on receiving the Serbian note, and left Belgrade, taking his whole staff along with him, I saw that now we were on the brink of the worst war we had had for forty-three years, a war which might become general and world-wide.   I began to realize also, with terror, that already we must be bound hand and foot to the policy of Count Leopold Berchtold, whose frivolous incapacity far exceeded even Austrian standards in such matters.

Next day (July 26th) on one of my rides I happened to meet Count Botho Wedel, who said he had come over for a holiday.   At that time he held the post of reporting councillor to the political department of the Foreign Office.   I was amazed to see him absent from Berlin in a general situation of such danger.   I told him so and he seemed rather surprised.   But that same evening he paid us a friendly call and, admitting that my remark had rather worried him, told me he had at once rung up the Foreign Office to ask a colleague and friend in the Political Section if he should return.   He had been answered that his presence was quite unnecessary; that all this was simply a false alarm and that everything would soon have blown over.   But the thunder clouds grew denser and denser. Two days later I ran into Erhard Wedel, Botho's brother, who had a seat in the Upper House, and asked him to tell me if I or his brother whom I saw over there on the beach, placidly sunning himself, were dreaming.   He answered, "I also am getting worried.   I've just been advising Botho to hurry back." And at last, on the following morning, Botho really did return to Berlin. He paid me a farewell call, in which he admitted that he and his friends had never really grasped how serious matters had become. But, in any case, there was no need for anxiety. England, he had just learned from Berlin, would almost certainly remain neutral. Italy and Roumania were our friends !

Three years after giving these proofs of perspicacity, this sagacious diplomat was appointed our Ambassador in Vienna, where he allowed himself to be equally duped by the Emperor Karl, the Empress Zita, the Duchess of Parma and the Archduchess Maria Josefa.

When Princess Victoria of Schaumburg-Lippe, the Emperor's sister, who also happened to be in Norderney, informed us that, in answer to her telegram, Her Majesty the Empress had wired back that "the situation was very serious", my wife and I said farewell to our beloved island, which we never were destined to see again. On August 1st war was declared on Russia.

In Hamburg, to the "Atlantic", at which we stayed, Ballin came hurrying to visit us. He was very shaken by the war and still more by the "enormous stupidity" with which we had stumbled into it. That in itself was enough to fill him with misgivings for the outcome, should the coachman, Bethmann, be left on his box. On August 3d came our declaration of war on France. On the fourth I was rung up by Herr von Eckardt, the editor of the *Hamburger Correspondent*, who told us that England had declared war on us. "This will be the rout of the Nibelungens," I answered him. Next morning I was told by some Hamburg journalists that, right up to August 1st, the Press Bureau of the Foreign Office had kept telephoning to warn them against publishing attacks on France or England, since there was still every reason to hope that the two Great Powers of the West would keep neutrality. On August 3d they had been warned above all to publish nothing against England, who would most probably remain a benevolent neutral. These directives were either consciously misleading or else the result of complete misapprehension — which, I have never been able to determine.

On August 6th, while still in Hamburg, I learned that my brother, Karl Ulrich, the commander of a cavalry division, had fallen before Liège, killed by the bullet of a *franc-tireur*. He was an officer of outstanding merit, a keen thinker, who could use his pen as effectively as his sword, and a very handsome man of exceptional courage. In his letter of condolence Bethmann wrote: "I have known few men in whom character and intellect united in so harmonious a whole — καλὸς καὶ ἀγαός."

As a young officer, in the 1st Uhlans of the Guard, he had attracted the attention of Count Schlieffen, his commanding officer, who later became Chief of the General Staff. With his *élan* and all his gifts, Count Schlieffen told me, my brother was one of the hopes of our army. He had been military attaché in Vienna, and later became the brilliant colonel of the 2d Uhlans of the Guard. He had died prematurely, at not quite fifty-two years of age; and a rumour, born no doubt, of the mad excitement at the Front, was spread that he had committed suicide. A scarcely conceivable lack of moral restraint allowed this rumour to reach my ears, and, naturally, I was very affected by it. In these hours of desperate anguish my old friend Lahusen, of Holy Trinity Church, stood by me and comforted me: a really good and pious man, a man of genuine delicacy of feeling. Later it was proved beyond a doubt that the rumour was utterly groundless. Lieutenant von Seydlitz, my brother's adjutant, told me that, fifteen minutes before his death, his general had been sitting quietly on a bench; that they had joked together about a tartine of bread and honey which a peasant woman had cut to give to the general, and which he was devouring ravenously. As he ate, my brother had said that he disapproved of the summary executions of Belgian priests, which had taken place on the previous day. He had given orders that no priest in soutane should be shot. Should any cleric be suspected of inflaming the population against us, he must be arrested and sent to Aix for examination, and so, if necessary, for judgment. A few minutes later the general rose and went off into a neighbouring copse; there was the sound of a shot, and he was discovered dead on the ground, grasping a revolver which lacked a cartridge.

Two hours after this Lieutenant von Seydlitz was grievously wounded in the foot, from behind a tree, by a *franc-tireur*, who was taken. When my brother's corpse reached Berlin, I caused the coffin to be opened and had the wound minutely examined by Privy Councillor Doctor Pütter, the director of the Königlichen Charité. He assured me that only a shotgun could have caused it; it was far too wide for any revolver wound. The bullet had entered behind the left ear, and it would have been impossible for the general, in whose right hand the revolver was discovered, to wound himself mortally from that angle. He must therefore have pressed his revolver trigger instinctively the instant another shot rang out. In any case, this minute examination finally disposed of the suicide story. I may add that my brother was always good-humoured — *mens sana in corpore sano* — and had a brilliant future in front of him.

On the day after the news of my brother's death, some Hamburg friends requested me to write for the *Hamburger Nachrichten*, the old Bismarck paper and traditional organ of Hamburg public opinion, an appeal, in this hour of fate and tribulation, to Hamburg, and through Hamburg to all Germany. It was published on August 6, 1914. I had written as follows:

On the 70th birthday of Prince Bismarck — the first of April, 1885 — I heard that mighty Chancellor say to his son, Count Herbert: "I really owe my greatest success in life to the fact that I could always remember these lines:

> *'Und setzet ihr nicht das Leben ein*
> *Nie wird euch das Leben gewonnen sein.'"* [1]

Schiller's words apply, to-day, to every German: they are the device of each one of our people. To-day we have staked our all — hearth and home, present and future, material goods and those still more precious goods of the spirit. We must risk all to gather the fruits of 1870; to gain what our fathers died for a century since. It is not only our young empire that is menaced, which has protected us for three and forty years. Old Prussia also is in peril, whose great king fought seven whole years to defend her. We fight to-day for our whole glorious German past, back from the very first instant of our two thousand year long history. It can-

---

[1] Unless you risk your life entire,
Life will ne'er answer your desire.

not and shall not be said that so much heroic valour and sacrifice, such
will and spirit, have been in vain.   Not in vain did many great and noble
minds think, struggle, toil and suffer, on our behalf.   Army and navy will
fight as only Germans fight, as they fought from the days of the Cherus-
cans to Leuthen, Leipzig, and Sedan.   The nation must stand steady
behind our arms, iron-willed, unshakeably resolute, quietly and heroically
determined.   We are right as we were right in 1870, when the German
people fought to build its house in such measurements and proportions as
seemed good to it, instead of letting foreigners dictate to them as they had
done at the Treaty of Westphalia, at the Congresses of Rastatt and Vienna.
To-day we are out to maintain that place in the world to which the German people has earned its right, by industry and service to mankind —
the place they deny and would grudge us.   The more enemies we see
surround us — the more hideously injustice, hate, above all envy, seem to
threaten, the firmer must our courage be set.   Let us remember the noble
face of the good old Kaiser, let us think of Bismarck, as he stands gazing
out from Hamburg harbour, his hands on the pommel of his sword.   Let
us recall the task and future announced to us by the heralds of the national idea, of all they taught us — from Körner, Arndt and Fichte, to
Treitschke.   Let us think of the goal to be achieved — a peace that shall
make good each grievous sacrifice the Fatherland demands of us at this
hour.   Our eyes steadily fixed on the one aim, let us neither be lulled in
false security by such victories as God may grant us, nor discouraged by
defeats, which may He avert !   No people was ever vanquished against
its will.   Never, since it has stood in unity, has the German people been
laid low.   We are one to-day, thanks to the iron circle Bismarck forged
for us; thanks too to the hatred of our enemies, which has hammered us
into still more unassailable unity.   All party discord is at an end.   To-
day we see how trivial it was in comparison with the thing which has
made us brothers.   The bearing of the German people, on this sudden
day of unexpected tempest, is noble beyond any word of praise.   This
must be admitted by every government — could the world be just, it
would be admitted by all mankind; it would be seen by those kindred
races which threatened our safety in the past and filled our minds with
care for the future.   Yet, though the world were full of devils, our people
will hold and assert their place in the sun.

The Head Burgermeister of the old free Hansa city, Doctor von
Melle, wrote next day: "From a full heart I have to thank Your

VISIT TO THE NAVY MANŒUVRES AT KIEL

Kaiser William II in the uniform of an Austrian Field Marshal, the Archduke Francis Ferdinand in the uniform of a German Admiral. Behind, Prince Henry of Prussia, the Austrian Admiral Count Montecuccoli and Grand Admiral von Tirpitz

Highness for your inspiring, manly words, the words of a thorough German, addressed in this solemn hour, to your Hamburg friends. They will find their resounding echo, since you have given most beautiful expression to emotions this moment of history awakens in all of us. May Germany never lack spiritual leaders such as yourself, to address her thus from the deepest heart."

From Hamburg we returned to Berlin. On arrival I wrote the Emperor a short letter, assuring him that, in this all-decisive hour, I was with him, body and soul: that no heart in Prussia or in Germany could pray God more earnestly than mine for the army, the Fatherland and himself. "May God be with our flag! May He grant Your Majesty victory and fame! Such is my deepest, loyal wish."

My wife, to whom William II had been consistently gracious and well-disposed, wrote to him:

YOUR MAJESTY,

In this solemn moment I feel I have to tell you that my heart is beating with all its strength for you and my dear Germany. My whole soul is given to my august Sovereign, to whom I am bound not only by patriotism, but by so many delightful personal memories of hours, grave and joyous, in the past. I knew Your Majesty in your younger days, and, since, not a day has passed without my having thought of you with devotion, and the wish that fortune, happiness and glory might accompany you through all the trials and dangers which fall to the lot of every sovereign. I assure Your Majesty that none will rejoice so much as I to see you triumph over your enemies, as gloriously as did your ancestors. Let me assure Your Majesty, our dear Empress and the dear Princes, of our most unchanging loyalty and affection.

Ever your devoted
MARIE BÜLOW.

Next day the Emperor received me in audience at the Schloss, where he welcomed me in the great courtyard. I was very moved by his pallor, his haggard, almost unnerved look. He looked excited, and yet exhausted. His eyes blinked restlessly. He might have been quite ten years older, and yet it was not five years since I had seen him last in the Neues Palais. As of old, he put his arm around my neck, very kindly, and began to tell me how the "terrible" events of the last two weeks had shaken him.   They had even affected him physically, so much so that he had stayed in bed for twenty-four hours.   "A little nerves rest cure," [1] he added with a haggard smile.   He expressed his most cordial regret for the death of my brother, Karl Ulrich, an excellent officer, and one he would always remember.   He went on to tell me that he had just been suggesting to the Chancellor and to the Secretary of State for Foreign Affairs my recall to the German Embassy in Rome.   "Of course, I know it sounds ridiculous to ask a retired Imperial Chancellor to go back to the post he occupied twenty years ago.   It's like asking a field marshal to take over the command of a division.   But I'm sure you won't mind doing it for my sake."   I said at once that I was ready to do anything he felt could be of use.   Then, with a certain embarrassment, he continued: "The Chancellor seems most anxious that Herr von Flotow, with whom he is very friendly, should not be recalled.   Even if I send you to Rome, he wants him to go on being our ambassador.   But he would have no objection at all to your going to Rome and making yourself useful there to Flotow."   I replied that, though it went without saying that I had laid aside all personal vanity, which in our present position could only be pitiable, I did not see what I could possibly do unless I were given direction of the Embassy.   Such divided authority would lead nowhere except to misunderstandings and intrigue.   Nobody would be able to understand my return to Rome, in mid-August, without official function or any clearly defined commission, for never once, since my retirement, had I stayed on in Rome through the heat.   In such circumstances my being in Rome would be less a help than a hindrance.   "That's what I thought at once," answered the Kaiser, "and I said so, too, to Bethmann and Jagow.   Between ourselves, they neither of them want to have you in Rome, so I suppose we must give up the idea."

But His Majesty said not a word of the real essence of the matter — how best to keep Italy and Roumania on our side.   He had evidently been well primed by Bethmann, who feared I might

[1] English in text.

destroy what he considered the finely woven threads of his own policy.

General Moltke, the Chief of Staff, was announced, and the Emperor brought our audience to an end, dismissing me with a cordial handshake. He left me, turned again and waved a farewell, with the same haunted look as when I arrived. In the distance I saw the tall figure and sorrowful face of Colonel General von Moltke. The Greeks might have said of Moltke and his Emperor that they had seen Medusa's head, forged by Hephaistos, on Zeus' shield, which the father of mortals and gods brandished to raise tempest and havoc.

Next day I visited my successor. Princess Marie Radziwill had just been with us — the daughter of the French Marshal, Castellane, who had come in her youth to Berlin, yet never ceased to feel as a Frenchwoman. Prince Anton Radziwill, her husband, the grandson of a Prussian princess and grand-nephew of the heroic Prince Louis Ferdinand, had served William I as his adjutant, and later as general aide-de-camp. It was he who, at Ems, before 1870, had been charged to notify the French Ambassador, Benedetti, that the king had nothing further to say to him. Princess Radziwill came into the room and burst into sobs. Already, she said, she had had to witness one war between Germany and France, and that had torn her heart in two. But this would be far worse, far more terrible. Her daughters, Betka the eldest, and Hélène, were married to Counts Josef and Roman Potocki — brothers, but one a Russian, the other an Austrian Pole. One of her sons was serving in the Russian army on account of the Radziwill properties in Russia, and she had relations fighting with the French. What she heard from France frightened her. The fury and hatred of Germany were already worse than any in 1870. Every one in Paris was saying: *"Cette fois nous les tenons; ce sera la grande revanche."*

An hour later Bethmann received me in the garden room at the Chancellor's Palace. In Bismarck's time this room had been a billiard room; later it was turned into an office, where chancellors usually worked through the summer heat. Bethmann stood in the centre of the room. Shall I ever forget his face, the look in his eyes !

The book of Leviticus tells of the scapegoat "on whom Aaron shall lay both his hands and confess over him all the iniquities of the children of Israel and all their transgressions and all their sins, putting them upon the head of the goat, and shall send him away by the hand of a fit man into the wilderness." There is also, I believe, a picture of this, by some celebrated English painter, which shows the wretched scapegoat with a look of ineffable anguish in its eyes — such pain as now I saw in Bethmann's. For an instant we neither of us spoke. At last I said to him: "Well, tell me, at least, how it all happened." He raised his long, thin arms to heaven and answered in a dull, exhausted voice: "Oh — if I only knew!" In many later polemics on "war guilt" I have often wished it had been possible to produce a snap-shot of Bethmann-Hollweg standing there at the moment he said those words. Such a photograph would have been the best proof that this wretched man had never "wanted war."

He mastered himself and said in a quick stutter: "This may be a violent storm, but short — very short. I count on a war of not more than three, or, perhaps at the very most, four months, and I 'm basing our whole policy on that. And I hope that, in spite of the war — or because of it, even — we may reach some really sound, friendly, trustful relationship with England — and then, through England, with France. An Anglo-German-French group would be our guarantee against the menace to civilization of that barbarian colossus, Russia. Under your direction, my dear prince, I was lucky enough to work at building the *bloc* which united our Liberals and Conservatives in the same domestic policy. Now higher tasks await me abroad. An alliance, for civilization, of England, Germany, and France would be still more important, beneficent, advantageous."

Amazed, horrified even, by so utter a misconception of our position, I described to Bethmann the state of mind in which I had just left Princess Radziwill. But my successor, who had by now regained his balance, could only answer with a smile: "My dear prince, we must hope that the princess, who, in spite of her years, seems still very passionate and emotional, will soon calm down —

and so will her former countrymen. But, provided our policy is the right one, it will be — above all — with England that I shall hope, very soon, to be reconciled. At present, of course, the Emperor is furious with her, but I trust we shall calm him by degrees."

To-day, as I think back on all this and remember our Chancellor's words in 1914, I ask myself if he really meant them. Or was he merely trying not to see his own grave errors in diplomacy? And yet there can be no doubt that in that August he really felt as he had spoken. A passage from the mediocre "Memoirs" which Baron Schön brought out in 1921 under the title "Erlebtes" [1] confirms me. Schön was our Ambassador in Paris from 1910 till war broke out. He says that on his recall to Berlin he visited Bethmann at once. The Chancellor, with whom, the day before, England had broken off relationships, asked his Ambassador, hot from Paris, whether he considered that Germany could ever make an alliance with the French. Schön, who, twenty-four hours previously, had left a Paris seething with hate, exultant and full of joyous lust for battle, answered that such an alliance seemed possible on two conditions:

1. That we did not invade French territory.

2. That we treated France with the greatest punctilio, especially on the *point d'honneur*, and perhaps even granted her a slight rectification of the Lorraine frontier.

This blindness of both Chancellor and Ambassador reminds me of de Gramont's illusions in 1870. When, in 1870, before his departure from Paris, Baron Werther, our German Ambassador, took leave of the Duc de Gramont at the Foreign Office, the latter offered him his hand with the following reassuring, confident words: "*Nous nous reverrons bientôt, mon cher baron. Nos souverains se livreront quelques galantes batailles, puis ils s'embrasseront, et nous redeviendrons les meilleurs amis du monde.*"

In this midsummer of 1914, our London Ambassador, Prince Lichnowsky, entertained equally foolish illusions, even after war had beeen declared. English troops were already in the field when I received from him a letter full of regrets at this sudden crumpling up of all the achievement of his brief London activities. Still, he

[1] "Things Experienced."

had every hope that his work would not have been in vain, and really felt that soon it might be possible to reunite the severed threads. England was not particularly hostile. Personally he was still very popular there; every one liked him and he had built up an excellent position.

Our whole lamentable diplomacy in those weeks of 1914, the mentality of the people in control, are perhaps revealed most unmistakably in a little-known work on Bethmann-Hollweg. This book, "Unser Reichskanzler, sein Leben und Wirken",[1] is by Pastor Kötschke, and has obviously been compiled from documents placed at its author's disposal by Bethmann's family. The many details which it gives of the Chancellor's youth and schooldays, his family, income even, go to prove this. Here is what the good pastor has to tell us of those weeks which brought the crash of the German Empire:

The Chancellor was extremely agitated. He had always considered that, if it came to war, England would certainly be neutral. For many years his efforts had been directed to this end; yet now all his painful achievement, the result of such skill and so much labour, had fallen "like a house of cards," as he himself expressed it to Herr Goschen. What a bitter moment for our Chancellor was this farewell visit of the English Ambassador! Such a thing ought never to have happened! The night that followed was a terrible one. "And yet," the Chancellor asked himself, "what other line of policy could I have followed? I can see no other course by which I might have guided the ship of state."

The pastor's book was written in 1916. He ends it on a note of prophecy. Bismarck, our first Chancellor, at Friedrichsruh, had welcomed many bands of reverent pilgrims. Our fifth would be equally acclaimed who, at that moment, guided the German people towards the happy termination of the World War. In Hohenfinow the cry would soon resound: "Throw wide your doors. See they come! To press his hand who once was so reviled."

Quo promissa cadant et somnia pythagoræa!

[1] "Our Chancellor, his Life and Work."

CHAPTER XII

German Policy on the Eve of the World War — William II's Attitude to the Crisis — Bethmann as Diplomat — His Offer to English Ambassador Goschen — State Secretary von Jagow — A Report of Baron Beyens, the Belgian Minister — Wilhelm Stumm — Zimmermann — Diego von Bergen — What Was the Diplomatic Position?

How had it all happened? To-day, when I repeat to myself this question, asked in my unforgettable talk with Bethmann, a résumé of which I set down forthwith, I am inclined to answer it in some words used by my old friend Alberto Pansa. He spoke them to me in the Villa Malta garden a few days before I left Rome and Italy declared war on Austria (May, 1915). Pansa had been formed in the school of Visconti-Venosta. He had been at the head of several legations, among them Bucharest, Belgrade, and Pekin; had served as Ambassador in London, Berlin, and Constantinople. He combined knowledge with *sang-froid*, had nothing of pedantry in him, was matter-of-fact and yet cultivated, prudent and calm without timidity, an observer whose attention never relaxed. He had followed the advice of Thiers and "*ne prenait rien au tragique, tout au sérieux.*" In May, 1915, he said to me: "*M. Bethmann et ses collaborateurs ont été beaucoup moins méchants, criminels, sanguinaires, belliqueux, que les ennemis de l'Allemagne ne le disent. Mais vos gouvernants ont été au mois de Juillet dernier cent mille fois plus bêtes qu'aucune fantaisie ne peut se le figurer. Sans vouloir la guerre, ils ont par leur maladresse jeté sur eux-mêmes et sur votre malheureux pays tout l'odieux de cette épouvantable catastrophe.*"

These words of an old and seasoned diplomat go straight to the heart of the matter. As an European who has known and rubbed shoulders with many races, I affirm of the Germans that we were the most pacific people in pre-war Europe. Through those forty-three years which divide the Treaty of Frankfurt from the World War,

every other nation — the French, the English, the Russians, the
Americans, the Spaniards, the Balkan peoples, the Japanese, had
made wars, either great or small. Not so Germany. Oblivious of
conquest and adventure, we thought only of building up our Fatherland, united at last, by hard and peaceful labour. William II did
not want war. He feared it. His bellicose marginal notes prove
nothing. His exaggerations were mainly intended to ring in the
ears of Privy Councillors at the Foreign Office, just as his more
menacing jingo speeches were intended to give the foreigner the
impression that here was another Frederick the Great or Napoleon.
Nobody had more chances than I of discussing war with him personally — and at moments when it seemed a probability, *e.g.* the
Moroccan affair, and the Bosnian crisis. I have therefore some
right to ask for credence when I affirm that William II did not want
war, if only because he did not trust his nerves not to give way under
the strain of any really critical situation. The moment there was
actual danger His Majesty would become uncomfortably conscious
that he could never lead an army in the field — in spite of the
marshal's baton he loved to handle, of the medals and uniforms he
adorned himself with, the pseudo-victories which, at manœuvres,
he counted on the judges to make him win. He was well aware that
he was neurasthenic, without real capacity as a general, and still less
able, in spite of his naval hobby, to have led a squadron or even
captained a ship. And neither Bethmann nor Jagow wanted war.

Albert Sorel, the author of that excellent book, "L'Europe et la
Révolution Française",[1] wrote to his mother at the time when he was
engaged on the research work for his "Histoire diplomatique de la
Guerre Franco-allemande": "*J'ai cherché consciencieusement, j'ai
cherché avec passion la cause de nos malheurs de 1870, et je suis arrivé
à cette conclusion: Ce qui manquait alors surtout chez nous ce fut
l'habilité.*"

This equally applied to German policy in the summer of 1914.
It repeats the truth of Montaigne's saying: "*que tous les maux de ce
monde viennent de l'ânerie.*"

The blunders of those who directed Germany were as numerous

[1] "Europe and the French Revolution."

LEOPOLD COUNT BERCHTOLD
Austro-Hungarian Foreign Minister

as they were grave. The worst was the secrecy allowed in preparing the ultimatum, and still maintained through the diplomatic crisis it provoked. In that fatal instant which changed the whole course of our history our future was in the hands of a few men. It was Bethmann who, first and foremost, directed the policy which the ultimatum had inaugurated. I have told how, when he took over the chancellorship, he said to me either sincerely or from vanity, in any case with astonishing simplicity, that, though he had no diplomatic training, he hoped that, with industry and good will, he would soon "get the hang" of foreign policy. He forgot the truth, so often expressed by Bismarck, that diplomacy is not a trade to be acquired, that it is far less a science than an art. "He who knows all ", the wisdom of the Brahmans teaches, "may be considered a happy man. He who knows nothing, it is well with him. He who knows half would govern Brahma himself." In reality Bethmann's temperament was too wooden for him to hope ever to be brilliant. Neither his antecedents nor his character qualified him to be a diplomat.

In Berlin, during the winter 1915–1916, I spent many evenings with Prince Guido Henckel-Donnersmarck, whom I had first got to know in the early 'eighties, in the days when I was serving in Paris. He had since lost his first wife, Paiva, left Paris, settled down, and been made a prince by William II, much impressed by his colossal wealth, although for many years he had cold-shouldered him and hated him as pro-Bismarck. Now he lived in Berlin, in a splendid flat in the Pariser Platz, with his second wife, a Russian by birth, but who had made of herself a patriotic German. The prince, who was eighty-five, had become almost monosyllabic, but was a man of clear perception and wide experience. He knew the world and its inhabitants. It was his way in speaking of Bismarck, with whom for many years he had been friendly, to describe him with a tinge of irony as "quite a gifted politician" or even as "a statesman of some experience." One evening, as I shall always remember, old Prince Donnersmarck turned to me and said: "Prince Bismarck, a statesman of some experience, once told me that the German Empire could stand any type of chancellor but a bureaucrat." The prince was silent; then he added, "And I 've also heard that not

ungifted politician, Otto Bismarck, say that it made no difference
what a chancellor was, if only he was n't a professor."

Another pause till, with a sigh, Prince Donnersmarck concluded:
"Well, now we 've got one who is both professor and bureaucrat."

It is typical of the bureaucratic mind that Bethmann should have
insisted on keeping sole direction of the whole affair of the Serbian
ultimatum, even when it had become a dangerous crisis. He
wanted, as, in the worst stage of this crisis, he himself admitted to a
colleague, to make of it his *pièce d'essai*, "my diplomatic masterpiece." Not only did he give special directives for every telegram
to London, he even wrote some of them himself. His professorial
side came out most strongly in the conceited, doctrinaire persuasion
that his personal "integrity" and "loyalty" had gained him the
undying support of the English; that thus, with England on his
side, no major conflagration was to be feared. The orthodox autocrat of the Russias would never, he was quite certain, draw his sword
on behalf of Serbian regicides and conspirators. As, one by one,
these preconceptions melted away in smoke, the innocent Bethmann,
on the edge of a precipice, lost his head. From that instant he was a
drowning man, gasping and clutching at every straw. In the end his
panic even drove him, on the day before we declared war on Russia,
into sending for Sir Edward Goschen, the British Ambassador, to
whom, in the Chancellor's Palace, *à brûle-pourpoint*, he proposed an
Anglo-German "understanding." All he gained was a sarcastic
reply, followed next day by a sharp personal call to order from Sir
Edward Grey, in whose answer to this strange offer there was mention of "a pact", a "bargain" — "a disgrace from which the good
name of this country would never recover."

And while, by his unskilled diplomacy, Bethmann exposed the
Empire to mortal danger, he took no measures for any war. I shall
never cease to assert that he did not want one. He and his colleagues were guilty of *stultitia*, not of *dolus*. At the end of June,
1914, the hard-worked Secretary of State for the Interior, Delbrück,
had gone on leave. His growing apprehension of the results of the
Sarajevo murder brought him back to Berlin by the 9th of July.
That same evening he went to see Bethmann, who gave him his

views on the situation. It was the day on which Jagow, as State Secretary, had received Szögyényi-Marich, the Austrian Ambassador, come to tender thanks from the Vienna Cabinet for the speed with which our Emperor and Chancellor had promised their unreserved support of the projected operations against the Serbs. These thanks Jagow had received, with an added recommendation to the Austrians to act as energetically as possible. Bethmann told all this to Delbrück, adding that he "did not know" the contents of the Serbian ultimatum, but that he and Jagow were both convinced that any war with Serbia could be "localized." Delbrück then asked whether the Chancellor did not consider it advisable to take all measures customary on the eve of war; to proceed, in particular, to the purchase of grain supplies in Rotterdam. Bethmann said that it was quite unpermissible for Germany to make the slightest show of active preparation against hostilities, but that Delbrück had better go and talk to Jagow. This Delbrück did the following day, but Jagow, in his turn, assured him that measures of economic precaution would be "entirely superfluous." Both Jagow and the Chancellor had seemed uncomfortable when Delbrück questioned them. Both assured him quite categorically that nothing in the political situation necessitated his presence in Berlin (as he himself informed me not long afterwards). He therefore went off again on leave, not returning until July 24th. No one, in this interval, had managed to buy provisions in Rotterdam. Kühn, the State Secretary to the Treasury, had refused all demands for credits with the words: "But there is n't going to be any war." Delbrück had to apply several times before he got the necessary funds, and when he received them, the market had been cleared by our enemies. Delbrück, in contrast to Bethmann, was of opinion that it would be a long war.

The waste of provisions on all Fronts disquieted him in the very first weeks. He suggested the immediate requisitioning and rationing of our whole food supply, but here again he met with opposition from Bethmann. The Berlin authorities had authorized this unreasonable, or, at the least, extremely risky Austrian ultimatum to Serbia without any preparations for possible war.

On the other hand, even in January, 1914, the Paris municipality had decided, with subventions from the military authorities, so fully to augment its flour supply that the city would not feel even a passing shortage, should mobilization hold up communications.   General Michel, the military governor of Paris, had declared at the meeting which passed this decision: "Time presses: this will be no ordinary year, and we can't say what may not be in store for us.   How do we know that by March or April we sha'n't be mobilized?"

Whereas both Bethmann and Jagow (neither of whom could be considered reckless — they were indeed inclined to timidity) pursued their imprudent policy with the guilelessness of children in a wood gathering mushrooms, the French saw clearly all the seriousness of the general situation in Europe.   Their own official post-war publications admit that Jules Cambon, the French Ambassador in Berlin, had said to Baron Beyens, the Belgian Minister there, on February 20, 1914: "The majority of both French and Germans want to be left alone and live in peace.   But both here and there there is a minority which dreams only of wars, *revanche* and conquests.   That is the danger, and we must live with it, as one lives by the side of a powder cask which any piece of carelessness may explode."

On March 10th M. Guillaume, the Belgian Minister in Paris, wrote in a report to his government that the fall of Barthou's chauvin cabinet had seriously annoyed President Poincaré.   His annoyance was an open secret.   Poincaré considered the fall of this cabinet a check to the militarist, nationalist policy he had systematically pursued since the day he became *Président du Conseil*.   In concert with Millerand, Delcassé and several others, Poincaré had never ceased to preach the regeneration, political and military, of France, at the same time making every effort to enflame Russian suspicions against Germany and to win over Russia, little by little, to the notion of a war against us.

The position internationally was so strained as to demand of the directors of Berlin's policy the uttermost care and circumspection.   No other country had so much to gain from peace as Germany.   Baron Beyens, who no more wanted a war than did the majority of his countrymen, and certainly not a war involving all Europe, sent in, on June 12, 1914, a fairly long report to his government, dealing with the fall of the Barthou Cabinet and the French vote on the three years' military service law.

He began by some severe criticisms of MM. Barthou and Poincaré, who, "misinformed", had precipitated the vote on the three years' military service bill and so increased the general uneasiness, the risks, already everywhere so considerable, of an European conflagration. "The great majority of the French people is certainly not desirous of war, and neither has Germany any need of it. A few years hence the present equilibrium of forces between the two nations will be impossible. Germany need only be patient, she need only peacefully augment her economic and financial strength, and await the results of her growing birth rate to dominate in Central Europe without a struggle, with no one to gainsay her."

This very sensible opinion had guided my whole policy while in office. It was in our interests to keep the peace. In a war, above all in any general war, we had all to lose and little to gain. This report from Baron Beyens concludes with further strictures on Barthou and Poincaré, who would have done far better to ask themselves calmly whether no safer method could be devised for keeping peace between France and Germany than the present insensate race of armaments and excessive augmentation of man power, a burden France was less able to bear than we. Our poor, misgoverned country was like a ship which, at the end of a long and difficult voyage, runs aground and sinks outside the harbour.

The fecklessness with which William II, led on by the Vienna Cabinet, allowed us to be dragged into war, fully equalled the innocence of his Chancellor and State Secretary for Foreign Affairs. On the evening of that fatal day when he had given the Austrian Emperor *carte blanche* for any adventure against Serbia, our Sovereign informed Von Falkenhayn, his War Minister, of the whole intended Austrian *démarche*, and asked if the forces were ready for all contingencies. Von Falkenhayn clicked his heels, saluted and answered in the accents of zeal: "Certainly, Your Majesty" — though, naturally, he proceeded to enquire if immediate preparations would be advisable. But all such notions His Majesty expressly opposed, and wished his War Minister a good summer (his last !). Next day, before leaving for Kiel, en route for his North Sea trip, he received representatives of the General Staff, Admiralty, and Naval Cabinet. He informed them that Austria intended to settle accounts with Serbia in the matter of the Sarajevo murder. There would be no need to fear grave complications. It was therefore entirely unnecessary to proceed to exceptional military or naval measures. I have compared Jagow and Bethmann to harmless children out picking mushrooms. I ought, perhaps, to have said that they were like a pair of wilful little urchins playing with what seems an empty shell case, which is liable to explode at any minute.

Bethmann had at least the excuse that he knew nothing of foreign politics or diplomacy. Jagow had no extenuating ignorance. He had been twenty years in the Service and could well have prevented his Chancellor from committing the most grievous of his blunders. Instead he encouraged every folly, in the reverent snobbery inspired in him by the greatness of "aristocratic" Austria. Jagow even (*horribile dictu*) did not believe in the least in war. Five days before the handing in of the ultimatum (July 18, 1914) he had written to our London Ambassador, informing him of the coming move against the Serbs. Austria, he had said, was insisting on a definite explanation from her small neighbour; we could not, nor would, attempt to restrain her, but must do our best to "localize" any conflict. The more decisive Austria's attitude, the more certain she felt of energetic German support, the less danger was there of Russian interference. There might be some fuss made in St. Petersburg, but Russia was not really prepared for war, and, for the moment, France and England did not want it. Jagow went on to repeat the specious arguments in favour of "prophylactic warfare" already several decades out of date, yet still, in spite of Bismarck, always repeated: a few years hence Russia would have grown more formidable, the Teutonic group would have weakened, the Slavs have become increasingly anti-German. Apart from all this, he declared: "I don't want preventative war. But if any one offered us battle we should have no right to draw back. I hope, and still believe, this war may be local-ized." He concludes with instructions to Lichnowsky to do all he can to prevent English public opinion from being enlisted on Serbia's side. Every effort in this direction would have to be made, though, of course, it was a very far cry from the sympathies or antipathies of a people to the blazing of an international trail. If Sir Edward Grey were logical and honourable, he, too, would help the Imperial Government to keep the conflict purely local. So Jagow to Lich-nowsky in London (July 18th).

And this same Jagow, that same day, had spoken in these very terms to Schön, the Ambassador's nephew and Bavarian *chargé d'affaires*, who came, in the name of his government, to inform him that a Herr von Boulatzuff, the Russian Minister in Munich, had sent word, *à titre d'ami*, by confidential messenger to Count Hertling, that: "*La Russie ne permettra jamais que la petite Serbie soit mangée par l'Autriche.*" This *chargé d'affaires* received the impression, as, in duty bound, he mentioned in a report, that, on hearing the above warning, the Secretary of State "had smiled." When the "fuss" in St. Petersburg was becoming a roar of artillery, little Jagow smiled on the other side of his face. His nerve gave way as utterly as his chief's. On August 2d he said to the deputy Heckscher, who told me the story not long afterwards: "My heart's like lead. You don't know how I feel."

In comparison to Bethmann and Jagow, Zimmermann, Stumm, and Bergen played minor parts. Wilhelm Stumm had, of the three, most influence, since he, in this Council of Ministers, alone knew London and Petersburg *de visu*. Prince Heinrich Carolath told me once in confidence how, at a secret session of the Budget Com-missions of the Reichstag, when the origins of the war were being discussed, a Socialist asked if it were true that the Counsellor of Legation, Wilhelm Stumm, had said, at the end of July, 1914, before witnesses, in the Union Club in Berlin: "By to-morrow morning I shall have brought the Russians to their knees." No official answer was given. There is, alas, no doubt that Stumm did not, like Bethmann, stupidly misconceive the gravity of the crisis; his arrogance blinded him to it.

In the case of Zimmermann things were different. He was an excellent fellow, who would have done very good and useful work had he stayed on in the consular service, or remained content to be the head of one of the Foreign Office departments. He might have done better still as Regierungspräsident, or public prosecutor, in a district of his own East Prussia, where he would certainly have been liked and esteemed. People would have greeted him on all sides as he came every morning to take his *apéritif* in the Hotel Zur Linde or The Prussian Eagle — "Good health, Herr Präsident — Good health, Herr Oberstaatsanwalt."

But Zimmermann knew little of foreign policy, had met none of the leading personalities in either St. Petersburg or London, and was, moreover, inclined to give himself airs. Very conscientious, which is more than could be said of Jagow or even Bethmann — honourable, a hater of intrigue, his "honest bluntness" none the less contributed to render the crisis more acute.

Diego von Bergen, who directed the Bureau of the Affairs of the Triple Alliance, was the son of a Pomeranian consular servant who had worked his way up to be German representative in some Central American republic, where he had married a daughter of far-off Guatemala. He never once gave a personal opinion on the crisis. In 1914, in a post of very great importance, he neither prevented nor wished to prevent developments, since his one fear was of giving offence to anybody. And certainly, later on, in war time, he succeeded in making himself *persona grata*, not merely with his chiefs, but even more — and this was far more important — with Erzberger. All through the War the latter's power kept increasing, till, at last, he strolled every day into the Foreign Office and demanded to be shown the notes received and sent. He was so indiscreet, so lacking in all *tenu* — and moreover kept the nuncio in Munich informed of every item he picked up — that the feeble Bethmann himself at last rebelled and refused him daily access to the *arcana imperii*. Privy Councillor of Legation, Von Bergen, was therefore charged to supply his daily welcome, to listen in patience for an hour or so to all the political "chit-chat" he poured forth, and to show him as few documents as possible. Bergen made the most of this duty to get himself appointed Minister to the Vatican, thanks to the patronage of Erzberger, who, with all his faults, was good-natured.

Such was the little group of men who dragged our country and people into the World War. The gravest fault of these blind leaders was their refusal to seek or take advice, share their intentions with any one, or confess the clumsy moves already made. If, after the murder at Sarajevo, Bethmann and his colleagues had turned to Mühlberg, an ex-State Secretary, at that time Minister to the Vatican, or to Bernstorff, our Ambassador in Washington, to Count Brockdorff-Rantzau, Mumm, or Metternich, the last of whom knew England from A to Z and had the clearest insight into her policy — there is no doubt that any one of these men, or all of them, might have stayed the Chancellor's hand and preached circumspection. My own retirement had kept me out of politics for five years. I did not know anything about the projects of my successor. But had my advice been asked, I should have tried to find out first if Berlin was aiming at preventative warfare. Had I learnt that this was our intention, I should have reminded Bethmann of a note, addressed by order of the Chancellor on February 16, 1887, through Count Bismarck, his Secretary of State, to Prince Henry VII of Reuss, then our Ambassador in Vienna. It runs as follows: "The Chancellor has read with interest Your Excellency's report (No. 99 of the 4th inst.), and entirely endorses your declaration, made to your Russian colleague, that in no case should we think of declaring war because it had seemed to us inevitable that, sooner or later, war would be certain to break out. None of us can see so clearly into the divine dispensations of Providence as to be sure of the course of future events. Incalculable incidents of all kinds might arise, with the process of time, which would prevent such a war from being declared."

So also, in an oft-quoted report, to William I, his good old Sovereign, did Prince Bismarck, categorically and in principle, reject the idea of "preventative warfare": "To-day, as in 1867, at the time of the Luxemburg question, I would not think of advising Your Majesty to any immediate declaration of war merely because it seems as though our adversaries would declare war on us later on, when they may be better armed than they are to-day. It is always impossible to know with sufficient certainty what the intentions of Divine Providence may be."

I should further have recalled that sharp reproof which Bismarck sent my friend and comrade Deines, the military attaché in Vienna, whom he suspected of egging on Austria to fight Russia. And when Bismarck conceived the same suspicion of Count Waldersee, the Chief of the General Staff, he wrote off at once to tell General Albedyll, the Head of our Military Cabinet, that Germany's task was to prevent declarations of war, or, should this seem impossible, to delay them; that he, Prince Bismarck, refused his consent to any other policy. I should have stressed, above all, the fact that this same Bismarck had said, again and again, that, of all contingencies, the most disadvantageous to Germany would be war between Austria and Russia.

Let us suppose that Bethmann and his colleagues had answered me that "prophylactic warfare" was an idea that had never crossed their minds — that they merely believed it might be possible to "localize" this Austro-Serbian conflict. Then I should naturally have warned them that theirs was a most dangerous illusion; that it could only have arisen from their ignorance of the whole situation in Russia, in England, France — all over the world! Never would the Russians allow the Austrians to organize punitive measures against the Serbs. Unless the most cautious diplomacy were employed, the antagonism created by such a measure between Russia on the one hand, and with her Serbia and the Dual Monarchy on the other, would have as its result a dangerous crisis. This, in its turn, would mean further armaments, that is to say, the menace of imminent World War.

France would at once champion Russia. For twenty-five years it had been an axiom that though, in any Franco-German conflict, Russia for a time might hesitate to take up arms against our Empire, the moment we were at war with Russia French rifles would go off automatically. And, I should have added, "once we are at war with Russia and France, it is more than likely that Great Britain will seize on such a favourable chance to strangle, without undue risks, her rival in commerce, navigation, and industry — the most powerful Continental State, and so, by British tradition, her enemy." I should have asked if we were really so certain that Italy and Roumania were our friends.

I repeat that such reasoning as this would have been no proof of unusual diplomatic experience, or exceptional political acumen. I am convinced that any normal German diplomat — Metternich, Bernstorff, Mumm or Rosen, Mühlberg or Brockdorff-Rantzau, would have said the same in July, 1914.

CHAPTER XIII

Bethmann Proposes to Resign — The Heroic Behaviour of Our People — Bethmann's Declaration of War on Russia; His Motives — Our Clumsy Handling of Italy — Roumania — Talks with Prince Wedel on Our Strategy — Lichnowsky's Telephone Conversation with Grey — The Fall of Liège — General Ludendorff — The First News of the Battle of the Marne — The Invasion of Belgium — Bethmann's Speech on Belgium (August 4th) — The "Scrap of Paper."

HISTORY has in it many instances of eleventh-hour escapes from catastrophe, when Providence has given statesmen and peoples their chance of avoiding mortal danger. Once, in the early 'eighties, Prince Bismarck said in my presence that, if Emile Ollivier and the Duc de Gramont had made good use of Leopold von Hohenzollern's renunciation, they could have prevented war in 1870, and gained a striking diplomatic success. Ollivier, Bismarck said, on receiving Prince Karl Anton von Hohenzollern's telegram renouncing the Spanish throne in his son's name, should have gone straight off to the *corps législatif* and spoken more or less as follows: "*Il y a peu de temps la candidature d'un prince prussien au trône de Charles Quint avait surgi. La France a élevé sa voix, la France a été obéie. Les bons rapports entre la France et sa noble sœur l'Espagne n'ont jamais été troublés. Quant à ceux, dont les ambitions, et les intrigues, ont mis en danger la paix européenne, nous espérons, et l'Europe espère avec nous, qu'ils ne recommenceront pas.*"

Having given the above sketch of the kind of speech which Emile Ollivier might have made if he had not been — Emile Ollivier, Bismarck continued: "What could I have said? I should have been in a very difficult fix. Both at home and abroad my position was far weaker in those days, than later. The old Emperor did not like war or risks, and neither did the Crown Prince. Queen Augusta and the Crown Princess were against me. All my domestic opponents, the Democrats all over Germany, the progress-mongers

In the north, the ultramontanes in the south, would have taken up the cry against 'the peace breaker.' I might have had to resign."

As late as on July 25th in the midsummer of 1914 we might have avoided war. It would have been quite enough to have told Vienna that we definitely refused our authorization of any breach between Serbia and Austria-Hungary until we had fully examined Serbia's answer. We could have added that if Austria wished to proceed to unauthorized military operations against the Serbs, she must do so *à ses propres risques et périls*. We should refuse her all assistance and leave her to work out her fate. Having examined the Serbian answer, we should have declared that we had perceived with satisfaction how, thanks to the wise counsels of the Powers, the Serbian Government had subscribed to nearly every Austrian demand. We should have proposed to submit such points as were still in dispute to the decision of the Hague tribunal. This would have given us nine chances to one of avoiding war. Even the unlucky William II saw this more clearly than Bethmann and his colleagues.

Bethmann, so as not to be disturbed in the achievement of his "diplomatic masterpiece", had advised his Sovereign on no account to abandon the usual North Sea trip. As the crisis became acute, he begged the Emperor most urgently not to recall the German fleet, then in Norwegian waters, or himself think of returning to Germany. When, in the far North, at Odde on the Utnefiord, William II heard the Serbian answer, he declared, in a marginal note, that he could not see what more the Austrian Government wanted: they had achieved a brilliant diplomatic *coup*. At the same time, and by the Emperor's order, Von Plessen, His Majesty's aide-de-camp, wired to Moltke, the Chief of the General Staff, that now all motives for war between Austria and Serbia had vanished, since the Serbs had accepted nearly every Austrian demand. The ancients affirmed that Fortune has a beautiful forelock, and the back of her head completely bald. Nobody, unless he grasped the forelock, could hope to win the favours of the goddess. Jagow and Bethmann let her turn her back on them. They gave the Austrians *carte blanche*. In the sheerest apathy and indifference they watched the Austrian Minister leave Belgrade as soon as he had received the Serbian answer, which he had not so much as examined, and so break off relations with Serbia.   That same evening they allowed the Austrian Government to proceed to partial mobilization against the Serbs.   For the sake of giving pleasure to Austria, of shielding her prestige and sparing the pride of His Apostolic Majesty, they stubbornly refused all English suggestions for a conference, thus exposing themselves, and with them Germany, to the reproach of not wanting a peaceful solution.   Would any statesmen worth the name have let slip every chance of avoiding a general catastrophe?   I answer: No!   The Government of 1914 allowed their boat to drift with the current without the slightest attempt to change her course — and so the good ship *Empire* sank.

When, at last, on July 27th, the Kaiser reached Berlin from Odde, his Chancellor awaited him on the platform, very humble, and with a pale and wretched face.   His Sovereign put, though far less amiably, the question I was to ask a few days later: "How did it all happen?"   His Majesty's ill temper was excusable since Bethmann had, to the last, kept on assuring him that peace was not threatened in the least, that he was in constant touch with England and on terms of complete understanding with her.   Count August Eulenburg was present at this scene between Chancellor and Emperor.   He told me later that Bethmann, utterly cowed, admitted that, all along, he had been deceived, and offered the Kaiser his resignation.   His Majesty answered: "You 've cooked this broth and now you 're going to eat it."

Our miserable diplomacy through the crisis made all the more heroic and admirable the spirit of the German people.   Her head up, without once flinching, without misgivings, our country faced a world of enemies.   In five days Germany had mobilized; everything went through without a hitch.   Then came the transport of troops to East and West, with not one single unforeseen delay!   Never once did the necessity arise of applying for further instructions to the General Staff in Berlin.   The armies, exactly as arranged, a fortnight after their mobilization orders, were in the positions assigned to them, concentrated, formed up for deployment.

Everything had "clicked", as officers have it. Put to the test, our whole organization, every cog in the administrative machine, functioned impeccably.

There was only one weak point — strategic direction. But this was almost as weak as our diplomacy. Moltke, like Bethmann, showed himself unequal to his task. So too the Emperor, who had never managed to choose the right generals for even the most essential posts. Two thousand years ago a Greek philosopher was already saying that an army of stags led by a lion is better than one of lions led by a stag.

Never shall I forget the spectacle of the glorious youth of 1914: the glow of sacrifice and pride with which it went out to meet its fate ! From far and wide volunteers came flocking to the colours, with blithe, heroic songs on their lips. As I lie on my deathbed I shall hear them, the songs of that *ver sacrum*, the consecrated spring of the Fatherland, those glad pæans of farewell with which youth faced a world in arms.

> *Gloria Victoria!*
> *Ja, mit Herz und Hand*
> *Fürs Vaterland!*
> *Die Vöglein im Walde*
> *Die sangen so wunder-wunderschön:*
> *In der Heimat, in der Heimat,*
> *Da gibt's ein Wiedersehen.*[1]

Thucydides, who, like no other writer, has the gift of the eternal image, has left us an imperishable description of the setting forth against Syracuse of the expedition sent by Athens. Men and women, clustered on the steps of the Parthenon, on the slopes of

[1] "Hurrah.
Victoria !
Yes, with heart and hand
        For the Fatherland.
The birds in the wood they sang,
        Sang — sang
        So beautiful,
        Beautiful — beautiful !
        Back home !   Back home !
Where we shall meet again."

Hymettos and Pentelicos, watch, with a thrill of melancholy and pride mingling with their joyous hope of victory, the sails dipping below the sky line. That was how all Germany felt as it watched its youth depart in 1914 — that army of which Marshal Foch, our bitterest enemy, has said that it was the best the world has seen: that army which, through four years in the field, was to earn imperishable laurels by its courage in attack, its iron defence. Whoever lived through that summer could only be silent and bare his head before the impetuous bravery, the grandeur, the virility and purity of spirit, the soaring idealism, of our people. His country, a nation in arms, was German virtue realized in flesh and blood.

And yet, any well-informed observer was forced, with misgiving, to ask himself if even such an army as ours could suffice to make good the faults of our ruling statesmen. In 1866, in '70 even, Prince Bismarck had found means to leave his enemies the odium of declaring war. Appearances govern the world. They, as the Greeks already knew, decide more easily than reality. Bismarck had secured the imponderable forces for his arms; Bethmann incurred men's hatred of aggressors. I admit that it is true, up to a point, that we had to attack France without loss of time, once we had declared war on Russia. The inconceivable blunder was that Germany should have let Russia force her declaration. This first declaration of war gave the whole world its chance to say of us that Germany had provoked the catastrophe. The verdict is unjust, but hard to refute. Moltke has assured me more than once that he considered our declaration of war on Russia premature; that he himself had urged against it — would rather have delayed it as long as possible.

And Tirpitz wished just as little "to let fly." He happened to be in Tarasp for a cure, whither Herr von Loebell, the Prussian Minister of the Interior, had also gone for the same purpose. Loebell has described Tirpitz' dismay to me, when telegrams, posted up in the Kursaal, gave him news that the Austrian ultimatum, considered so "local" and inoffensive both by the Foreign Office and Emperor, had provoked such a dangerous crisis. He and Tirpitz, Loebell continued, got into immediate touch with Berlin to ask if they were not to return. Bethmann begged them, most urgently, to remain — their return would only "cause a sensation." At last, and in spite of him, they left Tarasp, since they felt that their duty had forbidden them to remain abroad at such a time of danger.

Why was there this precipitate haste to declare war on Russia on August 1st? The reason for our blunder in diplomacy, like those for so many others we committed, must be sought in our domestic situation, or rather in the anxieties it caused the Chancellor. Albert Ballin gave me a very vivid description of a scene he witnessed that day, in the Chancellor's Palace. When he came into the ground-floor "garden room", in which these atrocious decisions were being taken, he saw the Chancellor — the "war chancellor" as people were already beginning to call him — pacing from end to end of it, in great strides. Geheimrat Kriege sat at a table covered with folio volumes. Kriege was a conscientious official, an excellent jurist, but without political insight consonant with his knowledge of the law. From time to time the agitated Bethmann would ask him, "Is that declaration of war on Russia ready yet? I must have my declaration at once!" Kriege, who looked a nervous wreck, was going through all the law books for a model — from Grotius' celebrated "De Jure Belli ac Pacis" to the well-known works of Bluntschli, Heffter, and Martens. Ballin allowed himself the question: "Why such haste to declare war on Russia, Your Excellency?" And Bethmann answered: "If I don't, we sha'n't get the Socialists to fight."

Ballin and I both gave this answer the same psychological explanation. The Chancellor had perceived the horrible situation he had brought upon himself and on Germany. He shrank from responsibility. His first instinctive reaction was the desire to disarm the Left Wing elements he so dreaded, and he felt that this could only be achieved by making the War look anti-tsarist, now that he had not managed to keep clear of it. Right up to his fall these were the tactics he pursued.

When on August 3, 1914, there followed our declaration of war on France, it was excused with the grossest misstatements. It was easy enough for the French to prove conclusively that no French airman had dropped bombs on the railway line from Nuremberg to Ingolstadt. To hurry on our rupture with France, which the previous declaration of war on Russia had made a strategic necessity, we presented the French with demands to occupy Belfort, Toul, and Verdun, and these were, of course, immediately published, by the French propaganda authorities, as a proof of our insatiable greed for conquest. The Ambassador Schön was, in any case, never able to carry out his instructions on this point, since the telegram sent by Berlin came into the hands of the French. It is sad to have to place it on record that our embassies, in the moment of unleashed tempest, were as lamentably unequal to their work as the central administration in Berlin — Jagow and Bethmann-Hollweg, Stumm, and Bergen.

Among other grievous errors of this July was the game of hide-and-seek we played with Italy. Bethmann and Jagow were both terrified that Italy would betray, in St. Petersburg, the secret of the Austrian ultimatum, that in Rome something might leak out of the secret plan of attack on Serbia, and this lead on to diplomatic protests. I may say at once that, in my view, such protests would have been a godsend. It would have been a most unmerited piece of luck had the whole insensate action against Serbia, begun with the ultimatum, been prevented. In the week before Austria delivered it Bollati, the Italian Ambassador, never ceased his demands, in the name of his government, to be informed if, as the rumour went in Bucharest, Constantinople, and elsewhere, Austria were really contriving a plot against Serbia. Jagow, to throw dust in Italy's eyes, answered him every day that this was a ridiculous suggestion ; that neither Berlin nor Vienna had any such project. It went, however, without saying that if, in any case of general war — war which the ultimatum would make most probable — the Central Powers wanted to keep Italy on their side, they must assure themselves of her help in good time. Without Austrian concessions this was impossible ; such concessions would even be indispensable to prevent Italy's going to the enemy. Since, when the moment came, they had not been made, Italy found herself faced with an alternative. Any operations begun by Austria without previous understanding with Italy violated both letter and spirit of the Triple Alliance. Moreover, up to the very last minute, we had kept the Italians in the dark. Finally, it was *we* who declared war on Russia, then on France, and so gave the Italian Government every excuse for remaining *ex nexu foederis*. All Bismarck's treaties had been defensive. To Bismarck it had seemed impossible that the Chancellor of such a country as Germany, a country whose major interest was peace, could ever be mad enough to *declare* war on either Russia or France.

On July 31st the Italian Council of Ministers voted neutrality. Giolitti, our best and surest Italian friend, had declared spontaneously to Salandra, the President of the Council, and to the Foreign Minister, the Marchese San Giuliano, his intimate, that he felt, having studied the position, and in view of Austria's rash, unheard-of action against the Serbs, that neutrality was the only possible attitude. It is easy enough to understand that all the Kaiser's telegrams and letters to King Victor Emanuel — so often snubbed and offended in the past by him — had no power to change the situation. This Italian declaration of neutrality brought France immense strategic advantages. She could withdraw all her troops from the Italian frontier and hurl them against us in the west. This modified our whole military outlook and prepared the Battle of the Marne. Military critics agree that this battle did much to change the decision of the war.

Such is the terrible Nemesis awaiting the blunderer in politics; since, in the end, there can be no doubt of it, policy, more than armies, must win wars. Not the generals who led us in the field but, above all, Jagow and Bethmann-Hollweg are the men who have to answer for our defeat.

Towards Roumania our behaviour was much the same. King Carol, who, throughout his whole reign, had considered it the first of his duties to give Germany and Austria his support in the event of any general conflagration, was put in such a position that this was impossible. It all came to pass as Carp had prophesied. Without ever having been duly warned or given any reasoned line of argument, the old, wise, and dignified King Carol was brusquely required

to aid us in a war which looked as though it would spread all over the
world — a war made possible by the frivolousness of Austrian
diplomacy and the purblind feebleness of our own.   The king's
dilemma was as follows : after nearly fifty years on the throne he
must abdicate and leave his adopted country, or else, a Hohenzollern
and Prussian officer, betray the country of his birth.   Within two
months the worry of it all had caused his death, or so Queen Elizabeth, his widow, said to Prince Wedel, sent from Berlin to the
funeral.

As our army marched on Paris, I could feel again, at sixty-five,
all the emotions I had known as a young man on the day when,
nearly fifty years before, I had hurried off to join the colours.   I
envied those with no anxieties, unvexed by any thought of politics,
who marched to the line, and should have been happy to go with
them.   Almost every morning I met my old friend, Prince Wedel,
who felt as I did.   He had been for over fifty years a soldier, and, to
long experience as an officer, he added the *coup d'œil* of leadership.
He was sure our troops would live up to their reputation, would do
all that was humanly possible.   But the Allies, he said, were greatly
superior in numbers.   Before the General Staff left Berlin, Wedel
had had a long talk with Moltke.   It was reckoned that the three
million men of the Central Powers had against them five millions
and a half — the combined strength of France, Russia, England,
Belgium, and Serbia.   Wedel deplored the fact that Germany, faced
as she had been with the recent uncertainty in Europe, had not
drawn more freely on her resources.   France, with a population
inferior by twenty-eight millions, opposed to us, thanks to her three
years' military service, an army of almost equal strength.   The
General Staff had demanded more extensive powers to recruit than
those afforded by the military law of 1913.   But Moltke, as Wedel
regretted, had not insisted urgently enough to conquer opposition
in various quarters.   The Finance Ministry had raised trumpery
objections, quite inadmissible in a vital question such as this.
Bethmann had lacked all vision, all power to make himself felt.

And our Ally had been even more neglectful.   Thanks to the
disorders then reigning in the Habsburg Monarchy, the ever-

increasing feebleness of her governments, the armaments and power of recruitment of this Austria for whom we drew the sword had remained well below the possibilities. From the August of 1914 Wedel could perceive that the Allies, who held the seas, would provision far more easily than Germany, obliged by her dense population to import vast quantities of foodstuffs; that our enemies had far greater resources of both man power and war material. Wedel, and I could only agree with him, did not share the Chancellor's opinion that "the storm would be short — very short." We asked ourselves whether our economic life, organized on the import of finished articles, would ever stand the strain of a long war. I expressed the fear that the feeble clumsiness of our policy might allow Roumania and Italy, even the United States, to join our enemies. Wedel, too, regretted that the close contact between the General Staff and our diplomacy which I had always managed to keep with Schlieffen, and then with Moltke, was no more. With Bethmann, Wedel said, Moltke was on very frigid terms; they were both easily offended and kept each other too much at arm's length.

In his talks with the Chief of the General Staff, Wedel had noticed, with anxiety, that Moltke himself was far from well. The general had told him of a fainting fit, brought on, he said, as the result of a political "misunderstanding", which in a really scarifying manner revealed all the disorder of our government. On August 1st, one day after official proclamation of "a state of danger of war", and a few hours before general mobilization, a telegram from London had been received. Prince Lichnowsky announced that England would be willing to guarantee French neutrality if Germany would abstain from attacking France. Emperor and Chancellor read this telegram not with mere sighs of relief, but in transports of such almost delirious joy as proved both their love of peace and political ignorance. William II sent off at once for Moltke, whom he ordered to hold up the advance to the west and turn back all our forces against Russia. When Moltke pointed out the confusion, the incalculable results of such a decision, the difficulties entailed in mobilization by it, the Emperor took him gruffly to task and ordered one of his own aides-de-camp to transmit to the 16th Division, advancing in the direction of Luxemburg, the order to call an instant halt. In conjunction with a triumphant Bethmann, who pointed out that all along he had been in the right about England, His Majesty wired off to King George V, accepting this English proposal with joy and gratitude. If England, the telegram said, would guarantee French neutrality with her arms, the Kaiser on his side would promise that the French frontier should not be crossed before seven o'clock on the night of August 3d. In the night of August 1–2 King George's answer was received. He declared himself entirely unable to understand these German suggestions. The German Ambassador in London must have made some very palpable mistake.

And Prince Lichnowsky had, in fact, misunderstood a telephone message from the Foreign Office. Instead of going straight off to Sir Edward Grey and obtaining his personal assurance, as the A.B.C. of diplomatic method should have indicated, our Ambassador, quite unnerved by the crisis, had wired direct to Berlin this misunderstood offer of neutrality. The Emperor was already in bed when King George's answer was received. His body servant, the faithful Schulz, aroused him out of his first sleep to read this afflicting telegram from his cousin. His Majesty sent at once for Moltke, received him in vest and pants, and announced that, unluckily, there had, after all, been no offer of neutrality from England, and that therefore mobilization must run its course. Moltke, so Wedel told me, had assured him that the shock of this announcement seemed to stifle him; that he had been overwhelmed by the sensation of standing on the brink of a gulf and felt as though he would have an apoplectic fit. This was, of course, exaggeration, but the expression proved that, physically and morally, poor Moltke was really a sick man.

Prince Wedel considered our advance on Paris too precipitate. Superhuman demands were being made on our troops. Yet both he and I hailed with delight the brilliant capture of Liège at the very outset of hostilities. It was essential to the success of our Western strategy that this fortress should be taken straight away, since it blocked the advance into Brussels of the whole right wing of our army. A siege would have taken far too long. Some one, therefore, hit on the idea of surprising Liège with an advance guard before the first advance had been carried through. On the night of August 5th a few brigades, in position before the line of forts, tried to pass the first defences in the dark and push on into the inner fort. This *coup de main* nearly failed. The shock troops did not advance; several detachments lost their officers and were taken prisoners. At this critical juncture Colonel Ludendorff, temporarily attached to the staff of General von Emmich, who directed the attack, took command of the 14th Infantry Brigade, whose leader had been killed in action. Sword in hand, by sheer force of personal example, he urged on a number of gallant men, and so, with a single brigade, forced his way through the first line of defences and on into the heart of the fortress, still entirely held by Belgians, whose numerous garrison gave way to a mere handful of Germans. Reinforcements did not come up for thirty-six hours. The General Staff began to breathe again. The whole right wing of the German army had been saved the danger of being held up south of the Meuse by Liège and Namur, two powerful obstacles. Namur could now be enveloped from the north and our movement presented no further difficulties. This first success was acclaimed all over Germany. That great general who, for the next four years, was to cover himself with glory and the flags of his country with fresh laurels, was first seen through the fumes of Liège by the German people: General Ludendorff. In spite of the jabber of blind demagogues, the childish criticism of pedants, ignorant of war and of reality, in spite of even his own political errors, he is, and will remain, one of the great figures in our history.

Through the following days Wedel and I could rejoice in the victories of Mülhausen, Saarburg, Neufchâteau, Mons, Charleroi, Maubeuge and St. Quentin. Uhlans, we heard, could already see the Eiffel tower. But, soon after, Wedel talked to a young officer who, in the early days of September, during the first check in our advance, had been attached to the Staff of General Moltke. He had come in one day to report, and the sight of our Chief of Staff had appalled him.   He had found him sitting hunched up over his table, his face buried in both hands.   Moltke looked up and turned a pale and tear-stained face on the officer.   Next day, or the day after that, some one in the suite of the Empress told Wedel that William II had sent her this telegram: "Pray for us."

It would be the very height of presumption if I let myself pronounce on strategy because I was once a lieutenant of hussars.   For all my keen interest in the army, whose uniform I have worn for half a century, I am fully aware of my inadequacy.   Yet I feel that even a layman has the right to affirm that, in strategy as in politics, no great project can be conceived and planned in advance, and then put into action a long time afterwards.   Plans of campaign are not like herrings which can be casked to preserve for several years.   No one said this more definitely than Bismarck.   Napoleon would frequently modify the strategic dispositions he had set down when, on the field, he faced a situation.   The conduct of war, as of policy, would be far easier than it is if either the general or the statesman had simply to pull out the right drawer and find in it a docketed prescription, guaranteed to bring success in a given circumstance.   The plan of attack drawn up by Count Alfred Schlieffen, some years before the outbreak of the World War, might suggest ideas, it might even lay down general principles applicable to such a war as confronted us.   But it was not to be considered a *ukase*, to be obeyed blindly and mechanically.   Once more I would repeat the apostle's warning that whereas the spirit gives life, the letter kills.   And Moltke, on many essential points, was untrue to the spirit of Schlieffen's plan.   Military experts have since proved it and even the profane are forced to agree with them.

It now became all too apparent how justified had been that self-mistrust expressed to me by the unfortunate Moltke on the day in September, 1905, when we rode together around the Hippodrome. All the peril of William II's tendency to give way to his own likes and dislikes in his choice of generals was revealed.   The victory or defeat of the Empire now depended on such choice as he had made. This nephew of the "thinker-out of battles", of the victor of Sadowa and Sedan, was a man of the most exemplary loyalty, full of

GIOVANNI GIOLITTI

the best intentions, and an idealist. Yet at the same time he was one of those luckless generals who, from Mardonius and Varus to Benedek and Trochu, excite our pity, but can expect no mercy with the historian.

It was soon officially admitted that our army had begun to retreat — a *communiqué* announced that we had "inflected" our right wing "to the rear." Wedel, informed by several intimate friends at the Front, no longer doubted the failure of our plan of attack. We both agreed that, as a result, our invasion of Belgium would necessarily prove a terrible blunder. There are acts which their success alone can justify. Machiavelli's saying that a bad action may seem useful if productive of any good consequence is sometimes proved. *Cosa fatta capo ha!* But a doubtful, or unsuccessful, bad action is far less easy to excuse.

It had proved as impossible to smash French resistance once and for all, by a lightning invasion of Belgian territory, as to "localize" the Serbian conflict, in the way Jagow and Bethmann had anticipated. We had clearly put ourselves in the wrong for nothing: *"Quand on fait des crasses, il faut au moins qu'elles réussissent,"* as a witty Petersburg friend, Missy Durnow, used to say.

There is no doubt that our invasion of Belgium, with the violation it entailed of that country's sovereign neutrality, and of treaties we ourselves had signed, and the world had respected for a century, was an act of the gravest political significance. Bad was made worse than ever by Bethmann-Hollweg's speech in the Reichstag (August 4, 1914). Never, perhaps, has any other statesman at the head of a great and civilized people for whose safety and future he had to answer, pronounced, in an hour of mortal crisis, a clumsier, a more terrible speech. Before the whole world — before his country, this spokesman of the German Government — not of the Belgian! — not of the French! — declared that, in invading Belgium we did wrong, but that necessity knows no law. Never shall I forget reading that speech! Seldom have I experienced such anguish. I could understand what the common people and children mean when they say: "My heart stood still."

I was aware that, with this one categorical statement, we had forfeited, at a blow, the imponderabilia; that this unbelievably stupid oration would set the whole world against Germany.

And on the very evening after he made it this Chancellor of the German Empire, in a talk with Sir Edward Goschen, the British Ambassador, referred to the international obligations on which Belgium relied for her neutrality as "*un chiffon de papier*", "a scrap of paper." Not since July 15, 1870, when the words "*cœur léger*" escaped the lips of Emile Ollivier, the French *président du Conseil*, had so fatal a slogan been coined. For Ollivier, who let fall his stupid phrase at a public session in a parliament, there had been nothing left but to sit down and compose a heavy tome in which he tried, in vain, to justify it. For Bethmann-Hollweg, whose blunder had been made *tête-à-tête*, the matter should have been far simpler. There is no need to be a Machiavelli to understand that if, in a moment of collapse, Bethmann really said these unlucky words, the whole *raison d'Etat*, the supreme interests of the nation, demanded his instant and formal denial of them. It should have been a case of statement for statement; the "no" would have weighed equally with the "yes." Bethmann had no right to lay on our people the burden of this terrible catchword, systematically, incessantly exploited, as long as the war lasted, by the Allies — and, after it, at the Treaty of Versailles — no right to brand us as the infamous violators of treaty rights, a nation against which mankind must protect itself. Imagine Bismarck in such a situation! Imagine even Talleyrand, or Metternich! How different was Metternich's attitude towards Napoleon, in 1813, at the celebrated Dresden interview. Or Talleyrand's, in 1814, towards the Tsar Alexander I, in the talk which he himself reproduces in his well-known report to Louis XVIII — Metternich, the *grand seigneur*, who was never known to lose his head; Talleyrand, the skilful diplomat, whose ease of manner, tact and aplomb, brought him through every encounter with flying colours.

CHAPTER XIV

Could the World War Have Been Avoided? — Why the Fleet Was Not Engaged — The High Command — Von Moltke — The Mission of Lieutenant Colonel Hentsch — The Battle of Tannenberg — Moltke's Successor, General von Falkenhayn — Unfavourable Developments in Rome — The Austro-Hungarian Ambassador, Herr von Merey — Passivity of the German Ambassador, Flotow — Italy's Declaration of Neutrality.

THIS fatal speech of August 4, 1914, had left me with the gloomiest presentiments. They returned to fill my mind as I read, in the political notes of the *Revue des Deux Mondes*, the arguments with which my old friend, Francis Charmes, a good Frenchman and the disciple of Gambetta, but, at the same time, a shrewd, unbiased politician, summed up our declaration of war. He wrote:

"La guerre s'est présentée à nous dans des conditions telles que, même dans nos rêves, nous n'aurions jamais pu en imaginer de plus favorables. Si une fée tutélaire était venue nous dire: 'la guerre est certaine, inévitable, prochaine; comment préférez-vous, comment souhaitez-vous qu'elle s'engage? qu'aurions-nous pu répondre, sinon en exprimant le désir que, dès le premier moment, la Russie, notre alliée, et l'Angleterre, notre amie, marchassent résolument avec nous, que l'Italie, notre sœur latine, désapprouvant l'agression dont nous aurions été l'objet, refusât de s'y associer et proclamât sa neutralité, en attendant mieux; que des puissances petites par leur territoire, mais très grandes par le cœur, fussent provoquées et envahies au mépris de la foi jurée, de manière à ce que leur cause se confondit avec la nôtre et à ce que l'opinion du monde civilisé, se prononçant en leur faveur, mit également son espoir en nous? Nous aurions demandé que ces milles "forces impondérables" dont Bismarck connaissait la valeur fussent de notre côté. Eh bien, tous ces vœux dont la réalisation totale paraissait si difficile que nous n'aurions pas osé les exprimer, tous ont été exaucés. Nous ne savons pas ce que sera la suite de la campagne, mais elle ne pouvait mieux commencer. Nous le disons hardiment, toutes les chances sont de notre côté.'"

Eheu ! — diplomatically and politically we had lost the war before the first shot.

Once, in every veterinary school, it was the fashion to hang up on the wall an anatomical chart of the horse, with above, the inscription "Equine Diseases." The chart set forth a list of all the ills to which that noble animal's flesh is heir — from spavin to foot-and-mouth disease. This method might be used with effect, for the benefit of our future diplomats, in the School for Higher Political Studies, recently opened. A special class might even be organized to study the mistakes of German statesmanship in July and August, 1914. Bethmann and Jagow should be our classic examples of how it ought never to be done. Study them, young men, and be warned ! In that fatal summer they proved themselves wrong on every point — wrong in supposing the Sarajevo murder such effective propaganda for Austria as would win her the sympathies of the world. In Russia, as I pointed out to Bethmann, it was most unlikely that this murder would cause any great revulsion of feeling. Even in the West, its moral effects had soon been dissipated by the sudden, arbitrary, and brutal Austrian demands. The men responsible for our foreign policy were equally wrong in their assumption that they could surprise and dupe Italy and Roumania, since these Powers, with France and Russia behind them, basing their attitude on the text of the Triple Alliance, could refuse to be circumvented or intimidated. Above all, Bethmann and Jagow were wrong about England. To every one — to William II, the Federal Council, the Austro-Hungarian Ambassador, to all our representatives abroad, Bethmann kept repeating his assurances that England would most certainly remain neutral, in any case in the first stage of the war. Illusion — pure illusion. As I have said, the very worst of all the errors of those four or five individuals who led their country to disaster was that of having taken such grave decisions in an hermetically sealed room in the Foreign Office, without once consulting a diplomat of experience, or any intelligent business man informed on international economics. Albert Ballin, Arthur Gwinner, Emil Rathenau, Max Warburg, Karl Fürstenberg, Paul von Schwabach, might all have been asked. In the second year of war Albert

Ballin said to me with a sigh : "Had I known the intentions of Beth-mann-Hollweg and Jagow in the summer of 1914 — had I even been given the barest hint of the terms of the proposed ultimatum to Serbia, I could at least have taken an off chance and got food supplies into Germany in time." The stupidity with which our committee — of public catastrophe, not safety — handled the crisis provoked by the ultimatum is inconceivable. At first every English suggestion of mediation was sabotaged, rejected, dawdled over.

And yet, I repeat, our leaders were not working for war. They were acting on the mad assumption that they could succeed in letting Austria "punish" Serbia, without risk of international complications. Their dream not only brought to a head the danger of that European conflict so desired by Poincaré and Delcassé, by Paléologue and Jules Cambon, by English jingoes, Montenegrin princesses, and the Grand Duke Nicholas of Russia — they exposed every German citizen to the utterly unmerited reproach of having willed, and deliberately provoked, the World War. While Germans fought in the persuasion that we were the victims of a sudden, sly aggression, the whole world saw in us the people that had thrown down the Serbian ultimatum, like a torch into a keg of high explosive; the nation which by infringing Belgian neutrality, did unheard-of violence to international law, to treaties we ourselves had sworn to maintain. We could find no striking, convincing formula to enlist the sympathies of the world. Our own unlucky diplomacy gave our enemies two arguments of unfailing appeal against us — big Austria had done violence to little Serbia; Germany had invaded Belgian territory in defiance of the promise she had made. And our wretched propaganda did the rest. We denied having known the precise terms of the ultimatum, although we ourselves were forced to admit that Count Berchtold, the Austro-Hungarian Foreign Minister, had handed its text to our own ambassador, Tschirschky, on the morning of July 21st. Tschirschky could never have doubted the grave implications of such a document. Had he sent it straight off to Berlin it should have been on the Chancellor's table, on the table of the Secretary of State, by the morning of July 22d.

We had therefore a full eighteen hours in which to have held up the ultimatum, since it was handed in, in Belgrade, on the 23d, at six P.M.

Here two further points are worth considering: first, that already, in actual fact, our Foreign Office knew its general tenor. This is proved, both by the well-known report of Councillor of Legation, Von Schön, the Bavarian *chargé d'affaires* in Berlin, and the no less celebrated declaration, made at the same time, in Munich, by the President of the Bavarian Council, Hertling, to M. Allizé, the French Minister there.

Secondly, the question arises: which was the more egregious blunder? Our permission, knowing the contents of the note, to Austria, to deliver it as it stood, or the *carte blanche* we gave the Vienna Cabinet for punitive measures against the Serbs? The wise Ballin has often told me that, to him at least, this last seemed our very worst stupidity. Had he, Ballin would say, found himself forced to let his partner go to Monte Carlo, for the purpose of risking their joint capital, on red or black, *pair* or *impair*, he would, at any rate, have insisted on going with him and standing at his side when he placed the stakes. But to send him off alone to Monte Carlo, with full permission to play as he liked there!! I too can only say over again that I consider this, of all, the least excusable — that Bethmann and Jagow, with plenty of time at their disposal to study the ultimatum from A to Z, should not, at least, have informed Vienna, categorically, that in no case must she break off relations and proceed to consequent military action, until we had examined Serbia's answer.

Yet that is just the opposite of what happened. The more critical grew the situation, the more blindly did Jagow and Bethmann, Stumm, and Von Bergen, in reverent awe of Count Berchtold, give way to the Ballplatz. This feeling in Jagow I have defined — the snobbish predilection of country squires for the "venerable and holy" Austrian Monarchy. The others of the Berlin group were what aristocratic pride describes as *"roturiers."* Count Leopold Berchtold could impress them: a "real aristocrat", a Knight of the Golden Fleece who owned a racing stable; a host whose shooting was so famous that he himself remarked of his career as a Minister that only two moments of it would really have satisfied him; the one when his peers came to congratulate him as the successor of Prince Clemens Metternich and Prince Felix Schwarzenberg; the other (still to be enjoyed) when he could hand in his resignation and devote himself entirely to racing.

Such a fool as this could so hypnotize Bethmann and his colleagues that they grew as wax within his hands. He dragged them into this terrible war, not because they themselves had ever wanted it, but because they were incapable of resistance.

Once only during the crisis did Bethmann-Hollweg summon up strength to make a somewhat forceful objection. This was on July 29th, when he demanded, in the following terms, of Austria, her resumption of direct *pourparlers*, already broken off, with St. Petersburg: "Most assuredly we are ready to stand by our treaty obligations but must refuse to let ourselves be drawn, without further reflection, by Vienna, into any general conflagration, because she has ignored our advice."

But Bethmann, Jagow, and unluckily the Emperor along with them had, from the first, given Austria a free hand, nay, encouraged her to pursue her action. This warning came ten days too late to be effective. It appears that, with the ultimatum to Serbia, Bethmann had some notion of repeating the tactics I had employed in the Bosnian crisis, some six years previously. As Bismarck said, there is no more doubtful method of foreign policy than "to make a copy" of any precedent. Circumstances, people, states of mind, the whole trend of ideas have changed with each situation. A chief of police, arranging to police a district on market day, may work from precedents; not a diplomat. Statesmen should have their own ideas. Already Kider'en had blundered in sending the *Panther* to Agadir, in an effort to copy the policy by which, thanks to the special circumstance that the Emperor happened to be at Tangier, I had managed to silence Delcassé for many years, at a time when he was Germany's worst enemy, the most dangerous troubler of the peace. Tangier succeeded. Agadir failed. Agadir was a set piece refusing to work, a rocket which, instead of mounting skywards, shoots out among the legs of the watching crowd.   But if Kiderlen's "*Panther* leap" finished lamely, Bethmann, with his ultimatum policy, so reminiscent of my handling of the Bosnian crisis, was more at fault even than Kiderlen.   Bethmann had the feeling that he too would enjoy a little diplomatic triumph.   But, as Sasonow had written so justly to the Russian Ambassador in Rome, the 1914 situation was in no way like that of 1908.   Russia, in 1908, had found herself hampered by a whole series of notes and conventions, in particular by the letter in which Isvolski, her own Foreign Minister, had extended a patent "invitation" to Austria.   In 1908 I had Austria well in hand : I had made quite certain that Vienna would not overstep the limits imposed on her.   Nor did I once lose contact with Russia or Italy.   As the French say : *Je jouais sur le velours.*

In 1914, on the other hand, Bethmann had nothing in reserve but the general indignation excited by the murder of the Archduke. This petered out as soon as the real motives of Berchtold and Von Hötzendorf were revealed — as soon as a general war began to seem probable.   *Si duo faciunt idem, non est idem.*   This, above all, is true of diplomacy, in which there can be only fluid elements.   I know many people are of the opinion that, had we avoided war in 1914, in '15, or in '16, we should have had it.   "The Great War was bound to come."   It was a kind of inevitable fate.   This seems to me an entirely false supposition.   I am no fatalist.   I think as Napoleon thought, in answering a defeated general, who had made "fatality" his excuse.   "*La fatalité — excuse des incapables et des maladroits!*"   With skill and clarity of vision, peace could have been kept in 1914, as we had managed to keep it in 1888, in 1905, in 1909. Nor had the German Empire, in any case, the slightest need of Austrian leading strings ; no need to go in the wake of those blind pilots who guided us, under the worst of all conditions, into the hurricane of the worst of all wars.

I had taken so great a share in naval construction that now it was not unnatural if I asked myself how the fleet would serve us in the World War.   Full of the highest hopes, I watched our navy.   And my confidence seemed amply justified.   We had excellent seamen,

HEINRICH LEONHARD VON TSCHIRSCHKY UND
BÖGENDORFF
German Ambassador at Vienna

our naval officers seemed keen and very intelligent. Admiral von Tirpitz, who commanded them, had inspired in me nothing but respect. I honoured this exceptional personality, with all his gifts of organization, his energy. And yet I had never rid myself of the feeling, since first we began to develop our fleet methodically — not, that is to say, since the days when Tirpitz had been State Secretary for the Naval Office, and I for Foreign Affairs — that the Admiral was attaching too much importance to the construction of the larger types of battleship. I would rather have seen him follow some advice given him by the aged Bismarck, who had suggested that he build light cruisers. Later, when these arms were invented, I had felt that he was neglecting the submarine and should pay more attention to aircraft. Although I am, in all such matters, a layman, without the least desire to instruct my betters, I still could never suppress the instinctive warning that, by building so many huge battleships, we could only irritate England more and more, with no hope of ever really surpassing her. To me, a mere looker-on, the submarine — the U-boat — seemed as the sling with which, if he is bold and lucky, little David may hope to slay Goliath. And after the War the English Admiral, Scott, wrote the following: "If, in 1914, the Emperor William had accepted some suggestions made to him for a submarine blockade of England, such a blockade could have brought the speediest disaster on us."

When, in December, 1914, Admiral Ingenohl wished to engage a British naval squadron in exceptionally favourable circumstances, the Emperor ordered him back to Wilhelmshaven. Admiral Scheer, the future victor of Skagerrak, observed: "We got the impression of having missed a first-rate chance, which probably would never be repeated." Tirpitz went so far as to add: "On December 16th, Ingenohl had in his hands the fate of Germany." Why did our fleet not engage at the right minute? Officers of the General Staff have told me that Moltke and Schlieffen had always attached supreme importance to the German and naval offensive. Tirpitz, who thought as they did, longed for a quick decision at sea, which he felt had every chance of success. He wished to know that the weapon he had forged was a good one. But the Emperor, the Chancellor, the languid Foreign Office, hesitating and timorous, thought otherwise. Never, since we began to build our fleet, had William II seriously considered that he might have to use it in a war. He had only felt that a strong German navy was our safest rampart against peace-breakers — that the fleet could also, now and then, be the pretext for magnificent manœuvres.

And that was all! His Majesty knew every battleship. On each he had his own luxurious staterooms, fitted out with special toilet apparatus by his faithful old body servant, Schulz. On the walls of each were portraits of his nearest and dearest. His heart sank at the thought of having to sacrifice even one of these toys that had meant so much to him. His feelings were those of the owner of a brilliant racing stud, expected to set his thoroughbreds to draw hay carts, at the risk of losing them all. William II wanted "to spare" the fleet. Bethmann-Hollweg did not want "to excite" the English. So that between them there arose a pact that the navy should be held in reserve, for use as our trump card at the peace conference. The end of it all was Scapa Flow.

I have said that the retrospective criticisms incurred by General Moltke would seem justified, even to those who themselves have never worn the crimson tabs of the staff officer. The General is most to be reproached with having let his reins become entangled, with not having kept a grip on his command; with having shifted his quarters to Luxemburg, from Coblenz, though either was too far removed from the right wing of our army — the strategic rôle of which was all-decisive. Moltke should have seen that he kept in constant liaison with the most important headquarters on this wing. Each separate army covered itself with glory, but there never was a central direction, and the actions were not properly concerted. At a time when, on the whole French Front, the position was becoming critical, Moltke should himself have visited the three commands of his right wing, collected his information on the spot, and made sure of our strategic unity. Instead, at the moment of decision (September 8th) he sent Lieutenant Colonel Hentsch to inspect it, leaving him free to take his own decisions, and even, in his last verbal instruction to him, mentioning "possible retirement", and adding some indications for a retreat. Hentsch, of all the officers on his staff, was the one most given to doubts and hesitations and had therefore gained the sympathy of his chief. When this officer — in his hands the fate of the battle, of the campaign, the army, the country — heard an unfavourable view of our position from the Headquarters Staff of the Second Army, he suggested to its commander, Field Marshal von Bülow, a retreat in the northeasterly direction. He went on, immediately after this, to the Chief of the First Army, General von Kluck, whom he also advised to retire. Both French and English felt so far from victory that they did not even harry our retreat. Only later, with their usual bragging effrontery, did the French manufacture "The Miracle of the Marne" which, so they boasted, had prevented them, and with them the civilized world, from becoming the prey of ravening Teutons.

And indeed, to the French, this retreat may well have seemed a miracle. They had seen (on September 2d), just forty-four years after Sedan, their government fly from Paris to Bordeaux. What had made the Germans turn back? The real, the disconcerting miracle was that any successor of Schlieffen and the first Moltke should have shown himself so far below his predecessors. The general had succumbed under the weight of his own responsibility. His weak hands had let go of the reins — and that at an all-decisive moment! The secondary commands and the army had won a victory for the High Command to throw away.

It is declared that Moltke, hoped, by a fresh offensive, to regain, a few days later, the advantage he had lost by retreating our right wing — that he meant to resume his advance with the help of the third, fourth, and fifth armies. But, by September 10th he had begun to relinquish this idea, and, on the 11th it seemed to him impossible even to keep these armies in position. Later, in tears, Moltke assured me that his health was then already so impaired that the agony of these days was "indescribable." The Emperor, not knowing what to make of this chief, who was at the same time his close friend, went, as usual, from one extreme to the other. He abruptly relieved Moltke of his command, to confer it on his War Minister, General von Falkenhayn. Provisionally this had to be kept secret, so as not to alarm the country. That is why Moltke, now a puppet, was still, for the look of the thing, obliged to be present every day at discussions of strategy at which nobody asked his advice or paid him any attention whatsoever. He was forced to sit without a word at the side of his former rival, now his successor. Later he told me that: "Dante's Hell cannot contain in it such torments as I was forced to undergo at that time."

But, for the moment, the country had forgotten the ruin of our highest hope and mightiest effort in the west, since Germany still rang with the news of the Battle of Tannenberg. That little town, where our people, five centuries before, had suffered the worst defeat in its history, was now the scene of one of the greatest victories of all time. The "Cannae idea" which, in the west, Moltke had in vain attempted to realize, had been carried through with all the daring, the amazing certainty, of genius. Ninety thousand Russians had been made prisoners; more still were dead, some drowned in the Masurian lakes. When the fogs upon those lakes had lifted, our people beheld a new hero, General von Hindenburg! This conqueror is one of our greatest soldiers: German to the marrow of his bones; German in physique, with his broad shoulders, his firm, resolute step, his wide, kind eyes, his perfect poise and naturalness of manner, the whole simple dignity of the man. Severe, where there is need of severity, but always kindly, always human, never personal, never vain or pettifogging, a supremely great example of moral force, that most salient trait of his own personality — Field Marshal von Hindenburg incarnates all that is good and fine in the German nature, in the German people as a whole, but especially in our Prussian army, and towers, a hero, in our history. All the greatness of the man was revealed in his dealings with his Chief of Staff, General Ludendorff. The utter freedom from jealousy and vainglory with which Hindenburg not merely supported, but continually encouraged this gifted, but often moody and not always conciliatory, brother officer, recalls Blücher's attitude to Gneisenau. All four have their lasting place in our Pantheon.

The failure of the Marne retreat had made a change in the High Command inevitable. Von Falkenhayn, the War Minister,

replaced Moltke.   Erich von Falkenhayn was what Goethe, and
after him Spielhagen, have described as an "enigmatic nature."
The type is not rare in other armies — the French, the Russian, the
Spanish, even the Austrian.   But we in Prussia have seldom bred it,
or not, at least, to form our greatest leaders.   This descendant of an
old Pomeranian family of nobles, endowed with all the virtues of
military squires; dashing, energetic, fearless, without hesitations or
anxiety in him, with the physical aspect of a war god, Falkenhayn,
while still a young officer, had been forced by debt to leave the
service.   He had gone to China, where he vegetated, on a very small
income indeed, as the military instructor of Chinese troops.   But
this had shown him the world.   Field Marshal Waldersee, struck
with his manliness and intelligence, had brought him back to Germany and the army, in which, once he had set foot on the ladder, his
new career was astonishingly rapid and brilliant.   He had been
General Moltke's protégé, so that the latter nourished in his bosom,
if not a serpent, a supplanter.

Falkenhayn, by his failings as by his virtues, was just the man to
find favour with the Emperor.   Moltke, already physically broken,
and inclined to mysticism and theosophy, had begun to depress the
All Highest, from the moment when our fortune seemed to turn.
The dashing Falkenhayn, on the other hand, full of *entrain*, and
never at a loss in any difficulty, acted on His Majesty like a tonic.
In him one could be sure of a vigorous chief, who would grip responsi-
bilities with both hands.   Of his military achievement I can say
nothing.   Was Verdun a mistake?   Ypres a blunder?   These battles cost us rivers of blood and neither brought decisive success.
It seems to me incontestable that Falkenhayn had not, like Hindenburg, the gift of forgetting all but the inspiration of whatever circumstance confronted him.   Lacking, perhaps, the other's moral
greatness, he is, in my opinion, much to be blamed for having, more
than once, responded half-heartedly, with a kind of sloth, if not with
actual envy, to demands from the Eastern Front for reinforcements.
On the other hand, it is only just to admit that Falkenhayn was more
aware than Ludendorff of the many dangerous inner workings of
politics and their bearing on the position as a whole.   Nor will our

people ever have the right to forget those heroes who held out at Verdun, in a hell of never-ending shell fire. Germans will ever recall the ardent pride with which, at Ypres and on the Yser, young regiments — students, most of them, even schoolboys — went to their deaths, singing "Die Wacht am Rhein" and "Deutschland über Alles." Always must we remember those young bodies, hiding an earth soaked in their blood. What German can think without a pang of that section of the Belgian coast? A quarter of a century before my wife and I had little thought, when we spent those delightful weeks at Nieuport, that one day the flower of German youth would be mown down upon this soil.

Among the many other grave mistakes made by our leaders in the summer of 1914 must be reckoned their whole policy in Italy. Here one may examine in detail every weakness, rashness, inconsequence — that singular mixture of perfidy and stupidity which then made our diplomacy what it was; mistakes that sent our quiet and peaceable Germans to the holocaust of a war which their rulers proceeded to make them lose.

The secret archives published by the Bolsheviks show that, at the end of the May of 1914, when the Russian naval cabinet were discussing the terms of an Anglo-Russian naval convention, the Russians had requested the English to put at their disposal some naval bases and so guard against an Austro-Italian attack in the Black Sea. At that time both the Russians and the English still felt that, if ever there were war, Italy would be sure to support the Central Powers. Then came the ultimatum and the crisis. What attitude did the Italian Foreign Minister, the Marchese San Giuliano, adopt? His own ambition had always pointed to an extension of Italy's power on the Mediterranean, more especially on the northeast coast of Africa. Now, on July 14, 1914, in a talk with our Roman Ambassador, Flotow, San Giuliano announced that Italy could never bring herself to reinforce these exorbitant Austro-Hungarian demands on Serbia. Three days later, again to Flotow, he repeated this, adding that Italy could approve no Austrian annexations of Serbian territory. Herr von Merey, the Austrian Ambassador in Rome, should have taken these statements as his warning and perceived that they wcre really addressed to Vicnna. On the contrary — he advised Count Berchtold to "surprise" the Italian Government, by a sudden descent on Serbia. By what I can only term fatality neither Germany nor Austria-Hungary was well represented in Rome, in 1914. Herr von Merey, with his insufferable manner and thinly veiled dislike of the new Italy, his continual pinpricks and chicane, was most unpopular with Italians. With San Giuliano, a man of the world and quite approachable, his personal relations were so strained that the two had almost ceased to meet unofficially. The Italian Foreign Minister often asked himself if it would not be as well to avoid all drawing-rooms in which he might see this emissary of the Habsburgs. Flotow, our own representative, was too timid to be aggressive and give offence. But, on the other hand, neither politically nor socially had he managed to build up a position. His wife, a pure-bred Russian, who spoke little German, had embellished her *salon* with a bust — a very lifelike bust — of Ivan the Tcrrible. Honcst German callers often mistook it for the portrait of Alaric, Theodoric, or some other primitive hero of Germanic descents on Rome.

Socially Flotow was eccentric and politically his influence was nil. To these drawbacks he added imaginary ill health, which would set him in a fever to leave Rome the instant the summer heats had really set in there. Barrère, Sir Rennell Rodd, Krupenski — all the representatives of the Allies — had naturally considered it their duty to remain on in Rome during the crisis. Not so Flotow, whose delicate health obliged him to take refuge in Fiuggi, a summer spa, a certain distance from the capital. He excused this desertion of his post to Jagow, his closest friend, and to the Chancellor, by saying that, if only he went to Fiuggi, he would have more chance of speaking to San Giuliano.

But in this he was quite mistaken. San Giuliano, a really sick, even a dying man, spent his nights in Fiuggi by doctor's orders. He remained there through the coolest hours, from nine P.M. till seven the next morning, and refused to let any one disturb him. Each evening Flotow made the same attempt to get himself asked to sit at the corner table, reserved, in the *sala da pranzo*, for the Minister.

Always, to the amusement of other visitors, he would find himself choked off by San Giuliano, who contended that, since all day long, in Rome, he had been at the disposal of diplomats, in Fiuggi he must insist on having peace.

Whereas Flotow could not manage to be well enough to attend even San Giuliano's funeral (who died at the beginning of October) Camille Barrère, our most dangerous adversary, had never been an hour out of Rome, but was paying official calls the whole day long, on senators, deputies, journalists, and ministers. Barrère, through it all, was in great pain, as the result of a recent motoring accident. It did not prevent his being seen at the funeral. Though at the requiem he fainted, he did his duty.

Very soon it had become fairly obvious that Italy would not join the Central Powers unless Austria cared to offer her compensations. I still think that, had these been guaranteed, we could have managed, in that summer of 1914, to have the Italians on our side. Our military prestige was very great and remained so till the Marne retreat. Many influential Italians were pro-German. If only Austria had, at the right moment, shown willingness to cede her the Trentino and admit the autonomy of Trieste — had we Germans aroused her hopes of Nice and Tunis — Italy would have been our ally. The organ in which Sidney Sonnino, who later induced his country to join the Allies, then published his daily propaganda, still violently exhorted Italians to guarantee the future of their country by linking up her strength to Germany. The Florentine, Sonnino, may have remembered some advice of his great fellow citizen always to be on the stronger side, since there glory, honour, riches, and all good things of earth are to be found. And, for the moment, we certainly looked stronger. Bethmann did, it is true, make feeble efforts with Count Berchtold to show Rome a more conciliatory spirit. The count snubbed such suggestions very haughtily, although, thanks to our possible aid in Serbia, we had then a first-rate diplomatic weapon and could easily have brought pressure to bear on him. And Berchtold instructed his own Ambassador in Rome to give "only superficial information" there, of the demands to be presented in Belgrade, not troubling to go into them in detail.

MARCHESE ANTONIO DI SAN GIULIANO
Italian Minister for Foreign Affairs

Merey carried out these instructions in gruff, almost insolent fashion. The Italian Prime Minister and Foreign Minister countered by expressing their disapproval of Austria's action against the Serbs and reserving their freedom of decision. This answer had in it all the germs of Italy's declaration of neutrality, and that of war on Austria which ensued. Yet, through all this, the Berlin Government, preening itself on its diplomatic finesse, left Italy free to decide her course with Austria, at a time when it was fully in our power to give Austria orders as to the method of putting into effect her Serbian plans. In the meantime, De Martino, the General Secretary of the Italian Foreign Ministry, had told Barrère that, had she known beforehand of its contents, Italy would never have approved the note to Serbia, and declared, almost immediately, to Merey, that his country felt in no way bound to Austria, who had not informed Italy in advance of her project of Serbian invasion.

Even this did not open Merey's eyes. He advised his government to reject, *a priori*, any Italian suggestion for compensation. Bethmann, at the instigation of Moltke, who, for military reasons alone, was very anxious to see Austria-Hungary achieve close understanding with Italy, managed again to find the courage to send Vienna a wire (July 26th), but made no further protest when Count Berchtold frigidly rejected all such suggestions. Jagow, our own State Secretary, more pro-Austrian even than his Chancellor, told Count Szögyényi, the Austrian Ambassador in Berlin, that he considered Count Berchtold perfectly right not to let himself be bluffed by Italian demands.

On July 29th San Giuliano informed both the German and Austrian ambassadors that, if Austria could not decide forthwith to promise Italy compensations, her whole anti-Serbian move must be considered so prejudicial to Italy's interests that his Government would find it quite impossible to give Vienna her support. The Marchese, with frigid detachment, a *desinvoltura* which Macchiavelli might have envied, added that his country's interests must be considered the sole motive by which Italy governed her policy. But that, after all, was what Berlin, and especially Vienna, might have expected. In the Franco-Prussian War it had been the same, when

Italy left the French in the lurch, without one thought of her previous obligations to France, merely because her interests made it advisable to crown the *Italia unita* by taking possession of Rome. The highly intelligent Marchese Visconti-Venosta had a saying: "*Pour un diplomate, il est fort important de savoir retirer à temps son épingle du jeu.*" Bismarck too would declare that it is a Prime Minister's duty to evade, with all the suavity he can muster, the obligations of any alliance no longer in the interests of the State. On this same July 29th Mr. Tyrrell, Grey's private secretary, was warning Prince Lichnowsky in London that, should Austria's conflict with Serbia be extended, Italy would abandon the Triple Alliance. Twenty-four hours later Merey, from Rome — Berchtold having asked him his opinion — strongly advised his chief in Vienna to admit no Italian aspirations or other suggestions for compensation. William II wired to Rome and Vienna, appealing to King Victor Emanuel's loyalty to the Triple Alliance, on the one hand, and, on the other, imploring the old Emperor Francis Joseph to give some consideration to Italy's wishes. Neither of these efforts was successful. For twenty-six years William II had made, in one direction, then in another, too many personal gestures to be effective. This Imperial telegram left San Giuliano quite unmoved. To Flotow he announced that, in the present instance, Italy could not admit herself bound, since Austria's move on Serbia was aggressive, and so an infringement of the spirit in which the Triple Alliance had been conceived — not to mention the harm to Italian interests involved by it. The Marchese also hinted that Roumania considered Vienna's action prejudicial.

On August 3d King Victor Emanuel wired his definite answer to the Kaiser. His Government had decided that Italy had no *casus foederis*. Simultaneously in Berlin, the Italian Ambassador handed in Italy's declaration of neutrality. A note to the same effect was delivered in Vienna, where Count Berchtold, fuming with rage, remarked to the Duke d'Avarna, who presented it, that Italy's policy was "a rash one", and one she might regret "very bitterly." Alas! — the event proved otherwise.

Now that we had declared war on Russia, Vienna, certain at last that the "Pomeranian grenadier" would have to leave his bones on the field, was more than ever determined to hear nothing on the subject of Italian aspirations. Count Berchtold instructed his Berlin Ambassador to inform the German Government categorically that never would he consent to negotiate compensations with Italy; Italian neutrality was enough. The brusque tone in which this declaration was made is, in part, explained by one of Merey's dispatches, where he informs his chief that San Giuliano had expressly mentioned parts of the Tyrol in which Italian is still spoken — the ancient territory of the Prince-Bishops of Trent.

The Germans fought with more than resolution — we fought in the assurance of victory. Our Prussian history holds proud memories: the Seven Years' War, when the great Frederick kept three Powers at bay with his little State: Prussia, diminished and exhausted by Tilsit and Jena, rising with a mighty effort to shake off the tyranny of Napoleon: the three great victories of Bismarck. All these, to the majority of Germans, made any prolonged series of setbacks, much more defeat, seem out of the question. In spite of the retreat from the Marne, the hecatombs of the Yser and Verdun, the nation's mood was one of defiant resolution. A poem by Rudolf Alexander Schröder gave fine expression to these emotions. Here are its opening cantos:

> *Wir reiten von Wäldern und Schluchten verborgen,*
> *Wir traben hinein in den dämmerenden Morgen,*
>   *Deutschland! Deutschland!*
> *Es wiehert und stampfet der Scheck und der Schimmel,*
> *Es klappert und trappelt der Hufe Gewimmel,*
> *Rot leuchtet der Himmel.*
> *Und deutet die blutige Röte Verderben,*
> *Für dich will ich leben, für dich will ich sterben,*
>   *Deutschland! Deutschland!*
>
> *Und wenn sie mit Eisen und Stahl dich umklammern,*
> *Wir schlagen die Bresche, wir brechen die Klammern,*
>   *Deutschland! Deutschland!*
> *Wir kommen wie Geier vom Felsen gestossen,*
> *Wir kommen wie Wasser vom Berge geschossen,*

Wie Hagel und Schlossen.
Da klirren der Stahl und das Eisen in Scherben;
Für dich will ich leben, für dich will ich sterben,
  Deutschland! Deutschland! [1]

[1] We ride hidden by woods and gullies,
  We canter on through the morning twilight,
    Germany! Germany!
  The grey and the dapple whinny and neigh,
  The swarm of hoofs clatters,
  The sky gleams red.
  Should this red mean my undoing
  I will die for you — live for you,
    Germany! Germany!

  Though they clamp you round with bands of iron and steel
  We will cleave a breach, we will burst your bonds,
    Germany! Germany!
  We come like vultures driven from their rocks,
  We come like drops, shot forth by a mountain torrent —
  Like a hailstorm.
  Steel and iron shall lie shattered beneath your strength;
  For you I will live — will die.
    Germany! Germany!

CHAPTER XV

My Roman Mission, 1914–1915 — A Letter from Bethmann and My Answer — I Go to Rome in the Middle of December, 1915 — Jagow and Flotow versus Bülow — A Letter from Ballin — Friendly Messages.

NOTWITHSTANDING the patriotic attitude of the very great majority of the German people and the valour and success of our armies, no calm and well-informed observer could help seeing the almost overwhelming difficulties of the task with which we were confronted. These were the result of diplomatic mistakes at the outset. England, on whose neutrality Bethmann had counted with so much certainty, was against us. The forces which she threw into the struggle were far greater than poor Moltke had supposed, who, hearing of England's declaration of war, had said phlegmatically that he preferred it. It was far better, he added, that the English should not remain doubtfully neutral, for the time being. Now that they had come out as our open enemies he would have no difficulty in beating them. Any one with eyes to see grew more and more convinced that Italy and Roumania, who had shirked their duty as our allies, might well end by becoming our enemies. In several quarters it was hoped that the Government might send me to Rome, there to make a last effort to keep Italy from declaring war on our Austrian ally. Every party in the Reichstag wished this to be done, from the Conservatives to the Socialists. But Jagow and Bethmann did their best to prevent my being sent to Rome, though they showed little open opposition. One of the Conservative party leaders, Count Schwerin-Löwitz, who had advised him to send me to Rome as soon as possible, was answered, by a seemingly astonished Jagow: "But it was just because of the Conservatives that I did n't want to send Prince Bülow to Rome. I imagined that after his quarrel with your party such a mission might seem a slight to the Conservatives." Schwerin-Löwitz, a man of honour and a patriot, answered that he much regretted my breach with the Conservative Party; that he, like many other Conservatives, could never feel me solely responsible for it; that, in any case, Conservatives were far too patriotically minded to let mere party rancour be their guide in the gravest questions of foreign policy — that they all were eager to see the Government send me to Rome.

Jagow could find no answer. Nor did any subsequent attempts to excite the Emperor against me meet with success, and so prevent my mission to Italy. Bethmann, on all sides harried by generals and deputies, decided, after many hesitations, to write to me, on November 30, 1914, at Hamburg, where I lived in the Hotel Atlantic:

When, soon after war had been declared, we discussed Italy, you told me that you would not object, in principle, to being sent to Rome to use your influence there, if ever I were to consider it advisable to charge you with a special mission. The necessity for this has just arisen. Our ambassador, whose health, as you know, is much impaired, has undergone great strain and emotion throughout the summer. He has written, as his duty dictated, informing me that his doctors urge him emphatically to leave Rome, and rest for at least some months. Although up to now Herr von Flotow has admirably defended our Italian interests, I am aware that all his zeal and talents will be of no avail if his health gives way. Since at the moment Rome is so important I can only consider for our embassy there some exceptionally well-qualified person. Need I add, my dear prince, that you, with all your intimate knowledge of Roman life, your position in Roman society, and many close relationships in Rome, seem eminently suitable for the post. Since therefore I have been told in many quarters that, from motives of patriotic devotion, you would still be willing to accept a mission to Italy, may I beg you, with the full consent of His Majesty, to go to Rome as ambassador extraordinary, there to direct our embassy for the time being? I hope that, in spite of all the fatigues such a mission will of necessity entail, all the personal sacrifice which you and the princess must make in accepting it will be, at this season, somewhat alleviated by the thought that you would both, in any case, be returning, just now, in normal times, to Rome. I am certain that whatever can be obtained you will manage to secure for us in Italy. May I beg you, my dear prince, to let me know your answer by telegram?

Should you accept I shall be most grateful if you can manage to be in Berlin for the few days which I myself am able to spend there, in order that we may talk this matter over. Since my time for the next few days will be almost entirely taken up by the Reichstag, you will, I am sure, excuse my not giving you a definite appointment at once. For the present I have one point to suggest to you. It has already begun to be rumoured that the War might be decided by a conference. You, I am sure, will agree that such a proceeding could never be to our advantage — or that of our Austrian ally. Should you find this suggestion current in Rome, I know you will have no difficulty in opposing it. But this, too, is one of the subjects I should like to talk over with you personally. In the hope that my request has not been in vain, and that this may find you ready as ever to do your country very great service, at a time of such exceptional gravity, may I assure Your Highness of my esteem, and ask you to believe me

Your ever devoted

VON BETHMANN-HOLLWEG.

I glanced with somewhat mixed sensations through these insincere and very involved sentences. It was easy enough to read between the lines. The Chancellor did not want to send me to Rome. His preoccupation was to spare his ambassador, Flotow, Jagow's bosom friend, whom he too esteemed so highly. If such was to be the feeling in Berlin, I could see that my task in Rome would be no easy one. Nevertheless, I did not hesitate to place myself at the Government's disposal, or, as King Ludwig III of Bavaria put it to Count Hertling, not merely myself, but my reputation. I felt at first that, while accepting this mission, it would be as well to impress it on Bethmann, in a letter, that I knew the position in Rome to be a most delicate one, and my task correspondingly ungrateful.

I wrote the following draft :

It goes without saying that I am willing to take over the embassy in Rome. I attach no importance whatsoever to the fact that, twenty-one years ago, I happen to have been the ambassador there, or that, since then, I directed our whole foreign policy for twelve years, during nine of which I was Chancellor. I feel entirely without *amour propre* or any kind of vanity or ambition. All that I have been able to gather from the most reliable sources on the Italian position makes me less than ever inclined to hesitate. It seems that in the last two years we have lost much ground there. The choice of Flotow has proved unfortunate. I say this all the more frankly since both my wife and I have done our best to make things easy for him in Rome, and see that he was well received there. But really he does not seem to have been able to build any kind of position for himself, to acquire the necessary influence, and make friends. When war had been declared on Russia, he found himself most awkwardly placed with the German colony — and not less oddly with Italians and the rest of his diplomatic colleagues, since he had married a Russian lady, attached to her country by old ties, traditions, and personal memories of every kind; a lady who had property in Russia and whose son (the ambassador's stepson) is fighting in the Russian army against us. This and his poor state of health, real or imaginary, have certainly so impaired his powers of work that he has shown himself inadequate to his task. This was particularly the case in those critical weeks immediately before, and after, war broke out, at a moment when, as many competent people have since assured me, we might, with a little more energy and a rather more influential ambassador, have secured the coöperation of Italy. Since then we have done nothing but lose ground, as many of my friends have frankly said to me — friends with a thorough knowledge of the country. It seems that already negotiations are in progress, unless they have already reached their conclusion, between the Italian Government and England. On pretext that the Turkish advance towards Egypt is damaging her interests in Cyrenaica, etc., and in Tripoli, Italy may declare war on Turkey next spring, and so would automatically be against us. I am, however, not a pessimist. Though I have no illusions as to the fact that, beneath its somewhat deceptive surface appearance, the position in Italy is very far from stable or encouraging, that will be for me an added incentive to do whatever is in my power to regain the ground recently lost there. In this I count, of course, on your kind support.

Always your very devoted
Prince von Bülow.

I showed this letter, already signed, to Ballin. He begged me not to add the Italian situation to the already numerous terrors of Bethmann-Hollweg; if I sent it I should demoralize completely the irresolute and over-fearful chancellor. I therefore contented myself with the following wire: "Your letter received. Naturally

I am ready to abandon my present intention of remaining on in Germany through the War and will gladly go to Rome as ambassador extraordinary, if you think I can be of use there. I take it that the length of my stay will not depend on the convalescence of Herr von Flotow, but that this mission is arranged to last for the whole duration of the War. Delighted to come to Berlin to settle details, including scope and date of my appointment."

The letter to Bethmann given above I deposited with my lawyer in Hamburg, Herr Heinrich Meinecke, in whose safe it remained until I sent for it to dictate these memoirs. Bethmann and Jagow were most unwilling to give up their first intention of letting Flotow choose his own time for returning to the Roman Embassy. They would much have preferred to have him report in a few weeks that he was well enough to resume his duties, with all his accustomed zeal and efficiency. Since this was no longer possible, they gave him leave to stay on indefinitely in Italy and await events near sunny Naples, not far from the delightful Posilipo. From there, during my whole Roman mission, he wrote private letters to them both, in which he developed the theme that Italy had not the slightest intention of taking active part in the War; that Prince Bülow painted everything, *en noir*, in the hope of scoring easy victories. For as long as he still had it in his power, Jagow seconded and supported his dearest friend.

On the day I set out for Rome, the Empress happened to receive Jagow. Her first lady-in-waiting, my cousin, Therese Brockdorff, was present. Our good Empress said to Jagow that she hoped I should be able to keep Italy neutral. He answered her: "But, Your Majesty, that ought to be so easy! We have packed the Trentino in Prince von Bülow's trunk. Anybody, with such a trump as that, should, of course, prevent Italy's coming into the war." This was a lie. So far we had received no kind of definite promise from Austria on the subject of the Trentino. Jagow was, however, doing his uttermost to prevent Austria's replying too soon or too amiably to Italian suggestions for compensation. Even later he made the same attempts — and for as long as my mission to Rome continued — in verbal declarations to the Austrian Ambassador in

Berlin, and finally by sending to Vienna Count Monts, who disliked Italians, and me still more, since so often he had covered me
with his flattery in a very undignified fashion. No doubt Flotow,
on his side, had spoken according to instructions both from his
chancellor and Jagow, his dear friend, when he said, before leaving
for sunny Naples, to the Councillor of the Roman Embassy, Hindenburg, a generous and upright man of honour : "Bülow has managed
to intrigue his way back to the embassy. Both the Chancellor and
the Secretary of State have had, most unwillingly, to give way to this
ridiculous clamour of incompetent journalists and deputies. But
I may as well tell you, as a friend, that the Foreign Office is not overanxious to have Bülow succeed in Rome." Hindenburg, surprised
and disconcerted, replied that he had not understood ; that his duty,
both to the service and as a gentleman, was the whole-hearted support of his new chief. Whereat Flotow, with a smile : "My dear
Hindenburg, you don't seem to *want* to understand ! I know the
world, and I 'm telling you for your own good. *Surtout pas trop de
zèle* on Prince Bülow's behalf. It would do your career no good."

To Italians Flotow said that, in Berlin, I had boasted that I would
not merely keep Italy neutral, but could make her declare war on
France and England — a contingency not to be hoped for, from
the time of the Battle of the Marne, and one that no Italian ever
considered. The only question they still asked themselves at the
moment when the Government sent me to Rome, was whether to
keep Italy neutral, or take the offensive against Austria.

Before leaving Hamburg for Berlin, I wrote Ballin a confidential
letter, in which I expressed to him the opinion that, since they
wanted me in Rome, it would have been less undignified for the
Government to have sent me there in the first weeks of August,
before we had lost so much ground in Italy. It would, I said, have
been far better to have turned to me between the ultimatum and our
declaration of war on Russia. That would have been the time at
which to ask me if I thought we could get Italy on our side. It
would even have done no harm to have consulted me on the situation
as a whole. I could at once have suggested modifications in the
text of the ultimatum — without in the least imperilling our honour

by so doing — had we wished to avoid this horrible war. Even after the ultimatum had been delivered, I could still have suggested means for keeping the peace, without the loss of a jot of our prestige, or the prestige of Austria-Hungary; with even, perhaps, a diplomatic victory, like that of 1908–1909. I had written this letter to Ballin, not in hope of any personal advantage, but simply because I felt the need to unburden myself and so clear my mind of certain thoughts that for several weeks had been tormenting me.

Albert Ballin, though a natural optimist, had been, from the very outset, inclined to view the War pessimistically. He wrote me the following letter before I left Berlin for Rome:

I have seen the Emperor, whom I found full of confidence in the future, though also of wrath against England, and, in this, the Empress encourages him. So that personal rancours and dislikes seem to play a considerable part in policy, and that appears to me very dangerous. I consider that both the Emperor and the Chancellor take far too rosy a view of our military prospects. To my mind the forces are about evenly distributed. We have Belgium, the English have the North Sea, Russia has Galicia, the Japanese Kiaochow, etc. Things might have gone far better strategically had our High Command not made mistakes. All the same I feel it a notable piece of military success that our armies, apart from a few raids into East Prussia and Alsace, should have succeeded in keeping the war on enemy soil, and that we hold our own so well in a world of enemies. Then, too, these recent successes of Hindenburg open up a number of favourable perspectives. But I cannot see yet what kind of a peace we are going to have. Our only hope of real advantage would be the conclusion of separate treaties with our various enemies. The Russians should be the easiest to deal with and to detach from their *entente* with England. Perhaps an arrangement with them might cause France also to want peace, and would, in any case, give us our chance of freeing Hindenburg, and a proportion of his forces in the East, so as to make sure of victory on the Western Front. But no doubt all that is far too good to be true, and, for the moment, I simply cannot believe in it. The best thing we can do is to make up our minds to go on fighting.

I reached Berlin to find there an embarrassed Chancellor, obviously not at one with himself. I could see at once how little he relished my return to official life. He asked me, almost naïvely, if I intended to receive any deputies or journalists before my departure for Rome, advising me "as your old and devoted friend" — this was his actual phrase — not to do so. I should, he added, risk reviving the irritation which His Majesty still, "most unluckily" felt against me — an emotion which had caused him, the Chancellor, not to wish my mission in Rome to be a permanent one, but merely the temporary replacement of Flotow, our Ambassador, absent on sick leave. These Imperial emotions, on which he dwelt, Bethmann was doing his best to keep alive; nor, as will be seen from the following telegram, just received by me, at Hamburg, from the Emperor, were they really so intense as he seemed to imagine: "I shall be most happy to see Your Excellency go to Rome as soon as possible, there to use your great personal influence on our behalf. Many kind regards to Princess Bülow."

But, on the other hand, Bethmann anxiously strove to convince me that I could count on his loyalty and support.

I found little Jagow full of spleen. Quite recently he had said to Prince Wedel, who had been urging him to have me sent to Rome, that nobody had any right to demand of him that he should give such pain to Flotow, his best friend. To me he remarked that he supposed I could not feel very enthusiastic at the task awaiting me in Rome: that nobody could do better there than Flotow, as even the *Corriere della Sera* had admitted, in a recent article, regretting his departure from the embassy. I answered that, of all Italian newspapers, the *Corriere* was most anti-German. Jagow had nothing more to say, but his face looked almost comic.

On every side I learned that the Foreign Office, and with it Bethmann, had done their best to prevent my being sent to Rome. Thus, at the beginning of November, Herr Eugen Zimmermann, of the staff of the Berlin *Lokalanzeiger*, had written: "The press bureau of the Foreign Office have announced, in reply to a question addressed to them by the Scherl publishing house, that Your Highness had refused to take over our Roman Embassy, and that perhaps, during the War, it would be as well to make no changes in Rome. From another quarter I hear that Jagow, in agreement with the Imperial Chancellor, refuses 'to raise his little finger' to have

Your Highness sent to Rome officially, and that the Chancellor has influenced His Majesty in that sense. It seems to me evident that the Government are afraid to put up more capable men than those who, for the moment, direct our policy. This is human enough, but, at present, it is very disturbing. We ought, without loss of time, to put every available statesman in the post in which he can be most useful. We shall never win the War unless we do."

At about the same time another journalist, Herbert von Berger, an extreme Conservative, who had written a most orthodox book on Stahl, the professor of constitutional law, told me in a letter that the Press was beginning to urge my dispatch to Rome, adding that this had given no pleasure in high places. Bergen also pointed out that the *Frankfurter Zeitung* was announcing, semi-officially, that Prince Bülow would, in any case, soon be returning to Rome, with or without official status there. This, according to him, was an attempt to make the public believe that I would be in Rome for the winter as usual, and that, though all possible use was being made of me there, there was no need to consecrate my journey officially. Such a policy of "shifty half measures" is eternally characteristic of Bethmann and all his tribe. Von Berger added: "But Your Highness will have seen through all that, and told them that it must be all or nothing. Both I, the most devoted of your adherents, and, with me, even your erstwhile enemies, can all only hope that very soon you will have received official intimation of your return to the service of the Fatherland."

At the end of November, 1914, a letter from Prince Wedel informed me that the prince had been pointing out to General von Plessen the "utter inadequacy" of the German Embassy in Rome, and especially the "scandalous position" of Frau von Flotow. This lady had taken refuge in Stockholm, not daring to acknowledge her German husband. She was in constant close touch with the Russian Embassy there; the stepson of a German Ambassador was fighting on the Russian side against us. Yet Jagow still resisted every suggestion that his dear Flotow should be recalled. "But," Wedel's letter concluded, "times are so grave that the whole crew must be forced to do its duty."

Loebell wrote: "You are making a very great sacrifice in accepting this mission to Rome, but I am sure you make it in all willingness, since the good of the Fatherland has been the sole guide of all your actions. It seems to me that the state of public opinion in Italy again leaves much to be desired. A great deal has been permanently lost there, and unnecessary harm has been done."

My brother Alfred, a man of sound good sense and deliberate judgment, wrote, as soon as ever he heard the rumour that I might perhaps be given a Roman mission, to tell me that, in spite of every difficulty, of all the intrigues to which I should possibly be exposed, of the insincerity of those who were now directing our foreign policy, I still could not refuse the appeal of the Emperor. He added: "May God grant that in so grave a matter those who direct the policy of our Foreign Office may be inspired only by thoughts of their country's welfare, and not by their own miserable ambitions and petty interests. Any other course would be a most guilty one. All Germany is indignant with our diplomatists. I have just heard the following joke: — The French Government had been trying to find out our peace conditions, so we answered: 'Rectification of the Vosges frontier; the dismantling of Toul, Nancy, Verdun, etc.' — none of which seemed insuperable to the French. But when we added a final clause that France must take five or six of our best and most qualified present diplomats, the French broke off negotiations."

These intrigues against me were pitiable, and so was the fashion in which Berlin conducted its policy. But the many proofs of sympathy and confidence which began to pour in on me from all sides had soon effaced the whole wretched business.

The Grand Duchess Louise of Baden wired to me in Berlin: "May I say how very pleased I am to learn that there is again some chance of securing your collaboration for the Fatherland at such a grave and difficult time as this."

Ernst Bassermann sent me a telegram: "I and all my friends most cordially welcome Your Highness's reinstatement in a post of the highest importance to the country."

Soon after this he wrote: "I must write to tell you once again how delighted I am at your decision to accept Rome. Italy is still a danger, and will remain so, but if any one can do us good there it is yourself. All Germany doubts that Bethmann-Hollweg is the right personality for a peace in the grand manner. In the west, for the moment, we founder in mud and swamps, and cannot advance. My impression, from many private talks, is that we lack unity of command, and a clear objective, on the Western Front. Moltke retired in disharmony with H.M. Falkenhayn had not the usual training of a Staff Officer; he seems to lack the necessary authority, and even, perhaps, any really outstanding strategic gift. In addition to this, Headquarters are a nest of intrigue. One therefore hears much that is unpleasant. Instead of thinking solely of one great aim, as our people does, with such wonderful and moving self-sacrifice, the authorities strive for personal advantage. I will say no more about all this, since Your Highness has, unfortunately, had all too much personal experience of the kind of atmosphere I mean."

Countess Christa Eickstedt, with whom I had played as a boy — the friend, for many years, of all the Bismarcks, and who had been at the deathbed of the great Prince, wrote to me:

DEAR PRINCE BERNHARD,

I have just heard that you will be a few days longer in Berlin, and so I can't refrain from sending you all my very best and most heartfelt blessings and wishes for the work you are to do beyond the Alps, in the cause of our dear Fatherland. I was indescribably delighted to hear that you had accepted this mission, and I think your great friend and predecessor, Prince Bismarck, would have been as pleased as I am. May his blessing go with you — and I don't think I could give you anything better to take on your journey!

Very best wishes from the old, faithful friend of your childhood.

CHRISTA EICKSTEDT.

Schwerin-Löwitz and Clemens Schorlemer both wrote to tell me how glad they were that I had announced myself willing to take direction of the Roman Embassy, in spite of all the difficulties in Italy, and the intrigues I should be certain to have to face. The widow of the President of the Reichstag, Udo Stolberg, wrote to my wife, expressing her relief at the thought that, notwithstanding all the rancour and unpleasantness, which she would not mention except *en passant*, I had not hesitated to make this great personal sacrifice — "Though, in a time such as this we are each of us ready with his sacrifice."

Naturally, Adolf Harnack, the Court theologian, was not behind-hand with his most enthusiastic good wishes. These, with the hope that, when the time came, I might also be entrusted with the peace conference, he delivered "from a joyful heart." Less insincere were the good wishes of Engelbert Humperdinck, the pleasant composer of that delicious fairy opera, "Hänsel and Gretel", who, on the two occasions when he lived in the Villa Falconieri, at Frascati, had been our close and charming associate. But what gave me most pleasure of all was a poem in my honour in the *Kladderadatsch*, written by its sub-editor, Paul Warncke, as much my friend as Trojan, his predecessor.

The *Kladderadatsch*, a complete set of which, from 1848, stands on my shelves, had remained true, even after his death, to Bismarck, my great predecessor. To me, while I was still a Chancellor, it would often tell the truth with a smile, in obedience to Horace's maxim : *ridendo dicere verum*. In my retirement, this old and excellent comic paper, full of German joviality and the keen, satiric spirit of Berlin, had still remained on very good terms with me. I feel I must also give a short letter from the widow of that very valuable Minister, Rudolf Delbrück, Bismarck's collaborator in the great days. She wrote to my wife : "In all circles there is real satisfaction at seeing the Prince return to Rome as our representative, with Your Highness. At last we have succeeded in getting realized this thing we had so long hoped and prayed for, for our Fatherland. I feel I must write to tell you how very pleased I am. May God bless you both, to the greater prosperity of Germany, and your own high satisfaction in serving her."

Walter Rathenau wired : "Delighted to hear Your Highness has decided to take an active share in the government, in these grave times. I place full faith in your old strength, and coming good fortune."

The German Press, without distinction of party, approved my mission unreservedly. Doctor Georg Oertel, a Reichstag deputy, and editor of the Agrarian *Deutsche Tageszeitung* did not exaggerate when he wrote: "Most heartily do I wish you all success! This deep wish is not only mine, it is that of every other German, whatever his party may be."

CHAPTER XVI

An Audience with William II — My Farewell Visit to Moltke — Flotow
Stays on in Italy to Intrigue against Me — Erzberger's Visit to Rome — His
Loyal Behaviour there — From the Archives of the Roman Embassy — My
Roman Activity — Letters from Germany — The Kaiser's Frame of Mind —
The German Colony — Count Greppi — The Austro-Hungarian Ambas-
sador, Von Merey, Replaced by Freiherr von Macchio.

AT Schloss Bellevue, before we left Berlin, the Emperor received
me in audience. Not without some inward emotion did I cross the
ancient park to enter this palace, whose apartments had beheld so
much. It was here that Prince Louis Ferdinand, before Saalfeld,
said his last good-bye to Princess Radziwill, his sister, in whose care
he placed his children. In this ancient park, after Jena, Arndt had
sought out secluded alleys, to meditate on the distresses of his country, and the means by which she might be saved. Here too, when,
in 1918, our tragic destiny was accomplished with the failure of the
last great thrust in the west, the Emperor, in harsh and boorish
terms, was to give General Ludendorff his dismissal.

But to-day William II was still all optimism. His mood was
almost one of exhilaration. As gracious, as cordial in manner, as
though there had been no cloud between us, he gave me his views
on the real origin of the War. In the May of 1913, at the celebration
festivities for the marriage of Princess Victoria Louise to the Duke
of Brunswick, the King of England, his cousin, and his other
cousin, the Tsar of Russia, had conspired together to betray him!
History showed no greater perfidy. His "cousins and colleagues"
had led the poor child to her marriage altar with guile and treachery
in their hearts! Together they had plotted his betrayal, for which
God would punish them, some day! His Majesty told how, on the
eve of the wedding, he had entered unawares, in Berlin Castle, the
apartment of his cousin, the King of England, whom he had sur-

prised in close conference with the Tsar. Both had started to their feet. He could see now that this had been the moment when the two were putting their final touches to a plot for falling upon Germany. The Tsar's ingratitude was revolting: he had always been the Tsar's close friend. As for "Georgie", all the Emperor had to say was that Queen Victoria, their grandmother, must have turned in her grave at the spectacle of her British grandson flinging down the gauntlet to the German. It was painful indeed to have to realize that even the bitter lessons of these war months had not taught William II to be objective, to see things as they are in reality, watch events and judge them with cold detachment. I ventured to suggest that British policy, especially since the succession of George V, was in the hands of Ministers and the Parliament. The Emperor glared; then he became as amiable as ever, seized my arm and said that it was time to go in to tea with the Empress, who was very anxious indeed to see me again. A few minutes later we were all three gathered round her tea-table, in an atmosphere of such gentle kindness as could only be conducive to peace and harmony.

Three days before this audience with His Majesty I had been to call on General Moltke. He had just moved from Homburg, to General Headquarters in Berlin, that "Red box" in the Königs-platz, opposite the Victory Column — a building which still keeps its great tradition, and one which I can never pass to-day without melancholy thoughts of a better past; the past in which we were free, proud, and happy. I found Moltke in bed, looking very ill, and paler than his sheets. He asked, with a melancholy smile: "Can you still remember that day when we trotted our two horses around the water-tower in the Hippodrome? Was n't I right not to want to accept the post they offered me?" But he uttered no word of recrimination and made no attempt to justify himself. He could only dwell on fears for the future, his ardent love of the Fatherland, his desire to see me return in Bethmann's place, since the storm was raging far too heavily for the strength of such a helmsman as the present one.

On leaving Moltke's bedroom I talked to his wife, who had come to the door to wait for me. She came of the Danish-Swedish branch of the Moltke family. Elisa von Moltke, "Lizzie" as they all used to call her, was a very pretty, very intelligent woman, entirely given up to her husband. Unluckily she "went in for" spiritualism, was preoccupied with all kinds of theosophical and occult phantasmagoria, and so had infected her husband, already rather inclined to be a mystic. I found her now trembling with grief at his sorrow and with indignation against those whom she accused of having caused the general's collapse. The Emperor, so she said, had taken away her husband's command at the very moment when he could have saved the western situation. She accused both Von Falkenhayn and His Majesty of neglecting Moltke's advice on the proper provisioning of the empire. This assertion was not unfounded, since the general, like Delbrück and others, had perceived that we must take early measures against the blockade.

Not long before this I had exchanged letters with Moltke. He was an old friend, whose sorrow really grieved me. Here is his answer to the few lines of sympathy I had sent him:

Your Highness has given me real pleasure by your kind letter of the 24th — the letter of a friend. I have done nothing to deserve your congratulations on our advance. The credit for that must go to the whole staff, to every one of the officers who worked so well to bring this army, a million strong, into position; but, especially to the staff of the transport section. As for the victories which ensued, they are due to the desperate valour of our men and the officers who led them, from the first soldier to the last; they were won by our entire people, a nation in arms, which had staked its life and was victorious. And the honour must not only go to combatants — it is due to the whole country, standing foursquare behind them, ready with any and every sacrifice, to that civilian strength which must always reinforce its soldiers, who are linked to it by millions of fibres, that strength which infuses them continually with its own spirit of valour and resistance. The German people is fighting for its holiest possessions, for its continued existence as a nation, for the protection of the Fatherland, threatened by a force which would overpower and annihilate. But this nation of seventy million souls is conscious not only of defending itself but of struggling on behalf of the human spirit. We must protect the soul of the German people, that soul which alone can guarantee the spiritual progress of all mankind. One would have to despair of progress if this supreme good were to be sacrificed to English materialism and Russian barbarity. That is why I too am assured that the German people is invincible. When I read what you say in your letter of the bad diplomatic preparation of this War, I thought of many former conversations with you. Since you relinquished control of our policy, our diplomats have had only one thought — peace at any price. They have seemed entirely to forget that the highest task of diplomacy is to guide the State in such a manner that at any given moment, if necessary, it may go to war in the best and most favourable circumstances. After all, for many years now, we have seen that this War was not far off. We did not seek it; we did not wish to prepare it; our whole effort was to prevent it; and yet it came. Our diplomats failed to perceive that history was entering a new phase, that this storm had to break over Europe. What other explanation can they offer of these two heavy and unexpected blows — our desertion by Roumania and Italy? I am convinced that we should have won the War had we kept the assistance of these two States. To have failed in that is the worst blunder with which historians will reproach us. You and I have often spoken of these things. They were a vivid reality to Your Highness and, from the day you went out of office, I was ever disquieted by the thought that henceforth we might lose sight of considerations and aims so full of grave significance to the empire. If God wills that, in spite of all, we emerge from this huge struggle victorious, there will still be one supremely important task — the strength for good which this War has aroused in our people, the idealism it has spread through all classes, this new, magnificent German unity, effacing every distinction of rank and party — these are the supreme treasures of the spirit. War will be to us as the fire which separates the fine gold from the dross. Our people has turned from that materialism which, through years of easy prosperity and well-being, threatened to clog our souls, and had already sown among the masses the seeds of party rancour, discord, and envy. It is our people's most precious jewel which this War has made our earth yield up. If that Highest of All Wills that guides the destinies of humanity means well by us, it will grant us men who no longer think in terms of the material benefits of peace, men who know how to keep intact in the life of Germany this spiritual gain the War has brought us.

Such is my ardent wish, and yet, at the same time, my anxiety. My fear is that the statesman who now guides may fail to perceive the depths of our spirit to-day, and so fail to lead us to our destiny. Your

Highness knows how much I honour you, but my wish that you may be the man to whose lot it falls to undertake this task is born of more than merely personal feeling. I know how well you understand these questions. Once before, and in very difficult circumstances, you appealed — and appealed successfully — to the latent idealism of our people. I know of no other man who could replace you. Forgive this long letter. Ill as I am, I can be of no further use in the War, and live, very quietly, here in the old castle at Homburg. But my heart and soul are bound up with the events of this great and holy time. The ardent wish that Germany may emerge, through darkness and struggle, into the light fills and enflames me. All my present thoughts and emotions are summed up in the one word "Fatherland", and I know that with you it is the same. May God send us victory, and may He grant our people such a peace as will leave us our most sacred treasure.

Your devoted and ever faithful

MOLTKE.

In this letter there is, of course, much to criticize. Bethmann was less to be reproached with having wanted "peace at any price" than with having blundered into war. It is also misleading to suggest that war in Europe had been inevitable. Bismarck no more believed in such shallow and unpleasing theories than he did in "prophylactic" warfare. But on the other hand, Moltke is perfectly right in saying that we should have won a speedy victory had Italy and Roumania not deserted us. They did, and the fault was diplomatic, the diplomacy of Vienna and Berlin. Moltke's letter reads, in its ensemble, like the generous, idealistic outpouring of some professor of ethical philosophy rather than the profession of faith of a leader. How different a spirit comes alive in the writings of Frederick II, or in the "Mémorial de Sainte Hélène !" Fate willed that we should embark on the worst of all wars with, in essential posts, not men of action, but two philosophers. I may add that history, with justice, will deal more harshly with Bethmann than with Moltke, his companion in misfortune.

On December 14, 1914, the express bore me back to Rome. There, a few days later, I had a letter from a journalist very conversant with our Foreign Office. He wrote: "Jagow, as soon as you left Berlin, began saying to whoever cared to listen, that we were quite certain of Italy. There could be no possible doubt that she would come into the War as our ally, etc." Clearly Jagow was spitting in my soup. On the platform at Rome the whole Embassy staff were waiting for me — all except Flotow, the Ambassador. I had decided to live in my own Villa Malta and not in the Palazzo Caffarelli, which had been my abode forty years before, in the days when I was a young attaché, and again when, twenty years later, I had the Embassy. That afternoon Flotow put in an appearance. His face and bearing might have served as models to an actor cast for the part of "Wurm", the secretary in Schiller's "Kabale und Liebe ",[1] that "Wurm" of whom another character "Miller" says: "The little quill driver freezes up your blood like a dose of arsenic." Herr von Flotow gave me fully to understand that, by kind permission of both Chancellor and Secretary of State, he intended to remain on in Italy, that here he would spend his whole leave, and live "till further orders" near Naples. A few days later the deputy, Erzberger, came to Rome. Since my break with the Centre, no other deputy of that party had attacked me so fiercely as he. It was he who had concocted the story, elaborated by ex-Privy Councillor Martin, and Gaston Calmette, the editor of the *Figaro*, of my having tried to force the Kaiser to abdicate and have myself proclaimed president of the German Republic. But I had never met Erzberger personally. When he came into my study, I saw before me a funny, dumpy little man, very clumsy in his movements and gestures, with blunt "honest-to-God" features. "Why, he looks like an ornamental beer cork !" remarked a Hungarian countess when, not long after, I introduced them. But in this first talk I had with Erzberger I found myself dealing with a man of very keen and vivid perceptions — no wit, and still less a man of culture, but obviously by no means a fool. Cleon would at once have recognized his brother demagogue in Erzberger, in spite of all the accidental differences between the Athenian and the German. To me Albert Ballin once remarked of him that he was industrious, but lacked originality. The subtle and cultivated provincial of the

[1] "Love and Intrigue."

Benedictine Order, Freiherr von Stotzingen, summed him up, after a long conversation: "He lacks the Humaniora"; while Pope Benedict XV, as I have said, expressed, after an audience, his surprise that Signor Erzberger, who, no doubt, was excellent in Parliament, should have tried to conduct diplomacy, a task for which he seemed in no way suited. Matthias Erzberger made many grave political mistakes, both during the last War years and after the Emperor's abdication. He did much damage, and I owe it him therefore all the more to say that, to me in Rome, his behaviour was, at least, entirely loyal, and that there he did me excellent service.

That day he began by saying that he had attacked me solely in the interests of the Centre Party, without personal animus of any kind, and that now he felt nothing but admiration for me. I could count in every way on his support. Bethmann and Jagow had sent him to Rome, with a special cipher code and told him to report to them in detail his observations of me and my behaviour. Naturally neither the Chancellor nor State Secretary had been well-disposed towards me when they commissioned him. But he would promise not to wire or write to Bethmann anything not previously inspected by me. And Erzberger kept his promise. No report or observation went to Berlin from him until I had had it through my hands. He would even keep me closely informed of his own political conversations in Rome. When, not without reason, since his many visits to the Vatican were beginning to be violently attacked by the whole of the Italian Press, he feared for his personal safety, I invited him to stay at the Villa Malta. At the same time I notified the Consulta that the deputy Erzberger was now attaché to the Embassy, and, as such, had extra-territorial status. This seemed to the worthy Matthias a happy presage of diplomatic advancement. I gave him two good rooms on the second floor, the windows of which afforded magnificent views of Rome — the glorious cupola of St. Peter's and the hills. He was a pleasant guest, and both my wife and I enjoyed his company, since he was natural, easy to get on with, and could, at times, be very funny indeed, when he let himself go on Berlin life. He had no notion why the Chancellor had taken such a fancy to him. He supposed he must dine there at least once a week. Not long ago the "Herr Kanschler"[1] had said to him: "How on earth do you manage to have such good ideas? I never seem to get an idea." Erzberger told this story quite simply, without the least hint of irony. When, later, the poor fellow ended, so tragically, his widow sent me a mourning card, inscribed with the quotation from St. Paul: "I have fought the good fight and have kept faith." That was the impression he had made on his best friends as well as on his family, on his fellow townsmen in Buttenhausen, and even on a considerable section of Democratic and Clerical Germany. The others saw a knave, even a criminal. A German court composed of unbiased, and in every way eminent judges, found him guilty of using his political status for private gain. The counsel for Helfferich, his opponent, tapped the portfolio in front of him and accused, point-blank, as follows: "There's enough material here for any assessor to make out a dozen cases against you — and win them all." Erzberger had no answer. Judged by the rigorous ethic of Kant, he would certainly have had little chance. But may he not appeal to the thief on Calvary? Let us hope that he too has managed to get into Paradise.

Wretchedly supported from Berlin and even less adequately from Vienna, through this difficult winter 1914–1915, and forced as I was to struggle against cross-currents, it was good to receive several further letters from Moltke — the letters of a patriot and true friend. Few men, I think, wished success to my Roman mission so wholeheartedly. And there was need enough of all his prayers and wishes. As I said in the course of my first talk with him, to our Councillor of Embassy, Hindenburg, I felt like a specialist called in too late to a deathbed. In July, 1914, we might still, with a little foresight, have won the coöperation of Italy. In the weeks leading up to the Marne we could still count on Italian neutrality. But now, to secure this bare neutrality it would have been necessary forthwith for Austria, *avec un beau geste*, quite unreservedly, to have sacrificed the Trentino and conceded the autonomy of Trieste. Austria did not care to make such concessions, nor had Bethmann and Jagow

---

[1] *I.e.* Kanzler — Chancellor.

the energy for any real pressure on Vienna. We Germans had given our assent, without reserve or hesitation, to the whole *démarche* against Serbia, leaving our allies free to choose their method. This made them perfectly sure of our support, and they felt in no way bound to consider us. With our blank cheque signed they proceeded to sit down to the gaming table and lose our money with their own. Had we not, after all, from the outset, given them leave to go to any lengths with Serbia — even to war, with all its consequences?

In Rome I found in our archives a letter received from Prince Stolberg, our Councillor of Embassy in Vienna, in which, during a brief absence of his chief, the Ambassador Tschirschky, he had, in the middle of July, about a week before the ultimatum was delivered, informed Berlin that, in obedience to orders received, he had asked Count Berchtold if the Vienna Cabinet persisted in its intention of demanding serious reparations from Serbia for the murder at Sarajevo. Berchtold having answered that this was so, Stolberg, still in obedience to instructions, had proceeded to inquire what would happen if Serbia should accept all the demands. With a smile (Berchtold, like Jagow, was given to smiling), the count had said he felt it most unlikely that even such a government as the Serbian would swallow the ultimatum whole. If, however, they did make up their minds to it, the only other course, after all its exactions had been fulfilled, would be so to harry and injure Serbia that, in the end, she gave Austria pretext for invading her. The archives further contained two copies of letters sent from G.H.Q. by Jagow, to Zimmermann, the Undersecretary of State. These furnished melancholy additional proof of the utter lack of clear objective with which, in that summer of 1914, our Foreign Office staff had behaved.

In one of these, written before the Marne retreat, Jagow exhorted the Foreign Office, and the German Ambassador in Rome, to make no kind of engagements to Italy — neither by promises, nor even conversations on possible eventual compensation. All this recalled to mind the Duc de Gramont in 1870. When told that the South-German States were coming into the war on Prussia's side, this French Foreign Minister jovially answered: *"Tant mieux. Nos armées se déployeront à leur aise dans les plaines de l'Allemagne méridionale, et nous aurons les coudées franches pour les négociations de la paix."*

Jagow's second letter had reached Rome a few weeks after the Marne retreat. By then he was wringing his hands and begging his friend to do anything to get Italy into the War on our side.

There is no doubt that, like every one else in politics, I have sometimes been mistaken in my judgments. I may even, as my opponents suggest, have made more mistakes than anything else. But at least I can lay my hand on my heart and affirm that, always, the one idea guiding my policy has been the greater good of the State. From that day in my youth, when I volunteered in the Bonn Hussars, as a lieutenant, and took my oath to serve my King and country, my entire strength has been used in that country's service — and never more fully and conscientiously than it was in Rome, in the winter of 1914–1915. And just because I was under no illusion as to the many perils of this contingency with which my successor's incapacity and that of his collaborators had faced us — five years after my retirement — I now strained every nerve to prevent our Empire, already surrounded by powerful enemies, from having to face one more, by no means negligible. All I could learn from Germany confirmed my realization of our danger. Albert Ballin wrote, soon after my arrival in Rome:

The position seems none too good. This idea of a submarine blockade strong enough to bring England to heel if it succeeds, has been riddled with criticism by jurists and the heads of the Foreign Office. Not much hope in Turkey either. They lack munitions, since Roumania is refusing passage to our transport. Neither Egypt nor the Suez Canal offer any very interesting objective. I really cannot see why we don't display more energy in Vienna, to make sure of an understanding with Italy, even at the cost of real sacrifice. It is absolutely essential to finish off Serbia by releasing Austrian troops from the Italian frontier. In my opinion the whole strategic position has been made considerably worse by this Austrian failure to overthrow Serbia quickly, since had they succeeded in this they might easily, with a few concessions, have made peace with that solid little people, and so even furnished the Tsar with a pretext for concluding a separate peace. May God improve it all. I shall be in Berlin shortly, for some time, and intend to advise Zimmermann most urgently to get all energy used in Vienna, with the object of an understanding with Italy. Our military successes will only drive the Allies to curry more and more favour with Italy and Roumania; while each military defeat we encounter will whet the present desire of Roumania and Italy to come into the war against Austria. So that therefore we are "between the devil and the deep sea", and what we really ought to be aiming at is a quick and honourable peace. After all it has been no small achievement to have kept the war on enemy soil as we have, and put up this brilliant defence against a world of enemies.

The Head of the Scherl Publishing House, Herr Eugen Zimmermann, who remained in closest contact with our headquarters, and was often asked to stay in the war zone — the same Zimmermann who, three years later, was to help the Kaiser with his book, " Gestalten und Erscheinungen ",[1] had already written before I left for Rome :

The general pessimism increases. Our armies can only advance by inches, and with huge losses. Our enemies gain far too much time in which to perfect their methods of defence. Russian artillery is being eked out by Japanese guns. The French bring up more and more black troops. The English are recruiting feverishly. On the Yser, after November 1st, we had lost, in round figures, fifty thousand officers and men. One often sees fifty-year old lieutenants and company commanders in the line. Sheer brute strength seems ever to increase in importance and the art of war to diminish. We have ceased to take the strategic initiative. In the west all our numerical superiority (of about 350,000 men) cannot achieve a break through. Nevertheless we can, we must, count on final success. Yet the more we owe this success to the ranks, the people, the resistance of the individual unit, instead of to superior leadership, the more demands will democracy make, after the War. When I talk here to members of the government, I am appalled at how little they seem to realize what is going on in the minds of the people.

The publicist, Herbert von Berger, who then still belonged to the Right Wing of the Conservative Party, wrote to me :

[1] " Silhouettes and Appearances."

I hope that the coming generation may live to see a time when the Prussian nobility will be asked to serve its country with heart and intellect, not merely to pour out its blood in wartime. Eighty per cent. of the Guards officers have been killed. Some are here wounded, and I often talk to them. They seem to feel that the nobleman's privilege of getting himself killed by the enemy has been extended to them more lavishly than was strictly necessary. Whole families of junkers have been wiped out. A disabled officer of high rank has asked me bitterly if political reasons had not made it convenient to kill off as many aristocratic officers and Civil servants as possible. I was forced to remember the saying of a well-known historian that Rome had been doomed because she let her aristocracy perish. It is curious that the present events, which have brought out all that is best in the German people, should be spoken of in the highest circles in a less hopeful, even pessimistic tone. It is said that we lack leaders and men of character. Hindenburg cannot do it all, etc. I really believe that, in certain exalted quarters there is unwillingness to give any one a chance to distinguish himself who shows signs of being more than a mere official, and might prove he had the qualities of a statesman. Every thinking German, possessed of any political consciousness, can see plainly that the present Chancellor will never do to negotiate peace, for which he would be no more adequate than he was to do the right thing when war came. The only reason for keeping him is that he shows himself an obliging servant. Is it surprising that our people, which has made such immense and willing sacrifices, begins to ask if the time has not arrived for serious constitutional reforms, so that, in future the appointment of Ministers may not solely depend on the wish of the Sovereign? Certainly such men as Bethmann and Jagow, as weak as they are lacking in ideas, are a menace to our whole foreign policy, while, at home, they endanger the constitution.

In contrast to the above grave warnings and patriotic anxieties, came the following, from Schloss Bellevue, by General Chelius, the Adjutant General, *de service*, to His Majesty:

The Emperor still refuses to believe that Italy can be seriously hostile to Austria, and hopes that Roumania, where there seems to be a fresh wave of opinion in favour of the Central Powers, will prevent her from taking any fatal decision. I may add, in the strictest confidence, that here they believe that, in the spring, the Pope will offer to mediate peace.

This idea appeals greatly to His Majesty. But he also, of course, feels that no peace can be concluded except on a basis of the then military *status quo*. He is sure that both France and England feel some need of peace. We are letting the English know our strength at sea, though, naturally, not without danger to our transports, especially those that go to Belgium. His Majesty is in excellent humour, and looks forward with the greatest confidence to the results of operations on the Eastern Front, which may bring us both the military and political decision.

One great consolation was my certainty, from the first day to the last of my mission, of having gained the trust and support of my fellow countrymen in Italy. A stream of telegrams and letters, from Rome, Florence, Milan, and Naples, gave touching proof that this was so. The German colony in Rome wired me their greeting as follows: "The whole colony is rejoiced and relieved." The banker, Joel, a native of Danzig, who had lived many years in Milan, where he was highly respected, sent me this telegram: "We are very gratified indeed by this generous decision of Your Highness, and firmly hope that its results for us will be of the best."

The first Italian friend I was to meet on my return, on the Pincio, was Count Giuseppe Greppi, an old man of ninety-five. Milanese by birth, he had entered diplomacy at seventeen, in 1836, in the Austrian service. He had lunched at Parma with the Empress Marie Louise, the widow of the Great Napoleon, whose charming bust and delicious little feet he still acclaimed. In Rome, in the Palazzo Buonaparte, on the Corso opposite the Gesù, he had kissed the hand of Madame Mère, the Corsican's mother. He had stood in the presence of Frederick William III of Prussia, and of Francis II, the last Holy Roman Emperor of German extraction, had met Wellington and the Archduke Charles, the victor of Aspern. For two years he had been *chef de cabinet*, for Italian affairs, to Prince Clemens Metternich, and could reëvoke, most vividly, the manner in which this dictator of Austrian policy and, up to a point, of the policy of all Europe, would, each evening, receive admirers and subordinates, leaning against a pillar in his great drawing-room, in the most ceremonious attitude, and discoursing, in a solemn voice, on the eternal principles of legitimacy, the rigidly Monarchist State, and that wise political immobility which should be the pattern for every government. These lectures of Metternich's — *le cocher de l'Europe*, as admirers called him — would usually end in the affirmation, delivered not without a hint of vanity, that: "*Je suis le rocher de l'ordre politique et sociale.*" Count Greppi had met De Musset and Chateaubriand; he had listened to the roulades of Henriette Sontag, had beheld the divine dancer, Fanny Elssler. In 1848, when the Habsburg Monarchy made war on Italian patriots, led by the house of Savoy, Count Greppi had left the Austrian service. A few years later he had entered Italian diplomacy, as Ambassador for the Kingdom of Italy, in Madrid, and St. Petersburg. He had seen much without ever losing his natural calm. One day I asked him how he had managed to go on living so many years. He answered: "I 've let nothing and no one upset me." With a curious little smile he added: "I did once, though! But only once. It was when I was Ambassador in St. Petersburg, and happened to be in Rome on leave, just about 1890. I had been spending the evening in Gianette Doria's charming palazzo, where he had given me a very good dinner. I went for a stroll down the Corso and they happened to be shouting the evening papers. I bought a *Tribuna* and read a huge announcement that Count Greppi, the Ambassador in St. Petersburg, had been retired. It was just one of Crispi's caddish moves — they were the only kind he ever made. He had got our good King Umberto to sign the document, and sent it straight off to the papers, without even troubling to inform me. I 'm sorry to say that, for a moment, I lost my temper. But it did n't last! I soon began to see that I should be happier and freer retired — that I could enjoy myself more in Rome and Milan, and on Lake Como, than abroad, as Italian Ambassador. *Ne jamais se faire du mauvais sang, voilà la vraie Eau de Jouvence.*"

Greppi lived to be a hundred and three. One evening in Milan, in the palazzo his father had left him, he simply drooped his head and died. That afternoon he had been, in great good humour, at the races. He had given his own centenary dinner, at the Grand Hotel, in Rome, to a hundred ladies of his choice, each lady selected for her beauty. Every guest found on her plate a magnificent rose.

When, that day in December, 1914, I met Count Greppi on the Pincio, he said: "*Cette guerre est différente de toutes les autres guerres que j'ai jamais vues dans ma longue vie: la guerre de Crimée, la guerre de 1859, entre l'Autriche et la France, vos guerres avec l'Autriche en 1866, et avec la France en 1870, les guerres de la Russie avec la Turquie et avec le Japon, la guerre entre l'Espagne et les Etats-Unis. La guerre actuelle n'est pas, à proprement parler, une guerre, c'est un terremoto, un immense tremblement de terre, qui changera non seulement la carte de L'Europe mais politiquement et socialement la face du monde.*"

At the moment when I took over our Embassy, Herr von Merey had just been recalled to Vienna. His personal relationships with Italian Ministers had ended by making Rome impossible for him. His post was taken over by Herr von Macchio, the First Chief of Section of the Austrian Foreign Office — a typical Austrian bureaucrat of the old — the very old — school; as slow in movement as in thought; formalist to the marrow of his bones; indolent, without initiative, without any personal opinions.

In my every conversation with Sonnino, the new Italian Foreign Minister, during my Roman mission, I would assure him that I was doing my very uttermost to make Austria consent to cede the Trentino. Herr von Macchio's interviews with Sonnino would usually follow mine. But whenever Sonnino asked him if he had any news of the Trentino, Von Macchio would answer woodenly that he had not understood the Minister's question. This was a kind of system with Von Macchio, who, no doubt, had learnt the method in Vienna. His plan was to say exactly the opposite of all I had just been suggesting to the Italian. Later I was to learn that this idiosyncrasy of the Imperial and Royal representative had also been, in part, due to the fact that Jagow had been taking malicious delight in submitting confidential reports in which, with the frankness incumbent on my position, I had given my views on the insufficiency of the Austrian Embassy in Rome, either to Prince Gottfried Hohenlohe, the Dual Monarchy's Berlin representative, or else, *via* Tschirschky, in Vienna, to the whole of the Austrian Cabinet. Against such stupidity and malice a demigod might well have striven in vain.

CHAPTER XVII

Sidney Sonnino, the Italian Foreign Minister — The Allies' Propaganda in Italy — How They Exploited the German Invasion of Belgium — King Victor Emanuel III — Queen Margherita; Her Confidential Question to Princess Bülow — The Councillor of Legation, Von Hindenburg — Giolitti's "Parecchio" — Pope Benedict XV — Bethmann's Miserable Policy — A Letter to Me from Bethmann — Flotow Reappears in Rome — My Farewell Audience with the King — Erzberger's Optimism.

On the day which followed my return, I presented myself to the Foreign Minister, Sidney Sonnino, at the Consulta. This splendid palace, the austere beauty of its lines in harmony with the spirit of Rome, still sheltered the Italian Foreign Ministry, which only after the War removed to the Palazzo Chigi, in the Corso, the former residence of ambassadors from the then extinct Habsburg Monarchy. I had often ascended the great double staircase of the Consulta. In its grand *salon de réception*, panelled with the yellow damask, I had seen, as a young attaché, in the winter of 1874–1875, Visconti-Venosta, enthroned. He had begun as secretary to the revolutionary agitator, Mazzini, but by then was already transformed into an orthodox Conservative statesman, and the pious son of Holy Mother Church. Later, in this same apartment, I was to meet Count Robilant, the son of a Prussian mother, a Countess Waldburg-Capustigall. When, as a young Piedmontese officer, he lost his arm at the battle of Novara, on March 23, 1849, Count Robilant had waved the bleeding stump, with a cry: "*Viva il Re!*" In the 'eighties they made him Ambassador in Vienna, where he married an Austrian, the daughter of Prince Clary. In the days of my first ambassadorship to Rome, from 1894–1897, I had often conferred, in the Consulta, with the fiery Baron Blanc, the prudent Marchese Rudini, and again with Visconti-Venosta, who now, with twenty-two more years on his shoulders, had grown still more orthodox, circumspect, and reserved.　To-day I attended Sidney Sonnino.

When I entered the Minister's antechamber, from which there is a wonderful view of the two colossi, Castor and Pollux, a view that, in Berlin and Tegel, Wilhelm von Humboldt still often regretted, I found myself face to face with three ambassadors of the Allies: Barrère, Rodd, and Krupenski.　The attitude of each towards me was characteristic of the spirit of his nation.　The good Krupenski hurried up to me, with the assurance that his personal friendship was in no way impaired by recent events.　The circumspect and highly intelligent Rodd shook me by the hand, with the words: "I wish to shake hands with you and beg you to give my very best compliments to Princess Bülow."　Of these three ambassadors it was Barrère who had been my best and oldest friend.　But no sooner was he aware of my presence than, with all the inborn histrionic talent which every Frenchman has at his command, he raised his arms to the heavens, then covered his eyes with both hands.　As he turned away, a French spectator might have exclaimed: *"C'est la France elle-même qui se dresse, irréconciliable devant l'ennemi."*

For a number of years I had been on the best of terms with Sonnino.　Born in the Levant, of an Israelite father and British mother, he was a mixture of Jewish acumen and penetrating subtlety in argument, with dogged English tenacity, even stubbornness.　Be it noted, by the way, as a proof of the tolerant spirit of Italians, that nobody in Italy raised objection to the fact that Italian foreign policy, even at so crucial a moment, should have been controlled by a Jew.　It is true that in his childhood that Jew had become a convert to Christianity — to the Protestant, not the Roman Catholic persuasion which, of course, is that of the vast majority of the Minister's Italian fellow citizens.　Yet not one Italian newspaper, not even the *Osservatore Romano*, the organ of the Curia, pointed out that Sonnino professed a faith which, in Italy, a country of nearly forty million inhabitants, can claim scarcely one hundred and thirty thousand adherents.　And still less objection was taken to the Jewish origin of the Minister.　In my account of the Emperor's journey to England, in 1899, I noted the British power of assimilation, at the same time recalling Goethe's saying that a language owes most of its vigour not to what it rejects but to what it can incorporate with itself. The same may be said of nations, which should assimilate, not reject, their Jews. Sonnino, at the outset of the War, had been actively in favour of an Italy in line with the Central Powers. But his chief hope was that the World War might not end without some territorial gain to his country. In 1866, in 1870, Italy had snatched her advantage from wars which other countries had waged, and this time too it must be the same.

Salandra, the President of the Council, played a secondary rôle compared with Sonnino. He had not the acute penetration, the seriousness, the strength of character, of the Minister for Foreign Affairs. His aim was merely to snatch some immediate advantage for his country out of the present confusion in the world. He owed his position in parliament to his Southern-Italian's "gift of the gab", whereas Sonnino, as a rule, would deliver clumsy speeches from notes, an unusual limitation in Latin parliaments.

Sonnino made no bones about giving me his views of the position and set them forth with clarity and candour. As war objective the Allies had promised Italy all Austrian territory peopled by Italian subjects. Should Austria wish to be assured that Italy would not enter the War against her, she must, in her turn, be willing to propose definite concessions, giving formal engagements to abide by them. These concessions would, moreover, have to be tendered in decent and dignified fashion — not thrown to Italy, like alms to an importunate beggar. They must show the sincere desire to establish between Austria and Italy, so long on terms of semi-friendship, a new bond of secure and reliable amity; durable, unequivocally affirmed. It was also essential that such concessions should be proposed without delay. The minimum offer must be the Trentino, not, in any case, an ancient Habsburg possession, since, until the Congress of Vienna, it had been, first an independent bishopric, then part of the former Kingdom of Italy, and administered by the Viceroy Eugene Beauharnais. Of course many Italians were demanding the annexation of Trieste, a city whose population was largely

Italian. But to this there were several sound objections, since either a prosperous Trieste would be bad for her neighbour, Venice, whose trade had just recently been revived, at the price only of great expense and effort, or Trieste, by losing her hinterland, as the consequence of incorporation with Italy, might find herself very badly placed. Against conceding Istria and Dalmatia — especially the latter — there was the fact that, in both these regions of the Dual Monarchy, the Italian-speaking element was out-numbered — a minority compared to the Serbo-Croatian. Nevertheless the indispensable minimum was immediate, unreserved cession of the Italian Tyrol; the Trentino; a promise of the autonomy of Trieste within the cadre of the Dual Monarchy, and better treatment for the Italians in Istria and Dalmatia.

In this connection Sonnino reminded me of the fact that, not very long before the War, a piece of clumsy Austrian legislation, expelling certain Italian nationals from Trieste, had caused such bitter feeling in Italy as still rankled when war was declared. This measure had been indeed a depressing instance of the fecklessness of Austrian policy, determined by the many intrigues, cross-currents, and ambitions of the Vienna Court. The Archduke Francis Ferdinand's betrothal to the Archduchess Isabella's pretty lady-in-waiting, Countess Sofie Chotek had, as I have said, caused much ill-feeling between the Archduke Frederick's household and that of the heir to the Throne, in alliance with little Sofie (meanwhile promoted Duchess of Hohenberg) whose husband was completely under her thumb. This rancour was especially marked in the case of the Archduchess Isabella, the Archduke Frederick's wife (*née* Princess Croy). On the failure of her scheme to marry off her daughter to the future Emperor of Austria, she had accepted Prince Gottfried Hohenlohe as son-in-law, though, judged by her standards, a most inadequate one. He was one of those Austrian aristocrats whose frivolity and incompetence did so much to bring about the fall of the Habsburg dynasty. As ambitious as he was useless, he suffered agonies at the displeasure of the violent and very susceptible Francis Ferdinand, whose dislike, besides the Archduchess Isabella, included all in any way connected with her. Prince Hohenlohe had pondered

long on means to mollify the Archduke, whose rancour had become
a real worry to him, and had at last hit on a happy inspiration.   His
brother, Konrad Hohenlohe, later Head Chamberlain, was in those
days Governor of Trieste.   Both Hohenlohe brothers were well aware
of the Archduke Francis Ferdinand's dislike — at times it became
an obsession — of the new Italy.   Gottfried therefore advised his
brother Konrad to seize the first opportunity of taking, as Governor
of Trieste, the most drastic and noisiest measures against the Italians
there.   This advice Konrad Hohenlohe followed, and, naturally, he
chose the very moment when a real improvement of feeling was
beginning between Austria and Italy — the moment when the
Italians had made advances, by sending an Italian general, as special
envoy from their king, to attend the jubilee celebrations of the
Austrian Military Academy, at Wiener Neustadt.   This general, an
ex-cadet of the Academy, had spoken most respectfully at the ceremony, on the training of Austrian officers.   Hohenlohe's silly
measure, coming as it did in answer to this Italian advance, was
considered by all Italy an affront, and had made bad blood there.
But the Archduke Francis Ferdinand was delighted: "Did n't
Konrad do that nicely?" he kept asking every one he met.   His
change of attitude towards the Hohenlohes threw that family into
transports of joy, but, politically, the prank was deplorable, coming
as it did so soon before the Serbian ultimatum.

Every talk I had with Sonnino, and many others with Roman
friends and acquaintance, made me feel it essential to act quickly,
if we wanted, at the eleventh hour, to keep Italy from declaring war
on Austria.   *Bis dat qui cito dat*, I kept telling the Austrian Ambassador von Macchio, and repeated this in every letter and communication to Berlin.   I could never manage to learn the exact
extent of Italian commitments, made before my arrival, to the
Allies; nor, above all, could I be certain that she had not definitely
and finally pledged herself.   My instinct told me that, though preliminaries might already have reached their final stage, there had
been, as yet, no binding official promise.   It was therefore a question
of giving Italian statesmen the speediest possible guarantee that
Austria would acknowledge, without *arrière pensée*, the minimum

at least of Italian aspirations and demands, while, at the same time, a current of opinion must be created which should lead the Italian Government to prefer the specific realization of its ambitions to all the hazards of a war. Whatever I might achieve in this direction, the freedom with which I would stake my personal credit, must do more, however, than merely serve to prevent an Austro-Italian conflict in the interests of the Habsburg Monarchy — it must profit my own German Fatherland, surrounded already with enemies. I knew that war by Italy on Austria would entail our further military support, a support which must cost us very dear. To-day I am still convinced that, had Italy refrained from war in 1915, she would later have had an excellent chance of obtaining the Trentino without bloodshed, as well as autonomy for Trieste, and better treatment for Italians under Austrian rule. Had Italy kept out of the War she would have been as a refuge for all nations and could have exported to every belligerent. The lira to-day would be on a par with the Swiss franc. I believe, moreover, that when, at Versailles, from the Allies, she received vast territories peopled by Southern Slavs and Germans, Italy not only ran counter to those principles of self-determination which she herself invoked so frequently, but did lasting disservice to her own true and permanent interests. Without Italy's help it is improbable that the Allies could have imposed the Versailles Treaty which, if it did not dismember Germany, maimed, and undoubtedly crippled her. Versailles has destroyed the balance of power in Europe and given France her European hegemony over the Mediterranean and in North Africa. These disastrous results of the peace were not really in Italy's interests, properly understood. Neither Crispi, Minghetti, nor Cavour would have been satisfied with such an achievement, as the price of all the blood and treasure poured out by Italy to secure it.

The Allied propaganda in Rome was not only very active but most intelligent. Their best weapon was the violence done to Belgium — done, as they never wearied of repeating, in defiance of time-honoured and solemn promises. One day soon after my arrival, I was crossing the Piazza di Spagna when I saw in a bookseller's window my coat-of-arms, displayed on a square of cardboard, well *en evidence*. Underneath, in huge red letters, the inscription: "*Le chiffon de papier.*" Closer inspection showed me that this was a reproduction of that article of the London Protocol of 1831 which had established Belgian independence. It had been drawn up in London by the various representatives of the Powers, each signing above his arms and seal. For Russia, unless I am mistaken, Pozzo di Borgo had signed it; for France, Talleyrand; Apponyi for Austria, Palmerston for Great Britain, and my great-uncle, Heinrich von Bülow, for Prussia.

But Belgian propaganda had devised more grossly effective methods than this — methods extremely well calculated to stir and enflame the Italian people, whose lower orders are still so simple-minded. Little statues of the Madonna were being sold, before her a kneeling child with its hands hacked off. It raised bleeding stumps to the Mother of God, and prayed: "Holy Mother, make my hands grow again, which the barbarous Germans have taken from me."

No German soldier ever mutilated a French or Belgian child! I do not think there was ever another army better disciplined or stricter than ours — nor one more essentially humane. On November 23, 1900, when the Socialists in the Reichstag had thrown mud at our German soldiers in China, I turned on Bebel and declared: "I say that the German private, for all his magnificent energy in warfare, is the superior of any in the world in matters of humanity and discipline. Our guarantee for what I assert is the character of our people as a whole. Through all the thousand years of our history, we have known how to be both valiant and humane." These words are equally true of the German armies in France and Belgium. But our neglect of our signed obligation in the matter of Belgian neutrality, the bad effect of which had only been aggravated by Bethmann's clumsy Reichstag speech of August 4, 1914, and made still worse by his wretched description of international treaties as "scraps of paper", was doing us very definite harm in Italy, as it was everywhere else in the world. The Belgian propaganda mission to Italy (its speakers included both an eloquent Socialist leader and that famous preacher Father Jansens, O.S.B.) had no difficulty at all in arousing sympathy for a Belgium "traitorously assailed", or in throwing our cause into disrepute.

I was received by King Victor Emanuel III, to whom I had to deliver my credentials. He welcomed me as follows: "*Si vous étiez resté au pouvoir, toutes ces bêtises ne seraient pas arrivées.*" In the audience which ensued, the King explained, calmly and objectively, avoiding all but the bare facts, that, surprised as they had been by the ultimatum, no Italian Government whatsoever could have come into the War on the side of the Central Powers. Germany, moreover, had run counter to the spirit in which the Triple Alliance was conceived, by leaving Austria free to proceed with her Serbian adventure — and had then herself taken the initiative by declaring war on Russia and on France. He was assured that all this entailed no German perfidy, and Signor Bollati, the Italian Ambassador in Berlin, had called special attention to this again and again. But clumsiness in politics often does more harm than mere bad faith. The King was, however, too polite to use the actual word "*maladresse*"; he only spoke of "*un certain manque d'habileté.*" Now, he concluded, it was for Austria to speed up the necessary concessions. *Fatte presto!*

Next day my wife and I were received in audience by the Queen Mother, Margherita. Before the War we had often been her private guests, both in her beautiful Roman palace and at Stupinigi, her château outside Turin. She was a lover of serious conversations. Born of a German mother, a Princess of Saxony and the sister of kings Albert and George of Saxony, she had, until war was declared, been as great an admirer of all things German as her chivalrous husband, King Umberto. She spoke and wrote German like a native.

But the ultimatum, Bethmann's oratorical *faux pas*, the invasion of Belgium, had all, I had been told, greatly displeased her. By the time I reached Rome, on my mission, many faithful servants of her house had long been assuring Queen Margherita that she had no right to oppose the national aspirations of Italy. She, as the queen, they had said to her, should be more ambitious for her country than any other Italian woman. These exhortations were scarcely neces-

ANTONIO SALANDRA

sary. The Queen Mother was already a passionately Italian patriot. Our present audience was conducted with all her usual graciousness and tact. The thing she most regretted about the War was that events would have made it very difficult for German princes and princesses to marry their equals in England and Russia. I answered that the policy of great countries could not, as had sometimes been the case, be determined by royal alliances. Her Majesty, with reason, pointed out that several royal marriages in the past, between Germany and Russia, England and Germany, had been conducive both to peace and the better promotion of German interests. As a second disagreeable result of the War, the Queen suggested the possible danger of a serious spread of democracy: it might affect every country and would certainly become an urgent problem in Austria, Germany, and Russia. She was not, she said, in any way *una codina* (a reactionary); still it was disturbing to see the democratic flood rise, as it does to-day, all over the world, and in particular the flood of Socialism.

Before she dismissed us the Queen Mother took my wife aside — they had played together as children — and asked her: "Maria, tell me the truth! Did you or did you not want the War?" My wife swore by all that was most sacred, by the Holy Mother of God herself, that neither the German Emperor nor his people had wanted war in the least. "Well, then, all I can say," answered the Queen, "is that the German Ministers and diplomats in power in the summer of 1914 are the biggest fools the world has ever known." I here anticipate to add that, about two years after this, I had my chance of repeating her remarks to the Emperor. It came in the late autumn of 1916, at my first and only audience with my Sovereign after my return from Rome. He had summoned me to the Neues Palais, unexpectedly and for no particular reason, and began to ask me about Queen Margherita, for whom he had cherished a youthful flame. "What does she think of the War?" he asked, and took no exception at all to the Queen's remarks on the political advantage of royal alliances, but disagreed entirely with Her Majesty as to the added power the War would give the Socialists. This prophecy seemed to hurt him very much, and he interrupted me, to exclaim:

"But it's just the opposite! Everybody says that the Berliners have never felt happier than they do under 'Isaak.' If the people were given a free hand, it would close down that talking-shop in the Reichstag, declare all Ministers superfluous, and petition that generals might go on managing it." "Isaak" was the nickname of General von Kessel, one of His Majesty's closest favourites, invested, for the period of the War, with the functions of Acting Commandant of the *corps de garde*, and Governor of Berlin. Unluckily future events were to prove that the Queen Mother had been a better prophet than the Emperor.

The Councillor of Embassy, Von Hindenburg, became my stay and support in this difficult winter. The son of an old General von Hindenburg, then no more, he had served in the Guards and was cousin to the great Field Marshal. On his mother's side he was the grandson of Prince Herbert Münster, for many years our ambassador in Paris and London. He had married an English wife, who behaved with great reserve, tact, and kindness, in the difficult position in which she found herself. Major von Schweinitz was our military attaché — his father had been our ambassador in Vienna and St. Petersburg.

How many hopes have been shattered by the War, and its result, the revolution! Wilhelm von Schweinitz was an exceptionally keen and capable officer and a man of unusual cultivation. He would have had a future; would have made as good a general as ambassador, adjutant general, or court chamberlain. By him I was often reminded of Goethe's saying that no one has so good a chance in society as the really well-read officer. And he combined the good points of two races. On his father's side he came of an old Silesian family, endowed with all the virtues of Prussian junkers; his American mother had bequeathed him her sound good sense and freedom from prejudice. At Wilhelm's birth, in the early 'seventies, his father, at that time German Ambassador at Vienna, had asked his father-in-law, Mr. Jay, the American Ambassador, as they stood looking down on his cradle: "What are we going to make of this youngster — Emperor of America, or President of the German Republic?" This first suggestion seems quite impossible, and the second not at all a likely one. Wilhelm von Schweinitz and Herbert von Hindenburg were my excellent and ever loyal collaborators.

But most of all, perhaps, did I find a never-failing source of comfort in Francis Xavier von Stockhammern, the Chamberlain and Privy Councillor appointed to the Bavarian Legation in Rome, only a few weeks before my own arrival there. With his fluent Italian, intimate knowledge of Italian culture and life, love of work and capacity for it — but even more by his dependable and exceptionally charming personality — he did both me and his country distinguished service, in a most responsible and in every way ticklish situation.

The tact and delicacy of feeling proper to all races of ancient culture characterized Italian society. Through the whole five months I was in Rome, I met with the same politeness everywhere — both from the partisans of Italian neutrality and the "*guerrifondaji*", as they were called — the people who were urging war on Austria. With the mass of the people it was the same. Even during the days when every newspaper was passionately debating future war — when the subject filled the air of Rome, Parliament, the cafés, the streets — not once, on my walks in the Corso, to the Villa Borghese, or on the Pincio, was I threatened, or even made the object of stares and impertinent curiosity.

Not many days before Italy's declaration of war, General Count Morra dined with me. He was one of the most impassioned "*guerrifondaji*", and had fought, as a very young officer, in the ranks of the Piedmontese at Novara, where he had seen King Carlo Alberto pass down the ranks on horseback, with just that air of melancholy grace expressed by his statue near the Quirinal. The king, catching sight of young Morra, the son of his *maréchal de cour*, offered him his hand with a smile, saying that he brought greetings from his father, who counted on his son to do him honour. From second lieutenant at Novara, Morra had attained the rank of general, was made tutor to King Victor Emanuel III, and finally Ambassador to St. Petersburg. From me he made no secret of his standpoint, expressed to his former pupil, and that pupil's mother, as the following: "The House of Savoy must always champion the Italian national idea. That idea should be its sole consideration, one from which nothing can distract it, and in promoting which no obstacle must hinder it." In those difficult days when King Carlo Alberto was asking himself whether, true to the former traditions of his house, he should follow the Austrians or oppose them at the head of revolutionary patriots, that monarch, so given to pessimism, had remarked to his *maréchal de cour: "Je suis entre le poignard des carbonari et le chocolat des jésuites."*

He had plumped for the Carbonaro's dagger, was beaten at Novara, and died in exile, at a Portuguese convent at Oporto. Yet, none the less, he had judged correctly. And, in spite of the Novara defeat, his son had been equally right to continue the nationalist policy. The greater part of the Piedmontese nobility were in violent opposition to Cavour, and so were nearly all the priests. But Cavour led us on to Milan, Florence, Naples, Palermo, and finally even to Rome. The breach of the Porta Pia raised storms of criticism and protest — as much in Northern Italy as anywhere, and notably in Piedmont itself, where, from time immemorial, the influence of the Church has been profound. Yet, in spite of these cross-currents, defeats, and obstacles, the House of Savoy still reigns in Italy, whereas both Habsburgs and Bourbons, who tried to oppose Italian national feeling, have been turned out of Florence and Naples, Parma, and Modena. Thus Count Morra.

It should be said that, till the day when war was declared, there were still, all over Italy, many patriots who strongly urged neutrality on their country. Not in Rome alone, but everywhere! Such pleaders for peace were less noisy than the urgers of war; yet they were, in the whole, more numerous. As late as in the May of 1915, a deputy of my acquaintance related how the Minister of the Interior had said to him that if there were a plebiscite, there would be no war. For many years Giolitti had been Italy's most powerful politician. Like all our foreign friends, he considered that we had blundered grievously in the whole ultimatum policy. Giolitti too, when war broke out, had suggested a demand for the Trentino, and the better treatment of Italian nationals in Austria. In a letter to his friend, Peano, the deputy, he had used the word "*Parecchio*" (something) to define the extent of Italian demands for compensa-

tion. The formula has since become a famous one. But Giolitti
had felt that all aspirations might be satisfied without the pouring
out of blood and treasure, the inevitable risk, of a great war. He
too had seen, from the beginning, that neutrality could only be
guaranteed by inevitable concessions, freely made, without *arrière-
pensée*, by Austria, in a dignified manner, and at once. The longer
she delayed, the more obscure and hesitant our policy, the greater
grew the danger of war.

Pope Benedict XV strove for peace — firmly and prudently, with
entire benevolence, great wisdom, without once overstepping the
limits set by his ecclesiastical function — as a true representative on
earth of the eternal Prince of Peace should strive for it. I shall
always remember it as an honour that my efforts received his support. He wished the Habsburg Monarchy to survive, since Austria
was the last great Catholic power. But he could see quite clearly
that war must come if the Dual Monarchy went on hesitating to
sacrifice at least the Trentino. The Pope, who loved Italy, his
country, really desired that her aspirations might be fulfilled, in so
far as this was in any way compatible with the survival of a Catholic
dynasty. But to him the supreme duty of the war was to end the
carnage as soon as possible or, in any case, limit its extension. He
charged Cardinal Piffl, the cardinal archbishop of Vienna, to speak
in this sense to the old Emperor. Francis Joseph, then eighty-four,
received the cardinal, who, modestly and timidly, repeated his
instruction of the Holy Father's wishes. The Emperor would not
even let him finish. His old face crimson with rage, he seized Piffl's
arm, and literally thrust him from the room. Francis Joseph was
a true son of the Church, a very devout and practising Catholic, but
his feelings as a Habsburg had got the better of him.

At Easter His Holiness sent my wife his apostolic blessing, with
a message to me that he prayed for the success of my mission. In
answer to my own respectful letter, in which I had already thanked
him for his very enlightened support, I received the following,
written in the Pope's own hand:

*Eccelenza, Accogliemmo con particolare gradimento la pregiata lettera che
l'Eccelenza Vostra si compiaceva indirizzarci in data de 21 corrente.*

Teniamo ora a significare personalmente all'Eccelenza Vostra quanto noi abbiamo apprezzato le nobili espressioni, nelle quali si traduceva l'ossequio cordiale che Ella professa alla Nostra persona ed a questa Sede Apostolica su cui, in circostanze così calamitose, volle il Signore collocarci; manifestazioni dell' animo di Lei grande e delicato, delle quali serberemo caro e perenne il ricordo.

L'alta stima, inoltre, che Noi sempre Le portammo ed il riconoscimento delle doti esimie che L'adornano, e delle non poche benemerenze che Ella, nella lunga Sua vita politica, seppe acquistarsi verso la Sua patria, avrebbero reso a Noi sommamente accetto l'omaggio che l'Eccelenza Vostra, insieme con la degnissima Sua Consorte, si riprometteva di presentarci personalmente alla Sua partenza da questa città, qualora le circostanze l'avessero consentito.

Ad ogni modo, accetiamo con animo grato l'augurio cortese che Ella, Signor Principe, sul finire della lettera affidava alla Provvidenza Divina, perchè propizia assista questa Sede, e alla Nostra volta Noi amiamo di volgerla con pieno ricambio del Nostro affetto paterno, alla di Lei Nazione, a Vostra Eccelenza stessa ed alla nobilissima Sua Sposa, Cui altresi concediamo ben di cuore la implorata benedizione apostolica. Benedictus P.P. XV. Roma, 30 Maggio 1915.

(Excellency: We welcome with especial pleasure the valued letter it has pleased you to send Us, dated the twenty-first of the present month. We consider Ourselves most bound to give you Our personal assurance that We appreciate the noble words in which Your Excellency has expressed such cordial homage to Our person and to this Our Apostolic Chair, to which, at such a time of calamity, it has pleased Almighty God to assign Us: proofs of Your Excellency's own strength and delicacy of spirit which We shall keep as an ever fresh and cherished memory. Moreover, the high esteem in which We have never failed to hold you, Our acknowledgment of Your Excellency's distinguished talents, no less than of the meritorious services which, in the course of a long political career, you have been able to render your country, would, in themselves, have made supremely acceptable to Us the homage which both you and your worthy Consort intended to render Us in person before your departure from this city, had circumstances permitted you to do so. However this may be, We welcome with a heart of gratitude the courteous wish which you, *Signor Principe*, express at the conclusion of your letter, that Almighty God may assist Our Throne, while in Our turn We express the like for your country, for Your Excellency's person, and the person of your noble Consort, to whom We accord with all Our heart the apostolic blessing she has asked of Us. Benedictus P.P. XV. Rome. May 30th 1915.)

This same generous spirit of peace had inspired another letter received shortly after my arrival in Rome, by Donna Laura Minghetti, my wife's mother, from Princess Leonille Wittgenstein. The Princess, nearly as old as Count Greppi, was ninety-nine at the time she wrote it. She died in 1918, at the age of a hundred and one, at Ouchy, near Lausanne, where she had built herself a villa and a little chapel to St. Joseph. She was the mother-in-law of my predecessor, Chlodwig Hohenlohe, at whose house in Paris I had often met her, thirty years before. She and I had discussed many subjects, and she had been as kind to me as to her son-in-law. By origin a Russian (*née* Princess Bariatinsky), she had married a Prince Louis von Sayn-Wittgenstein, who lived in the Rhineland, where she heard the Rhenish carillons, was influenced profoundly by Rhenish piety, and became a fervent convert to Catholicism. She had written as follows, in French, to Donna Laura :

Chère et très charmante donna Laura,

Bonne année, année réparatrice! Après celle-ci, effroyable, qui finit noyée dans le sang et les torrents de larmes! Je grille de vous dire un mot tout petit, mais brûlant du sentiment qui l'inspire. Je vous le confie, afin que vous le transmettiez à votre illustre et très aimé gendre, le prince de Bülow. Au milieu du chaos qui bouleverse le monde et creuse des abîmes entre les peuples, la réapparition du Prince est un coup de grâce de la Providence, et le signe évident de sa prédestination à l'accomplissement, du salut de l'humanité, de sa dignité, de son honneur et de son équilibre. Je prie Dieu, seul juste, bon, et tout-puissant, de présider aux inspirations du Prince, de l'assister et de bénir ses efforts. Je vous quitte sur cette pensée et vous embrasse aussi tendrement que je vous aime.

In most afflicting contrast to this spirit of peace and generosity was the petty spite of Berlin diplomats, of whose letters I give, as characteristic, the following, received from Bethmann-Hollweg, dated March 16, 1915. He had just received a report from the military attaché, Von Schweinitz, whose candour and precision seem to have riled him :

I was about to write when I received your interesting telegram, relative to your interview with Signor Sonnino. It appears, from this Italian attitude, that Austria, as she herself has told us repeatedly, has every reason for her fears that the more response she makes to Italian demands the more these demands are sure to increase. Italy asks for a treaty of cession, to be put into immediate effect. Naturally Austria could not accept such a suggestion, nor, I insist on this point, could Germany. Italian policy seems one of blackmail, without example in all history. But to practical concessions there is a limit, and one which we could never overstep without detriment, of the most serious kind, to the dignity and prestige of our two empires, allied in a victorious struggle. Your Highness will, I am sure, agree in this, and will not fail to bring all your energy, and all your well-known diplomatic skill, to bear on the Italian Government to get them to renounce so exigent an attitude. I am, however, perfectly well aware that, should we fail to obtain of her this concession, Italy will inevitably join our enemies. In Berlin we have done all that is humanly possible to persuade the Cabinet in Vienna to abandon the uncompromising tone adopted by it when the Trentino question was first raised. The results we have so far managed to obtain prove that our methods were the right ones. It would, no doubt, have been desirable to have reached these results more speedily, but you know the factors which have retarded us. To begin with, there is that ancient Austro-Italian antagonism which makes any sacrifice to Italy so difficult for Austrian pride to accept; there were then the erroneous reports of the Austrian Ambassador in Rome; finally we must reckon the exaggerated hopes aroused by our joint successes on the Eastern Front. In these circumstances, I am more than surprised that our military attaché in Rome, Major von Schweinitz, should permit himself to criticize as he does our present policy towards Austria. I read in his reports expressions, the good taste or competence of which I need not discuss, such as "with a little more energy", "*Berlin est faible*", etc. Major von Schweinitz' use of such phraseology may be excused by the fact that, insufficiently versed in politics, he is unable to form a just idea of what may, or may not, be gained by diplomatic pressure. In actual fact we are saying in Vienna as much as is at all permissible with an ally: had we proceeded further, and used threats, we should only have brought the Austrians to the point of laying down their arms and might so have been left to face our enemies alone. At Teschen I myself made every effort to influence Baron Burian, though without success, since the Baron was most energetically supported by the Austrian Chief of the General Staff, also present. This officer maintained his attitude, although fully in agree-

POPE BENEDICT XV

ment with his German colleague that, should Italy and Roumania join
our enemies, it would be tantamount to our losing the whole War.   Herr
von Schweinitz seems to overlook my efforts, and had, it appears, received
previous information from Your Highness of all that passed at the Teschen
interview, since one of his reports, in reference to the attitude of these
staff officers, qualifies Baron Burian as our worst enemy.   Yet he seems
entirely oblivious of my difficulties, although, in the matter of Italy, he
has before him palpable examples of the limits set to all diplomacy, not
supported by real military preponderance.   He will in future, I hope,
confine himself more strictly to his military duties, though at the same
time supporting Your Highness to the uttermost by using whatever
influence he commands in the military and social circles with which these
bring him into contact.

> In old esteem I remain, with heartiest greetings
>
> > Your very devoted
> >
> > > BETHMANN-HOLLWEG.

Herr von Bethmann seemed quite unaware that at present he was
merely condemning his own policy, inaugurated at the time of the
ultimatum, since now he expressed the fear that Austria might "lay
down their arms", and leave us to face our enemies alone.   Yet had
he not involved us in this struggle simply and solely on Austria's
behalf?   And if these two Staff Officers, the German and the Austro-
Hungarian, both admitted that, with Italy and Roumania against
us, we might feel that we had lost the War, had not, in heaven's
name, this German Chancellor the duty of avoiding such a contingency, by any means — at any cost?

From Naples at the end of March, Flotow turned up in Rome
unexpectedly.   He stayed at the Palazzo Caffarelli, where he had my
reports submitted to him, and took notes, evidently in order to pull
them to pieces and, in private correspondence with Jagow, throw
discredit on everything I had said in them.   He paid two lengthy
calls on the Austrian Ambassador, Herr von Macchio.   Later I was
to hear he had told this ambassador with emphasis that Italy would
never dare attack so powerful a State as Austria-Hungary.   For
him all that Salandra and Sonnino were saying was "humbug", the
bellicose articles in every Italian newspaper were "so much stage

thunder", etc. He was equally emphatic in warning Herr von Macchio that neither the Austrian Government nor, in particular, the old Emperor, Francis Joseph, would ever forgive his discussing, or so much as suggesting to the Italians, such a step as the cession of the Trentino. As for me, during the ten days of his stay, Herr von Flotow did not once approach me. He contented himself with spreading the rumour that nothing I might say or do in Rome would have any real support from my government.

To-day, as I look back on this indescribable behaviour, I feel that I was wrong in not having wired straight off to Berlin, resigning. I am still amazed at my own patience. Brought up as I had been in the Bismarck tradition by my father, a tradition of absolute devotion to the duty I owed my country, I wished, after so many years at the head of the diplomatic service, to give one last example of selfless detachment. But I saw in advance where this Flotow-Jagow intrigue was leading us, and, in this conviction, addressed a confidential circular to the consulates, warning all German subjects domiciled in Italy to be prepared for eventual hostilities between the Central Powers and the Peninsula. A fortnight later I repeated this warning more urgently. By the end of April, in my conversations with Sonnino, I was beginning to feel he had crossed the Rubicon. Of this I had no tangible proof, but could sense it in the tone of his voice, and read his intentions in his eyes. Then I remembered the Bülow device, *"Nil desperandum"*, and some heartening words of the heroic French sailor, Jean Bart, inscribed on his monument at Dunkerque, that, while there is still a bullet, it must be fired. On May 9th I sent word to Baron von Macchio to come to the Villa Malta for an interview, and forced him to write, from my dictation, a note to the effect that the Austrian Government would be willing to cede that part of the Tyrol inhabited by Italians, Gradisca, and the west bank of the Isonzo, in so far as its population was Italian. Trieste was to become a free city within the cadre of the Austro-Hungarian Empire, with an Italian municipal council and university; Austria was to recognize Italian sovereignty in Valona and declare that she had no political interest in Albania. This note was confidentially transmitted to the Italian

Government, that same day. It had needed the uttermost pressure to determine the hesitant Von Macchio to a step, at the eleventh hour, which in January might well have succeeded, at the moment when Giolitti's "*Parecchio*" was still the slogan of the day. But once again Napoleon's saying was proved true. Austria was still "*en retard.*" Since April 24, 1915, the Italian Government had been secretly committed to the Allies, and, nine days later, on May 3d, had publicly denounced the Triple Alliance. Though these Austrian offers had made a deep impression on the mass of the Italian people their effect, by now, was insufficient to create any real popular movement, more especially since the "*guerrifondaji*" had begun to strain every nerve and were doing their best to mobilize the streets. And Von Macchio, whom I had scared into publishing them, had soon begun to regret having done so. He declared that there had been a misapprehension, that his government had not given its formal assent, either on May 9th or later; the whole Trentino question, he said, could receive no definite settlement till the peace conference. The secretaries of both the Austrian embassies said the same, whenever they got a chance to do so.

From Berlin I received instructions to request one last audience of King Victor Emanuel III. I was to transmit to him a letter from the Kaiser — a last appeal to his feelings of personal friendship and sense of his treaty obligations. This audience was granted immediately. The King received me amiably enough: he was calm, but obviously resolved — had taken his decision and burnt his boats. To me he explained that there are moments at which constitutional monarchs are powerless against the reasoned opinion of their Ministers, supported by a majority in Parliament, by public opinion, tradition, and the highest interests of the State. He thanked me for the loyal manner in which I had discharged my mission. "At least," he said, "if war comes, it won't be your fault."

Baron von Macchio still refused to believe in any serious danger of war with Italy. I told him that, by the first week of May, before another fortnight was up, she would have presented her declaration to Austria. He answered me: "Not a bit of it! The Italians are always excitable. They'll calm down."

Our Foreign Office staff were equally blind. A few days before war was declared, I received from Berlin, for my instruction, some "impressions" of a journey in Italy, written by a German who, the Wilhelmstrasse assured me, was "highly intelligent." This poor man, having travelled all through Italy, from the Austrian frontier down to Naples, declared that nowhere had he seen signs of serious preparation for war; this in those feverish days when, from morning to night, in every Italian city, the streets were full of transports and marching troops: when, in Rome, there was all the stir and activity proper to the eve of grand manœuvres, or of mobilization itself.

Three days before Italy entered the War a highly placed official of the Vienna Foreign Office, Count Nemes, who had just arrived in Rome, telephoned to know if he might call on me. I asked him to luncheon. He said he felt bewildered. Count Burian, the Austrian Foreign Minister, had sent him to Rome with instructions to request me to remain on there through the summer and continue my efforts for peace. The Minister was sure that with my "remarkable powers of dialect", I could succeed in pacifying the Italians. Such was the feeling in Vienna, added Count Nemes, but here things seemed to be so different! He had come to stay with his Italian mother-in-law, Contessa Spaletti. With tears in her eyes she had embraced him, asking why in the world he had come to Rome at a moment when war was just beginning. The prospect seemed doubly appalling to her, since her daughter was the wife of an Austrian diplomat. She advised her son-in-law not to unpack. I could only suggest to Count Nemes that he should follow his mother-in-law's advice.

The deputy, Erzberger, thanks to his understanding with the Vatican, had supported me most valiantly in Rome, in my efforts to preserve the peace. He had also highly praised my activities in every report he sent to Berlin. His intentions were always of the best, but he lacked political acumen. He too had refused to believe that war was possible. In spite of all my urgent reports to the contrary, he kept telling Berlin I had saved the peace and that everything would now be for the best. In passing through Munich, a few days before Italy's breach with Austria, he called there on the mother of Von Stockhammern, my distinguished colleague, the Councillor of Legation. He had come like a whirlwind into her drawing-room: "I have all sorts of messages from your son. He 'll be here himself within a few days. He has been doing so much to save the peace — and now we 're certain of it, etc." When the lady, twenty-four hours later, read in the *Münchener Neueste Nachrichten*, that Italy had declared war on Austria, she wrote to her son: "The thought that this muddle-headed little Swabian is now in a leading position in Berlin has been making me quite melancholy."

On May 25th I left Rome, taking with me the whole Embassy staff. All secret archives had preceded me, a fortnight earlier, by courier. My departure went through without an incident. The people outside the Villa Malta, and in all the streets my car had to traverse to reach the station, bowed to me in very courteous fashion. An hour before I left I had said good-bye to my wife's mother, a woman of the highest intelligence and greatest generosity of feeling, who had been as a second mother to me. I was never to see her again. From my brother-in-law, Prince Paolo Camporeale, this also was to be my last farewell. They both were dead before the Armistice! The Prince was the only member of the Italian Parliament who had given his vote against war.

I left Italy full of sorrow at having failed to keep her at peace with the Central Powers. I was well aware that, in December, the position might easily have been saved. More energy and, alas, more loyalty from the Berlin Government, might have saved it. It had been lost by the vacillations of Bethmann, Berchtold, and Burian, the intrigues of Jagow and Flotow. At the time of their insensate step against Serbia, our diplomats, in deference to senile susceptibilities, had treated *en quantité négligeable* our ally in the Triple Alliance. They had continued to do so undisturbed. My hands were only freed when Italy's had been tied by the *Patto di Londra*. That was too late.

CHAPTER XVIII

Back to Berlin — A Dinner Party at Bethmann-Hollweg's — But I Am not Received by the Emperor — Bethmann Writes to Me — My Answer and His Reply — My Reception at Hamburg — The War Develops — Bethmann-Hollweg Indicates the Future Establishment of an Independent Poland.

But the Foreign Office did not share these regrets. In Berlin, in the days of my Chancellorship, a book had appeared, under the title, "Kaiser Wilhelm II und die Schwarzseher." [1] After the war it was republished in a new and much enlarged edition. It is said to have been written by a Herr Nebel, a publicist of a certain reputation, who had been in closest contact with the Foreign Office, and had also visited Rome for several weeks in the winter of 1914–1915 — though I do not remember having met him there. In this second edition of his book, which appeared in 1919, the author says of my Roman mission: "Nothing could give a better idea of the spirit and atmosphere of our Foreign Office than the rumour, so generally believed, that there was never a day of greater rejoicing in the Wilhelmstrasse than that on which Italy declared war on us. Her declaration had given the reigning clique their weapon. They could rid themselves once and for all of Prince von Bülow, who had staked his reputation in Rome, and made use of all his very important connections there, to prevent our having to face yet another enemy. All his efforts were scandalously betrayed by the Wilhelmstrasse, and this from entirely personal motives."

This "Pessimist" is perfectly right in adding that, at the time when the World War was declared, a small clique of minor officials had gained control of the Foreign Office — people whose sole idea of German policy was that they themselves should achieve decorations and titles by it. Raymond Recouly, a French diplomatist and historian, published, after the War, under the title, "Le Duel entre

[1] "The Emperor William II and the Pessimists."

Bülow et Barrère", some very interesting observations : *"Ce duel fut très vif. Politiquement, il nous faut le reconnaître aujourd'hui, Bülow aurait peut-être gagné la partie, mais psychologiquement, elle était perdue d'avance. Etant donné la situation crée par la diplomatie de Vienne et de Berlin, même le genie diplomatique d'un Prince de Bülow ne pouvait obtenir aucun résultat."*

On my journey back into Germany, the Swiss authorities welcomed me most courteously at the frontier. At Karlsruhe I was met by a representative of the Grand Duchess Louise, who tendered me that Sovereign's thanks for my patriotic efforts in Rome. Jagow, in Berlin, had spread a report that I should not be returning immediately. He hoped by this to prevent any reception, at the Anhalter Bahnhof, in my honour, although I myself had not wanted one. Next day, in every paper it could command, the Foreign Office published sarcastic little paragraphs, to the effect that, at the station, the only people there to receive me had been a hall porter and the proprietor of the Hotel Adlon. But I had already heard from Eugen Zimmermann : "There has been some talk of your possible reappointment to the chancellorship. Herr von Jagow remarked, à propos of it, that such a step would scarcely be possible, since nobody believes you nowadays. He said this to Count Schwerin-Löwitz. Such foolery is surely quite superfluous ! You, I think, would be the last man to wish to come back just at present. Of all the funny little stories Herr von Jagow has been spreading to harm you, the most amusing is his assertion that you can no longer manage more than half an hour's work a day. It seems that the rest of your time is spent asleep, on a sofa, in a dressing gown." Zimmermann added that though he was doing all he could to show the absurdity of this gossip he felt it as well that I should be warned. These accounts of my health and personal habits had been invented by Flotow, for Jagow to repeat in Berlin. Actually, never in my life, which till then had been anything but an idle one, had I had to work so hard or see so many people as in Rome during the winter of 1914–1915. Nor have I ever worn a dressing gown or been in the habit of sleeping on sofas. If I had, I should not feel in the least ashamed of it. No less a man than Bismarck in his old age would

lie down on the sofa after lunch, to smoke his post-prandial pipe on
it. And in his young days he wore a dressing gown — a flowered
dressing gown, even! I can see him in it still! He looked most
eighteenth-century in it, though every whit as powerful and dignified
as he did in his Halberstädt Cuirassiers' tunic. The ambassador
Schweinitz once described to me the manner in which Bismarck had
received him, soon after being appointed Prime Minister and Minister
for Foreign Affairs. While expounding his plans for the new government, the great man had swung the tassels of his dressing gown!

"In home affairs I am royalist to the backbone. If necessary,
I would follow the king to La Vendée, and fight for him side by side
with the peasants of the old March of Brandenburg. But in foreign policy I would not stop short of revolution. *Flectere si nequeo
superos, Acheronta movebo!*"

Not one of these schemes should I have mentioned in my account
of the portentous and terrible happenings which transformed the
history of Germany at the time of my mission to Rome, had I alone
been made to suffer by them. Their deep significance lies in this —
that they laid bare the most deep-seated cancer, a veritable state of
moral rot, in the various departments of the Foreign Office. Mean
and silly personal ambitions, lamentably devoid of all patriotic
scruple, appear to have determined our policy at a time when in
every trench there were dying soldiers.

For the evening of my return to Berlin I had accepted an invitation to dine with the Chancellor. He thanked me in the most
pathetic fashion for all my "self-sacrificing efforts." Jagow, who
sat next my wife, told her that he did not understand how I ever
could have advised the Austrian Government to cede the Trentino.
She answered that I was still persuaded that Italy might have been
kept out of the War had concessions been made in time. Jagow
continued: "But surely you forget that to give up the Trentino
would have broken the heart of His Apostolic Majesty, the venerable
Emperor Francis Joseph, the eldest Sovereign in Europe. You
should remember that Austria is the last stronghold of the aristocratic tradition and Conservative principles, whereas Italy is a
democratic and revolutionary structure."

After the meal Jagow, whom I had seemed not to notice, came sidling nervously towards me with an air of such extreme discomfort as showed plainly that his conscience was not clear. Before the whole room I turned my back on him and can think of few moments in my life which have given me deeper satisfaction! Is there any more perfect sensation than to be free to show a man one detests one's feelings? Next day he went to call on my friend, Prince Wedel, whom he begged to put in a word with me in his favour. He well knew he owed me his career, I had been his benefactor, etc. — but Flotow was his "dearest friend." This attempt to curry favour was unsuccessful. I continued not to notice Jagow. I even cut him in the Upper House, to which, on Bethmann's suggestion, the Emperor had just promoted him — an august assembly with a great patriotic tradition, in which he was as much out of place as ever Pilate in the Creed.

Soon after my return, an aide-de-camp told me in the closest confidence that the Emperor had wanted to receive me on my arrival back from Rome and thank me. Bethmann and Jagow had dissuaded him. To grant me any special sign of favour, even so much as an audience, they had said, would make a bad impression on Vienna. It is not hard to imagine the satisfaction with which the Austrian Ambassador, Gottfried Hohenlohe, kept always closely informed by Reischach, the *maréchal de cour*, informed Vienna of this discourtesy. It is equally easy to see how Bethmann's weakness encouraged the reckless Austrian Cabinet. A few days later the Kaiserin did us the honour of asking us both to luncheon. The only other guests at table were the Duchess of Brunswick and her husband. Her Majesty thanked us most touchingly for all I had managed to do in Rome, but did not conceal from me the fact that the Chancellor and Jagow between them had prevented the Emperor from receiving me. Not long after this I received the following from Bethmann:

MOST ESTEEMED PRINCE,

In our talk the other day at my house I attempted to give you some account of the degree of pressure we were able to exercise from here on the Vienna Cabinet, throughout the Italian crisis. Now that we are at war with Italy, people are looking for a scapegoat, and, as I hear, are less inclined to accuse Rome or Vienna than Berlin. I fear that all such discussion will be to the detriment of our country. Your Highness' established popularity, the attitude of the whole Press towards you, and the applause with which the Reichstag received my speech, must all confirm you in the assurance that no possible doubts can arise as to the nature of your own unflagging efforts in Rome. They need no defence. As for the Cabinet in Vienna it is clear that, so long as we are at war, the most obvious *raison d'Etat* will prevent me or any other person in a high official position from letting the public know the full extent of Viennese responsibility. These are not the days in which to indicate the many grievous errors of Austrian policy in its treatment of the whole Italian question — errors which go back several decades. Nor can I make known the limitations set to our power of swaying the Austrian Cabinet by the fact that, to protect Silesia, Austria had detached great masses of troops, at the cost to herself of East Galicia. It is equally impossible to point out the obstinacy of Austro-Hungarian Ministers who, up to the very end of the crisis, remained proof against all our persuasion, since they stubbornly persisted in ignoring every view of the Italian situation other than those set forth in memoranda from their own representatives in Rome, rejecting both advice from Berlin and Your Highness' reports, conceived in a very different sense. Finally I dare not even mention the brusque and uncompromising attitude of the Emperor, Francis Joseph himself, who remained deaf to letters and special envoys from our own All Gracious Sovereign, and to the pleas even of the Pope.

So that Berlin is condemned to silence, no matter what reproaches we may incur, until such time as we find ourselves at liberty to speak. Unluckily, all this may do much damage to the *morale* of the German people, should it come to be at all widely felt that my policy, or that of my associates, has resulted in war with Italy.

This weakening of *morale* might develop into a very serious matter, it might release a veritable hurricane, should criticism, once directed along these channels, retrace the same argument step by step, back to those events which led to war. Such reflections as that this war was avoidable; that we declared it at an inauspicious moment, and might easily have fought it in better circumstances; that this has all the look of being a "preventative war", etc. — may plant in the mind that entertains them a barb, which will enter all the more deeply the consciousness of unreflective people the less they know the true complexity of the facts. The formidable events we have to witness may easily blur the vision of the past. All those various steps may be forgotten which led on — either through our fault or in spite of us — to the grouping of so many Powers against Germany. People may easily cease to remember the fact that German isolation presented ever greater dangers as the position of Austria grew more weak, and the strength of the Allied Powers increased; they may forget all the reasons which forced on Germany a policy of exceptional risks, risks more apparent with every step: in 1905, with Morocco; then throughout the whole Bosnian crisis; then with Morocco again — a whole network of events, which can only be unravelled thread by thread when peace returns, since this war is of world-wide significance, and far too gigantic to be attributed to any immediate, petty cause. Your own wide knowledge of history and politics will, I am sure, enable Your Highness to appreciate all this far better than I. If I write to you of possible dangers it is because I am filled with patriotic anxiety when I hear, on every side, the comments of even quite serious politicians. Your Highness' views command the widest acceptance, and you well understand the methods by which opinion may be directed and controlled. I must therefore beg you to be so kind as to help me to take some action to stifle any premature strictures on our policy, since, for the moment, these can be neither frank nor sincere; must, of necessity, remain loose and fragmentary, and can only serve to paralyse the strength we need so much to hold out for final victory.

In old esteem

Your Highness' most obedient servant

BETHMANN-HOLLWEG.

Wounded susceptibilities, anxiety, but, most of all, a bad conscience speak from this letter. I answered:

MY DEAR FRIEND,

I gather with regret, from your letter, received yesterday, that the intrigues I had to encounter, again and again, in the course of my short official stay in Rome, are still being spun around my activities, even though I have retired into private life. It is nearly six years now since I relinquished the direction of affairs. Through the whole of this time I have imposed on myself the strictest discretion on every political topic. My silence, as you know, remained unbroken, even when I was being made the object of the basest, most insensate detraction. Even latterly, on hearing Italy mentioned, especially if the subject under discussion was Austria's attitude towards her, I have been careful to avoid any comment, either in Rome, or here in Berlin, which might hamper the activities of those whose business it is to guide our policy. I may say that I am too tactful to make such slips (in no circumstance has it been my habit to make them) and that, moreover, I have too great an appreciation of the value of our Austrian alliance, an alliance which, for so long as I was Chancellor, secured, as I am sure you admit, to Austria many notable advantages abroad, while at home, although we never ceased to be, of the two, the dominant partner, it gave her a sense of security. In Rome, though I of course could never forget that Prussian and German interests must come first, I have also just been making every effort to shield the Austrian Empire from all harm while at the same time defending her vital interests and endorsing any reasonable standpoint.

I have, I think, the right to express an opinion on events which are now common property, which are being judged by all who have knowledge of Italy; by the members of our missions in Rome, the representatives there of every neutral, and Germans either resident or on holiday there. But whatever I may have said has been said with diplomatic discretion. Of that I am sure you can have no doubt when you remember that you are dealing with a man whose father was Secretary of State for Foreign Affairs, a man who at twenty-four was in diplomacy, who has spent twenty-six years in the service, and directed that service for twelve. Neither did I abandon this discretion when I strove in Rome to contradict an assertion — from what quarter it sprang I am not ignorant — that I was taking too gloomy a view; nor when, as my duty dictated, I pointed out the very real danger of an Italian declaration of war on Austria. In spite of every kind of difficulty, of mistakes made before I arrived in Rome, I can say, at least, that I succeeded in retarding that declaration by several months. This fact alone should go to prove that my personal status in Rome, which I used as well as I could for the good of my country, was better than certain people, also known to you, had made it out to be before you sent me there.

You seem, my dear Herr von Bethmann, to be alluding to something I am supposed to have said on events leading up to the war. I shall be most grateful if you will send me the name of any person who dares suggest that my remarks on such a subject were inexact, or in any way exceeded the limits imposed on my expressions by my patriotism, my past, my sense of personal dignity. I reject such an assertion with all my strength. It is quite unnecessary to tell me that, in this present terrible struggle, the unity of all Germans is essential. I myself have taken every chance of saying so — such unity is the primary condition of victory and a peace we can accept. Somebody may perhaps have been suggesting to you that I had described this war as "having all the look of a preventative war", etc. If this is so my denouncer is either too ill-informed to see the exact implications of any political statement — or else he is a conscious liar.

As to what you say of my years as Chancellor, I must content myself with simply pointing out to you that it is impossible you should be perfectly informed of all the events of 1905, or of 1908–1909. I would also remind you of the fact that I managed to keep peace with France, with Japan, but especially with England; to be on excellent terms with Russia, to maintain the strength of Austria-Hungary, and also the integrity of Turkey, while at the same time, I assembled the conditions necessary to build up our fleet successfully, through twelve very critical years — years which brought increasing accumulation of riches and power to the German Empire.

I am sure that you will not deny all this; you who, from June, 1909, to the July of 1914, insisted so often on our peaceful and amicable relations, scarcely troubled save by an occasional minor difference, with Russia, England, and even France — a harmony marked by the Potsdam interview, by your journey to Russia, the Congo Treaty with France, and the conventions to be suggested to England; that is to say by numerous indications of a happy future. Of course this terrible conflict has some origins far back in the past. Antagonism between Germany and England was bound to become more defined as our industry and commerce assumed such unlooked-for dimensions, above all as we began to be a naval Power. On several occasions our relations with Russia have been strained, from the days of the first great Eastern crisis which ended in the Congress of Berlin, to those of Austro-Hungarian opposition to her. Finally, since the Peace of Frankfurt, and annexation of Alsace-Lorraine, antagonism from France has seemed inevitable. Yet, in spite of all these very real dangers, our policy kept us at peace for many years, and the day will probably come when we shall ask ourselves if it was necessary to deviate from that policy. You are, however, perfectly right in saying that for the moment our only tasks must be peace and victory — a victory worthy of the heroism and sacrifice of the German people. No one — you may rest assured — is more deeply convinced of this than I.

Please believe that I am doing all in my power to help us secure these two main objects.

At once Bethmann rejoined: "I thank Your Highness for your letter of the 12th inst. received yesterday, and perceive that, in essentials, we do not differ. You, like myself, desire that the critical spirit, so deeply a part of the German mind, may not be allowed to trouble the unanimous resolve of the nation, at a moment when the union of all is indispensable. I thank you heartily for your promise to act in such a way as will promote it, faithful to the line of conduct you have imposed on yourself since 1909, in the national interest, at the cost of so much personal sacrifice."

I showed this correspondence, in confidence, to the wise Ballin. He returned me the letters with the following: "I herewith return Your Highness the letters you were good enough to show me. I found them extremely interesting, and most characteristic of the state of mind of our Berlin rulers." I had already won Ballin's approval for my summing up of our war-time situation: "*Morale and attitude of German people — A1. Political leadership — Z minus.*"

I went to Hamburg, where Herr von Melle, the acting burgomaster, received me at a very friendly dinner, to which Hamburg senators and many prominent citizens were invited. Melle, in the name of Hamburg, thanked me in terms which moved me to the heart, for the services I had done in Rome. Not long after this I settled down in the Elbpark Villa, where, again, I met with a rousing reception. From all over the district a great crowd had flocked in to welcome us. Bouquets were presented to my wife, the ladies of the Flottbek Society for the Relief of Combatants' Dependents, aided by many children, gave a concert. The Landrat of the Pinneberg district made a speech. My answer expressed all the gladness which I felt at returning to my birthplace, where I had spent the greater part of my boyhood — a land whose every stick and stone were familiar to me. How often, of a Sunday morning, had I been with my parents to church here — either to Ottensen, up the Elbe, or down it to Nienstedten, along that charming Flottbek "Chaussée", which my late friend, Detlev von Liliencron, the poet, had rightly called the most beautiful road in Germany. I was, I said, and should always remain, a good Prussian, and as such it rejoiced my heart to be here in Flottbek, on Prussian soil. But I was also pleased to be near Hamburg. The steamer would take me over there in an hour, and there in the harbour I could see the Bismarck monument, the colossal statue we had raised in honour of that gigantic German genius. I could see the high towers of the city in which I had so many friends, to which it always rejoiced me to come back, where my wife was as happy as I, since she too loved the land of oaks and elms. I thanked them all, in particular those whose fathers were at the front. I had read with real grief, at Flottbek station, the names of those sons of Flottbek who had already laid down their lives for King and Country, Empire and Emperor. I finished up with three cheers for His Majesty !

Our exploits in the field, through this summer of 1915, filled me with ever-renewed enthusiasm. In the west, with a much weaker force, we had repelled, at the battle of Loretto, Marshal Joffre's powerful attempt at a break-through. In Artois and the Champagne district every enemy offensive was still in vain. But, against this, Bethmann's attitude on the Polish question made me more uneasy every day. In the Reichstag, in this same summer, he expressed the quite unnecessary hope that our occupation, to its eastern limit, of Polish territory, marked the first stage of an evolution destined, in the end, to resolve the old German-Polish antagonism. Poland, free of her Russian yoke, was entering a new and happy epoch, an epoch in which her national life would flourish. This, in the eyes of Herr von Bethmann, appeared to be the first war aim of Germany. The "happy evolution" prepared by him was to lead to the artificial strengthening of a national enemy on our frontiers, an enemy who has wrested from us provinces which we had held for over a century — a mercenary of France, her knife for ever to our throats !

Even in 1915 I was told that this illogical and ill-omened speech for Poland had been delivered against the advice of every Minister, of Conservative and National Liberal deputies, even of some clear-sighted representatives of the Centre and Liberal parties. And, no sooner had the possible consequences of setting up an independent Polish State become most deplorably evident, than Bethmann and Jagow, true to their unpleasant tradition, did their best to unload on other people the onus of their own absurd initiative. This time Field Marshal von Hindenburg, and his Chief of Staff, General von Ludendorff, were the sufferers. My old friend and colleague, the Minister of Public Worship, Studt, had written to know the truth from the Field Marshal. On September 24, 1917, Hindenburg answered him in this letter. I had it in my hand and made a copy of it with the authorization of Studt:

I hear that in Berlin there is a rumour that the creation of an independent Poland has been undertaken at Ludendorff's and my request. I beg you to take every opportunity of denying this inexactitude. The creation of an independent Poland was decided on the 12th and 13th of August, 1916, by Bethmann-Hollweg and Burian. It was not until August 29th that I was appointed Chief of the General Staff, and only some little while afterwards was I told of the birth of this monster. Beseler came over to Pless for a conference. At that time, for the spring of 1917, he was promising us, as the result of reëstablishing Poland, huge new contingents of Polish troops — five divisions of volunteers, and a million of men if there were conscription. For 1917 such reinforcements could only seem a godsend, and that was all in the business that really interested us and all we ever emphasized in the matter. But Beseler had been very wide of the mark, since the summer has brought us only three thousand Poles, in the Polish Legion, and nine thousand others — Galicians, sent me by the Austrians, who could only be used behind the line. Naturally I said "Thank you" for the contingent. But neither Ludendorff nor I have further connection with the new "Kingdom" of Poland. They always thrust forward the High Command, every time they feel they 've been making fools of themselves, and then, if one asks that the Press should be told the truth, one is only informed that Staff Officers must never be exposed to public criticism.

In January, 1918, at a public meeting in Hannover, Herr Tramm, the burgomaster of that city, declared, with direct authorization from the Field Marshal, that: "It is entirely false to describe the establishment of the new Polish State as having been the result of any wish expressed by the High Command, or as having had that Command's full approbation."

Herr Tramm continued: "The political treaty dealing with Poland was arranged between the German and Austrian governments several weeks before Hindenburg and Ludendorff had been given full command of our armies, and therefore they knew nothing about it. It had been estimated in the treaty that the Polish State could supply us with two hundred and fifty thousand recruits, and when our new chiefs received this appointment they said: 'If these reinforcements really exist, they will come in very useful just at present.' We were on the eve of Roumania's declaration of war, and Brussilow was developing his offensive. Our chiefs could only say: 'If you have so many troops to dispose of, send them along.' I do not know if you remember the wretched results of the treaty. Though I have not the exact figures, I don't believe that more than ten thousand Poles volunteered. But, as I have said, the High Command was in no way answerable for the establishment of the Polish State."

Herr Tramm, added, most justly, that it was essential to have these facts well known, since the attempt was being made to cast a slur on Germany's two most popular heroes by suggesting that the High Command were the true begetters of the abortion. They were being accused of a grave political lapse, of an error in reality due to others. It was necessary to scotch these lies, if the image in people's minds of our two great leaders were to retain its essential purity.

To the above I may add that General von Beseler, the German Governor General of Warsaw, certainly allowed the Poles to trick him. He was not the man to resist Polish duplicity. Yet Von Beseler even did not embark on this Polish experiment till Bethmann had done everything to encourage him in it. He soon found out his mistake, and I hope regretted it, when the Poles, who till then had flattered him, deserted overnight to the Allies, with whom they had long been in secret contact, the moment the tides of battle turned against us. Bismarck's truth had received fresh confirmation who, from the first day to the last of his career, insisted that the Poles were our born enemies, the most dangerous haters of the Prussian State and all its ideals.

I do not deny that poor Bethmann was committed, more and more deeply, to his ridiculous Polish policy by his familiars, Privy Councillor Riezler (alias "Ruedorffer") and Doctor Hans Delbrück. Riezler maintained a thesis that the bad impression we had made by our breach of Belgian neutrality might be "morally readjusted" if we set up an independent Poland. I have several times mentioned Doctor Delbrück. I think the best accounts I ever heard of him were given me by the poor Empress Frederick, who knew him well, since he lived several years in her household as tutor to her son, the young Prince Waldemar, who died. Once, at a luncheon-party, in the Crown Prince's palace, to which I also had been asked, Delbrück, whose manners were atrocious, sat arguing at the top of his voice with a guest at the other end of the table, so carried away by what he was saying that he had planted his elbows squarely on it, and gripped his knife in one hand, his fork in the other. Lord Ampthill, then Ambassador in Berlin, a most cultivated, intelligent Englishman, with perfect manners, eyed disapprovingly this very badly brought up tutor. The Crown Princess tried to smooth things over a little by remarking, in a conciliatory whisper: "He is not a bad man, but awfully tactless." [1] Unluckily, to his inadequate table manners Delbrück added far more dangerous failings — an utter lack of political discernment, of feeling for direction in politics, of political caution, *doigté* — or even the merest common sense.

[1] English in text.

CHAPTER XIX

The Winter of 1915–1916 in Lucerne — Count Ledochowski, the General of the Society of Jesus — The Central Powers Make a Clumsy Offer of Peace — My Last Audience with William II — The Tactics of Defeatism in Germany — Energy of the French Government towards Similar Manifestations among the French — Prince Lichnowsky's Brochure — A Conversation with Bethmann-Hollweg — Conscription Introduced in England.

IN December, 1915, the doctors ordered my wife a long spell of fresh mountain air. They advised Switzerland. I have always been fond of Lake Leman, but this time we decided to avoid it on account of the ridiculous pro-French attitude of the Vaudois. It was the boast of the whole Canton de Vaud that *"les Boches"* were even more hated there than in France. *"Paris peut pardonner, Lausanne jamais."* The Engadine seemed to us too restless, too much a fashion resort, for these grave times. We decided at last on Lucerne which, for me, had in it many early memories. I had been there twice with my beloved parents, as a boy, and well remembered the old bridge, with its Dance of Death, its quaint inscriptions, its pictures of the history of the town. Nor had I forgotten Thorwaldsen's "Lion", the impression of which, in its ensemble, I can only compare to that of the Bismarck monument in Hamburg. How well that lion is placed at the foot of the dark crag, overlooking the little pond! A dying lion, shielding with its paw a lily: a very beautiful symbol of the soldier's fidelity to the end. The old *Vierwaldstätter*, the steamer I had known as a boy, still journeyed up and down the lake, just as it had done sixty years before.

In Lucerne I scrupulously avoided all expression of political opinion. Bethmann's uneasiness at the thought of me, partly due to natural anxiety, partly to the prickings of his conscience, was really not necessary in the least. But I followed events most carefully in every great European newspaper. I would read both *Le Temps* and *The Times*, to be sure of forming a just idea of the state of feeling in France and England. My wife and I were always interested to receive the staff of the German Legation in Berne, and glad to see my old friend, Herr von Mühlberg, once Assistant State Secretary to the Foreign Office, and later Minister to the Vatican. From Lugano, where he had settled down, he would often run across to Lucerne to stay with us. In other ways there was also much to be learned, in this neutral country, into which, from every belligerent, there flowed a constant stream of fact and opinion. It was in Lucerne that I received confidential information of some remarks made by Count Ledochowski, the General of the Society of Jesus, who, with the whole Mother House of his Order, had moved to Zizers, near Chur, when war broke out. When, in February, 1916, the Tsar chose Stürmer, a Conservative, as his Prime Minister, Count Ledochowski said to one of my Swiss friends: "I think that now there is some chance of peace. I hear that the Emperor Nicholas is eager for it; not, of course, from any love of the Central Powers, but because he is convinced that, if war continues, his throne, and even his life, may be in danger. Stürmer, who in spite of his German-sounding name, is a pure-bred Russian, shares the opinion of his Sovereign. He, too, fears that, unless the war ends now, the fall of the Romanovs is a certainty."

Ledochowski added: "Now everything will depend on whether Berlin and, naturally, also Vienna, can make the most of this great chance as quickly and skilfully as possible."

If Berlin had any sense, it would have given the greatest weight to these opinions, which were, of course, repeated word for word to Bethmann. That was in February, 1916. Yet two months later, at a moment when the new Russian Prime Minister had had scarcely time to feel his seat in the saddle, Bethmann, with his incorrigible doctrinaire obstinacy, was, on April 5th, saying the following: "Poland, now abandoned by the Russian Tschinownik and the Cossack — the first pocketing a last, hasty bribe, the second burning and laying waste — old Poland, bent and yoked under Russia, belongs already to the past. History knows no *status quo ante*, after all the stupendous events which we are witnessing. Russia herself will have to acknowledge this. The thought of that Tschinownik's return to lands in which a German, a Pole, an Austrian, have worked so well on behalf of unhappy Poland, is inconceivable to the world. Never will we hand back to Russian despotism the peoples Germany has freed — from the Baltic to the Marshes of Wolhynia — Poles, Balts, Lithuanians, or Letts."

That was a slap in the face for the Tsar and Stürmer. Six months later (November 5, 1916) there appeared the Austro-German declaration on the setting up of an independent Poland. Within fifteen days, as the result of the wave of anger aroused by it, in the Duma and all over Russia, Nicholas found himself forced to dismiss Stürmer. I heard from a reliable source that the Tsar had said to a Russian friend, who favoured peace: "*Après ce coup de pied de Guillaume la paix devient impossible.*" The pacific Stürmer was succeeded by General Trepow who wanted the war to continue. When the wise Count Ledochowski got news of it he said: "Berlin must either have lost its head or lost control of its nerves. Probably both." This criticism is by no means too severe. I had thought of Talleyrand's well-known saying on the murder of the Duc d'Enghien: "*C'est pire qu'un crime, c'est une faute.*" But this restoration of Poland, at a moment when it seemed quite possible to achieve a satisfactory peace with Russia, was a crime committed against all Germany, as well as the most egregious of blunders. Later I heard it confirmed on all sides that the Tsar and Stürmer had really wanted peace.

Eight years after this I was so fortunate as to meet Count Ledochowski in Rome. He lived in a flat, in the Via San Nicolo di Tolentino, at the top of a very modest house, altogether different in appearance from the magnificent churches and palaces and picturesque convents of the rest of ecclesiastical Rome. A long passage led to the flat of the General of the Society of Jesus. Its walls were hung with portraits of his predecessors, among them many interesting faces. They included those Vicars General who, from 1773, the date at which the Order had been suppressed, had kept the Jesuits together, saving what was left to save through the years of storm and persecution till their reëstablishment in 1814. A lay brother, who told me he came from the Bavarian Palatinate and certainly seemed not to have forgotten its patois, ushered me into the room where the Count received me. This room was bare, except for a statue of the Virgin and a few portraits of Popes. The General is a man of middle height with unusually intelligent eyes, the wrinkled and moulded features of a savant, and the certainty of manner of a born aristocrat. In measured terms, frankly, without reticence or evasion, he discussed the international situation, showed extensive knowledge of all that was going on in every country, and seemed well able to appraise the driving forces at work within each people. His judgments were acute and individual. I was very much struck with his remark that ideas are, in the last analysis, stronger than material forces. Violence always discovers its limitations. In the end it is ideas that shake the world. This applied, he said, even to such false and pernicious theories as Marxism. He gave me the impression of a man of wide intellectual horizons. I began to see why, up to now, every General of the Jesuit Order has refrained from accepting the purple. Their own function is more interesting, they see more, have more influence in the Church than most Roman Catholic cardinals.

Coming at the moment it did, this creation of an independent Poland lost us every chance of securing separate peace with Russia. But, apart from that, it was soon obvious that a terrible blunder had been committed — the worst, without exaggeration, for which any German statesman has been responsible. As for our offer of peace of December 12, 1916, it was inopportune and clumsily made. William II's personal letter to Bethmann, of October 31, 1916, by which the Emperor hoped to end the War, was well-intentioned enough. But it was too sentimental, too naïve, almost childish! And children in politics have rarely that "quality of divine beauty" which Schiller's *Don Carlos* ascribes to them. Moreover, there was far too much vanity in this, as in so many other Imperial manifestations.

"Such an initiative as this needs a Monarch whose conscience is awake, one who knows himself responsible to God, who acknowledges his duty to all men — even his enemies : a Monarch who feels no fear because his intentions may be misinterpreted; who has in him the will to deliver the world from its agony. I have that courage. I can dare this thing, with God. Quick, Mr. Chancellor ! Submit me the notes. Make everything ready." This is not the style of a statesman.

The joy called forth by this Imperial letter and the offer of peace presented by the Central Powers on December 12, 1916 — that *naïveté* with which, even in Berlin, many people seriously imagined that this would mean the end of hostilities — merely showed our enemies that Germany, reputed so unshakeable, so resolute, was war-weary, and more inwardly disintegrated than, up to then, they had believed. Nor was this open manifesto, couched in the terms of melodrama and sentiment, in the least effective in assuaging our coldly implacable enemies.

I have said already that, after my despatch to Rome in the December of 1914, I had only once again the honour of being received by William II. That was in the late autumn of 1916. I was then commanded to spend the evening in the Neues Palais in Potsdam. Each time I returned to Berlin I had, as usual, announced my arrival to the Emperor. Each time word had been sent back that important affairs, to his regret, would prevent His Majesty's receiving me. Yet this seemed not to tally with what I heard from anxious friends in the suite. The Emperor, even in war time, still lived, they said, exactly the same life, did little work, strove to amuse himself, thought far too much of his personal pleasures. In obedience therefore, to his command — the only one I ever received from him through all the last four years of the War — I set out for the Neues Palais. I found him alone, without the Kaiserin, or any member of the suite, his only other guest being Baron von Bissing, the cavalry commander, and Governor General of Belgium. His Majesty was in excellent spirits. I received the sensation that he had sent for me to impress me, as a man of iron resolve. As I have said, he told me he was convinced that the German people wanted no parliaments; they were "thoroughly fed up" with the Reichstag, and would much rather be governed by generals, etc.

Von Bissing's presence then inspired him to pronounce on the Belgian question. To the baron who, rightly no doubt, was said to desire that Belgium should be annexed, the All Highest explained that it was not his intention to turn the King of the Belgians off his throne. He was, above all else, a legitimist. He very much regretted the fact that, prompted by the wicked Bismarck, his grandfather, in 1866, had deposed the legitimate sovereigns of Hannover, Electoral Hesse, and Nassau. No King by the Grace of God should be deposed. Von Bissing and I stared open-mouthed at the Emperor, who had for decades felt so much the master in Hannover, who had so enjoyed occasional trips to both Wilhelmshöhe and Wiesbaden. His Majesty continued: "What has been, has been! Nothing can be altered now in Hannover, Nassau, or Hesse. But Albert shall keep his Belgium, since he too is king by Right Divine . . . though, of course, he'll have to toe the line there. I imagine our future relationship as rather that of the Egyptian Khedive to the King of England."

That was the last pronouncement on politics I heard from the lips of William II. He changed the subject, and told us of the Castle of Pless, the charming "*Residenz*" of Prince Hans Heinrich of Pless, which had left on him a very good impression.

Prince Hans, he said, had had the most attractive cretonne borders hung round every washing stand in the castle. He, the Emperor, intended to do likewise, in every one of all his numerous palaces.

He dismissed us both fairly early. We had been from nine till shortly after ten in this Neues Palais, the splendid creation of the Great King, most beautiful, perhaps, of all Prussian palaces. This was my last sight of my Sovereign, with whom I had faced so much of good and ill. My first was in this very apartment of this same Neues Palais at Potsdam, and had taken place forty-one years earlier. In those days he was the sixteen-year-old Prince Wilhelm, and I an attaché of twenty-six. I had been commanded with my parents to dinner at the Neues Palais. How clearly I can still see before me the impressive figure, gracious, knightly bearing, and kind eyes of the future Emperor Frederick. And I hear, as though it had been yesterday, the lively, witty talk of Crown Princess Victoria. I hear Prince Wilhelm too, who, in a clear — in perhaps too clear a voice — lectures the assembled guests on the Bremer Lloyd and Hamburg-America steamship companies. Yet he had a real, inborn love of the sea. It may have been the deepest of all his instincts. What an age, and how many events, between our first meeting and our last !

Among new German friends in Lucerne I was interested in General Count Max Montgelas, the Bavarian. He had resigned from the General's Staff and worked until almost the eve of war in the Operation's Section of the War Office; had commanded a division and led it bravely. His personal courage was as unmistakable as his patriotism. I was therefore somewhat surprised when he asked me whether I blamed him for the share he had had in the final strategic preparations to invade Belgium — operations carried out in defiance of international law. I naturally replied that, whatever might be said of the political aspect of the matter, a soldier need only think of his orders, and that for officers more than all other ranks the maxim "Right or wrong, my country" holds good.[1] Montgelas had also moral scruples as to the use of poison gas in warfare, and Zeppelin raids. I did not conceal from him my opinion that the shooting of Nurse Cavell and Captain Fryatt had seemed to me acts the usefulness of which was incommensurate with the moral obloquy incurred by them and, on that account, not justifiable. I told him that, in my opinion, "frightfulness" is a bad method of waging war, but that the leading statesman's business and duty is to prevent soldiers making these mistakes. A Chancellor should guide, not be guided by those who have no duty except to fight. Unless I am deceived, General Montgelas managed, as the War proceeded, to overcome the morbid moral doubts which go, as a rule, with too much introspection. His polemic against Kautsky is written with the courage and dignity of a patriot.

It is depressing to have to admit that Germany was the only belligerent in which there were individuals so base as to stab in the back their own compatriots, engaged in a life or death struggle.

[1] English [*sic*] in text.

The first of these wretched traitors was Grelling, the author of
"J'Accuse", a pamphlet which the Allies sold by the hundred thousand, in enemy and neutral countries and, whenever they could do
so, in Germany.   It would, however, be wrong to include under the
head of such catch-penny scribbling Prince Lichnowsky's brochure,
"Meine Londoner Mission."   He did not wish it ever to reach the
public, but should certainly not have composed such an effusion,
since, quite apart from the opinions expressed, it is worthless.   In
the course of a debate on Lichnowsky's expulsion from the Upper
House, many serious accusations were made against him.   Yet
much was also said, and said with justice, in his defence.   The most
effective point made in his favour was the simple reading, in lieu of
any other *apologia*, by Prince Alexander Münster, since deceased —
the son of a man for many years our ambassador in London and
Paris — of the opening paragraph of his brochure.   Its sense was
more or less as follows: Among the many mistakes made by Bismarck in his foreign policy was to be reckoned the Berlin Congress,
without which there could never have been a World War.   The
Berlin Foreign Office had made an unfortunate choice when it sent
Baron Marschall to London as our ambassador, though it had
been an inspiration of the Kaiser's to appoint the author, Prince
Lichnowsky, to this very important position.

When Prince Alexander Münster reached this point, a storm of
laughter interrupted him.   He ended his speech in the hope that
the Upper House would not show itself so hard-hearted as to visit
with disgraceful punishment any member whose political harmless-
ness was so obvious.   A majority of very worthy gentlemen, myself
among them, were so tickled that we decided to place a white ball
in the box. The final majority, however, decided to expel poor
Lichnowsky, who in consequence also lost his right to wear a
Prussian officer's uniform.

We Germans have ever been inclined to set the part above the
whole, group interest above the general good.   It was therefore only
to be expected that so long and rigorous a war would increase the
demands of every party.   In these circumstances it ought to have
been obvious that speedy concessions were now necessary, in so far

as they were in line with the *salus publica*. Members of every party
in the Reichstag should have been given their chance in important
posts — Radicals, Clericals, even Socialists — and the rulers should
then have kept a tight hand on them. I should have considered it
perfectly natural had all laws of exception been repealed on the 4th
of August, 1914, including the law against the Jesuits, and every
law of expropriation. Such a reorientation of our home policy
would only have been an obvious consequence, as well as the best
practical illustration of the meaning of the Kaiser's excellent saying
that now, as Head of the Empire and leader of the whole German
nation, he refused any longer to recognize parties in the State. But
at the same time, as was done in England and France, we should
have kept a sharp look-out for any attempt to undermine the war
morale of the nation, to sow seeds of civil discord and revolution.
If necessary, such attempts should have been stamped out ruthlessly. A definite line of demarcation should have been drawn
between Socialist patriots and Socialists whose only aim was to get
their party into power. While Wolfgang Heine, Südekum, David,
Noske, and many other excellent Socialists placed themselves at
once in their country's service, and while the great mass of the German people followed their country's flag with courage and loyalty,
it soon became apparent that there were traitors within the ranks of
German Socialism. And only there! Not among the French or
English, Italian or Belgian Socialists! Karl Liebknecht was the
one German deputy who voted against war credits in the Reichstag,
on December 2, 1914. He was merely an isolated fanatic. But
not long after this the deputy Haase, the head of the Socialist Party,
declared: "We will undermine the army to inaugurate world
revolution."

And unluckily Haase and his accomplices really managed to shake
the discipline of certain divisions and sowed sedition among the
crews of a few ships. It was quite beyond the power of these infamous persons to "inaugurate world revolution." They could only
succeed in delivering their country into the hands of French generals
and English admirals. In February, 1915, the Socialist deputy,
Stroebel, the editor of *Vorwärts*, said in the Prussian Chamber of

Deputies : "I frankly admit that a complete German victory would not be in the interests of Socialism."

Never, through the whole course of the World War, was any French, English, Italian, or Belgian Socialist guilty of such a profession of faith — whose baseness only equals its stupidity. And at the time when Haase and Stroebel were speaking thus, the whole of French, Belgian, Italian, and British democracy, including their extreme left wings, had sunk all party considerations and kept one only object before their eyes — a crushing Allied victory.

By March 20, 1915, two deputies, besides the Communist, Liebknecht, one of them the Saxon, Otto Rühle, a "man of letters" of scarcely thirty, whose theories also tended in this direction, had voted against the second instalment of war credits. In January, 1916, a majority of the Socialist party, then still orthodox, had decided on Liebknecht's expulsion. He revenged himself by the secret publication of his "Spartakus-Briefe"[1] in which, in conjunction with the Russian nihilist, Rosa Luxemburg, he indulges in Communist propaganda. In the following spring he organized a revolutionary demonstration in the Potsdamer Platz in Berlin, with the slogan, "Down with the War ! Down with the Government !" He was sentenced to thirty months' hard labour. But his followers went on organizing, in Berlin and various other cities, their "demonstrations against war and hunger" — openly declaring that revolution would break out as soon as the position on the Fronts grew really bad.

To bring that about as soon as possible, they kept up their agitation in every depot, in military hospitals, in the streets, from mouth to mouth. And the Government took no steps ! Herr von Bethmann's sole preoccupation was his own most effective answer to the pamphlets written against him by Kapp, and other Pan-German nonentities, which had pierced his vanity to the quick. He was then denouncing these scribblers as "the pirates of public opinion" (an expression coined by Riezler — "Ruedorffer" — who was not a little proud of having invented it) in the most vigorous Reichstag speech he ever made, the only one I have ever known him make

[1] " Letters of Spartacus."

with anything like passion or inspiration in it. "Bethmann," a Liberal deputy remarked to me, "is obviously one of those Ministers who can only attack when their own precious skin has been scratched." He had certainly found nothing to equal it in denouncing his country's enemies and still less for putting us on our guard against revolution at home.

Among the several other concessions we ought to have made the instant war broke out, I should like especially to mention the reform of the Prussian electoral system. Such reform was long overdue, but my successor always managed to postpone it. In my last year in office, it would have been feasible to achieve some working rearrangement of conditions for election to the Landtag. This would have had the support not only of National Liberals but of Liberals. When war broke out we should have granted universal suffrage, with secret ballot for the Landtag, perhaps with a few restrictions of voting age, eligibility to stand as candidate, and period of residence in an area. But, in all the first three years of war, Bethmann did not raise a finger in this. Not until the spring of 1917 did he feel the waters rising to his chin. And then the same Bethmann-Hollweg who had started his career as Chancellor with a violent philippic against those who were "trying to drag the Prussian State over into the parliamentary camp" — the statesman who had ruthlessly opposed the most modest extension of our suffrage, suddenly apprised an astonished country, by means of the "Royal Easter message", of the establishment of a system of secret and universal suffrage for election to the Prussian Chamber of Deputies. This, like so many of his decisions, was inspired by the Chancellor's own fear — and fear is the worst counsellor in politics. He had seen, in this sudden concession, his only hope of keeping the Socialists in check a little longer. The sole result of such tactics was the transformation of the "Labour Party" into the "Independent Socialist Party of Germany" — that all too famous U.S.P.D.[1] which at once began an open battle for the instant cessation of hostilities, and revolution, and, from then on, did everything in its power to bring to earth the old powerful, prosperous Germany. Not content with

[1] *Unabhängige Sozialdemokratische Partei Deutschlands.*

his "Easter message", Bethmann induced the King of Prussia to send forth another "message" in July, announcing that the reform of the Prussian electoral system would entail universal suffrage, and that such reform would be put through in time for the next election.

Naturally these hasty concessions could produce no great effect in the German people. It was evident that Bethmann only made them to retain his post a little longer. And it was all the other way in enemy countries, especially in France, whose rulers tightened the bridle more and more. Paris had been made to feel again the rough spirit of the Convention and of Napoleon. Grave mutinies broke out in the French army in the May of 1917, as the result of the check to General Nivelle's offensive whom the ranks had nick-named "*buveur de sang.*" His troops refused their orders, formed Soldiers' Councils, on the Russian lines, barricaded themselves into their camps and raised red flags, with the cry: "*À bas la guerre !*"

The French Government acted at once, with drastic energy, pro-ceeded to mass executions, and soon had the movement flattened out. At the same time it drafted a law, decreeing the direst penal-ties for "pacifist and defeatist propaganda." The editor of the Socialist *Bonnet Rouge*, Almereyda, was clapped into gaol, where, a few days later he was found dead, most probably strangled, in his cell. Malvy, the *Ministre de l'Interieur*, accused by Clemenceau of not having shown enough energy in opposing defeatist propa-ganda, was deported. Caillaux, the ex-Minister of Foreign Affairs and erstwhile *President du Conseil*, was imprisoned as a defeatist, and for some time went in justified terror of his life. Bolo Pasha, a banker grown rich in Egypt, a man in a very good position, was arrested on the (trumped-up) charge of being in the pay of Germany as an agent for pacifist propaganda. The *Conseil de guerre* con-demned him to death, amid the applause of the whole court, and, twenty-four hours later, he was executed at Vincennes.

When Herr von Bethmann induced the Emperor to promulgate his "Easter message" Ballin remarked: "The Chancellor reminds me of a business man who, although he knows himself bankrupt, refuses to admit that he is so, and has used a deposit in order to seem to honour his signature a few weeks longer."

Each time I came to Berlin from Flottbek, or from visiting my wife at Lucerne, I would be sure to pay Bethmann a visit. He knew that I was always ready to offer him or the Emperor my services or advice in whatever way he cared to make use of them. Yet never once did he ask me my opinion. From his remarks, or rather his lectures, on our position, I gathered that he still had hopes that England would not want to go on fighting. "The English will be the first to come back to us," he said on several occasions. I could not conceal my disagreement. "I believe," I told him, "that had our policy been properly directed at the outset, we need never have had war with England. But now that she has her teeth into us she won't let go in a hurry. The British bulldog, you know!"

Poor Bethmann could never refrain from little allusions to his "difficult political legacy." Naturally I could not let him rearrange history like that. I told him that, though no doubt it was convenient, it was both amateurish and unjust to saddle one's predecessor with one's mistakes. "When I was Secretary of State and Chancellor, and found that I had difficulties to cope with, did I ever accuse my predecessors of having caused them? Did I, for instance, complain that they had failed to renew the Reinsurance Treaty and so brought about the Franco-Russian alliance? Did I seek excuses in the Krüger telegram or the Far Eastern Triple Alliance? It was always my aim to make the most of any given situation — 'to make the best of it.' [1] Moreover, unless I am mistaken, you, my dear Bethmann, said yourself, in a recent circular to the Press, that foreign policy is finally controlled by His Majesty, and that to criticize it is therefore tantamount to a criticism of the person of the Sovereign. This thesis is perhaps not unassailable but, in any case, if formulated at all, it must not be for the benefit of one Chancellor. Above all, I cannot accept the actual facts brought forward in your unjust recriminations against the political legacy you inherited from me, since, thanks to this legacy, you managed for five whole years — and five years, my dear Bethmann, are something, even in the life of a nation — to keep on good terms with Russia, which you made better still by the Potsdam interview and your journey to

[1] English in text.

St. Petersburg and Moscow, as you yourself have often boasted.
On the conclusion of the Morocco and Congo understanding, you
announced to me such an amelioration of the whole Franco-German
position as might conceivably end in an *entente*, while with England,
on the very eve of war, we were negotiating two important questions — the Bagdad Railway and the Portuguese Colonies. The
treaties in view, for which I myself had assembled the conditions,
were on the point of being ratified at the end of July, 1914. And
it was in just these two years directly preceding the War that you
so emphatically proclaimed the amelioration of our relationship
with the Western Powers."

Bethmann was silent. Though I read annoyance in his face, it
seemed to me even more uneasy, especially when, still in the friendliest tone imaginable, I begged him, in drawing up his balance sheet
of responsibility for the World War, not to diminish his debit side
unduly by foisting some of its items on to other people. But he
seemed to cheer up when I told him that I feared the English might
be quite capable of introducing conscription. When I suggested
this, he gave me such a look of pity that his thought was easy enough
to read : "The poor dear prince really seems to be getting very old
— he 's beginning to dither." He said : "But, my dear and estimable prince, have n't you read the 'History of England' by your
Hamburg compatriot, Johann Martin Lappenberg? Or Macau-
lay? Or the quite fundamental work of Von Gneist? Surely you
know that Britons would never allow the yoke of conscription to be
laid on them."

Influential financiers in Switzerland, the business representatives
of the Curia, were at that very moment receiving news from England that the Government there had made up its mind to pass the
Compulsory Military Service Act, and, as I heard later at Lucerne,
had no reason to doubt this news authentic. It was left to the
responsible head of German policy, strong in the dusty wisdom
of old tomes, to err as to the attitude of England at this crucial
turning-point of the War. A few weeks after our conversation,
conscription was the law of Great Britain.

IMPERIAL CHANCELLOR THEOBALD VON BETHMANN-
HOLLWEG IN CONVERSATION WITH VICE-CHANCEL-
LOR DOCTOR KARL HELFFERICH

Behind, Secretary of State for Foreign Affairs Gottlieb von Jagow

CHAPTER XX

Submarine Warfare — The Crown Prince Interviews Leading Politicians — Bethmann's Retirement — My Recall Is Considered — Intrigues against Me in Berlin and Vienna — The Diplomatic Possibilities of Peace — Assistant State Secretary Michaelis, Imperial Chancellor — Count Czernin's Memorandum — A Peace Resolution in the Reichstag — Erzberger — The First Signs of Demoralization in the Fleet at Kiel — State Secretary Zimmermann — Michaelis Replaced by Hertling — State Secretary Kühlmann — The Peace of Brest-Litovsk — The State of Mind in Berlin — Adolf von Harnack.

By more and still more concessions to the Left Wing, the Chancellor hoped to keep his head above water. Through his intimate friend, the Cabinet Councillor, Valentini, he had managed to convince the Emperor that he alone, Bethmann, was the man to stem the on-coming tides of revolution. In reality he could only hesitate; and most fatal of all were his vacillations in the matter of submarine warfare. These in particular reminded me of the oft-quoted message in the Book of Revelation, to the angel of the church of the Laodiceans: "I know thy works, that thou art neither cold nor hot: I would thou wert cold or hot. So then because thou art lukewarm, and neither cold nor hot, I will spew thee out of my mouth."

Obviously there were many grave reasons against the full employment of the U-boat. If, however, it was decided to use this weapon, its use should have been placed unreservedly in the hands of Chief Admiral von Tirpitz, the creator of our navy, our first authority on naval matters. Instead of which, aided by Admirals Müller and Holtzendorff, Bethmann began an intrigue against Von Tirpitz, which ended in a brusque telegram from the Emperor, retiring, at the very height of the war, the admiral who had made of us a naval power. And the right moment for submarine warfare had been let pass. When at last we made up our minds to it, we were not only too late but very clumsy. Unrestricted submarine warfare was decided at the Castle of Pless, in the absence of the Imperial Chancellor, who only heard *post festum* of the decision, tried to resign, but was easily dissuaded by the Emperor.

At the time when the decision still hung by a thread, I was lunching one day with Albert Ballin at the Hotel Continental, in Berlin. We were still at table when Ballin was called away to the telephone. He was away a quarter of an hour and returned with an anxious face. "They 've made up their minds at last to unrestricted U-boat warfare. But now it 's too late. If they wanted to do it at all, they ought to have started it long ago. And they ought to have kept Tirpitz. Now England has had nearly two years to arm almost all her steamers against it, and organize her defence with chasers, Q-ships, motor boats, aircraft, anti-submarine escorts, depth charges, mines, and naval patrols." I asked Ballin if he thought Bethmann could ever stay in office, after having so incessantly opposed submarine warfare. He answered: "Oh, yes — he 's stopping on. That man is our misfortune. He 's just been telling me how, for the sake of the Fatherland, he feels that, even now, he must stick to his post."

Never, or very seldom, did Bethmann show the same resolution as he did in sticking to office through the summer of 1917. I admit that the Emperor hated parting with him, not only because he had been persuaded that Bethmann, and only he, could save him from revolution and abdication, but also because he felt it most unlikely that he would ever again find so submissive a Chancellor.

A Crown Council was called to debate the reform of the Prussian electoral system. Partisans and opponents spoke interminably. The Emperor, transported by so much eloquence, exclaimed: "I had no idea that I had such clever Ministers."

The best, most intelligent speech was that of the Minister for the Interior, Herr von Loebell. He presented the reform as a serious step, but one which, all things considered, would have to be taken. But it would be most unwise, he added, to confide the application of such a measure to the present Chancellor, now grown stale and overfatigued. New wine should never be poured into old bottles. It is untrue that Herr von Loebell had told me the gist of his speech; nor was it prearranged between us. He was freely expressing his personal opinion in the matter and I did not hear his remarks till after he made them. When the sitting rose, the general concensus of opinion was still that Bethmann had won the day. He himself, that same afternoon, was receiving congratulations from his friends, while at the same time he expressed, to those among his colleagues who had opposed him, his regret at having to dispense with them. Who gave the final push to Bethmann? The Crown Prince had already become aware that we could neither win the War nor yet make peace with this chancellor. Hindenburg and Ludendorff thought the same, and, *au fond*, the parties agreed with them. This the Crown Prince had been discovering, in a series of interviews, given at the beginning of July to several leading parliamentarians, whom he had, moreover, greatly pleased by his tact and the intelligence of his questions. Erzberger, in the course of one of these interviews, had expressed his opinion rather happily: "Bethmann cannot possibly sit at the Conference table with a dribble of stains all down his waistcoat." It was Erzberger who gave Bethmann his *coup de grâce*.

When this Chancellor learned that his Emperor had gone back on him, he did not, as Bismarck is said to have done, exclaim: "*Le roi me reverra.*" He only sighed: "Now revolution is unavoidable."

When it was certain Bethmann would resign, His Majesty said to Count August Eulenburg: "Go and find my wife and tell her she'll have her Bülow back again." William II knew that the Empress and Count Eulenburg were eager to have me reinstated. Should I have been fortunate in office? Or rather, since here it was a case of nothing except the *salus publica*, could I have been of use to the country? Naturally, had I found myself once more Chancellor, I should have felt it my duty to secure an acceptable peace. Before the senseless restoration of Poland a separate peace with Russia would have been possible and, this achieved, we might either, under favourable auspices, have continued the War in the west or, better still, might have arranged an acceptable general conclusion of hostilities. Prior to the Polish folly, I should not have hesitated an instant to negotiate peace with Russia, on the basis of restoring to the Tsar every inch of Polish territory we had taken from him. Had the Government in Vienna made difficulties, I should have raised Russia's hopes of getting Galicia into the bargain; and I should have waited. With a satisfied Russia at our backs, we could have been certain of the Italians and Roumanians. In 1917, though the whole position had grown much worse, it was not by any means a desperate one. I do not wish to trade on conjectures, but I will say this — in 1917 peace would have been perfectly feasible on condition that our enemies saw no weakness in us. That is to say, we could have made it, if we had not seemed to them overanxious for it, had we abstained from all naïve peace demonstrations, and puerile peace resolutions. It had literally then become a case of showing the world a bold front — a face of unshakeable resolution, with a hint of defiance in it. Yet at the same time, through some suitably chosen agent, we ought to have made it clear to the Allies that we should not refuse an equal peace, a peace by mutual understanding.

Our ideal mediator would have been Pope Benedict XV, assuredly not hostile to Germany, or her Austrian and Hungarian allies; a sincere striver after peace and a man of great wisdom and enlightenment. But since, by the Patto di Londra in which she engaged herself to the Allies, Italy had received their assurance that the Pope would in no circumstance be invited to take a share in the peace conference, this choice was already ruled out. There remained the Queen of Holland, the President of the Federation of Swiss Republics, the kings of Spain, Sweden, and Denmark. It ought at least to have been obvious that we must make a serious offer of peace, through a recognized diplomatic channel, and not, as Bethmann did so frequently, give permission to sundry individuals without experience in diplomacy to "get the lie of the land", and so, by their clumsy efforts, compromise the business from the outset.

I would have offered more or less the following terms: Complete reëstablishment of Belgian independence. Integrity of Belgium guaranteed, with solemn reaffirmation of her neutrality. A generous indemnity to Belgium. The cession to Italy of the Trentino, together with autonomy for Trieste. Reëstablishment and fresh recognition of the independence and neutrality of the Grand Duchy of Luxemburg. If necessary, the evacuation of French Lorraine, after dismantlement of the fortifications at Metz. In case of extreme necessity, the constitution of Alsace-Lorraine as an independent, demilitarized, buffer State, recognized by international law.

Many post-war conversations with neutral, and even ex-enemy politicians, have all confirmed me in the assurance that peace on such terms could have been obtained. No doubt it is still more certain that, had I concluded such a peace, the Germans would have slung rotten apples at me. A hundred leading articles would have told me that a stroke of my feeble pen had forfeited what steel had so gloriously won. But I would have braved even rotten apples and scribblers for the sake of preserving my country from utter ruin and defeat, disintegration and revolution.

Before saying good-bye to Bethmann in these "Memoirs" I owe it him to place on record the last political declaration I heard from him. Not very long before his retirement I returned from a walk in the Tiergarten to the Hotel Adlon, where we were staying, to find him in conversation with my wife. He had, he told us, just returned from a visit to the front where, at Charleville, he had stayed a second time in the house of the same *brave bourgeoise* who had put him up, in the first year of the War there. And she had said to him: "*Revenez souvent nous voir quand la paix sera rétablie, monsieur le Chancelier, vous trouverez chez nous des mains prêtes à serrer votre main, des cœurs qui vous estiment et vous aiment.*"

"That," added Theobald," gave me a better idea of what the French people are really feeling than all the hatred in the newspapers. And it is n't any different in England or Belgium!"

An old French comedy has the line in it: "*Faut de la naïveté, pas trop n'en faut.*"

What decided William II to appoint, as his new Imperial Chancellor, at such a terrible crisis in Germany history, Michaelis, that

Assistant State Secretary whom Lucanus, who possessed so thorough a knowledge of the Prussian administrative machine, had considered, only a few years previously, unequal to the post of Oberregierungsrat in Breslau? One of the equerries gave me the following explanation of it:

We were all sitting together in the Marble Hall, discussing suggestions for a successor to the now impossible Bethmann-Hollweg. Each of us had suggested a name, but we did n't seem to be getting much further. Then suddenly General von Plessen came bursting into the room and shouted: "I 've thought of a Chancellor! I forget exactly what his name is — Michel, or something like that. He deals in bread supplies, and the other day he made a famous speech, saying he 'd stick his blade through the carcass of anybody who barred his way." Valentini, who had been sitting there saying nothing, got up at the back of the room, and said: "His name is n't Michel — it 's Michaelis. And he does n't deal in bread supplies either; he 's Assistant State Secretary to the Prussian Civil Commissariat. He did n't say he 'd stick his blade through any one's carcass — all he said was that he had a legal weapon in his hand and intended to use it ruthlessly if need be. It would n't be such a bad idea to make that man Imperial Chancellor. I 'll go straight over to Schloss Bellevue and see His Majesty about it. How pleased he 'll be to think he need n't have Bülow back."

So in a quarter of an hour Valentini was at Schloss Bellevue, in audience with William II, to whom he suggested Michaelis as his new Chancellor. The Emperor replied very graciously: "Of course I shall be delighted to make his acquaintance. For the moment I have no idea who he is, or what sort of person he is."

Doctor Michaelis, Bismarck's fifth successor, was summoned at once and presented himself. The Kaiser shook him by the hand and asked him if he cared to take over the Highest Imperial Office. For a few moments Michaelis stood covering his eyes, then answered in a very solemn voice: "I feel that help from Above will not fail me. I accept."

He was an excellent fellow. I had noticed him particularly, because of his unusually forthright manner, at the time when he was Assistant State Secretary to the Finance Ministry. Assistant

State Secretaries were, of course, expected to be present at the sittings of the Ministers of State, where they deputized for unavoidably absent chiefs. Once, on such an occasion, Doctor Michaelis had to speak in the name of his Minister, Baron von Rheinbaben. He stood up, put his thumbs to the seams of his trousers, and began, in a rather grating voice: "With the gracious permission of His Highness the Prince, and Imperial Chancellor, I, as representative of my exalted Chief, Baron von Rheinbaben, have to state, most humbly, etc. . . ."

The Federal Council's feeling about him is best illustrated by the following little episode. Count Hertling had come to Berlin, to speak at one of the Council debates. He was dining one night at Borchardt's, with Count Hugo Lerchenfeld, the Bavarian Minister, and some other people, when a young attaché of the Bavarian Legation approached Count Lerchenfeld to announce to him the appointment of Doctor Michaelis. Count Hertling asked Count Lerchenfeld who this Michaelis might be. He did not seem to have heard the name. Count Lerchenfeld, with true Bavarian pawkiness, answered, amid general hilarity: "This Doctor Michaelis is what we in Munich call an animal with buttocks to it — and that 's about all I can tell you."

Assistant State Secretary Michaelis was not only a very sound official but an exceptionally pious man — member of the "League for Resolute Christianity", a society of believers, of slightly pietistic tendency, who wore a badge, inscribed with the letters E.C. (*Entschiedenes Christentum*), which device they also stamped on their notepaper. Of international relations or foreign policy he had not the haziest notion. The Emperor gave Valentini the Black Eagle as his reward for having suggested this alternative!

The Wilhelmstrasse too had done its uttermost to prevent my having to be recalled. The moment Bethmann's position seemed insecure, it had set Vienna in motion and telephoned the following questions to the Austrian ambassador in Berlin: 1. Does the Austrian Government wish the retention of the present Imperial Chancellor, Bethmann-Hollweg? 2. Is it in favour of the recall of Prince von Bülow? The Austrians were not long in answering through our ambassador, Botho Wedel: "First point: Yes. Second point: No."

It was indeed quite understandable that Vienna should not have wanted me back in power, since Austria tried again and again to conclude, at Germany's expense, her own separate peace with the Allies. Vienna knew that I should soon have got wind of these attempts and opposed them with every force at my disposal. Those exalted ladies into whose hands the control of Austrian policy had fallen since the accession of the new Emperor, Charles, feared me as much as did the Ballplatz. They either knew or vaguely felt that within twenty-four hours I could have got a tight grip on the Dual Monarchy. The Archduchess Maria Josefa, the mother of the inexperienced Emperor, a Saxon princess, the Duchess of Parma, his mother-in-law, and his Consort, the Empress Zita, all equally detested the German Empire, Prussia, and the power of the Hohenzollerns. Freiherr von Tucher, the Bavarian Minister to Vienna, the highly capable son of an old Nuremberg family, of which Hans Sachs and Albrecht Dürer had been the guests, gave me, in his own bluff way, his impressions of these three ladies, supreme at the Vienna Court since November 21, 1916, the day of the old Emperor Francis Joseph's decease: "Maria Josefa is an idiot; Zita a little intriguer; and her mother is simply a malicious cow."

Baron, later Count Burian, had been appointed successor to Count Berchtold, one of the people chiefly responsible for presenting the ultimatum to Serbia. Berchtold had been a frivolous, shallow aristocrat; Burian was a good, conscientious official, but very mediocre politically. In December, 1916, he was replaced by Count Czernin, the decided intellectual superior of both his immediate predecessors, a man who would never have conceived such a folly as the Serbian ultimatum. Having been an intimate of the Archduke Francis Ferdinand, he could perceive the many dangers of too great a Magyar influence on the foreign policy of the Dual Monarchy. For some years he had been Austro-Hungarian Minister to Bucharest, where he had learned how necessary it was for Austria to keep on good terms with the Roumanians. He knew the ramshackle quality of the Austro-Hungarian State, which Austrians themselves would jokingly call the "Conglomeration", and saw how little reliance was to be placed on the Poles, the Czechs, the Southern Slavs. His aim was peace as speedily as possible, but peace in conjunction with Germany. He would have liked us to facilitate this by ceding Alsace-Lorraine to the French. But Czernin desired no base and open treachery to the Ally who had gone to war for Austria's sake. He mistrusted the Emperor Charles and the ladies whom that young Monarch allowed to rule him.

But he made the mistake of using Erzberger to further his wishes in Berlin. He had found means to secure that worthy Buttenhäuser an invitation to the most straight-laced and exclusive Court in Europe. The Hofburg went to Erzberger's head. Count Czernin had told Zita it would be necessary to put up for an hour or so with the society of "this rather common little Swabian" — the interests of the dynasty required it of her ! The pretty Empress gave Erzberger her hand to kiss, and he was hers ! When later she even allowed him to attend Mass, in the private chapel at the Hofburg side by side with Their Imperial Majesties, he had become her slave for evermore.

Shortly before Erzberger reached Vienna, Czernin had drawn up an immediate report for his Sovereign, to the effect that, in his opinion, Austria was in no state to go on fighting. Her choice was immediate peace or utter and final catastrophe. This report was intended first for the Emperor Charles, and only through him for William II, and the German High Command, who must in this fashion be won over to the idea of peace by understanding. It is almost proved that the Duchess of Parma, to whom the document was communicated, showed a special copy of it to Erzberger, who, in his turn, soon afterwards, at Frankfurt, read it out to a meeting of Centre Party delegates. Erzberger, before letting them hear it, had insisted that it was strictly confidential and forbidden his hearers to take notes. Nevertheless, a certain number of them managed to get down extracts in shorthand. These copies had soon reached Switzerland and, from there, come to the knowledge of Allied governments, whose assurance of victory they redoubled.

Later, by 214 Liberal, Socialist, and Centre Party votes, against
116 votes and 17 abstentions, the Reichstag passed a peace resolution.   Deputies, this resolution insisted, aimed at a peace by understanding, and the lasting reconciliation of peoples — a peace with
no brutal annexations of territory, without political, economic, or
financial measures of constraint.   France and England were heartened even more by it and it determined them to fight on to the bitter
end.   This peace resolution of 1917 had therefore prepared the
ground for Versailles, for a treaty in utter contradiction to the puerile
hopes of these three "ruling parties", as they styled themselves.
Versailles has brought no "lasting reconciliation of peoples"; it
has merely imposed unheard-of territorial sacrifices on Germany,
laying on our wretched people the most shameful exactions of every
kind — political, economic, financial.

By July, 1917, it had come to mutiny in our fleet.   This was engi-
neered, there can be no doubt of it — had been long and methodically prepared, by the agents of the U.S.P.D.   Naval officers of
judgment and perspicacity all agree that it could never have happened had our fleet been sent into action at the beginning; that this
mutiny itself, and the traitorous undermining of *morale* by such
creatures as Haase, Vogtherr, and the Dittmanns, which led up to
it, had both been very much facilitated by the long inaction of the
crews, the boring routine of peace-time duty, made still more
exasperating, no doubt, by useless and despotic red tape.

Before Bethmann's fall, a change had also been made at the
Foreign Office.   Jagow, at last, in November, 1916, was relieved of
the post of State Secretary in which he had done so much harm.
His successor was Assistant State Secretary Zimmermann.   Filled
with the best intentions, a man of honour and a patriot, Zimmermann, none the less, was very clumsy in his handling of our relations
with America, the importance of which, to us, daily increased.   He
was one of those Germans who mean so well, whose industry is so
unquestionable, whose virtues are solid and apparent, but who never
can manage to see that, in diplomacy, it is skill and the knowledge of
"how to take people" that count.   That was how Prince Bismarck
once put it, in my presence, in a talk with my father in January,

1874, three months after I first came to the Foreign Office: and later, in 1879, I heard Gambetta express the same view at a Paris dinner party, to which the excellent Comte Roger du Nord had invited me. The honest Zimmermann assured Gerard, the Ambassador of the United States, that Germany would certainly not extend, *à outrance*, her submarine warfare, without first having reached an understanding with America on the subject, and so gave this Ambassador his pretext for saying, in a solemn speech at a banquet of the American Chamber of Commerce in Berlin, that German-American relations had never before been more cordial. "For so long as such men as Doctors Solf and Helfferich, as Hindenburg and Ludendorff, as Admirals Von Müller, Von Capelle, and Von Holtzendorff, and as the State Secretary Zimmermann, are at the head of the civil, military, and naval services in Germany, it will undoubtedly be possible to keep these good relations intact."

Three weeks later, without due warning to America, we extended our submarine warfare. Simultaneously Zimmermann sent instructions to the German Minister in Mexico by which he was to propose to that republic, torn with civil dissension and half disintegrated, an alliance on the following terms: Mexico was to take back all the territories she had been forced to abandon to the States, *i.e.* Texas, New Mexico, Arizona (in all five hundred thousand English square miles, with nearly five million inhabitants), in exchange for which she should try to win over Japan to an alliance with Mexico and Germany. War was to be waged in common; peace to be signed in common. Important financial assistance to be extended to Mexico by Germany.

To make it even more ridiculous, this grotesque offer was technically badly drawn up. When it had got into the hands of the Americans, who promptly decoded and published it, a Swiss friend with whom, back in Lucerne again, I was walking beside the Lake of the Four Cantons, said to me: "The notion of using little Mexico to assail such a Colossus as the States strikes me as much about the same as a project to sink the British fleet with the three pleasure steamers on this lake."

On August 5, 1917, Zimmermann was replaced at the Foreign

Office by that same Herr von Kühlmann who, at Tangier, had won the Emperor's heart by his nimbleness in clambering up and down the rope ladder of the *Hohenzollern*. But the Imperial predilection for this young diplomat quickly waned, becoming in fact a source of misfortune to him, since it induced him to take as his guides to diplomacy the not always happy inspirations which would suddenly be vouchsafed to his Sovereign.

When Michaelis had grown not merely impossible, but had made himself the universal laughingstock, William II, once again, was faced with the horrible necessity of having to appoint a new Chancellor, the sixth successor to Prince Bismarck. He, who had been so glad to be rid of that prince, who had never shed a tear over Caprivi, had let Hohenlohe depart without a sigh, and seen the last of me with one of relief, found it hard to dismiss Doctor Michaelis. No other Chancellor, save Bethmann, had really been in such deep contact. A witness told me how, a few weeks after having put him in Bismarck's seat, His Majesty said with glee to the King of Saxony: "You can congratulate me on having discovered Michaelis. He really is the best I've ever had!" And the Emperor did his best to keep Michaelis at least his First Prussian Minister, but met with such unanimous opposition that he had to relinquish the idea.

Thus Doctor Georg Michaelis made his exit, to whom, not long after his appointment, the *Times* had devoted an article in more or less the following strain: "When Herr von Bethmann-Hollweg blundered out of the chancellorship, in the same clumsy manner in which he had blundered into war, the Kaiser summoned a mediocre official, entirely unknown in Germany or abroad, to whom he said: 'I promote you major. Nothing further should be necessary to make you, by the grace of God, an excellent Imperial Chancellor.'" Unhappily even his promotion to the rank of major in the *Landwehr*, which did, in fact, soon follow his appointment to the chancellorship, was not enough to secure Doctor Michaelis from prompt political demise. Once more, at the height of the storm, William II had no pilot. Once more, firmly resolved to do without me, he conceived the idea of appointing the Bavarian Prime Minister, Hertling, already considered for the chancellorship in July, 1917, but who then had refused, pleading ill health. This was that same Hertling to whom His Majesty had been with such difficulty persuaded to say a few words at a Court ball, twenty years before — unluckily, also, that same Hertling whose colleagues and subordinates in Munich, the former scene of his activities, as well as all his personal friends, were alike persuaded that he would soon be unequal to his duties there, though his task in Munich was far less arduous than that of an Imperial Chancellor. I do not wish to be misunderstood. Hertling was thoroughly efficient, a serious and dignified figure, as well as an alert and expert statesman. But he had aged before his time. Rapid arterio-sclerosis had hold of him. In Munich he had found it too great a strain to listen to reports for longer than an hour on end. His appointment caused astonishment in that city, where his state of health was perfectly well known.

Soon after he took over his new duties, I went to pay him a long call, which I owed him, if only because he had been the one Centre deputy, who, even when I broke with his party, had maintained with me his usual courtesy. In his mind he seemed as lucid as ever, but physically broken and used up. He was a great lover of books, so I advised him to send for his wonderful library to Munich, saying I was afraid he must miss his hobby. He only answered: "I might be dead before the books could reach me. I'm very ill." He went on, without turning a hair, to tell me how, a few months previously, he had written from Munich to tell the Emperor that he no longer felt well enough to accept his eventual appointment to the chancellorship. But that had made no difference to William II.

Hertling had come up to Berlin, where Count Lerchenfeld besought him on no account to suggest a cabinet of deputies to His Majesty, who had no further use for such people. He had answered: "Well, that's just what I shall do then." He was received in audience by his Sovereign and at once opened proceedings with the remark that it would be quite essential to appoint a more parliamentary cabinet. But William II had merely answered: "Well, do what you can't avoid doing." Hertling had gone on to say that he, personally, an old parliamentarian, had little use for parliamentary government as such; that he hated party hegemonies; that parliamentary methods were wrong for Germany, but that, with things in their present state, there was no alternative. The Emperor had approved all this with a nod and told him he could have a free hand. He had even accepted Hertling's further suggestion that he would have to get the support of all the parties, a proceeding till then rejected by William II as an intolerable insult to the Crown. Then Hertling had got into touch with the party chiefs. All, except one he did not name, had promised an old colleague their support. The one who refused did not conceal it from him that, in spite of all his personal friendship for Hertling, he would be bound to oppose him politically. Hertling shook this colleague by the hand and said to him: "I 've always liked you. But now I like you even more, since you 've given me some hope of getting out of this awful chancellorship." Later he had sent further word to His Majesty that he felt quite definitely obliged to renounce the honour of being his new Chancellor, while at the same time requesting the Chancellery to place once more at his disposal the saloon car which had brought him from Munich. But on this, Herr von Kühlmann had come hurrying to see him, with Count Lerchenfeld, pointing out that he could not abandon the Emperor; that to leave Berlin at such a juncture would be tantamount to positive desertion, and both had spoken so long and so persuasively that at last he consented to the post.

Kühlmann had, in particular, done his best to get Hertling appointed Chancellor. He did not follow him, however, to the "big box" at Number 77 Wilhelmstrasse. Nevertheless he found time, in his short spell of office as Foreign Secretary, to make several quite notable mistakes. The peace of Brest-Litovsk was the most salient. It needed no extraordinary valour to impose an exorbitant peace on the Bolsheviks. They were eager for peace at any price, so as to give themselves happily up to exterminating their enemies at home. In any case Trotski and his associates believed themselves on the eve of world revolution, and so considered all mere peace treaties provisional. But the treaty of Brest-Litovsk did harm in two ways to Germany. First, it gave the world the impression that we were a nation of insatiable brutes, thus furnishing French and English propaganda with new and specious arguments in support of their myth of a German plot for world hegemony. Second, the looseness of this treaty, which seemed to open up boundless perspectives, aroused all too many dynastic hopes of territorial aggrandisement. In Württemberg the Duke of Urach strove, with Erzberger's help, to get himself crowned King of Lithuania. This notion tickled Erzberger's fancy almost as much as another of his projects — the establishment of a neutral zone for the Papacy between Città Leonina and Cività Vecchia, so as to give the Holy Father full freedom to establish his own relationships abroad. Prince Frederick Charles of Hesse, the Emperor's brother-in-law, aspired to the throne of Finland. William II had been told of the magnificent bison in which Kurland forests abound, and wanted that country for himself, as a personal preserve, in which to hunt. The Emperor, a fairly good draughtsman, had already designed the coat-of-arms he intended to use as Duke of Kurland. In the West, there were also raised dynastic pretensions. Bavaria wanted the re-partition of Alsace-Lorraine — Lorraine to go to Prussia, Alsace to Bavaria. Württemberg declared that, in that case, she would claim the Sigmaringen district in compensation. Saxony refused to be left empty-handed and gave it to be understood that Upper Alsace might very well be governed from Dresden. The old dynastic trunk of German dynasties, twisted and gnarled by many centuries of passion for territorial aggrandisement, put forth fresh sprigs of hope after Brest-Litovsk, before the final tempest swept it away. It was sad indeed, in this winter of 1917–1918, to live in Berlin and witness these petty and absurd ambitions, this narrow egotism, at so terrible a moment in our history. The German princelings shared out land in advance exactly as, in Schiller's "Piccolomini", Wallenstein's generals distribute princely coronets.

Nor did a better spirit reign at the Foreign Office, especially among its minor officials. I had managed to keep a diary, with many gaps in it, ever since the beginning of the War. I here reproduce the following extracts, entered during this winter in Berlin: "Lunched in Hotel Adlon, the big dining room. At the table next me two young fellows from the Foreign Office. Was obliged to overhear the following talk. '*A*. Any news from the Front? *B*. Oh, shut up — you and your Front! I 'd much rather know if Jagow has managed to pick up an embassy.' An elderly man, who looked like a half-pay general, happened to be passing these eager young diplomats' table. He stopped, laid his hand on the last speaker's shoulder, and said sardonically: 'That 's right. Keep in the picture!'"

My second entry: "*X* tells me that a young Foreign Office official had asked the officer dining opposite him if he knew who had lunched with Prince Bülow yesterday. The officer answered: 'If I were you I 'd ask the Head Waiter.'"

Since then I have heard from every side that my movements at that time were closely watched. When Von Tirpitz had called at the Hotel Adlon to see me, in the winter of 1915–1916, Bethmann said reproachfully, next day: "You 've been seeing Prince von Bülow again!"

At a sitting of the Prussian Ministry, the Chancellor handed Herr von Loebell, the Minister of the Interior, a French illustrated paper, containing my photograph as I strolled along the quayside at Lucerne, where an adroit French journalist had "snapped" me. He asked in an anxious voice: "Why is it that the foreign Press is always making so much of Prince von Bülow? Surely it does n't happen as a rule, with foreign ministers, out of office!" Loebell reassured the Chancellor. I was not in the least anxious to get his post, etc. But Bethmann shook his melancholy head: "They 're all anxious to get my post! And yet I 'm the only one who, in spite of everything, can still gain the confidence of Europe — especially England."

The following is also from my diary: "To-day Harnack and his wife dined with us. This invitation was to make up to him for a great disappointment. For a long time Harnack has been trying to get himself made Minister of Public Worship. Bethmann had given him endless promises, and the Emperor, whom Harnack flatters more than any one — and, I must say, better and more wittily than any one — had also given his consent. But then unluckily some one published a letter, written by Harnack to a pretty, but indiscreet niece who lives in Munich, in which he had said that the Chancellor had been telling him in confidence that he would really like to go much further Left than he is at present, but is afraid of doing so for fear of annoying the Conservatives, and also, especially, the Emperor. But this letter had in it even worse: 'I, Adolf Harnack, consider the will to power a sin!'" Yet Harnack had been one of the noisiest jingoes among German savants, all through the War.

To be sure, many learned men sinned with him. I need only recall Professor Lasson, the last exponent of Hegelian philosophy in the University of Berlin. Hegel, it is said, asserted that only one disciple had understood him, and that he had understood in the wrong way. I do not know whether Hegel had a prophetic vision of Lasson's exegesis. But I am sure that of the profound and all-embracing Hegelian spirit, not a breath had passed into Lasson's mind. Soon after the declaration of war, Lasson had answered a Dutch colleague who, with the best of intentions, had written him his ideas for the progressive reconciliation of warring peoples as the result of peace by understanding, more or less as follows:

If he, Lasson, had been a Dutchman, he could have felt nothing but shame at being a neutral; at living on the fat of the land, in a country clogged with well-being. And his Dutch correspondent need never trouble his head about Germany. The epithet once bestowed on Titus applied equally well to William II: *Deliciae generis humani.* Bethmann-Hollweg was a statesman whom future ages well might envy us, etc.! The National Economist, Werner Sombart, would also have been better advised not to call his war-book "Helden und Händler." [1] His "heroes" were, of course, the Germans; his "shopkeepers" the English. But the English, all through their history, have displayed the most unquestionable heroism, and showed it again in the World War, whereas, on the other hand, we Germans have not lacked many brilliant commercial qualities — all the qualities associated with the best sense of the word "shopkeeper" and have been noted for them, both in the

[1] "Heroes and Shopkeepers."

Hansa period and after the restoration of the Empire.   The warning of the wise and patient Boethius, given in his "Consolationes", may well be applied to Sombart : *"O, si tacuisses, philosophus mansisses."*

But in grandiloquence Harnack surpassed all his colleagues. In Munich, when War was at its height, he made a speech in which he declared that only Germans were ready to die for the State — a death of which our enemies were incapable — and went on to explain this by adding that the Germans alone possessed any real culture. It is amusing to note that this same Harnack who, in the manner of Homeric braves, taunted and flouted the enemy, was writing, not long afterwards, to his niece, that he considered the will to power a sin.   "Get thee to a nunnery, get thee to a nunnery, Ophelia !"   That is what his students ought to have shouted at Harnack, the Court theologian.   Or, better still, they might have reminded him of those magnificent words of Disraeli, spoken as leader of the Conservative opposition : "Professors and rhetoricians invent systems and principles.   Real statesmen are inspired by nothing else than their instinct for power and love of country. These are the emotions and methods which make great Empires." Thus, in the House of Commons, Benjamin Disraeli, Earl of Beaconsfield.

CHAPTER XXI

Bad News from Austria — Our Ambassador there, Count Botho Wedel —
Roumania Comes into the War — Hindenburg, Ludendorff — The Develop-
ment of Their Strategy — Our Great Offensive in France in the Spring of 1918
— The Increasing War Weariness in Germany — Lamentable Weakness
of Our Government — Ballin Visits Me at Klein-Flottbek — His Last
Attempt to Open the Emperor's Eyes — A Letter from the Deputy Heckscher
on Our Defeat — My Answer — The Soviet Ambassador, Joffe.

MEANWHILE the political horizon was obscured by ever darker
clouds. The news from Austria above all, and relative to Austria,
was of the worst. Only Count Botho Wedel, our new Ambassador
in Vienna, could still manage to see everything *couleur de rose*. His
reports were the incessant confirmation of the optimistic views
expressed by him, whenever they had come to Vienna, to Michaelis,
innocent as a baby, and Hertling, sick and old before his time.
These reports, to Germany's misfortune, lulled into false security
the responsible directors of our policy. They were never led to
suppose that Austria-Hungary would not be loyal to her alliance.

But Wedel himself had been completely taken in by the fact that
Countess Louise Gröben, his mother-in-law, on a visit to her children
by the banks of the blue Danube, had actually received that rare
distinction, the Austrian Order of Elizabeth, with brilliants, from
the Empress Zita's own hand!

Yet this mark of signal favour to the Countess had not prevented
the Emperor Charles from betraying us, at the very moment it was
accorded, by a secret promise to Poincaré, transmitted through
Prince Sixtus of Parma, his brother-in-law, that he would support
by every means at his disposal, and the use of all the influence he
possessed, the "just" demands of the French for Alsace-Lorraine.
In exchange the Emperor Charles had begged for a separate peace.

Later he tried to deny his treachery, but was soon exposed for the insolent liar he was by Clemenceau, who published his letter in facsimile. That was where the blind reverence for Austria of Bethmann and Jagow had led us, and the Emperor's misconceived chivalry towards the aged Emperor Francis Joseph. Berlin had only the uncompromising spirit in which Sonnino upheld Italian claims to Trieste and the Trentino to thank for the circumstance that, as early as in 1917, the Habsburgs had not left Germany in the lurch. The Emperor Charles was willing enough to see us vacate Alsace-Lorraine, but felt that it would be a different matter to cede the Trentino and Trieste to "godless Italians."

Roumania's entry into the War had also greatly increased our burden. The Hungarian Government, even after 1914, could still not make up its mind to better treatment of Roumanians under the Crown of St. Stephen, or to promise them parliamentary representation in Hungary, corresponding to the nearly three millions of that country's Roumanian inhabitants. As to the Berlin Government, it failed as signally in the Roumanian question as it had in Italy, a year previously. Berlin could no more persuade Hungary to adopt a conciliatory tone to Roumania than it had managed to make Vienna change her mind on the subject of Italian concessions. In vain did the courageous Carp in Bucharest, and in Berlin the active Roumanian Minister, Beldiman, plead the German cause in direct reports to their king. The pro-Allies, led by Take Jonescu and Nikolaus Philipescu, won the day, since they could always point to the fact that, whereas the Central Powers maintained a never-changing reserve, the Allies had already promised Roumania the whole of Transylvania, Bukowina, and the Banat.

Roumania therefore followed Italy and, on August 27, 1916, King Ferdinand of Roumania declared war on Austria-Hungary. This king was a Hohenzollern who had served in the first Guards' Regiment. He betrayed Prussia, the army, and his country. Forty-eight hours after this declaration William II, at last, had the good sense to place Hindenburg and Ludendorff in supreme control of our forces. These new chiefs not only succeeded in paralysing the Roumanian attack; they gave a fresh impulse to our arms.

While at the Hofburg, unperceived by German statesmen, the cancer of treachery spread and spread; while secret, but never-remitting propaganda in Germany undermined and sapped the *morale* of the nation, our armies, led by Hindenburg, won imperishable laurels on every front. Nineteen eighteen brought tragic contrasts: in the trenches incomparable valour; at home the sinister growth of defeatism, the slow exhaustion of our strength.

Nowhere in all military history is there anything more shiningly heroic than the German offensive of March, 1918, conceived by Hindenburg as a series of closely combined attacks which, first in one sector, then another, should hammer at the enemy defences till at last they crumpled up before it. Preceded by creeping barrage, the German infantry made stormy and victorious assaults on the positions of the English. Bapaume, where half a century earlier I had fought as a young hussar, was snatched from them, with much capture of war material, and so we pushed on to Albert and Mont-didier, to which I had ridden out on patrols. But in the west we stopped short of Amiens. Two English armies had been routed by us; our men had taken nearly a hundred thousand prisoners and captured more than a thousand guns, yet no strategic result had been achieved. The enemy had outnumbered us too heavily! They could dispose of the war material and man power of almost the entire world. The last decision was given by American reinforcements to Europe.

Faced with such valour, criticism finds it difficult to speak. Yet I cannot deny that, at the time, I often wondered if we were right to extend our forces as we did, from the Somme to the Vistula, the Vosges to the Carpathians, Kurland to the Ukraine, the Isonzo to the Euphrates, Roumania to Palestine. I often said, and even wrote to Berlin, that Napoleon, in spite of all his genius — of the almost inexhaustible strength with which subject peoples, Germany and Italy, Holland and Belgium, had to supply him — had owed his final defeat to the fact that he kept troops in Madrid and Moscow, in Rome and Amsterdam. *Qui trop embrasse, mal étreint.* We should have done better to relinquish the Eastern Front and concentrate our whole strength in the west.

I followed with a beating heart the second German offensive in France, the battle of the Lys; and the third, the taking of Soissons by our gallant Crown Prince. Our fourth offensive had as objective Rheims, which would fall to us automatically if we could take Epernay to the west, Châlons-sur-Marne to the east of it. It brought the military decision, and with it the end. The passage of the Marne (July, 1918) succeeded brilliantly. But the German plans had been betrayed. The enemy, who knew our intentions, had shifted his defence to the second line. I had news for the first time in this offensive that there were signs of demoralization in our armies. Many units were refusing their orders. Regiments, gallantly advancing, were insulted by others with the shout: "Streik-brecher!"[1] It is well known that after the War an English general declared that the German army had not been conquered — it had been "stabbed in the back." German Socialists raised vehement protests; and the loudest of all were just those Socialist publicists and leaders who had most incurred such a reproach. No impartial witness will assert that Socialists fought any less bravely than did their non-Socialist comrades. Yet it cannot be denied that the party chiefs, not one of whom had ever left his fireside, behaved in a very different fashion from their political co-religionists at the front. The nearer we seemed to a decision, the more efforts did these blind fanatics make to involve us in irremediable disaster. The slacker the grip upon his reins of one feeble chancellor after the other, the bolder revolutionaries became.

In France, as I have said, defeatists and pacificists were put down at once, and with an iron hand. They were shot, imprisoned, sent into exile — though the guardians of the nation's *morale* were Socialist or Radical Ministers. In England, a Liberal Government repressed Sinn Fein with bloodshed and brutality. In the Tower of London, the seat of many another gruesome incident in English history, Sir Roger Casement, the Irish leader, was hanged by them. Yet whereas, in both these countries, the penalties, not only for high treason but for any attempt at peace propaganda and defeatism, were daily sharpened, there was, in Germany, a tendency to

[1] "Strike-breakers."

relax such excellent measures against treachery at home as we possessed, or else to apply them only rarely. At the moment even of final decision — the moment when we had staked our all — that *petit bourgeois* mentality which Bismarck, who fought it so hard for thirty years, has christened "Der Standpunkt des Philisters",[1] was triumphant in German politics. I was often seized with pity for Germany, as I read in *Le Temps* the details of executions for high treason — details which gave a clear idea of how little it needed among the French to get oneself tried by court-martial — at a time when, with us, the pacifist spirit was spreading like some repulsive mildew.

But while, in France, this mildew was being swept out of the way, while bad citizens there were being killed off like vermin, I received the following curious answer from one of our Foreign Office officials, a man not otherwise lacking in solid qualities, to whom I had written that, no doubt, at such a time of crisis, he would not have a minute to spare in which to reply to my letter. He wrote : "Certainly we are very busy. We are engaged in drawing up German suggestions for a League of Nations which will, it is to be hoped, be the best result of this War !"

At Flottbek, where, since 1915, I had spent a few weeks every summer, I received many visits from Albert Ballin, especially in 1918. At the end of August he had been to stay at Headquarters, invited there by the wish of the High Command, which had begged him to say straight out to His Majesty how serious our position was becoming. Both Hindenburg and Ludendorff had often attempted this in vain. But Ballin had found it impossible ever to be alone with the Emperor. Either the Kaiserin or the new Cabinet Councillor, Von Berg, had always managed to choke him off.

Herr von Berg, soon after Bethmann's departure, had replaced Herr von Valentini as Head of His Majesty's Civil Cabinet. Valentini's general narrow-mindedness and, even more, his lack of character, had done much to harm his Imperial Master and the Fatherland. Yet William II had hated having to part with him, since he had been a humble, timorous flunkey, going in wholesome

[1] "The Standpoint of the Philistine."

awe of his master, whom, on principle, he never contradicted. Bethmann also had done his best to keep Valentini, who had been the companion of his youth and to whom his soul was so akin. It was thanks to the Crown Prince that, at last, Valentini was given his *congé*, not long after Bethmann's retirement, and this should be accounted to him as merit. Herr von Berg was about the Emperor's own age, and they had been members of the same students' corps. He was the best type of East Prussian squire's son, and a very decent sort of man, who would not mince words, even with the Emperor; upright, a good official and, better still, a true patriot.

Both Ludendorff and Hindenburg trusted Von Berg. But even he was not quite equal to the very trying position in which he found himself in the autumn of 1918. Ballin, always indulgent with other people because he could see into their minds, related, therefore, his unsuccessful visit: "I'm not blaming either Von Berg or the Empress. She is the very best of women, the ideal of a German *hausfrau* — and Von Berg is a gentleman and a patriot. But they're both convinced that if the Emperor is forced to see things as they really are, the result will be his utter collapse, and so they ask themselves: 'What use would that be to us?' The result is that the Emperor lives more 'in a fool's paradise' than ever he did, and a great many or, let us say, the majority of Germans along with him."

Ballin told me all this in the course of the last talk we ever had. For twenty years we had often exchanged ideas and together we had witnessed many events. I have liked few people so much, for few have I felt such respect, as I did for Ballin! Not only was he very clear-sighted but — a quality far rarer with us than in Italy — he was gifted with a most resourceful mind. *Il était plein d'expédients*, could almost always suggest a way out of difficulties, and possessed that practical common sense more often met with in Englishmen, in Americans, in Frenchmen even, than in Germans. At the same time, although he was self-taught, he had the profound sense of what intellectual culture really means. Above all, he was the kindest of men, and many indeed are the lame dogs he has helped over stiles, demanding nothing in exchange, nor attaching the least importance to what he had done for them.

GENERAL FIELD MARSHAL PAUL VON BENECKENDORF
UND HINDENBURG

Ballin died suddenly, at the moment when revolution was breaking out. It is said his death was self-inflicted, but I am convinced he did not actually kill himself. The ruin of Germany had shaken him to the very depths. He believed, as his dear wife afterwards told me, that his whole life's work had been destroyed. The fate of the Emperor also affected him profoundly, to whom, though he did not always agree with him, he remained devoted and loyal in spite of all, and whom, if I may so put it, he loved as a father. The best proof that he did not commit suicide is the long letter I received from him, written twenty-four hours before his death, in which he had sketched out suggestions for the country's economic reconstruction, and that of the German merchant service. On the morning of his last day he had been sitting alone in his private office, in the imposing "Hapag"[1] building, on the Binnenalster, which bears, carved on its front, the proud inscription : *"Mein Feld ist die Welt."*[2] Sailors, wearing red brassards and cockades, burst into the room and threatened this sensitive, ailing man with a thrashing. They bawled into his ears that the German Republic had been proclaimed, that a great new time was beginning; that this would be a glorious age, an age when it would be all over with capitalism, with Ballin and his Hamburg-America Line. Ballin, who suffered much from insomnia, had a very strong sleeping draught on his writing table. When these ruffians had gone, he felt so upset that he emptied the bottle at a draught, then, seized with instant regret, telephoned at once for his doctor. The doctor came hurrying; did not consider the case a desperate one, but declared that the stomach must be emptied and ordered Ballin to walk with him at once to his clinic, since movement was the thing he needed most. Ballin reached the clinic and fell dead of heart failure.

Ballin was born in Hamburg, at the Steinhöft. From his earliest boyhood he had lived under "the forest of masts", as the old Hamburg song, which I too heard as a boy, expresses it. He came of a Jewish family, domiciled on the banks of the Elbe for centuries, which had produced many active merchants and also some scholars of repute. He never forsook the faith of his ancestors. I

[1] Hamburg-America Line.   [2] The world is my field.

have met few men who knew humanity better than he; few more adroit and assured in their human relationships, few who could be at once so kind and dignified. He was, which is even rarer, a good man. Few have done so much good all their lives as Ballin. His weakness was perhaps a certain tendency in him to wish to please every one he met, a trait which caused those who disagreed with him to say that he was lacking in character, and which did, in actual fact, sometimes give one a feeling of insecurity with him. But, all things considered, he was a man; a true representative of the bold mercantile genius, ever resourceful and full of enterprise, which distinguishes our largest German port, the ancient, yet undying, Hamburg.

Five weeks before Ballin's death I had received the following at Flottbek, from the Liberal deputy, Doctor Siegfried Heckscher:

Most esteemed Prince,

On September 30, 1918, even foreigners had begun to hear the knell of the German Empire founded by Bismarck, developed and maintained by Prince von Bülow. The High Command has unluckily made the fatal mistake of underestimating the strength of our enemies. But the chief cause of our defeat is the shameful — the criminal — manner in which our foreign policy has been guided, ever since July, 1914, and right on, to Hertling's resignation. We might still, in spite of all, have pulled up at the edge of the precipice, had the Crown, even in September, been advised by men of character and wisdom. But Herr von Berg was utterly insufficient. First he was for Bülow, then against him, because Bülow wanted to work with Scheidemann. Von Berg began by advising dictatorship; then he relinquished, without a blow, every constitutional right of the Crown, and, in the end, made an amateurish attempt to regain what he had irrevocably lost.

All this reminds me of Charles I of England, that king who once inspired me to write a poem; but with this difference that, in addition to the struggle between a king and his parliament, we are faced with this terrible loss of the War. The reversal is so catastrophic that with few, very few, exceptions, people seem to be losing their heads completely. One of these exceptions is old Count August Eulenburg, who has kept his judgment clear, and his head cool. Had he, and not Von Berg, advised the Sovereign, the worst could most likely have been avoided. I do not, even to-day, attempt to conceal from you that I am, and shall ever remain, a convinced believer in parliaments.   But what I utterly deplore, what seems to me a very real danger, is the revolutionary tone in which we have begun our parliamentary government.   To-morrow, I suppose, the new Chancellor will be announcing to our people, and to the world, that Germany has sent a request for peace to Wilson.   By to-morrow evening the whole country will be wrapped in a dark cloud of national sorrow.   Here and there perhaps there may be people who can only feel it a relief — the few who say they prefer a horrible end to a never-ending horror — but it will not be long before we hear cries of : "Who were the guilty ones?"   Our real danger will be on us with the return of our gallant men, all demanding shelter, work, and bread.   Every clear-sighted, self-controlled German ought already to be concentrating on that, if utter disaster at home is to be avoided.   I can only respect Prince Max of Baden for his courage; but he must make a clean sweep of all such hysterical advisers as Conrad Haussmann, who rushes about, as red as a tomato, with others like him, through the Wilhelmstrasse and into the lobbies of the Reichstag.

In any case I don't imagine that Prince Max's government will last. Yet although I am perfectly conscious of dangers, present and to come, I still hope that, after decades of toil, Germany may build up anew her strength and greatness.

Much will depend on the skill of those who negotiate our peace for us; I am thinking of the France of 1814 and 1815, and of the results of the Congress of Vienna.   But let come what may !   For four years we have held our fortress unflinchingly, against all comers, in the face of over-whelming odds.   *Si fractus illabatur orbis, impavidum ferient ruinae.*

In inexpressible sorrow for the Fatherland, I remain

Your Highness' most devoted

HECKSCHER.

Since the death of my only sister, a little angel whom, in January, 1870, the Celestial Gardener took into His garden in Paradise, while she was still a girl of twelve, I had shed no tears.   Nor did I ever weep again till the death of my darling wife, whom I loved more dearly than anything else in the world.   Yet, as I finished this letter, I broke down !   Certain defeat !   Unavoidable, instant capitu-lation, after four years of such resistance, of the finest, most glorious army the world has seen — the army of Fehrbellin and Leuthen ;

of Leipzig, Waterloo, Sadowa, Sedan ! But keener still the sudden intuition, which came upon me like a lightning flash, that all my past uneasiness had been justified — every fear of the last nine years, that one day I might live to see the fall of Ilium. I knew so well the character of our enemies ! All the sadism, the vindictiveness, the thirst for power, of French generals and *avocats;* all the cold cruelty of the English ! Recent declarations from Washington, received by us within the last few weeks, showed me plainly that President Wilson, faced by all these European complications, would be as credulous, as naïve, as the good "Huron", in Voltaire's immortal "Ingénu." And I knew the miserable, petty spirit, the narrow selfishness of our party politics ! I was well aware how completely the average German is lacking in all political awareness. I could scarcely believe in that resistance which, according to a section of our Press, would at once be organized when democracy had come into its own.

On October 7th I wrote Herr von Heckscher a long letter, given in part below. I have only suppressed certain criticisms of the last few years of German policy :

For two days your letter has lain on my desk, with its terrible news that Germany will have to give in. You know me too well to need any description of the effect which such a letter has had on me. Would to God I had never lived to see this day ! Why could I not have died while Germany was still in her greatness? When, last July, I heard on good authority that the High Command wanted peace, I said that, in that case, it would be essential, by the use of diplomatic skill, to reach an understanding with our enemies, before our military position had ceased, in their eyes, to be still tenable. But what was ever done in that direction? The most highly placed members of the government made contradictory speeches, one after the other, and, if any diplomatic steps were taken, if any one really attempted to put out feelers, such efforts have been without result. Why was our people never warned of the inevitable *débâcle* in Bulgaria, and so saved the panic which it caused? Weeks ago I had heard the rumour that King Ferdinand was hinting to all and sundry that he would find it hard to keep his throne if he remained true to his alliance with us. Any one with knowledge of near-Eastern affairs ought to have seen that Radoslavov's retirement and replacement by Malinov were a serious warning to Germany. What hurts me most is this apathy and discouragement on all sides and, with them, every sign of panic. Have things really got to such a point that we must lose our heads altogether? Did not the French go on fighting desperately, enduring defeat after defeat, at a time when we were already threatening Paris? Have our enemies reached the left bank of the Rhine? Are they in Alsace-Lorraine — in Baden? Are Aix-la-Chapelle, Coblenz, Freiburg, or Mannheim in ruins? Is Cologne cathedral being shelled? It would need all this to place us in a similar situation to that in which the French have gone on fighting us for four years. Did not little Prussia, crushed at Jena, arise and continue her struggle? Did not Courbière, summoned by the French to surrender Graudenz, on the pretext that there was no longer a king of Prussia, answer that, in that case, he was himself the king of Graudenz? Where is the spirit of Arndt, of Theodor Körner, of Stein, of Schleier-macher? Was Gerard, the American Ambassador, right when he said last year, in his spiteful book, "Face to Face with Kaiserism": "The nerve of Germany will break; there is a suicide point in the German character."

And even if the military position had become desperate, that was no reason at all for our sudden change of political attitude towards the foreigner. I don't suggest that this new government was not well chosen for its purpose: but, since, on August 4, 1914, the Emperor said that he no longer knew parties, only Germans, surely it would have been better to set up a coalition, as they did in France and England, in Belgium, and later in Italy — a government which could have brought us through the War! You know how, from the very first day, I have felt that such a war as this could only be waged with the full approval of the masses, above all of the workmen's organizations, and with Socialist leaders in the government. If democracy can produce such chiefs as it did forty-eight years ago in Gambetta, and has done again to-day in Clemenceau — leaders who can march at the head of the nation, with the flag unfurled — I shall be the first to thank it. I will make no prophecies as to the probable reception of our peace offer. The French, who already see the cathedral spires of Metz and Strassburg within reach, and who have been roused to fury by four years of German occupation of their soil, will be the most relentless of all.

The more I ponder this situation, the more deeply do I admire our people, with its splendid powers of sacrifice, its energy — that people which we should cherish all the more since the road which it must tread will be a stony one. Let us wish it better times with all our hearts!

A few days after this we settled down again, in our usual suite at the Hotel Adlon, with a view over the Pariser Platz. I went out, on the evening of our arrival, for a walk in Unter den Linden, and was astonished to see every first-floor window of the Russian Embassy lighted up. I knew these apartments well, having talked in them to Paul von Oubril and Peter Saburov, to Bismarck's friend, Prince Orlov, who had lost an eye in the Crimean War, at the storming of Silistria; to my friend, General Shuvalov, and, during my chancellorship, to the good Count Osten-Sacken, all Tsarist ambassadors. When I asked a newspaper seller what was going on at the Russian Embassy she answered: "There's some sort of a big how-de-do among the Russians, for the U.S.P. comrades." And, to be sure, the Russian and German "comrades" were mingling in true brotherly fashion. They had been on intimate terms for some time past. The Russian ruble which, under Tsardom, had come rolling into so many French newspaper offices, and into the pockets of so many of France's leading politicians — which had achieved such widespread corruption in the Balkans, Galicia, and Bohemia — had now, under the Soviets, found its way into the hands of our Left Wing Socialists, whose criminal designs had been furthered, for months, with Russian money. A year later the giver of this feast, the Ambassador Joffe, reminded Oskar Cohn, the Reichstag deputy, in a rather brusque open letter to him, that even he, Cohn, might have found it hard to prepare the naval mutiny at Kiel, the revolutions in Munich and Berlin, without subsidies from Russia.

Soon after this return to Berlin, I began to hear strange rumours of the Emperor. The deputy Heckscher related how he had happened to meet him in the Königgrätzer Strasse, coming out of the gardens of the Hausministerium, where His Majesty went nearly every day, for a conference with his Minister, Eulenburg. The Emperor had turned an eagle eye on Heckscher, and shouted, in a tragic voice: "Protect my Imperial rights!"

Stranger still was another little episode confided by a member of the Spanish Embassy: A person sent in confidence by the Emperor had enquired, at the Spanish Embassy, if, in case he should be forced to leave Germany, His Majesty might count on a good reception in

Spain. The Ambassador had sent back the assurance that both the Spanish people and their king, who throughout the War had made no secret of the sympathy they felt for the German cause, would, of course, tender His Majesty hospitality, in accordance with all the traditions of Spanish chivalry. But how did William II propose to reach Spain from Berlin? It would be difficult to go by the usual route, via Paris-Hendaye-Irun, and equally hard to travel via Italy, and so, by sea, to Barcelona. The Kaiser had replied that he intended to reach San Sebastian in a submarine, as had been done, not long since, by the hardy commander of one of our U-boats. It seems that William II gave up the idea almost as soon as he had conceived it. But it is certain he felt most anxious to leave Berlin.

The Emperor never lacked courage in facing danger. This he had proved, as I have noted, in those grave days when he was faced with an operation on his throat, the thought of which, together with the memory of the cancer that had afflicted not only both his parents, but several other members of his house, might well have caused a stronger man to quail. He was also an intrepid rider, though, with him, riding was always dangerous, since he had not the use of his left arm. Finally I have often walked with him unescorted in the streets of Wilhelmshöhe, at Wiesbaden, Homburg, Kiel, and on our numerous journeys together, and have never known him even a little uneasy. But imagination, Schiller's bold adventurer, was at times stronger in him than μῆτις, the calm reflection of the Greeks. Does not the Olympian Goethe himself boast his allegiance to fantasy, the most cherished daughter of great Jove — the eternally mobile, vivid, capricious! With such a nature as this, it was essential that William II should have about him the calm, balanced advisers he so needed. His mind was ever pregnant of images, which filled him, now with boundless hope, now with the most abysmal despair. He could not ever manage to rid his thoughts of the tragic fate of Nicholas II; was persuaded that the Tsar had died so horribly because he had remained too long in Petrograd, instead of taking refuge at once with the headquarters of his army. These delays, he felt, had given the revolutionaries their chance to capture the Tsar *en route*, force his abdication, and afterwards slaughter him.

William II could not perceive how different our German temperament is from the Russian; or, indeed, from that of any other people ! No German sovereign yet has been forced to the scaffold, as were Charles I and Louis XVI; nor have we assassinated our monarchs, as did the Swedes, the Italians, and, several times over, the Russians.

In any case it was the gravest of political errors for the Emperor to abandon his capital in the autumn of 1918. He ought to have remained where he was, keeping in closest touch with his Ministers, receiving only serious people, maintaining his power, and organizing the defences of Berlin. Revolution was in no sense inevitable. At the worst, William II could have taken the advice of Prince Bismarck, and died, sword in hand, on the steps of his throne.

CHAPTER XXII

Prince Max of Baden, Imperial Chancellor — His Personality, His Unfitness for Office — My Name Comes up for the Chancellorship — The Question of William II's Abdication — His Flight into Holland and Letter to the Crown Prince — The Kaiser Abdicates — Philistine Character of the German Revolution — The Naval Mutiny in Kiel — Events in Munich — The Flight of Ludwig III of Bavaria — King Frederick Augustus of Saxony's Farewell to His People.

ON October 3, 1918, Prince Max of Baden replaced Count Hertling, whose illness gained on him so swiftly that soon he found it utterly impossible to continue in office.

When, not long before his resignation, a messenger from headquarters presented himself at the Count's, with a very important communication, demanding instant and vigorous political decisions, he entered the room to find himself choked with incense. The Chancellor had just had a seizure and had demanded the last sacraments. Four months after this he died, on January 4, 1919, in his châlet at Ruhpolding in Upper Bavaria.

His successor, Prince Max of Baden, deserved neither the premature laurels bestowed on him at the moment of his appointment nor the hail of invective which pattered on his retreating back: *ni cet excès d'honneur il ne méritait, ni ces indignités,* as the French poet remarks. I think I may say that I am able to judge the Prince impartially since, though he never impressed me, I did not dislike him, and we were bound by a friendship of some years' standing. He was, above all else, an amateur — a princely amateur. Without any particular knowledge of his subject he had received the honorary degree of Doctor of Political Science; was a cavalry general whose only experience of the army had been a few years' service in the Cuirassiers of the Guard, followed by a brief spell as Colonel of a regiment of Baden Dragoons. As a prince of his house he had been named President of the Baden Upper Chamber, where, every two years, he was in the habit of making a little speech, on entering on his term of presidency, since the Baden *Landtag* had the sense only to meet every other year. A few months before these auspicious events fell due, the Prince would get some Professor of Heidelberg or Freiburg University to write his speech for him, and he always found time to learn it by heart. These inaugural addresses, delivered with impeccable elocution, replete with Liberal sentiments, and "progressive" generalities, were sure of the cordial reception which such innocent eloquence always receives in Germany. Let us remember Herr Willy Helpach, who, on the death, in 1925, of the excellent Ebert, dreamed himself President of the Reich. Prince Max's "war work" had been the care and instruction of Germans interned in Switzerland, where he had displayed great tact and affability in his relationships with the Swiss authorities, and the interned nationals of every belligerent. To-day I still believe that had the Prince been given a good Staff Officer to support him, and a skilful Foreign Office official, he would have done his work as head of the Armistice Commission very well. He was far better fitted to negotiate with foreign diplomats, ministers, and generals than the "independent Germans" who so kindly went to Versailles on our behalf, where they played indeed a sorry part; or than Erzberger, whom we sent to the Forest of Compiègne.

Prince Max had perfect manners; his French and English were both fluent. A descendant of the ancient house of Zähringen, he had married into an even older Guelph house and was closely related to the sovereigns of England, Russia, and Denmark. Through his mother, a Leuchtenberg-Romanowsky, he was a great-grandson of Nicholas I. But, in addition to this magnificent autocrat, he numbered among his ancestral connections the Vicomte Alexandre Beauharnais, who had gone over to the French Revolution, been named Commander of the Rhine Army and, for losing Mainz, was guillotined in Thermidor, 1794, a few days before Robespierre suffered the same fate. Young General Beauharnais would have been astonished indeed if, as the tumbril rattled him to the guillotine, some *voyante* such as the Westphalian Velleda, or a prophet like the Greek Teiresias, had appeared before him and predicted: "Your pretty widow Josephine will become Empress of the French. . . . Your young son Eugène will be a Viceroy in Italy, and son-in-law to the first King of Bavaria, and this son's son will marry the eldest daughter of a Tsar. Your little daughter Hortense will be Queen of the Low Countries, and the mother of the third Emperor of the French, who will be taken prisoner at Sedan by a German Emperor. Your descendants will sit on the thrones of Sweden, Norway, Denmark, and Brazil, and even Anhalt-Dessau, Köthen, and Bernburg. Your little niece Stéphanie will become Grand Duchess of Baden, and one of her great-grandsons will be the last Chancellor of the powerful, the Imperial Germany." Georges Sand was perfectly right when she said, "*La vie ressemble plus au roman que le roman à la vie.*"

I can only repeat that "Bademax" as they called him in the Cuirassiers of the Guard, though, by connections, family, personality, he was designed to be the ideal diplomat, even in affairs of some consequence, was in no sense fitted for the chancellorship, especially at a moment of such crisis. He gave way utterly before Wilson and, with his advisers the Democrats, swallowed every phrase sent from Washington. When the Emperor, according to custom, had sent to ask Frederick II, the Grand Duke of Baden, if he had any objections to offer to his cousin Prince Max's appointment, the Grand Duke merely enquired if the dispatch had been wrongly deciphered — or was this simply another Imperial whim which need not be considered as really serious? William II replied that his choice had been most carefully thought out; he was therefore quite in the wrong when, a few weeks later, he showered all those zoölogical epithets which would flow from his lips in moments of ill-temper on the Chancellor he himself had selected.

An old friend, who was also very intimate with the Emperor, had been asked to stay with our erstwhile sovereigns two months after the Imperial flight to Holland, at the château of Amerongen, the property of the Bentincks. He told me how one night at dinner, His Majesty had seemed especially sombre. He had sat in silence. The poor Empress gazed up at him anxiously. Suddenly, with a shout, William II had thumped the table. "That 'Bademax' is a scoundrel — a traitor!" The Empress gave a sigh of relief and murmured, "Thank Heavens, he 's beginning to speak again !"

Yet these accusations were quite unmerited, since the Prince might have answered with Molière: "*Tu l'as voulu, Georges Dandin, tu l'as voulu.*"

The pressure of events had led to the abandonment of surprise appointments to the chancellorship and, at the Emperor's order, Herr von Berg had asked the party chiefs to give their views on this choice of a successor to Hertling. Several deputies, in particular Erzberger, have told me that my name was mentioned, since it was generally admitted by the Reichstag that, when it came to negotiating the peace, my experience of foreign affairs might be useful. The suggestion worried Herr von Berg. He answered nervously that he deeply respected Prince von Bülow and was personally on the very best of terms with him. He would even go so far as to admit that my appointment might be considered the right solution. "But I should never," he added, "get the Prince accepted by the Emperor. It would be out of the question."

This verdict was natural enough. And it would, at such a moment of danger, have been quite impossible to work with William II on any terms save those of absolute and mutual trust. But people who imagined that by so doing they would be giving pleasure to His Majesty, while at the same time they assured themselves of his favour, had taken good care to keep his mind inflamed against me, and he had not enough self-control, a sufficiently strong sense of duty, to overcome the personal rancour, fed from so many sources, for nearly ten years.

I do not know if I could have managed to save William II, or in any case to save his dynasty. I do not imagine that I should have stepped into Wilson's trap, as did Prince Max, and such inexperienced people as Haussmann and Erzberger. I must not incur the reproach of cheap hypotheses, in face of the established facts. But for me, as for every loyal Prussian, every clear-sighted German, there was only one thing left for us to do in October, 1918 — we should have gone on fighting, fighting resolutely. We had no choice! At home we should have tightened up discipline; the war zone should have been reduced to order; every available man should have been despatched at once to the Western Front. Competent soldiers have since assured me that many of our positions were still quite tenable; that, in any case, we could have held the Rhine. And this according to these experts, was the concensus of declared opinion of our Corps Commanders, summoned from every sector to G.H.Q. to report to the High Command on the state of *morale* in their trenches. In contrast to the commanders of divisions and army corps, both colonels and brigadiers pronounced for the continuance of hostilities and had guaranteed the fighting spirit of their subordinates. At the moment when our Government gave in, we were perfectly well able to go on fighting and should even have fought in not too adverse strategic positions. This has been several times admitted by Marshal Foch, the most valiant of our enemies. In the interview which, in July, 1928, he gave the editor of the *Wiener Neue Freie Presse,* he declared that, in September, 1918, Germany might have held out behind the Rhine: "Had the Germans possessed a Gambetta the war would have gone on; and who knows?" To the suggestion that Gambetta's example merely showed that even the most heroic resistance of a people defeated in the field serves to prolong a war unnecessarily, Marshal Foch replied: "Nevertheless, I am convinced that a nation which does not wish its own defeat need not, inevitably, be beaten. In November, 1918, Germany had obviously lost all hope of possible victory. Had her armies made a stand behind the Rhine, much might not have happened as it did."

If Ludendorff himself had come to tell me that he considered further resistance out of the question, I should have answered him: "I can well understand that your nerves are strained to breaking point with all the exhaustion your tremendous efforts must have cost you. Both Frederick the Great and Napoleon had their moments of utter discouragement. Go home and sleep for twenty-four hours, then come back and we will discuss it again."

I am persuaded that, within twenty-four hours, the General would have become the old Ludendorff, and that we should have gone on fighting — fighting to the last ditch, in the spirit in which both Hindenburg and Ludendorff had fought ever since they obtained command of our forces. I would at least have forced the Emperor back to Berlin. I would not have allowed him to run across the frontier! And in Berlin I should have seen to it that order was maintained. We might be defeated, but we had no right to collapse. Prince Max was certainly not the traitor that William II and other "right-thinking" people have accused him of being. But like Bethmann, he was too weak to be really straightforward. There can be no doubt that he took over the direction of affairs with the intention of sacrificing the Emperor in order to save the Prussian dynasty as a whole, and with it, all the other princely houses. Already, several months before he was made Chancellor, he had said, in a letter to the Crown Prince Ruprecht of Bavaria, with whom he was in continuous correspondence, that the Emperor's abdication was inevitable. King Ludwig III, feeling no doubt that if the Emperor went, he would go too, had sharply reprimanded his son for having even discussed the possibility. As Wilson's hints grew ever broader, Prince Max, now Chancellor, said straight out to the Bavarian Prime Minister, Herr von Dandl, that he considered it the most important part of his task to convince the Kaiser that he must abdicate. Herr von Dandl, highly indignant, had passed on these assertions to his Sovereign, so that consequently the Prince was soon in very bad odour in Munich. Later Prince Max tried hard to bring the Grand Duke Ernst von Hesse to the point of tell-ing the Emperor to abdicate. This the Grand Duke refused to do, reminding Prince Max that William II was his first cousin, who in his boyhood had often come over to Darmstadt, from Kassel and Bonn, to spend his holidays. He could not possibly be party to any such suggestion as that he, the Grand Duke, should be made the bearer of the bowstring. Finally, Prince Max succeeded in persuad-ing Herr Drews, the Prussian Minister of the Interior, to try to make the Emperor realize that he could no longer remain on his throne. Herr Drews prepared his *exposé* with great care, but had scarcely begun it when the Emperor, whose kingly pride revolted at the sight of this rather subordinate bureaucrat, showed him the door. Yet

William II had no need of any ministerial admonition to make him aware that, both in Parliament and in the very heart of his own Cabinet, efforts were being made to force him to relinquish the throne. When he left Berlin for Army Headquarters at Spa, he knew that his own fate hung in the balance and that the future of his dynasty was uncertain. Outwardly, however, he gave no sign that he did not consider himself the Emperor. As late as on November 6th or 7th the aide-de-camp, General Löwenfeld, told me how His Majesty had wired to him from Spa inviting him to proclaim "to all true-hearted Germans" that "the King of Prussia and German Emperor" would resist "to the last drop of his blood."

When news reached us of the mutiny at Kiel and revolution in Munich and Berlin, and rumours were floating through the capital that the army in the west had refused its orders, Count August Eulenburg came to me, and said : "Please God our Sovereign will have the courage to get himelf killed by the enemy." That would indeed have been the only hope of giving fate a turn that could save the dynasty.

Prince Max, who could only keep going with the aid of bromide and chloral, was by then on the edge of a breakdown and had begun to lose his head completely. Announcing the possibility of bloody civil collisions in Berlin, he had wired, and finally telephoned to Spa that the Emperor must abdicate at once. His Majesty was no longer in any state to have these announcements properly verified or find out for himself how much in them was due to neurasthenia. Prince Max made haste to give Berlin the news of his sovereign's precipitate abdication. The thought that the "chief war lord" had abdicated was disastrous to the army's *morale*.

Soon it was made known to Berlin that William II, in flight, had crossed the frontier into Holland, where he had been received at the château of Amerongen by Count Bentinck. Of all the accounts which have been given of the Emperor's arrival in Holland, the most reliable seems to me that of Lady Norah Bentinck, a close connection of the Count's, who happened to be staying in Amerongen at the time. She says :

"On the journey, through driving rain, to Amerongen the Kaiser had said scarcely a word. It was easy to see that this sudden catastrophe had stupefied him almost to the point of coma; added to which he was tired out with forty hours of flight, travelling, and delays. He was obviously eager to be alone, in some quiet place, as soon as possible, to recover himself. But when the car, crossing the inner drawbridge of the château, had pulled up before the main entrance, he gave a deep sigh of relief. 'Now,' he said to Count Godard, rubbing his hands together, 'you must let me have a cup of real, good, hot, strong English tea.' The Count, with a smile, promised to see to it at once — and soon the Emperor got his tea. It was not so much an ordinary English tea as a real Scots high tea. One of the many treasures of Amerongen is a Scots housekeeper, an expert at the preparation of Scots biscuits, scones, shortbread, and all the delicacies which most travellers in the Highlands have enjoyed. The Kaiser was soon acknowledging her exceptional culinary skill."

Nobody who knew William II could doubt that this eyewitness saw the reality. The Emperor who, since the day he dismissed Bismarck, had all too often shown himself presumptuous, showed himself dwarfish, alas, when real misfortune overtook him. In peace he had wanted to be "war lord", as he only too frequently asserted. In war he was content to remain an onlooker; was seldom seen at the Front, more seldom still in his capital, and spent most of his time in such luxurious châteaux as Pless, Homburg, Coblenz. He, who in peace had for ever striven to play the chief part, evaded every decision in war. He could not even manage to preserve a good, harmonious understanding between the High Command and his political chiefs. He had wanted to control and manage everything, had chosen his most important advisers solely because he liked them personally — and his choice had never been a fortunate one. Moltke, Bethmann, Michaelis, Hertling, Prince Max of Baden were all mistakes: mistakes which, in one way or another, made possible the disaster of 1918. William II had proclaimed himself the Chosen of God, the ruler who would lead the German Empire on into a splendid future. He ended as a fugitive from his country.

Another document, also related to those days, contains in it the essence of William II. It is the letter he wrote to the Crown Prince, at the moment when he decided on flight.

My DEAR BOY,

The F.M. can no longer assure me that I am safe here, and refuses to guarantee the loyalty of the troops. I have therefore, after a hard inner struggle, decided to leave the army, which has gone to bits. Berlin is completely lost, in the hands of the Socialists, and already two rival governments have been formed there, one by Ebert, who is made Chancellor, the other by the Independents. I advise you to stick to your post till the armies retreat into Germany, and prevent the dislocation of the troops. We shall meet again, by God's will! General von Marschall will tell you more.

> Your deeply afflicted father
> (Signed) WILLIAM.

No one except William II could have stated so baldly, so naturally, with so candid an absence of all embarrassment, his true reasons for running into Holland — or rather his own neurasthenic feeling of the dangers his imagination suggested to him. Such terrors were to him far more a reality than any dread of the verdict of history, than any thoughts of the glorious tradition of his house, of his father or grandfather, of the Great King or the Great Elector. When the Emperor had just dismissed Bismarck, my brother Adolf, then aide-de-camp to His Majesty, said: "This terrible decision is quite without moral justification. May it be at least politically expiated by a happy reign — above all, by a reign which ends well." To have dismissed Prince Bismarck at the beginning and escaped into Holland at the end is more than history can forgive or the shoulders of William II bear. Well-intentioned people have done their best to absolve the Emperor of his flight and saddle others with the burden of it. Such excuses will not bear examination. There comes in the life of every man a moment at which he only can decide; when he is thrown back utterly on himself. This, above all, is true of princes. An Emperor and King, at such a moment, could make no other living man responsible: he had to decide. This successor of the Great Elector, of the Great King, the Great Emperor had, of necessity, to choose his own path: he more than any other sovereign, since he, a hundred times, had told the world that as a monarch he would answer only to God; that no one, no minister, parliament, adviser — could lift his obligation from himself. The man who for thirty years had spoken thus, in so solemn a voice, and with such seeming deep conviction, had no right, when the hour of trial came, to shuffle off his burden on to others. He had no right to say that Admiral Hintze had advised him to do this or that, that General Groener had said one thing, and Councillor of Legation Grünau another. Still less should he have dared to try to hide himself behind the mighty figure of Marshal von Hindenburg. To fly or to remain? Only the Emperor could answer. He chose flight into Holland and, this responsibility once taken, not all the perfumes of Arabia, to speak with Lady Macbeth, can sweeten it.

I, like many another, had to pass through three phases with the Emperor. The first was one of cordial sympathy with him, a sympathy which bordered on admiration. I could see that he was endowed with many and exceptional gifts, capable in the highest degree of assimilating knowledge of all kinds, full of the best intentions, unprejudiced, natural. When I compared him with other German and foreign princes, with my colleagues, the ministers, with deputies, with innumerable people of my acquaintance, I felt myself to be working with a sovereign who, despite certain dangerous tendencies, gave promise of the highest achievement. But as I lived and laboured at his side, I saw his faults grow more and more pronounced: an open mind, but one that would never concentrate; a quick, but superficial intelligence; a natural manner, but no tact, with, at times, the lack of all dignity or control. More and more, like quicksands at low tide, the ugly traits began to show themselves — his excessive vanity, naïve egotism, lack of discernment, insufficient regard for truth, either with himself or other people. Field Marshal Count Waldersee said one day to me: "The Emperor often lies to other people, but still more often to himself."

Waldersee, like Von Tirpitz and so many others, had, little by little, turned against the Emperor, till in the end they had grown to hate him. As for me, though he caused me much pain, it was soon assuaged by the thought that, in William II, I beheld the son of his father, the grandson of William the Great, the bearer of the Prussian Crown, of the crown of Imperial Germany. I never hated him.

In the end I only deeply, sincerely pitied him, as I watched so pitiful a conclusion to a reign that had begun so brilliantly. But stronger far than such compassion in me was my pity for our glorious Prussia, whose past and spirit William II had betrayed; for the splendid Empire, founded under William I by Bismarck, to crash to earth with William II.

Even before the fatal November 9th, the blackest day in all German history, I had been told that Prince Max of Baden's insufficiency was becoming hourly more apparent; that, even physically, he was quite inadequate to his task. To be sure, it was harder to steer through such a storm than to arrange the affairs of interned Germans in Switzerland, and far harder than the good prince had expected to find it. He had soon become a prey to sleepless nights, caused by all the emotion and fatigue, and so had had recourse to sedatives. But, on the day which followed a bad night, he could never manage to work till the afternoon. His colleagues at the Ministry, the Socialists, Scheidemann and Bauer; the Clericals, Erzberger, Groeber, and Trimborn; the Democrats, Haussmann and Payer, were no Jacobins, *à la française*, no revolutionaries in the grand manner; they did not, God be praised, set up any guillotines in Germany — but neither did they inspire a *levée en masse*, nor, by stamping on the earth, summon up from it fourteen armies: no "Marseillaise" thundered and flashed before them. It ought, with a little skill and decision, to have been quite easy to manipulate these honest folk. One day, on the eve of revolution, I happened to meet a Left Wing deputy — a deputy, indeed, of the deepest Red — whom I asked if, in his opinion, Herr Scheidemann would rather become a German republican minister, or remain one, under William II. He answered, after an instant's reflection: "I think he would rather be one of the Emperor's ministers; that is to say, if he saw his chance of getting the title 'Excellency', and perhaps a bit of ribbon to wear along with it." Erzberger beamed with joy when he found himself invested with all the dignity of a *Wirklicher Geheimer Rat* (Privy Councillor), and so with the right to be called "Excellency", and insisted, even after revolution, on being so addressed, in his quality of republican minister! It was a red-letter day to the good

Payer when, in honour of his appointment to a state secretaryship, his sovereign, King William of Württemberg, most graciously conferred on him the grand cross of the Württemberg Order of Frederick, which made of him a noble for life. Haussmann has confided to me his pleasure to think he had become a real live minister, though, unluckily, he foresaw that, in the new Germany, this dignity might become a trifle tarnished — a premonition which seems to have spoilt the pleasure of a number of other worthy men. Haussmann's one desire was to die to the ministry, in order to resurrect as a diplomat. A southern German, he felt himself peculiarly fitted to conduct our embassy in Vienna. Should he manage to enter the service he would never, he declared with a little bow, fail to come to me for advice. He "well knew me a master of diplomacy."

Meanwhile the Spartacists, led by Liebknecht, fresh from prison, by Paul Levi and Rosa Luxemburg, and subventioned by the Soviet ambassador, Joffe, continued their shameless agitation. The *Vorwärts* too, the organ of the Majority Socialists, dared to print at the head of one of its articles: "Germany, we are firmly resolved, shall haul down her war flag for all time, without having brought it home victoriously." I say with regret that in no other people had a great party fallen so low; that in no other would such baseness have been conceivable! I do not consider it impossible that a great many German Socialists, and a certain number of Centre Party and Democrats, may have felt that they could mollify our enemies by this mixture of cowardice and treachery. They may have thought they could win them over and so shield their country from the worst, while they prepared the fraternization of the peoples. It is inconceivable how utterly the three parties then at the helm, their chiefs, and an important part of the nation, ignored the true enemy mentality, or the real intentions of enemy statesmen. At the moment when Germans were at once so simple and so abject, Georges Clemenceau, in the French Chamber, was scoffing at the "*moutons bêlants du pacificisme*", and proclaiming in a voice of thunder: "*Je me presente à vous avec l'unique pensée de la guerre intégrale. Tous les défaitistes devant le conseil de guerre! Plus de campagne pacifiste, ni trahison, ni demi-trahison! Ma formule est la même partout.*

Politique intérieure, je fais la guerre. Politique extérieure, je fais la guerre. Je continue la guerre et continuerai jusqu'au dernier quart d'heure, car c'est nous qui aurons le dernier quart d'heure."

And when this *"dernier quart d'heure"* was upon us, Clemenceau, our fateful telegram in his hand, broke into a pæan of victory. *"Enfin! Il est arrivé, ce jour que j'attends depuis un demi-siècle! Il est arrivé le jour de la revanche! Nous leur reprendrons l'Alsace et la Lorraine, nous rétablirons la Pologne, nous forcerons les Boches à nous payer dix, vingt, cinquante milliards. Est-ce assez? Non! Nous leur fouterons la République!"*

That is how the incident was described to me by an old French friend, who was also one of Clemenceau's intimates. And to the last item Clemenceau carried through his programme! Our disaster entailed the Republic, a form of government most unsuited to us. To Clemenceau, the protagonist of war to the knife, *la guerre à outrance*, it seemed the supremest honour when in every French school a plaque was hung on the wall to celebrate the shameful peace of Versailles, with the inscription: *Georges Clemenceau a bien mérité de la France."*

Naturally the Government's spineless attitude redoubled the insolence of the Spartacists. The last days of October saw the outbreak of the Kiel mutiny, provoked by the Socialist Left Wing, with the help of money from Russia. By November 4th revolution had triumphed in Kiel. The red flag was hoisted on all ships. The garrison went over to the rebels. Prince Adalbert and Prince Henry left Kiel. On November 5th the Soviet Ambassador, Joffe, was at last expelled from Berlin for his propaganda. Some defective post bags, addressed to his embassy, had burst open on the station platform, discharging a shower of revolutionary pamphlets in German, and so had furnished irrefutable proof that Joffe considered it his mission to foment revolution in Germany. The stable door was then carefully locked, long after the horse had bolted, since by now revolution had broken out. The Kiel conflagration had spread to Hamburg, Bremen, Lübeck, the whole coast — then on through North Germany, from west to centre. At Munich the Prime Minister, Dandl, lost control. He had allowed the Socialist,

Auer, to persuade him that a big demonstration, organized for
November 8th, by Right Wing Socialists in the Theresienwiese,
would pass off without any incidents. He had no idea that Auer
had failed to keep his grip on the movement. It was now in the
hands of an erstwhile editor of the *Vorwärts*, the Galician adventurer, Kurt Eisner, an utter stranger to Munich, into which he had
drifted via Nuremberg. Eisner stirred up this mass demonstration
to proclaim the Bavarian Republic, and declare the Wittelsbach
dynasty at an end, though it had reigned for over a thousand years
in Bavaria, and the majority of Bavarians were attached to it by ties
of loyalty and gratitude. With a truly grotesque simplicity, the two
leading Munich statesmen, Dandl and Brettreich, had recently been
using all their influence to secure Eisner's release from prison, by
the supreme court of Leipzig, which had detained him, on a charge
of high treason, at Stadelheim, near Munich. Only a few days
before, when the public prosecutor at Leipzig had answered his
request for Eisner's release unfavourably, Herr von Dandl had
telephoned over to say that both he and Brettreich were convinced
that Eisner's release would "calm" the Munich population. A
person in the confidence of the Imperial Government, who happened
just then to be in Munich for the purpose of collecting information
there, had occasion to interview Von Fuchs, the President of the
Bavarian Chamber. The latter told him that Herr von Dandl had
advised the king not to receive the head burgomaster of Nuremberg,
Gessler, the future Minister of the Reichswehr, adding that he
thought Dandl perfectly right. "That alarmist busybody Gessler
has been trying to persuade the king that Eisner is hatching revolution; that we ought to intervene at once, if the king is to be saved
from having to abdicate. But Dandl knows his way about all
right! He gave that gossiping fool a flea in his ear. He would n't
even let him into the room, etc. . . ." *Difficile est satiram non
scribere.*

King Ludwig III had his ministers' incapacity to thank for the
fact that he was the first German sovereign obliged to leave the
throne of his fathers in a hurry and in very undignified circumstances. Nobody dared offer shelter to him or his queen, who was

seriously ill. His suite had arranged his escape by motor, during the night. The car overturned in a ditch. A peasant had to be found who, with the help of his cow, set it on the road again. Then a Bavarian landowner, with whom the sovereigns had sought shelter, replied that he could not possibly take them in. The unrest in the country made it too dangerous.

"Her princes are become like harts that find no pasture; and they are gone without strength before the pursuer." Thus mourned Jeremiah, the son of Hilkiah, of the priests that were in Anathoth, in the land of Benjamin.

If the fate of the King of Bavaria was a tragic one, King Frederick Augustus of Saxony's farewell to his people was more in the nature of burlesque. Clio records immortal farewells. *"Plaudite amici, bene egi actum vitae,"* said the Emperor Augustus to the friends surrounding his deathbed. To his legions stationed in Caledonia Septimus Severus gave the last, immortal watchword: *"Laboremus !"* Napoleon's farewell to the *vieille garde*, in the courtyard at Fontainebleau, is famous. As for King Frederick Augustus, the grandson of Johann, the delicate translator of the "Divine Comedy" into German, and nephew of King Albert, that great captain and wise prince, he left his subjects with the words: "Well, make your dirt by yourselves then" (*So macht denn Euern Dreck alleene !*).

It is a relief to be able to add that both the good King William of Wurtemberg, and the noble Grand Duke Frederick of Baden, with many another German prince, descended with dignity from their thrones.

CHAPTER XXIII

The Triumph of Revolution in Berlin — Prince Max Leaves the Capital for Baden — The Spartacus Agitation — Ebert and Noske — My Experiences in the Hotel Adlon — Countess Treauberg, Doctor Stampfer, Doctor Breitscheid — The Troops Return from the Front — The Armistice Negotiations in Compiègne; Erzberger's Business Methods as Head of the Armistice Commission — The Shameful and Dictated Peace of Versailles — The Publication of Our Archives.

In Berlin on November 9th, I witnessed the beginnings of revolution. Alas, she did not come as Ferdinand Lassalle had envisaged her in his moments of giddiest ambition, in the shape of a radiant goddess, her hair flowing in the wind, and shod with sandals of iron. She was more like an old hag, toothless and bald, her great feet slipshod and down at heel. The German revolution was drearily Philistine, lacking in all fire or inspiration. It revealed no such figures as the Danton whose statue in bronze stands on a Paris boulevard : erect, with clenched fist, to the left of his plinth a *sansculotte* with fixed bayonet, to his right a tambour, beating up the levee *en masse*. Our revolution brought us no Gambetta to proclaim war to the knife and prolong our resistance by five months, not even a Delescluse, to get himself killed at the barricades. I have never in my life seen anything more brutally vulgar than those straggling lines of tanks and lorries, manned by drunken sailors and deserters from reserve formations, which trailed through the Berlin streets on November 9th. That afternoon, from the window of my suite at the Adlon, I had a view both of the Linden and the Pariser Platz. I have seldom witnessed anything so nauseating, so maddeningly revolting and base, as the spectacle of half-grown louts, tricked out with the red armlets of Social Democracy, who, in bands of several at a time, came creeping up behind any officer wearing the Iron Cross or the order *Pour le mérite*, to pin down his elbows at his side and tear off his epaulettes.

When young Captain Bonaparte stood watching the attack on the Tuileries of August 10, 1792, the sight inspired his well-known exclamation: *"Avec un bataillon on balayerait toute cette canaille"* — and there can be no possible doubt that on November 9, 1918, the Berlin streets could easily have been cleared with a few battalions of storm troops. Such battalions would have been easy enough to form from the N.C.O.'s and officers of Berlin, who were positively itching for such an order. With a few machine guns set in position simultaneously at the Brandenburger Tor, in the Schloss Platz, and the Alexander Platz; a few tanks, each with a crew of sharpshooters, set going through the streets of the town, the Berlin *canaille* would soon have scuttled back to their holes. But for this, not an authorization, but the formal order to fire with ball ammunition would have been necessary. Prince Max had not the courage to give this order, especially since he feared it might disqualify him from succeeding to the Baden throne.

While the populace gained possession of Berlin streets, endless telephone conversations were in progress between Berlin and Spa, Spa and Berlin. At the Berlin mouthpiece sat Privy Councillor Wahnschaffe, at Spa, Von Grünau, the Councillor of Legation, Wahnschaffe; as a rule a sound official, had managed to lose his head completely under the enervating influence of Prince Max. As for Grünau he had no head to lose. He was a young and very callow diplomat, with neither knowledge nor practical experience, utterly ignorant of the questions of civil law to be decided. The fruit of a morganatic marriage between a Prince von Löwenstein and a governess, he was on fairly intimate terms with the Court at Karlsruhe, and therefore in the confidence of Prince Max, who had attached him to the Emperor's person at Spa. In this hour of deadly peril to his dynasty, a tragic fate had given the King of Prussia, as his sole adviser, a young man, possibly endowed with every talent, but not, in any case as yet, a prudent and vigilant guardian of the glorious and menaced Prussian throne. The result of all this ringing of telephone bells was that Prince Max began to placard every kiosk and every street corner in Berlin with the official announcement to Berliners that their Emperor and King had abdi-

cated. The truth, as it later was established, was that William II
had only wished to divest himself of his Imperial dignities, while
at the same time remaining King of Prussia. The announcement
was either hysterical or a blunder — but, in either case, entirely
characteristic of this last Chancellor whom the Emperor had seen
fit to appoint. Prince Max, without consulting one of his colleagues
or those military chiefs who for the last twenty-four hours had been
longing for their orders to intervene, wrote off to the Socialist leader,
Fritz Ebert, into whose hands he gave the affairs of the Empire,
relinquishing to the Socialist Party the business of forming another
government.

Ebert assumed the title of People's Commissar, which he further
bestowed on several of his revolutionary friends, the Socialist leaders
of Berlin, and began to govern. The energy which they all, especially Noske, displayed in the next few days in keeping down the
Spartacists, grown too insolent, might have served as example to
Prince Max. But, careless of what happened in Berlin, the Prince
was on his way to Baden, the dynastic interests of which seemed to
him far more important than all the destinies of the Empire. Whatever Chancellor William II had cared to select, in that fatal October,
1918 — general, diplomat, civil servant, or deputy — none could
have served him worse at the critical moment than this neurasthenic
prince, whose egotism and family interests entirely outweighed his
sense of duty. Prince Max, however, had miscalculated in supposing that he could save himself or his house. He lives to-day as a
private citizen on Lake Constance.

But our new masters were equally unfitted to govern. Most
characteristic of their mentality was the speech from the Reichstag
steps, delivered by Scheidemann, an ex-Imperial State Secretary,
who, in proclaiming the Republic, began his oration with the following: "The German people has won all along the line." A stupid
lie ! And a very cruel piece of self-deception ! No, alas, the German people had not "won" — it had been conquered ; overpowered
by a host of enemies, wretchedly misled politically, reduced by
famine — "stabbed in the back !"

To any unbiased spectator of these events, to whoever watched it all in the one hope that the German nation might not perish, these first days of our Republic were days of the return to chaos. Children could scarely have done worse. The new régime was so constituted that the Council of People's Commissaries (*Rat der Volksbeauftragten*) gave an equal number of seats to the Majority and Independent Socialists — the S.P.D. and U.S.P.D. Two mandates therefore; two executives! Such a system had never been seen, since the two quaestors, two consuls, of ancient Rome, which certainly did not resemble modern Germany! And above the Council of Peoples' Commissaries throned the Executive Committee of Workers' and Soldiers' Councils, in whose hands lay the real power. In "modern art", as it is called, there was for a time a certain vogue for "dadaism", whose aim was a complete return to the lispings and gurglings of sucklings. The beginnings of the German Republic were a kind of political "dadaism." Such phenomena as Müller made their appearance. Müller had been nicknamed "corpse-Müller" for declaring that there should be no more Reichstag elections, unless they were held over his dead body. Herr Müller is to-day in the best of health, yet since he spoke his memorable words there has been more than one election to the Reichstag.

The Socialist Left was all for suppressing the Reichstag out of hand and replacing it by Workers' and Soldiers' Councils, though even this suggestion was not original, but a miserable, servile copy of Bolshevik Russia. Bethmann, from the very start, had given an anti-Tsarist turn to our war propaganda, and every fool had applauded him. Now our own people, become like apes, could only try to imitate forms of government set up in Russia by the Bolsheviks, and unworkable even there on such a passive herd as the Russians.

In Prussia there were at first two ministers for each department; the one Majority (S.P.D.) and the other (U.S.P.D.) Independent Socialist. Conrad Hänisch and Adolf Hoffman were the simultaneous Ministers of Education. The first had risen from the ranks by becoming *cavaliere servente* to Rosa Luxemburg, then he had sloughed off his Communist skin and emerged, by degrees, a moderate Socialist. He was "moderate" when I made his acquaintance.

He seemed not a bad sort of fellow, jovial and very good-natured, the usual type of dyed-in-the-wool Bohemian, certainly without wide and delicate culture, and still less with any profundity of thought; the ordinary half-educated mind. His political Siamese twin, the Berlin publican, Adolf Hoffmann, was, at least, what Countess Terzky, in Schiller's "Wallenstein", desires her step-brother to become, that is to say, a truly self-integrated personality, since he never cared to bother about such trifles as bad grammar in a Reichstag speech. On the premature termination of his minis-terial activities, Hoffmann became the spokesman of revolution, on the Municipal Council of Berlin, and for years he set the tone to that assembly. The Berlin City Fathers hurled invectives, at moments they even came to blows, while, from every tribune, there were cat-calls, stink bombs, and similar intellectual weapons of the young Republic. This noble Hoffman-Hänisch administration had in its care the Ministry of Public Worship — those departments of public instruction and medicine directed, from 1817 to 1838, by Baron von Altenstein, the great organizer of our Prussian elementary schools, gymnasia, and universities — in a word that whole *"Cultus-Ministerium"* founded by Wilhelm von Humboldt as the instru-ment of a Prussian intellectual renaissance, and which had had as former directors, a Falk, a Bosse; Gustav von Gossler, Count Robert Zedlitz, and Studt. A basic antipathy in Socialists to the humanist, the only real intellectual discipline, the true foundation of all our culture, has always seemed to me one of the gravest dangers to which these men expose our Fatherland. Such dislike found blatant expression in a certain article in the *Vorwärts*, published not long after the revolution, and of which the most typical sentiment was the following: "The spirit of Bebel is out of harmony with the spirit of Julius Cæsar." As the natural consequence of its precept the *Vorwärts* went on to demand the gradual reduction, then abolition, of all our classical gymnasia — that is to say the total suppression of the teaching of Latin and Greek in German schools. It is true that the assertion was perfectly justified. The spirit of August Bebel is certainly not that of Julius Cæsar! I would even go further, and suggest that the spirit of Pericles has very little in common with that of Scheidemann, that Plato and Gustav Bauer, Joseph Wirth and Scipio Africanus, Virgil and Ledebour, Comrade Zubeil and Thucydides would not find they had many thoughts in common.   The Republic which emerged from our revolution was, as I have said, flatly amenable.   It was *petit-bourgeois* and philistine ; its leaders the perfection of mediocrity.   But at least there were no serious disorders.   More than once I was enabled to realize all the calm and placidity of the movement, the phlegmatic nature of the Berliner.   I took daily walks through every quarter of the city and, although fairly well known, I was never molested.   I can only remember one incident which might perhaps have ended unpleasantly.   I was returning from a long walk out to Charlotten-burg, and was just about to step off the pavement and cross over into Unter den Linden, through the Brandenburger Tor, when a tall, broad-shouldered fellow, with a rather uninviting cast of counte-nance, pointed me out and shouted : "That's Prince von Bülow ! He dares to show himself in the streets after the people's victory !" I went quietly on and did not turn until I had reached Unter den Linden.   When I looked back my friend had vanished.   I saw the same fellow a few weeks later, in front of the Hotel Eden, in other circumstances.   This time he was handcuffed, and was being led by an escort into the hotel before the court-martial of the Cavalry Division of the Guard.   He looked at me in the most unfriendly way — his expression, I will admit, was less one of fear than of defiance.   I asked his name, and was told that he was a Com-munist called Jogisches.   It appears that next day he was shot while trying to escape.

The elements which, in Berlin, in these first months, gave revo-lution its own peculiar character, were mostly callow, half-grown youths.   At that time we were still at the Hotel Adlon.   A self-styled "Republican Commissar" forced his way into our suite.   I had been asked to a bachelor dinner and was out.   The "commissar" enquired of my wife whether we had any officers in hiding.   Had I brought my uniform to the Adlon?   Did I keep a revolver about me?   My wife insisted politely that she knew nothing at all of any such anti-Republican plots and secret armings, and the embarrassed "commissar" made his excuses and departed. Another day, as we walked down the long corridor, a youth, of not more than seventeen, emerged from the lift and pursued us, in either hand a revolver. My wife asked why he wanted to shoot us and he answered in a piping treble: "You must excuse me, Madame, but we are all so terribly nervy and strung-up. We have the Republic to defend and the least you can carry is a revolver. But we don't want to do you any harm. If you like we'll even come out with you for walks, and protect you." With a smile of thanks I declined this Republican Guard of Honour.

On another day as, from the Linden, we were about to enter the Wilhelmstrasse, that street in which I had lived twelve years as Chancellor and Secretary of State, where my father had worked as Secretary of State to Bismarck, and where Bismarck himself had fixed his residence, there was a whistle of bullets. A few ricochetted along the pavement. Others clattered down into the courts, or lodged in the stonework of the houses. I might have imagined myself back in the good old days of our victory over the French. I led my wife aside into a doorway. As we stood there, a car drew up in front of us, and the chauffeur, who had recognized my face, asked me where I wished to be taken. I thanked him and asked him to put us down at the Adlon. When we reached it, after a detour, via the Leipziger Strasse and the Bellevue Strasse, he removed, as we were getting out of his car, the little red flag which he had stuck into the driver's seat beside him. With all the delightful good nature of the true Berliner, he told me that he had not asked my permission to use his flag because he had known I should never have allowed him to do it, but that, all the same, he had put it out, to make sure that nothing happened to my wife.

It seemed likely that there would be fighting in the Pariser Platz and the proprietor of the Adlon asked me to vacate our suite. He feared for the precious glass of his windows and wanted to keep the shutters closed. I decided to change my hotel. For some time I had known of the Hotel Eden, very well situated near the Tiergarten, and designed by Scharfenberg, a talented architect, the son of an old regimental comrade whom I mention in my early account of my war experiences. During my chancellorship I had several times inspected this hotel, since the building had been offered to the State, for use as the Ministry of Agriculture and *Oberpräsidium* of the Province of Brandenburg. Its proprietor eagerly offered us a suitable front floor suite, with a charming view out over the Tiergarten, but could not let us have it immediately, and so, while we were waiting to take possession, he procured us a more modest habitation, in a pension in the Kurfürstenstrasse, near his hotel. It was there I met that much talked-of lady, Countess Treuberg, about whom so many unpleasant things have been said. Her parents, rich and very cultured Israelites, had married her off, while still a girl, to a Bavarian officer who, though he behaved well in the War, was not precisely the ideal husband to strew roses along the path of a mate with intellectual demands on existence. Solomon says, "spare the rod and spoil the child"—but he does not suggest that with one's wife this method of approach is the right one or even that it is permissible.

Finding herself thus handled by an aristocrat, Countess Treuberg had gone over to the Reds. She made a great display of Communist sentiments and had, for that reason, been interned in a little Pomeranian town through the whole last year of the War. But the poor lady was also destined to be turned out of Berlin, under the drastic Republican régime of Ebert and Bauer. She made every effort to render our stay in the pension a pleasant one and was especially eager to introduce me to some of her Left Wing friends. It was through her that I made the acquaintance of Herr Stampfer, the editor of the *Vorwärts*, and of the Deputy Breitscheid, of whom so much has been said. In Stampfer I met a man of subtle and acute intelligence, with excellent manners. As for Breitscheid, although he argued very well, and with perfect courtesy, he seemed to me the usual type of Radical, frequent enough in Latin countries, though less familiar to Germany, who makes a great parade of advanced ideas till a minister's portfolio is within reach.

As soon as our promised suite at the Hotel Eden was vacant, we moved from the Kurfürstenstrasse to the Kurfürstendamm. A few days after our arrival there I noticed some uniforms in the corridor and learned that the General Staff of the Cavalry Division of the Guard had been transferred to our hotel. Next morning we were told that during the night Liebknecht and Rosa Luxemburg had been summoned before the court-martial of this division. Liebknecht had tried to escape into the Tiergarten, on their way to the hotel, and had been shot. Rosa Luxemburg had begun to scream sedition at the top of her voice and a soldier had cracked her skull with a rifle butt. But we had noticed nothing of all this.

During our stay in the Eden I saw one of the most melancholy and painful sights I have ever witnessed : the return of our troops after a lost campaign and the fall of the Prussian monarchy. Shall I ever forget the march past of those officers at the head of their gallant men? Their whole aspect was that of insurmountable fatigue, of deeply ingrained suffering and privation. In their faces and the faces of their men there was all the pride of four years' desperate resistance against an overwhelming number of enemies; but with it their agony and rage that no final triumph crowned their heroism, greater than any yet recorded in the military annals of the nations.

When, in 1840, Nikolaus Becker answered the French threat of war with his *Rheinlied* — "Sie sollen ihn nicht haben" [1] — Alfred de Musset countered with : *"Nous l'avons eu, votre Rhin allemand !"* And of the powers co-allied against France in the War of Liberation, the French poet asks : *"Combien, au jour de la curée, étiez-vous de corbeaux contre l'Aigle expirant?"*

That is a question which the German braves of the Great War might well have asked of the Powers and forces massed against them. How many vultures had it needed to subdue the German eagle? In England, in Italy, in France, memorials have been raised to the Unknown Warrior. The body of a dead hero, picked by lot, has been laid, in Italy, by his countrymen, under the memorial to King Victor Emanuel II — *Padre della Patria*. In France, under the Arc de Triomphe, which recalls the *Grande Armée* and Napoleon, lies a soldier. An Unknown Warrior lies in the heart of London, the capital of the British Empire. Wreaths are still laid daily on

[1] "They Shall Never Have It."

all these monuments.   No such grave adorns the German capital!
This is one more afflicting proof of that weakness in our national
sentiment which our present Republican leaders have not known
how to reawaken and fortify: a proof of all our lack of piety and
gratitude for what the German people and its army did in the
greatest war in history.

All the harder, therefore, should each German worthy of the name
try to keep alive in his heart the memory of our old Imperial army
in the full refulgence of its heroism.   The French, in 1871, coined
their proud and beautiful epithet: *"Glorieux vaincu."*   But such
words as these would mean nothing to the mass of our Socialists.
They keep aloof, indifferent, silently hostile, when veterans of our
glorious regiments assemble to revive in us the spark of just feeling,
military honour, pride, and patriotism.   Only in Bavaria, where
salutary reaction has succeeded the Bolshevik wave, has it been
possible to hold memorial services with inspiring military displays.
Defeated France, soon after 1870, set up Mercié's beautiful monument — a vigorous woman, dressed in the costume of Alsace, who,
armed with a rifle, braves the enemy, while her son, mortally
wounded, lies stretched half-conscious at her feet.   That statue
is all pride, beauty, strength !   Frankfurt, on the other hand — the
city where German Emperors of the Roman Empire were crowned
— is disfigured by a hideous piece of sculpture.   A shapeless female,
apparently composed of one great rump, crouches on the earth, as
though she were expecting a few more kicks on it.

Moments of public crisis, and not long periods of tranquillity,
reveal the strength or weakness of individuals.   When, soon after
the revolution, the provincial Landtag of Brandenburg held its customary banquet, its Oberpräsident, Von Loebell, a man not in the
habit of currying favour, did as he had done for some years past,
and reminded his hearers, in his speech, of all that the March of
Brandenburg, Prussia, and Germany owed to the Hohenzollern
dynasty.   The new régime then made itself exceptionally ridiculous
by relieving Von Loebell of his post.   He was one of our best admin-
istrators, a man who had been liked by every one.   Nor had he ever
been an especial favourite with His Majesty.   Harnack, on the

other hand, the Emperor's toady and favourite, had taken a very different line. Shortly before the revolution he had sent me a book, recently published, containing a series of lectures by various university professors, all criticizing Wilson's wrong estimate of Germany. Harnack had supplied the introduction. It was a gushing pæan of praise of the Hohenzollerns from whom, His Excellency declared, no power on earth should ever separate us. But this "theologian versed in the ways of the profane", as the *Kladderadatsch* had once so justly styled him, knew how to turn his coat when necessary. A few days after the revolution this devoted panegyrist of Imperialism had sent his son to me with a message of regret that he himself would be unable to call since, as director of the once-Royal Library (now the National Library of Prussia), he had his respects to pay to his new chiefs — Their Excellencies, Konrad Haenisch and Adolf Hoffmann. "Papa," the young man added in explanation, "is seeing things strictly as they are, and I've become a Socialist myself." Though Doctor Harnack had soon repaired his Royalist indiscretions, he did not discard his quality of Excellency, conferred by especial favour of the Emperor.

The birth of the German Republic coincides with the Armistice of Compiègne, signed on November 11, 1918. This laid on us the first of our chains and prepared the way to the shameful Peace of Versailles. We had sent Erzberger to Compiègne. The lords of Republican Germany saw in him an expert in foreign politics — mainly because of his many trips abroad during the War, either on official business or impelled by his own roving spirit. He reached Compiègne in the mistaken notion that, together with strictly military conventions, he might also arrange the preliminaries of peace. His voice and pen had both been very active in advertising a future League of Nations, and with it, the hope that we might conclude provisional peace. He was also persuaded that his brochures, which abroad were almost unread, had made our enemies see their own true interests. For him, his intimates and colleagues, a demilitarized Republican Germany on virtuously democratic lines would, of necessity, be welcomed by the Allies with open arms, and might count on universal help and sympathy in her task of economic reconstruction. This candid hope, together with his utter ignorance of foreign and enemy mentality, were the source to him of much cruel disillusionment. Marshal Foch began the *pourparler* by requesting one of his officers to hand the German envoy a vast document, in duplicate, to which Erzberger had to reply by six that evening. The time at his disposal would have been short, even for a man whose French was fluent, and who, therefore, could have read the original text and discussed it at once with his subordinates. Unluckily poor Erzberger "had not the French" — not even enough of it to read a short advertisement in *Le Temps*. This string of official technicalities left him completely flummoxed. It is terrible to reflect that the man upon whom, in the days of our misfortune, it devolved to answer the drastic stipulations of our enemies, had to await the irksome business of translation, before he could form any idea of what the Allies really required of us. Some precious hours were squandered in this way.

Foch's method, begun at Compiègne, had, at Treves, Mainz, and Spa, been reduced to a system : give the enemy the shortest time to answer in ; leave at the very second it has elapsed. We shall never be able to estimate or repair the damage done to German interests by Erzberger's utter ineptitude in the conduct of this kind of negotiation. He had felt that as a civilian "man of the people" he would inspire the kindly Marshal with sympathy ; but in Foch he only encountered brusque disdain. Pressed hard by the Marshal, who seems to have taken a sadistic delight in his discomfiture, he foundered from one concession to the next.

But it took some time for the rumour of his incompetence to get any farther than the saloon coach which bore him hither and thither to these encounters. The first sustained and reasoned complaints against him were raised by German freight and shipping interests, too ill defended to be able to restrain their protests. Foch had requested Erzberger's presence in Treves, for a conference, timed to last three days. Erzberger, unreflective as usual, sent back word that two days would be enough for him. His reason for this singular answer was the desire to reach Treves, via Switzerland, where he intended to meet one of his paid agents, kept there in the lap of luxury, though they brought us nothing substantial to show for it. When the Armistice Commission got to Treves, it soon became clear why Marshal Foch had suggested three whole days for his Conference. He intended to negotiate the modalities for the transfer of the German Merchant Fleet. Since it was not the Marshal's habit to state beforehand which subject he proposed to discuss, this came as a great shock to Erzberger and, thanks to his clumsy handling of the business, the experts, hastily summoned by telegram, could only manage to reach Treves an hour before the time conceded for signing the documents had expired. Marshal Foch would entertain no thought of delay.

In such circumstances as these, it was impossible that, for all the advertisement he could give himself, Erzberger should be able to satisfy even Ebert and Scheidemann for ever. They profited by his absence in Switzerland to transfer to Count Brockdorff-Rantzau the preliminaries for negotiating peace. To the fussy and vain Matthias this was a blow, who had already seen himself in the limelight at Paris, with the eyes of the world upon him. But he plucked up courage soon enough. If they would not let him shine at Versailles he could at least make things as difficult as possible, in Berlin and Weimar, for his supplanter. He therefore neglected nothing which conceivably might persuade the Allies that the Reichstag majority he controlled would accept any peace they cared to offer. I admit that with his political incapacity Erzberger may have imagined he helped Germany by this trustful and amenable spirit. I admit that he was sincerely zealous in maintaining his thesis that, for the moment, no sacrifice we made could be too great, if only we managed to save German unity. But his zeal in preaching such a doctrine did the greatest harm to the German cause, since the Allies had always, in Weimar, agents and journalists enough, to report to them from day to day on the state of mind of "the great Matthias."

When Count Brockdorff-Rantzau, to his credit, refused to sign the Treaty and withdrew, Herr Erzberger looked about for a substitute. He succeeded at last in persuading Hermann Müller, who consented to sign together with Herr Bell, the Centre Deputy. Never, on no other people, has so crushing, so ignominious a peace been so brutally imposed as was the shameful peace of Versailles! Every war for the last two centuries had necessarily been brought to its conclusion in negotiations of victor with vanquished, prior to the signing of the treaty. The Treaty of Westphalia, which concluded the Thirty Years' War, was negotiated for three whole years, at Münster and Osnabrück, before signature. Before the Peace of Hubertusburg, which brought the Seven Years' War to an end, there had been long and secret negotiations between Maria Theresa and Frederick the Great. Each of Napoleon's most decisive victories was followed by negotiations for peace. He negotiated at Campo-Formio, at Lunéville, Amiens, Pressburg, and Vienna. When at last the great Corsican fell, the Vienna Congress worked for nine months, laying the new foundations of Europe. The Crimean War was followed by the Congress of Paris, the Russo-Turkish War of 1877 to 1878 was followed by the Congress of Berlin. Prince Bismarck, after the campaign in Bohemia, treated with the South German and Austrian delegates. He treated long, minutely, and courteously, after our great victory over the French, both at Frankfurt and Versailles, with Jules Favre and Thiers. There were negotiations at the end of the Spanish-American War, at the end of the Russo-Japanese. But such an unnegotiated agreement as this dictated Peace of Versailles is as little a true agreement between nations as would be a transfer of property for an individual whom a footpad had knocked down and forced to give up his purse.

The Peace of Versailles has cost us over seventy thousand square kilometres and more than seven million German nationals. Not only have we had to forfeit the "*Reichslande*", Strassbourg, the "*wunderschöne Stadt*", the Fortress of Metz, before whose walls so much valuable German blood had been poured out in order that we might make it ours, but we have lost our granary, Posen. We have lost the greater part of West Prussia, conquered by the German race as long ago as in the thireenth and fourteenth centuries, by the Knights of the Teutonic Order, and retaken by the Great King in the eighteenth. We lost parts of East Prussia and even of Pomerania. We have lost most of Upper Silesia, one of the chief centres of German industry. We have even lost the ever-German city of Danzig, the city of Fahrenheit, of Schopenhauer, of that great engraver and painter Chodowiecki, one of the most ancient and beautiful cities in all Germany. We have forfeited much of Northern Schleswig, the little Huldschinen country whose heart was German, Eupen, and Malmédy, peopled by Walloons, but ever loyal to Germany and Prussia. And, to guard the fettered giant, two warders have been set on either side of him — Poland and Czecho-Slovakia — who have received the right, retained by the victor States, to increase their military strength as they see fit, whereas our army, once the bravest and strongest in the world, is diminished to the level of a constabulary, scarcely strong enough to maintain order at home. Our beautiful navy has been reduced to a few cruisers and ships of the line, and our coastal fortifications destroyed. We alone are not allowed to have U-Boats, Kiel became an open harbour, and Heligoland was dismantled. The one ray of light to pierce this gloom was the sinking at Scapa Flow, by our own men, of our armoured cruisers. But, worst and most insulting of all, they have forced from us a declaration of "war guilt", by the terms of which, in denial of the intimate conviction of our whole people, we have admitted ourselves the sole instigators of the war, answerable for all the loss and damage sustained by the Allied and Associated Powers, in a conflict forced upon them by German aggression. Surely I need scarcely say again that we imposed no such conflict on the Allies: that the stupidity and blindness of our rulers in that summer of 1914 caused our fall into the trap set for us.

The men of the new régime seem to imagine that they have done much to advance the German cause in this matter of "war guilt" by their publication of Foreign Office archives in a work containing every political document, from the foundation of the Empire to the Great War, which now appears to have reached its last instalment. Apart from the Bolsheviks, whose avowed object it is to discredit the old social and political order, for the benefit of World Communism, no other Great Power has dreamt of publishing its archives. Was this German official publication, begun with so touching a zeal, inspired by any just idea? It has, in any case, been of no use to us. It has disarmed neither the hatred of the French, grown deeper than ever as they perceive, and begin to fear, our latent strength, the cold egotism of the English, nor the national animosity of the Poles, who dread and have always disliked us. The indiscretion with which, in all these documents, the most confidential pronouncements of foreign diplomats and statesmen have been dragged to light and given to all to read : the imprudence of publishing certain criticisms of foreign institutions, notabilities, habits, made by our own political chiefs, will in future render every foreign diplomat most chary of speaking his mind in conversation with a representative of Germany. But all diplomatic relations, as Bismarck was for ever telling us, must have, as their first condition, absolute trust in the discretion of the opposite party. Without such trust there can be no fruitful diplomacy.

To be sure, this publication confirms the fact that, ever since the Treaty of Frankfurt, Bismarck and each of his successors had striven imperturbably for peace. But to our enemies that is not a merit ! The French have a very good phrase to describe the gambler who pockets his winnings, gets up, and leaves the game. They call that *"faire Charlemagne."* Abroad it was generally felt as a proof of our wisdom and, from our point of view a perfectly natural one, that we did not feel inclined to risk again our enormous winnings of 1864, of 1866, and 1871. But nobody saw in that a sign of heroic virtue on our part. On the whole, the world is no longer interested in our policy prior to 1914. All that people really want to find out is why, in that disastrous summer, we behaved as, unluckily, we did.

The most candid souls, politically speaking, I have met in the whole of my long life were, I may add, Professor Ernst Hasse, the president of the *Alldeutscher Verband*, and Doctor Friedrich Thimme, who edited these Foreign Office archives. I have already given Hasse's reply to me, when I met him one day in the Berlin Tiergarten, at the critical point in the Boer War. I had pointed out how difficult he was making it for me to create any real understanding between the German people and the English, by his tactless and ill-regulated press campaign in favour of the Boers. The good Hasse answered that he considered it both his duty and his right to express what the German people were feeling; my business as minister was to see to it that our diplomatic relations with England were not prejudiced by anything he might say !

Many years later I told Herr Thimme that his all-too-conscientious publications were making even harder than it already was the task of our foreign representatives — who had the interests of a defeated country to defend. He replied: "Truth, Excellency — truth! Diplomats may let themselves be guided by reasons of an opportunistic character. Statesmen may obey only reasons of State — real or supposed. But history has only one aim — the truth. And I intend to serve the truth, and her alone, whatever the consequence." He spoke the word "*Wahrheit*" with heavy emphasis — *ore rotundo: "Die Wooorheit."* I suggested, with an amiable smile, that neither England, France, nor Italy had made such lavish displays of their foreign archives, and was reproved by him: "Well, then all I can say is that those countries may be victorious, but morally they are far below Germany." And proudly, from his moral pinnacle, he gazed down upon me.

These retrospective sidelights on history, published by us after our defeat are, however, less striking than numerous. As the German proverb says: "One who comes out of the Town Hall is generally wiser than when he entered." Historians too find it easy to criticize the events of the past; far easier than it is for statesmen to guide and control those of the present. Were historians really such sages as they would have their readers believe, there would be no better course than to entrust them with the direction of our foreign policy and the conduct of foreign negotiations. Would they be any more likely to succeed than our delegates to Geneva, Locarno, Genoa, than Marx and Luther, Lathenau and, especially, Gustav Stresemann? I am willing enough to admit that they would avoid such stupidity as Bethmann's in the tragic July and August of 1914, since for that only a little common sense, some prudence and reflection, would be necessary. But would the censors of our policy whom we nourished through the twenty difficult years from Bismarck's retirement to the World War really have done any better than we did? To most of these retrospective musings, these censures our activity has incurred, two commonplaces drawn from the poets, though oft-quoted, remain forever applicable: "Art is hard and criticism easy." "Ideas may live at peace side by side, but facts clash eternally in space."

CHAPTER XXIV

The Weimar Spirit — Erzberger — The Political Incapacity of the Leading Politicians at Weimar — Defects of the Old System, Its Attitude to Parliamentary Government — How Many Chancellors since the Revolution? — Did Bismarck Give too Much Power to the Crown? — Retrospect — No laudator temporis acti! — Symptoms of Gradual Improvement in Germany — Hindenburg — Germany's Future.

THE spirit in which these Foreign Office archives were published was that of Weimar. Not of Goethe's Weimar nor Schiller's, but the Weimar of the National Assembly, whose task was to conclude the peace with the Allied and Associated Powers, and to inaugurate the new régime in Germany. It was this spirit which the worthy Ebert intended to express when, as first-elected President of the Reich, he ordered a wreath to be laid at the foot of the twin statues of our two greatest German poets, bearing the inscription: *Genio loci.* His Weimar was the Weimar of self-deception; its spirit that which in 1918 and 1919 befogged the minds of all those men who, for the moment, ruled over Germany. The spirit of false peace, a vain expectation of that chimera, the universal brotherhood of nations; a loosely democratic doctrine, improvised, and half-understood. With it all went the crazy notion that Germans might reckon on the sympathy of yesterday's enemies, on their help in retrieving our economic position, if only they would depose every sovereign, disband their army, sacrifice their war fleet, surrender the whole merchant service, cut loose from every great tradition, give their proofs of sincere democracy.

Drunk with their own imaginings, our Weimar rulers could not see that the Allies were taking careful stock of all the latent forces in our country; that they knew well enough that our industrious and disciplined people, a nation of technicians and organizers, would soon have recovered its old strength, and had therefore resolved to do their best to chain us down as long as possible in political and economic subservience. These ignorant guides into Utopia failed to perceive how much sadism underlay the hatred of the French; they had no clear realization of the morbid fears in the French mind, terrified by the automatic increase in our birth rate. Nor could they see that, by giving way, as we did, on every point, we could only encourage the insolence of our enemies, their longing to destroy us systematically. This spirit of Weimar was responsible for much of the pain and bitter sacrifice to which we were perpetually subjected, even after the Treaty had been signed: for the unexampled suffering we endured, which reached its acutest point with the Ruhr invasion of 1923, and all its monstrous violence and atrocities. If the will to subject, to annihilate, incarnated in Poincaré and Foch, was broken on the stubborn resistance and loyalty of the Rhine and Rhineland Germans; if the plots and agitations of the Separatists did not succeed, as Paris hoped, in detaching the Rhineland from the Reich, the thanks are due to the innate good sense of the population which, sinking every party difference in face of such unutterable oppression, defended the land against invaders, checkmating the brutal action of such French Generals as De Metz and Mangin. The spirit in which the Rhine and Rhineland opposed these Armies of Occupation was not the pseudo-spirit of Weimar, it was the old, true spirit of Germany.

I think with envy of the debates of the National Assembly of Bordeaux in the spring of 1871. They preceded the French decision to accept the Treaty of Frankfurt. In magnificent words the great French poet, Victor Hugo, proclaimed his unshakeable faith in his country's future. "Yes," he cried to that assembly, "a day will come when France shall arise again! In one mighty leap we shall seize on Strassburg and Metz. Only these cities? No, we shall take Cologne and Mainz, Coblenz, and Treves!" A section of the house interrupted, and the poet, with a cry that France only asked what in reality was her due, answered his critics with the words: "Why do you hedge round my patriotism?" And when Thiers, the great historian, the mighty statesman and patriot, burst into tears whilst reading out our conditions of peace, the whole chamber rose and bowed in silence to him. In the admirable conclusion to his speech, Thiers, like Victor Hugo, affirmed his entire faith in France, whose resurrection, the splendour of her past guaranteed, the burning love of her sons, her own "*admirable unité.*" To sign such a Treaty, he said, would be the deepest sorrow of his whole life, yet that sorrow held no despair of a French future. In the course of these debates, General Chanzy, the Commander in Chief of the Army of the Loire under Gambetta, had registered his protest against peace. The assembly heard him with emotion, with sympathy and profound respect. And yet it would have needed far more than Chanzy to reap such laurels as our generals have reaped in the last Great War. The French in 1870 had no such soldiers as Kluck, as Below, Marshal Mackensen and Marshal Bülow, Eichhorn and Woyrsch, Scholz and Litzmann, as our Crown Prince, and the Crown Prince of Bavaria, Marshal Leopold of Bavaria, and many another — not to mention our great Hindenburg and Ludendorff. The glory of Chanzy, of Faidherbe, of Jauréguiberry, of Léon Gambetta above all, was, and remains to-day, that they wished to go on fighting to the end: *Envers et contre tout et tous.* That is why victorious France has had Gambetta's heart removed to the Panthéon, though his body lies buried in Nice. Thus did the Roman Senate come out to meet the Consul Varro, beaten by Hannibal at Cannae, to thank him for not having despaired of his country.

Our attitude in defeat was a very different one. It was an insult to any public man to say of him that he was a "war prolonger", whilst this was an honourable title in France and ancient Rome. Our rulers accepted their fate with far less courage, a less unanimous sorrow, far less patriotism.

No German can remember without a pang the fashion in which the Weimar Assembly received the news that peace had been dictated at Versailles. Not one member of that Assembly, and therefore, of course, not a member of the three German parties then in power — still less any minister — was inspired by this event to a speech, to a thought even, in keeping with the tragedy of that moment! Not one who from the blackest of this cloud could cry out the hope of better days, proclaiming our future restoration to all our past splendour and prosperity! On the contrary, these majority deputies seemed to feel a kind of relief. This peace, for many among them, only meant the abolition, once and for all, of the old Imperialist régime, that "militarist" régime of Bismarck, which nevertheless had made us a powerful State. These men, no doubt, could see that for Right Wing patriots, condemned to look on and suffer impotently, its abolition must be painful; but, as for them, they did not care overmuch, since democratic Germany seemed to promise a new and better future for simple men. This state of mind is luminously revealed in the couplet which our most powerful politician, then the real lord of Republican Germany, Erzberger, scribbled, on that tragic July 8th, on the evening after the vote had been taken, at the end of a copious meal, in the Visitors' Book of a Weimar Hotel:

> *Erst schaff dein Sach*
> *Dann trink und lach.*[1]

My courage fails, and I cannot bear to recall these years of shame and misery, of the cruelties of implacable enemies, of anarchy and national paralysis. Our degradation has been so marked that to-day, I am almost certain, not one German in six could give the name of every Chancellor since the Revolution. No hymn, no book of national heroes, will ever record for future generations, the names of Gustav Bauer and Hermann Müller, of Joseph Wirth and Konstantine Fehrenbach. By 1925, seven years after the Revolution, there had been two hundred and fifty ministers, either retired or still in office. Since we have had the good fortune to be a republic, one German in every two hundred and fifty thousand has been a minister! Yet these innumerable changes in the ministry have not averted governmental crises lasting for months at a time.

Herodotus, the father of history, tells in the first book of his "Historia" how Croesus asked the wise Solon which man he held to be the happiest. Solon answered: "Tellus of Athens," since he, in

[1] First do your whack
Then booze and laugh.

that city's prosperity, had led a calm and happy life, and later, when the men of Athens were at war against their neighbours of Eleusis, he had come to the rescue, routed the enemy, and, at the very instant of victory, had "died by the fairest of all deaths." Such happiness fate has denied me. And Herodotus in his Ninth Book of Histories reproduces an account, given by Thersander of Orchomenus, one of the chief citizens of the town, whose mind had been formed by travel and experience, and who had told the poet that, when Mardonius, at the head of the Persian Army, marched on the Greeks, who were destined to rout him at Platæa, the Bœotians who were at one with the Persian cause, offered them a banquet at Orchomenus. The guests at this feast lay side by side, in the Greek fashion, a Persian to each Greek. One Persian began to weep and told the Bœotian at his side that he was convinced that of the Persian army, few would return from the battle. The surprised Bœotian asked him why he did not speak his thought to Mardonius or another of the Persian leaders. And the Persian answered: "Worst of all the sorrows in the world is to see a future misfortune and yet be impotent to avert it." This worst of all sorrows has been mine.

Was this People's State set up by the Revolution to supplant the old authoritarian Empire equal to the Herculean task imposed upon it by the disastrous end of the Great War? Could it, rising from the ruins, lead on our country with strength towards its destinies, force other nations to respect us, even in the days of our calamity, and show itself the worthy inheritor of a great and splendid German past? My answer can only be, no: yet none the less, justice demands of us that we recognize the fact that the system of political ideas in which we had lived in peace and strength till 1914 had crumpled up too suddenly for our people to be able to react with the necessary judgment and calm to the National Assembly of Weimar, and the earliest years of the new Republic. Left to themselves, as they were at Weimar, the men who had seized power had no idea what to do with it. Certainly such a situation was in part the fault of the old régime which had always been too anti-parliamentarian. A deputy in pre-war Germany had every chance of finding himself excluded from important legislative office.

Whoever wished to succeed and be a minister did well to keep clear of the Reichstag. Government and Reichstag, therefore, had become two opposing camps, living in a state of armed neutrality. Even retired ministers, with nothing either to hope or fear, held aloof from parliamentary activity. They would have considered it disloyal to Empire and Emperor to criticize their Government, as deputies; and these were no mere individual scruples, but implicit in the whole political order. In England and in France a Prime Minister, out of office, does not hesitate to attack his successor if the interests of his country seem to demand it. In Germany a minister, once retired, was condemned to watch events in silence. All the experience he had gained, his knowledge of affairs, was lost to Parliament. This certainly was never an advantage. Already I have spoken of the difficulties I encountered more than once, during my chancellorship, whenever I wished to bring William II to the point by inviting any deputy to take an important post, by way of experiment. The few deputies of the old régime who found their way to a portfolio were the exceptions which prove the rule.

So that, in consequence, when the German people came to elect its National Assembly, when later, it elected the new Reichstag, it lacked a political élite, versed in the technique of state affairs. Those first politicians who set their seal on the government of Republican Germany were all new to the game. Till then they had been in the habit of treating every question of national interest from the point of view of sterile criticism; of utterly unscrupulous opposition. The idea "State", "*salus publica*", meant far less to these *homines novi* than the sectional interests and points of view drilled into them in the school of party politics. Power had fallen too suddenly into their hands to give them any chance of adapting themselves. Lacking any vivid realization of the essential dignity of the State, they themselves lacked all dignity in their methods and, at times, in their deepest mentality. A striking proof of this was their introduction of that black-red-gold national flag, imposed on the German people at Weimar in a moment of moral exhaustion. The old Imperial flag, those colours which for half a century had waved with honour in the world, the flag which every sea had beheld,

which had won itself respect in every land, was sacrificed to the
"Weimar spirit", without any jot of realization how lamentable
a spectacle we offered when we tore into shreds, in an act of undignified self-abasement, the emblem of our worth and glory. The pro-
cession of ministers we beheld through these first years of the
Republic, all made the most unfortunate impression even on foreign
countries that wished us well. With neutrals in particular, this
was the case. Many foreign diplomats, my friends, with whom I
had long been on excellent terms, though, in all our personal conversations, they remained as correct and friendly as ever, showed, to
my deep pain, with every word that, even in countries best-disposed
to Germany, nobody seemed able to understand why she should be
so poor in men of political distinction, men who could maintain their
country's interests with dignity; though in London and Paris the
sight was welcome.

If I cast a backward glance at the glorious Bismarckian Empire,
I am forced to ask myself one question. Did not that greatest German statesman place too much power in the hands of the King of
Prussia and German Emperor and give too little influence to
Parliament? This essential question Bismarck, as was ever his way,
answered from his personal experience. By birth, habit of life,
family tradition, sentiment, and *influence du milieu*, he was very
deeply a Prussian loyalist. In this he was instinctive, he did not
reason. As a young man he had known Frederick William III, had
heard much of this reserved and taciturn sovereign, who never said
an unreflective word, whose duty was forever paramount, who after
Jena and Tilsit had not despaired, nor been made proud by Leipzig
and Waterloo. Certainly Bismarck had known Frederick William IV, unstable, fantastic, not always entirely dependable, but a
man of generous instincts and wide culture. And Bismarck all too
frequently differed from that Crown Prince destined to be the
Emperor Frederick, yet, more than he himself would admit, he
could appreciate all his chivalry, gentleness, honour, his soul, inac-
cessible to fear. Above all, Prince Bismarck had sounded the very
depths of William I, that monarch at once so noble and so modest,
so strict in the performance of his duty, so tender in all his affec-

tions, never indiscreet, never tactless, never forgetting that he was a king, yet never misusing his authority, never ungrateful or vindictive — the William I in whose praise, a few hours after his death, Bismarck had delivered a Reichstag speech in magnificent eulogy of his heroism, his elevated sense of national honour, his diligence in the service of his people. As for William II, the grandson of this truly great Emperor, Prince Bismarck did not know him really well. He could never feel quite at his ease with this somewhat singular monarch, whose character seemed to have nothing of his father, nothing of his grandfather or great-grandfather, little of his mother, and all too much of Ernst II of Koburg, his great-uncle. Each word our greatest Chancellor has written in volume III of his "Gedanken und Errinnerungen",[1] shows that the forty-four years between them had prevented his ever really grasping the Kaiser's somewhat complex mentality. He would not have believed such immaturity possible. In laying the foundations of his Empire he had not foreseen a William II. Yet could he have foreseen such a sovereign, and so diminished, even by a little, the height of the Imperial Crown, Bismarck would have found it a sour business to give more scope to any Parliament, or make concessions to any German democrat. In many ways his estimate was the right one, but he was inclined to go too far in his contempt of all German parliamentarians. Honest but inexpert, and quite out of touch with all reality, German parliamentarianism, for Bismarck, meant only two types of German dabbler in politics — the County Court judge, and the professor. From the first day to the last of his career he held these types in very low esteem. Bismarck was the greatest of all junkers, but he was, and remained, a junker of the March; a squire to the marrow of his bones, and officer to the tips of his finger nails.

The misfortune was that William II, having given Bismarck his dismissal, should have been unable to discipline himself, while at the same time he set about the development of our German political system in the direction of parliamentary Liberalism. But no — the young Emperor cherished the illusion that he was fitted to be his own Chancellor, and play, before the eyes of the world, such a part

[1] "Thoughts and Memories."

PRINCE VON BÜLOW

After the funeral of the Princess, with Felix von Eckardt

as Bismarck had sustained for eight and twenty years with magnificent genius. It was also a misfortune that the Emperor could never understand my intention of preparing, little by little but progressively, and without once halting or looking back, a system of parliamentary government, after the Reichstag elections of 1907, by the reform of the Prussian electoral system, and with it the appointment of deputies as ministers or secretaries of state. Such appointments would have been experimental. But William II could never see that it was necessary to anoint the forehead of Germania, our common mother, with a rather bigger drop of the oil of democracy, and when, at last, he perceived that this was my objective, that I wished to guide both him and my country in that direction, he turned against me and, by my dismissal, prevented the slow, methodical evolution I had dreamed. Instead of evolution came revolution! The Great War which gave such scope to Bethmann's and his colleagues' incapacity, and which, from the political standpoint, was so disastrously conducted, has forced on us a change of régime — a change which more than ever isolates us, which at home has disorganized the State, and made of what was once the best organized country in Europe, a country very badly administered. Yet even in such sombre days as these, it behoves us to cry with St. Paul: ". . . As chastened, and not killed; as sorrowful, yet alway rejoicing. . . . As having nothing, and yet possessing all things!"

Let us take a glance at other nations. It is just a hundred years since Prince Metternich, who in those days not only governed Austria, but also, in a sense, all Europe — *le cocher de l'Europe*, as he was called — solemnly declared that Italy was neither a nation nor a State, but simply a geographical expression. To-day the Habsburgs are no more, and Italy is one of the great Powers, with all her national aspirations realized. France, fifty years ago, was defeated, her Emperor had become our prisoner. Yet, by following Gambetta's advice to speak of *la revanche* as little as possible without ever ceasing to think of it, she has managed — alas, that I should write it! — to fly her tricolour from the ancient cathedral built by Master Erwin, and jostles us on the Rhine and the Moselle. Poland, a hundred and fifty years ago, was divided up between three great Powers, yet now she has arisen from her sepulchre to rob and harry us in the east. Every Balkan people — the Serbs, Bulgarians, Greeks, Roumanians, and Albanians — has been bowed under the yoke for centuries — mishandled, massacred — and yet they have survived their tyrants. Human life is in perpetual flux. Peoples may decline, but they arise again.

Having set down this record of my memories, I have reëxamined many times in spirit the age in which God has permitted me to live. I have forced myself to review the justice of my estimate of the German people and the men who controlled its fate before and after me. I have asked myself whether I write more leniently of the days during which I was in office than of those which, after my retirement, led on to the Great War, and our defeat. And in thus examining my conscience, I have striven to keep my spirit detached from all of which I myself was the eyewitness, to weigh things with careful objectivity, seeing them, as it were, from outside.

My life has been of such a sort that to-day two feelings live in me together: joy, as I remember our great past; grief, for the heavy shadows of the present. My memories reach far back, prolonged beyond my own existence by the things of which my father would often talk to me; back to the days when the German people was still without unity and impotent; back to the foundation of the Empire, the birth of our unity as a nation, that crown of hitherto undreamed-of political and military success. Then on through those few decades in which the German people put forth its strength, developed in peace its economic forces, fortified its position in the world, consolidated its national sentiment — and so to the four disastrous years when we fought a world in arms and collapsed.

My father had been most careful to form my mind, he had jealously superintended my education; later he became my friend and adviser. He, in his youth, had had to behold our weakness. He had seen, in the prime of life, our degradation of 1848, one of the lowest points in German history. At the zenith of his powers, soon after the foundation of the Empire, it had been granted him to work with Prince Bismarck and, as Secretary of State, receive his confidence. But his many recollections had in them always a shadow which still overcast my boyhood, the shadow of a disunited Germany. Later my years as a young man were brightened by the effulgence of Prince Bismarck, whose mighty figure stood for the new time. My most formative years, intellectually and politically speaking, were those of that magnificent spate of energy which had begun for us, thanks to Bismarck, in the year 1864. My father's first activities had been circumscribed. Now, under the eyes of the great Chancellor — eyes which nothing ever escaped — he had the interests abroad of the new German Empire to defend. His sphere of activity, his political horizon, widened immeasurably, as, step by step, he saw our national unity being prepared, saw the Empire born, watched Germany consolidate her position among the great Powers of Europe. I had observed at the closest possible quarters, in the microcosm, as it were, of my father's house, that macrocosm, the German Empire, grow stronger and stronger every day.

Military prowess, national greatness, dynastic splendour, an Imperial future — these were the noble inspirations that surrounded me as a growing boy. They became to me as the anchor of my youth; in the years of my early manhood they gave my life its urge and its direction; they remained the guides of my activity through my twelve years of ministerial office. A man whose mind had been formed by the glories of the old régime, whose activities and personal life were both very closely interwoven with that Imperial greatness, strength and splendour, which remained with us till our final defeat, has the right, I think, to affirm himself no mere *laudator temporis acti*, even if he regrets the brilliant past so clouded by the sombre present; if to him the Germany of the fathers seems more estimable than that of the sons; if that buckler of glory once set before the body of the Empire strikes him as a nobler accoutrement than the ill-adjusted toga in which democracy has enveloped the Germany of to-day.

But I have not been blind to the faults of the old régime. Some of them, as I show in detail, resulted from the system itself. Others, as I have never ceased to point out, were personal. The Monarchy was made for the German people. It suited our temperament exactly. It only showed itself weak in William II. For many

years incessant efforts had been made to strengthen and develop
our army, build up our fleet, foster art and science, encourage our
economic development, awaken and reaffirm our national sense.
But the World War took William II by surprise, with at his side
two men, of whom the one, Moltke, had himself declared that he
would not be equal to the task of leading our armies in the field,
while Bethmann-Hollweg, the other, soon showed himself all too
lamentably unable to resolve an international crisis. William II
had chosen both these men. Each in his way began the downfall
of Germany. Michaelis and Hertling, both also chosen by the
Emperor, hastened on the final catastrophe, and Prince Max of
Baden achieved it. What Hindenburg, Ludendorff, and every German soldier had won for us, was either never used, or frittered away,
by the incapable statesmanship imposed on a great people by
its Emperor — on a people that had long come of age.

William II had an absurdly disproportionate notion of the
attributes and prerogatives of a sovereign, and this conception, I
affirm, was disastrous to the German Empire. But none the less
I have felt bound to criticize severely the lack of all capacity for
government and, worse, of any sense of national dignity, apparent
in Germany's new rulers, in that moment of German disaster, when
those democratic parties who had formed the Weimar coalition were
wallowing in the sense of their new power. That democracy flung
overboard the most sacred possessions of any nation, even a nation
in defeat: the goods it was our highest duty to save. It tried systematically to suppress all memory of a noble past; it did nothing
to foster the virtues which alone can guarantee us a better future —
courage, devotion to the Fatherland. There was something very
repulsive indeed in the scramble for salaries and posts which we
witnessed at the moment when we set up our first half-dozen republican governments, in the brutal fight for the spoils of office between
the parties, in the heartrending scandals and corruption which sul-
lied the first years of the Republic. That justice which commands
that each thing shall be given its due forbids me to pass over without
full censure these shameful aspects of the public life of latter-day
Germany.

As a close observer of events, in touch with many foreigners, and a daily reader of the newspapers of every country and shade of opinion, I have observed with delight the early signs of political and economic improvement. At home the flood of the November revolution begins to ebb. In foreign affairs the horizon is far clearer than it was. Reason has begun to make herself heard, and hope to flower in us again. The Germans, a fundamentally stable people, a people full of calm good sense, have set themselves to repair the dykes which anarchy had threatened to destroy. Those ignorant and soulless politicians who, in the first years, seized power, one after the other, have disappeared. Their places are being taken by men of knowledge and capacity, more than one of whom would have made an excellent minister, even in pre-war Germany. First among them I should like to mention Stresemann who, guiding as he does our foreign policy in circumstances of peculiar difficulty, has known how to win confidence abroad, secure for himself the respect of former enemies, and so open up the possibility of our gradual rehabilitation. Hindenburg, our great military leader, who had given a hundred proofs in the field as the glorious commander of our forces, has consented to guide the civil destinies of the Reich, and assumed with us the tasks of reconstruction. Since he lent our people the splendour and strength of his personality, we have begun to recover our lost prestige and, now, to call oneself a German, means once again to command respect.

When, each spring, I return from Rome to the banks of the Lower Elbe, my birthplace, I am always rejoiced to perceive how, little by little, things improve. But no real or durable prosperity will ever be the lot of our people until we can bring ourselves to cure some inherited defects in the German character: our bitter party rancour, our doctrinaire particularist ambitions — and return to those ways of thinking and feeling which had made our forefathers great men.

But my deepest conviction is that we too shall see better days; days when Germany once again is imbued with the national spirit. It is impossible that a nation with such a past, the nation that has seen *Fredericus Rex*, the rising of 1813, Blücher, and Scharnhorst,

Baron von Stein, and half a century later, William I, the Emperor Frederick, Bismarck, Roon and Moltke, Düppel, Sadowa and Sedan — a people that could put up such a defence as the German defence in the Great War; which has given the world a Kant, a Luther, the Humboldt brothers, Schiller and Goethe, Bach and Beethoven, Richard Wagner, Fichte, Hegel, Schopenhauer and Nietzsche, so many works of such imperishable genius — it is, I say, impossible that Germany should remain forever stultified and oppressed, forever condemned to act a minor part, eternally the plaything of the forces of international politics.

Shall I live to see the day when Germany takes her rightful place in the world again? When my country is honoured as of old? I cannot tell. But I shall close my eyes in the hope, the certainty even, that such a day is bound to dawn for her. My last thought, my last prayer to Heaven, my last wish, will be for the German future.

BERNHARD PRINCE VON BÜLOW.

SUPPLEMENT

SUPPLEMENT

Letters and Addresses Received by Prince von Bülow on His Retirement

The address presented to me on retirement by the Federal Council was a source to me of peculiar satisfaction. Its members learned "with deep regret" that I had relinquished the Imperial chancellorship, and with it my duties as their president.

For twelve years the Federal Council has congratulated itself on the fact that it worked under your direction. This whole period has been marked by the successes obtained by Your Highness, as His Imperial Majesty's adviser in the domain of foreign policy, as well as in the economic development, the commercial relations and domestic legislation of Germany, and not least in your careful attention to the interests of the Federal States. Though now this bond, forged by our work in common, is to be loosened, let Your Highness be assured that the Federal Council will always keep a grateful recollection of this brilliant period of successful effort. May we beg you to accept our most devoted and respectful farewells.

Every German Federal Prince without exception expressed his deep regret at my resignation, and thanks for what I had achieved. The Prince-Regent Luitpold of Bavaria, then in his eighty-eighth year, wrote to say that the news of my definite retirement from the chancellorship had come as a very real shock to him.

"I am well aware," his letter continued, "of the exceptional services which you have rendered for so many years to Emperor and Empire, and of how devoted your work has been. With all your careful attention to the rights of the Confederation as a whole, you have never failed to show a perfect understanding of the wishes and desires of the separate States, especially Bavaria."

King Wilhelm of Württemberg wrote to me from Schloss Friederichshafen, on the Lake of Constance:

On this occasion, so deeply deplored by me, of your retirement, from the service of the Empire, I feel it, as a Federal Prince, especially incumbent on me to express to you my warmest, sincerest thanks for all you have done, in a career rich in brilliant successes as the First Official of the Empire, for the well-being of the German Fatherland as a whole, and its separate States; and not least for that friendship for the Confederation exemplified in your attitude towards my government. May I wish you most heartily many years of future happiness and ask you to believe me, in sincerest esteem

Your thankfully devoted
WILHELM.

From Dresden, King Frederick Augustus wired:

Must assure Your Highness of my deep regret that unfavourable political circumstances have necessitated your resignation. I thank Your Highness for all the especial services which you have rendered my country. I know myself at one with my government in my esteem and affection for the departing Chancellor, as well as in the opinion that Your Highness' suggestions for the reform of Imperial Finances were the best for the Empire as a whole and the most acceptable to the Federal States individually.

Rüger, the Saxon Finance Minister, both a statesman and a very distinguished specialist, had already written, during the crisis which led to my retirement:

May I, in the name of the Saxon government, most urgently implore Your Highness to remain in your difficult post of Imperial Chancellor, in spite of the endless annoyances of these last months? Unless you do so, the Conservatives and Centre will be able to boast with some show of right that they have succeeded in bringing about a change in the chancellorship, and would be reaffirmed in the belief that victory is to be gained by persistence in their own plans and intentions in spite of all opposition on the Federal Council.

The Grand Duke Frederick of Baden wired from Stockholm, where he was on a visit to his sister, Queen Victoria of Sweden: "Have just learned with deep regret that your resignation has been accepted. This occasion of your retirement fills me with gratitude as I remember your exceptional services to our Fatherland. My very best wishes go with you on your path into the future."

I received the following official report from Von Eisendecher, for many years the Minister in Karlsruhe:

On all sides I hear expressions of the deepest regret that Your Highness has found it necessary to decide to give your high office, as First Imperial Official, into the hands of a successor. Indignation is universal at the ingratitude, the blind egotism, of just those people who owe Your Highness only thanks, and who yet are primarily responsible for this step you have taken. Their mistake is bound to have bitter consequences. More and more is public opinion becoming convinced that Your Highness has rendered most distinguished services to the Empire, that you have earned the sincerest gratitude, and that it will be hard to find any one to replace you. All perceptive Germans regard the future with misgivings — misgivings which certainly seem to be not unfounded — and doubt whether the new Chancellor will be competent to resolve possible difficulties and conflicts with such effortless success and distinction as so often attended Your Highness. Moreover, a select and chosen few must certainly have an inkling of the obstacles, the resistances, which you had to encounter, and of which the general public knew nothing, and so must perceive what immense political damage Your Highness' quiet judgment knew how to avert. The financial wisdom of the Reichstag majority is considered here to be very doubtful. This new taxation scheme is felt to be far too complicated, too costly to be carried out in practice, and not conducive to economic advancement. It is generally beginning to be perceived, by all whose judgment is worth having, that the original proposals of the government were both juster and cheaper, as well as being less onerous, and therefore much to be preferred. Her Royal Highness the Grand Duchess Louise, and her Minister of State, Von Dusch, were both particularly regretful in their talks with me, on hearing of Your Highness' decision. I have not yet seen His Royal Highness the Grand Duke, but he also, as I hear, has expressed himself in this sense, while there can be no doubt that the whole Grand Ducal Government feels the same.

In a private letter, addressed to me a week later, Herr von Eisendecher wrote as follows:

"Will Your Highness please believe me when I tell you that, in the interests of Emperor and Government, I regret very deeply indeed your resignation from your high office? May Your Highness' distinguished services on behalf of Emperor and Fatherland come to be acknowledged on <u>all</u> sides." The word "all", twice underlined, was naturally aimed at William II.

Prince Max of Baden wrote from Schloss Salem, on Lake Constance:

MY DEAR PRINCE:

Our connection of so many years' standing, keeping me so happily in touch with you and the Princess, gives me the right, I think, to say too how sorry I am to hear that you intend to retire from the Chancellorship. It seems so impossible to realize that you are actually relinquishing your high office that, again and again, I am forced to remember it afresh. And the more real it becomes the less it pleases me. All my very best wishes for the future in your incomparable Villa Malta; — behind you, struggle and authority; but before you beauty and peace, to enrich your thought, and give it fresh significance! In old esteem I remain

Always Your Highness' most devoted,

PRINCE MAX OF BADEN.

Prince Max's mother, née Princess Leuchtenberg Romanowsky, a granddaughter of Tsar Nicholas I, wired:

Prie accepter l'expression de tous mes regrets sincères de vous voir quitter votre position et l'assurance que ma vive sympathie vous entourait tous ces derniers temps. J'espère que les chemins de nos vies se croiseront encore. Mes compliments sincères à la Princesse.

The Grand Duke Ernst Ludwig of Hesse wired:

"I feel I must express to you my thanks for the distinguished services you have given the Fatherland. May it be granted you to enjoy for many years yet, the fruits of so successful a life."

The Grand Duke of Weimar expressed his keen regret that I had retired from the direction of the high office whose activity I had controlled for many years, "at times in very difficult circumstances" to the greater good of the German Empire. He signed himself: "Your Highness' constant well-wisher."

Even Duke George of Saxe-Meiningen, the talented founder of the celebrated Saxe-Meiningen State Theatre, directed under his supervision by Ludwig Chronegk, thanked me for my meritorious service of Germany. The Duke, then in his eighty-third year, had been, through no fault of his own, at loggerheads with William II.

The Duke of Saxe-Altenburg thanked me especially for the intelligence, in the highest sense of the term — the impartial justice ever displayed by me in my guidance of Imperial relationships "even in the most difficult circumstances." He hoped that the pleasing sense of "duties chivalrously and faithfully performed would for many years to come rejoice the evening of my life."

The Prince of Lippe-Detmold thanked me for the "invaluable services" I had rendered our German Fatherland, but even more for the excellent support I had given him and his little country, in a moment of crisis. He signed his letter: "Your gratefully devoted." The Prince of Waldeck also especially insisted on the "wisdom and circumspection" with which I had directed affairs "in excessively difficult circumstances" and stressed the "universal" esteem and gratitude in which I was held all over Germany. Even the Prince of Schaumburg-Lippe, who had got the worst of the quarrel between Schaumburg-Lippe and Lippe-Biesterfeld, insisted in his letter to me that throughout my whole term of office I had done great things for the Empire and the German Confederation. The German princes and people, he added, owed me deep gratitude; I should always remain an honoured and grateful memory, and he wished me: "many years' untroubled enjoyment of the peace and quiet you have earned so well."

From Hamburg the burgomaster Burchard wrote that the Municipal Senate of his city had heard the news of my resignation "with the keenest regrets" and in the unanimous conviction that the Fatherland "owed me deep gratitude" for my long years of successful effort in many branches of activity. The German Empire, in losing me, had forfeited a predominance and authority reminiscent of the days of the Great Bismarck. It was good news to the Senate that I should soon be in Flottbek for the summer, and so within reach of Hamburg. From Bremen the Head Burgomaster joined his regrets to those of Hamburg. The Bremen City Fathers felt "keenly sorry" that I had seen the necessity for resigning the chancellorship — a post which I had filled for many years and "at times in the most difficult of all circumstances." Abroad I had kept the peace while consolidating the prestige of the Reich; at home my guiding principle had been " a statesmanly effort to reconcile differences, to smooth the path which leads to mutual understanding in politics and so to work in the direction of less narrowness and party rancour in German affairs."

I do not deny that this trust which I encountered from all the Federal governments, and German princes, the satisfaction they both expressed at the fashion in which, for long, I had guided our policy, came as a very grateful compensation for the capricious, relentless, and — in the last days of my chancellorship — almost ill-bred behaviour of the Emperor. Bismarck, in founding the Empire, based our unity, and with it our security and future, on the German princes. His decision in this had been deliberate and the fruit of long and careful meditation. Was it a mistake? Did he go too far in his contempt of German party politics and parliaments? His action finds its explanation both in the traditions in which he had lived as a young man, and in the spirit in which the eighty-three-year-old Bismarck caused it to be engraved on his tombstone that he had been a true servant of his master. Bismarck's own experience inspired him with the deepest mistrust of each and all of the German parties, which, from the ultra Left Wing to the ultra Right, had disgusted him by their narrowness of spirit, their doctrinaire preconceptions, and, last not least, by their miserable *petit bourgeois* ideology. He sought in vain among the German factions that sound good sense, knowledge of humanity, respect for the past and reverence for tradition, inherited love of order and skill in practice which for centuries have distinguished the English Parliament. Even more must he have been conscious of the absence of that glowing, passionate love of country, displayed by every French and Italian party, once it has the government in its hands. More than once he had had to warn them all — Conservatives and Liberals; Democrats and Aristocrats — to keep the national idea as a clear and guiding light over Germany. And more than once he had warned in vain ! Our "carpet knights", as Bismarck ironically called them, did not impress him.   This was not altogether surprising, after the fiasco of German parliamentarianism in 1848–1849, after the feebleness it had displayed to Bismarck, both in the days of the conflict and more than once in later years.   When, with the "Kulturkampf" Bismarck made a great mistake in domestic policy, the German Democrats, Virchow at their head, had acclaimed him, only to leave him in the lurch soon afterwards.   His best and most inspired strokes of policy — from his attitude to the Polish rising of 1863 to his cool refusal to participate in the German enthusiasm for Alexander Battenberg ("the Battenberg rumpus", he called it scornfully) ; from his handling of the Schleswig-Holstein question to his change of opinion on tariffs—had one and all, from a depth of inner conviction been opposed "heart and soul" by the German Democrats.   But Bismarck was the only man who could rule in such contempt of parties and parliaments.   When, in another age, decades later, William II, lacking Bismarck's stubborn tenacity, attacked all parties with equal vehemence, with hasty expressions and theatrically exaggerated gestures, and lost no chance of treading on the corns of the parliaments, the effect was not only vulgar, it was also politically mistaken.

I myself had always been very careful not to harry or annoy the parties unnecessarily, to treat the people's representatives with respect and courtesy.   Especially in this department of my activities did the *fortiter in re* seem to me to necessitate the *suaviter in modo*.   I was therefore very pleased at the recognition of the value of my activities as Chancellor which I received from the National Liberal party, whose leader, Bassermann, wired to me, on July 15, 1909 :

The National Liberal Reichstag deputies, to whom, through so many years of collaboration with you, it has been granted to support Your Highness' policy, regret, from the sincerest depths of their patriotism, your relinquishment of the post of Imperial Chancellor.   Your activities, always concerned with the well-being of the Fatherland as a whole, ever striving for the greater power and happiness of Germany, have been rewarded with an abundance of success.   We thank Your Highness for these faithful efforts on behalf of our people.   Your name and achievement will never be forgotten by the National-Liberal party in the Reichstag.

For the Empire Party the deputy Gamp expressed regrets that my activities as Imperial Chancellor, so successful both at home and abroad, would soon have reached their termination. "We shall keep always in our hearts the grateful memory of Your Highness' incomparable services on behalf of the German Empire. It is a particularly gratifying reflection that we, as a party, ever supported your policy, and continued to support it to the last."

One of the ablest leaders of the Independents, a Rhinelander, the deputy Reinhart Schmidt-Elberfeld, for many years the second Vice President of the Reichstag, wrote to me:

The German people can only profit by the participation of every competent German in the work of administration and legislation. The achievement of this lay in the direction of Your Highness' domestic policy. As part of the bloc the bourgeois Liberals have striven to do their duty to the country and, far removed from all callow radicalism, show themselves both able and entitled to take their share in legislation and government. This Conservative-Liberal entente was also the right line for the bourgeoisie to take against the overthrow of our social order. That, in 1907, the Socialists should have been reduced to half their former number of seats in the Reichstag is a clear proof of how necessary it has become to develop the popular strength of middle-class solidarity. Only thus shall we get the better of Socialism. Your Highness may well look back, in proud and tranquil satisfaction, both on your work and on the purblind opposition to it.

If, in addition to these, I reproduce more letters and addresses received, on my retirement, from many quarters in which the opinion merited a hearing, I do so merely in order to give as true a picture as possible of the state of opinion at the time; the instinctive tendencies and reactions prevalent in leading intellectual and political circles throughout Germany, in the year 1909 — a turning-point in the nation's development. The Admiral of the Fleet, Von Tirpitz, wrote from St. Blas:

It has caused me much regret to have been unable to have one last detailed conversation with Your Excellency on the methods by which, in my opinion, we may best allay the feeling in England against us. I believe I should have managed to persuade you that those differences which seem to have arisen between us were more a matter of the form which such procedure should take than of its essentials. If, as I firmly believe, we shall soon have achieved our object in setting out to develop our fleet, and see that, by means of it, we have consolidated the political power of Germany, the thanks of the German people will not be withheld from Your Excellency, since you will have been among the first who contributed to the foundation of our naval power, and this will set an additional seal of honour on all that you have done for the German people.

The Bülow epoch comprises the development of German interests at sea, our achievement of strength as a naval power. The years during which the naval cabinet could work, under Your Excellency's direction, on behalf of Emperor and Fatherland, will be both for myself and for my subordinate officers and officials an unforgettable memory.

My respect for the Admiral's glowing patriotism, and admiration for his exceptional gift as an organizer, had never prevented me from insisting again and again on my first warning — the warning I gave in 1897, the year in which we both took office together — not to create unnecessary friction with England or test too heavily our relationship with her by excessive concentration on big battleships. *Non propter vitam vivendi perdere causas!* One of the reasons for Tirpitz' noncommittal and dilatory attitude towards my desire to reach an agreement with England was his certainty that any resistance on his part would be sure to receive the full support of the Emperor. But, although William II was not aware of all the political dangers and disadvantages entailed in forcing on the construction of big battleships, he could never, since he had ceased to be well-disposed towards me, let slip the chance of making himself unpleasant.

Baron von Marschall, my predecessor as Secretary of State for Foreign Affairs, wrote:

I feel I must write a few lines to tell you how well I appreciate your reasons for feeling it impossible to remain any longer at your post, while at the same time I assure Your Highness how deeply I regret your retirement whenever I consider the interests of our great Fatherland.

Although by conviction a Conservative, at one time a Conservative deputy, and deeply attached to that party, I am nevertheless quite clear in my mind that German domestic policy cannot for long be properly directed solely by Conservative standards, and still less by any Conservative-Centre coalition. It was imperative in the case of legislation of so drastic an economic and socio-political character as the reform of Imperial finances, to secure the active coöperation of the Liberal bourgeoisie. May Your Highness' resignation impress this fact even on those political circles which have to answer for it. Unless this happens, it will be hard to preserve our social order from acute crises and upheavals. This present occasion impels me to tender Your Highness sincerest thanks for your never-failing friendship and benevolence; to assure you from the depth of my heart that the memory of those years in which it was granted me to collaborate, under your direction, in the great tasks which the Fatherland imposes on us all, will ever remain a very grateful one. Your Highness can look back on long years of faithful, arduous, and, in every department, successful labour. I wish you with all my heart the full and tranquil enjoyment of that *otium cum dignitate* for the moment imposed by political circumstances.

Count Eberhard Solms, my predecessor at the Roman Embassy, who had served his country with distinction, first as a young diplomat in Vienna, and later, in the second half of the sixties, as Councillor of Embassy in Paris, where he had gained deep insight into affairs, wrote :

You will forgive me, and not take it amiss, if, as a diplomat of many years' service, I feel myself confident to pronounce on the state of our foreign policy. I cannot find words in which to express to you the really profound regret with which I read the news of Your Highness' retirement from your responsible position as Chancellor. It comes at the very moment when Your Highness had at last succeeded in so enhancing the prestige of the German Empire that once more we are beginning to be treated with that respect, bordering on fear, which Germany had not known in the world since Bismarck's retirement.

From the right bank of the Tiber my wife received a letter from Herr von Mühlberg, for many years my very distinguished collaborator; in Bismarck's time a chief of department at the Foreign

Office, later Undersecretary of State and now Minister to the Vatican:

I do not know whether to be pleased or sorry. "The pleasure of all creatures is mingled with bitterness," sings Walter von der Vogelweide, whose pleasant monument is so welcome a sight to Germans on the picturesque market square in Bozen. It is at least pleasant to think that it will not be so very long before I see you in Rome. But my somewhat egotistical pleasure is really being spoilt by deep regret, mixed with a certain patriotic anxiety, which the Prince's retirement arouses in me, and of which I cannot rid my mind. This uneasiness increased perceptibly as, this morning, I read in the papers of all the changes and new appointments made in consequence of Prince Bülow's resignation. Whither are we steering? What is happening to the really important thing — our future? The Italian Press is quite unanimous in its regret. And this morning the Pope expressed to me his disappointment, and with it a certain surprise. Correspondents in Germany had, for months past, left me in no doubt as to the attempts being made to undermine the Prince's position. And while I feel this change of Chancellor as a decided loss to the Fatherland and German prestige abroad, it is also a source of personal anxiety. I know that I have lost a powerful friend, a friend to whom I owe much, if not all, the success that has attended these last years of my career. May I beg you, my dear Princess, to tell this to His Highness.

Count Wilhelm Hohenthal, once Saxon Minister in Berlin and later Saxon Prime Minister, wired:

"I much regret that Your Highness should have been forced to deprive the Fatherland of your valuable services so prematurely."

Countess Hohenthal wrote to my wife, reminding her of the fate of my great predecessor:

You may perhaps feel a certain relief at the thought that the Prince has been freed from all the wearing anxieties of office. We, on our side, have wished his retirement to take place in other circumstances. As it is, when he looks back on his brilliant career, his pleasure will be darkened by these clouds, and for his sake that is deeply to be regretted, who had devoted so much time and strength to his Fatherland. But such has been the lot of many statesmen. We need not look many years back — and that I suppose consoles Prince Bülow.

His Excellency Otto, the Acting Minister in Brunswick, wrote to my brother Alfred, his old friend:

"Your brother's resignation from the Chancellorship came as a shock to me. As a German I can only deplore it. He will be a great loss to the foreign policy of the Empire."

Count Max Berchem, Under State Secretary for the Foreign Office in Bismarck's time, wrote to me:

As one who has served in the great army, I look up with pride at the leadership which, in the good old tradition of diplomacy, secured to us those two splendid conquests, Delcassé and Iswolski, as well as so many other victories. To my deep regret that such a leadership has passed into other hands I join the hope that you, most honoured Prince, will remain in touch with the future destinies of the Fatherland.

Arthur von Brauer was one of the most brilliant servants of the little model State of Baden. His career had begun in the consular service. He had then become a Councillor to the Foreign Office, had succeeded Von Marschall in 1890, as Baden Minister to Berlin. In 1893 he became Baden Minister of the Grand Ducal House and Foreign Affairs; in 1901 the Baden Prime Minister. We had known each other first in St. Petersburg, as young men, in the winter of 1875 to 1876, he as the German Consul and I as the third Secretary of the Embassy. On my retirement he wrote:

Now that we have received official intimation of your retirement from active service, I could no longer delay my expression of the keenest regret that in future we shall have to forego your brilliant leadership. Your skill, throughout last winter and the spring, in reconciling Conservatives with Liberals was so often shown that I firmly believed that in the end you would have managed to bring about even so difficult a measure as the reform of Imperial finances. I gave the Conservatives credit, I will not say for more political insight, since in Germany "insight" is a word inapplicable to any political party, — but at least I gave them credit for enough patriotic feeling not to land us in the position in which we find ourselves, merely because of an inconvenient tax. However, the unanimous recognition your achievement received on every side, must show you that Germany knows how much it will lose in you. You can retire in the consciousness of having guided our affairs to a pinnacle of success both at home and abroad, which they had never reached since Bismarck's retirement. I say this as your old friend and admirer.

Count Crailsheim, from 1880 to 1903 the first Bavarian Foreign Minister, then Prime Minister, — a statesman who had enjoyed the confidence and esteem of Prince Bismarck and whose loyalty to the Empire was undoubted, wrote :

The news that Your Highness is soon to resign the chancellorship has filled me with the deepest sorrow. Though for six years I have not had the pleasure of personal collaboration with Your Highness, I have, nevertheless, followed with the closest attention the domestic and foreign policies of the German Empire, and always acclaimed Your Highness' many successes in both these departments. As a German patriot, I can only look forward with anxiety to a future bereft of such a statesman. When it is too late, many of those who made possible the present situation will perceive what they, and with them Germany, have forfeited in losing Your Highness. Deeply as I regret Your Highness' decision, I can only congratulate you heartily on retiring in a blaze of glory, and as I hope only temporarily. All true lovers of their country will see you go with real regret.

From Stora Sundby in Södermanland, his wife's Swedish castle, I heard from Count Karl Wedel, in turn the distinguished military plenipotentiary in Vienna, Minister in Stockholm, and then Chief Adjutant to the Emperor, Cavalry General, and Governor of Berlin. From 1899 to 1902 Wedel had been Ambassador in Rome; from 1902 to 1907 in Vienna, and since 1907 had been the Statthalter of Alsace-Lorraine :

DEAR BÜLOW:

Since here I live far from all news, I have only just heard definitely of this change decided two days ago. It did not come as a surprise to me. I regret it for the Kaiser's sake, and the Empire, and personally you cannot doubt how sorry I am. I am sincerely glad, however, to gather that the whole party press is paying you unreserved tribute and acknowledging your services as it should. These thanks you receive from public opinion must afford you the satisfaction you so richly deserve. Now that you are about to retire, I feel I must tell you how grateful I am for the friendship and trust you have always shown me, both personally and as my chief, and for all the posts which I owe to your kindness and recommendations.   Please continue to be my valued friend and be sure that I am always sincerely yours.   My kindest regards to the Princess.

Prince von Solms-Baruth wrote me :

DEAREST, MOST HONOURED PRINCE:

Now that this fatal decision has been taken, and the first wave of sympathy and regret has ebbed, I can no longer refrain from letting you know very briefly how deeply I deplore this turn of events.   I more than any one else am in a position to appraise without any preconceptions the services you have rendered the Crown and our domestic and foreign relationships.   You have this to console you, and us along with you, as well as millions of true patriots, that the manner in which you gave in your resignation leaves us conscious that both we and the King may still count, in any crisis, on the renewed services of one of our best citizens. It is unnecessary to dwell at length on the short-sighted stupidity of certain people, but, since there will always be fools, the stupid ones, and, alas, many of the less stupid along with them, will have to learn by bitter experience what they could not or did not want to perceive.

Ever your most devoted,
PRINCE SOLMS-BARUTH.

Baron Clemens von Schorlemer, then Oberpräsident of the Rhine Province, and a year later Prussian Minister of Agriculture, wrote to me from Schloss Lieser, on the Moselle :

So Your Highness has got to Norderney at last, in the best of health, after all these days of strain !   May I disturb your peace after the storm for a minute — just long enough to tell you how deeply and sincerely I regret that the Reichstag's attitude towards financial reform has made it impossible for Your Highness to continue as Chancellor.   In the Rhine province everybody regrets this culmination of the crisis — not only your numerous admirers but even, with an ever-decreasing number of exceptions, your political opponents, all who remember with gratitude how much Your Highness has achieved for the preservation of peace and the maintenance of German power, for the betterment of German industry and Agriculture, in so many years of successful activity.   It is scarcely necessary for me to say how particularly sorry I am personally to see Your Highness go out of office.   The understanding spirit always shown by you towards my official activities, and my point of view in matters of ecclesiastical and civil policy, will always remain a source of grateful remembrance.

From the Province of Posen, the scene of his courageous and clear-headed championship of the German cause, I heard from Prince Hermann Stolberg, the son of Prince Otto zu Stolberg-Wernigerode, deceased thirteen years previously, who had been so delightful a chief in my Vienna days:

"The Fatherland will never forget how much you have done for it. I write to tell you this from the province which always engrossed so much of your interest."

Baron von Mirbach, the Kaiserin's Master of Ceremonies, whose pious zeal in the cause of religion had sometimes compelled me to oppose him, since it tended to overstep the limits of political expediency, wrote from Potsdam:

After long, difficult, and successful endeavour Your Highness has set down your burden of exacting service to the State, a burden which demanded your whole strength and health, freely given to the Emperor and Fatherland, in a spirit of self-sacrificing devotion, of which the multitude can form no concept. I was one of those who still continued to hope that we might keep you. Our time is one of terrible gravity and danger, both at home and abroad, and nothing is to be gained by trying to blink the fact as so many people do who strive to cover it up with phrases or forget in pleasure and self-indulgence. Party strife, the evil influence of by far the largest section of the Press, the spread of irreligion among the masses and even among people of education, must fill every one who loves his King and country with deep anxiety. But with all the noise and all the struggle, one must perceive ever more clearly and unmistakably that there is only one sure rock of salvation, one fixed immovable star, Our Lord Jesus Christ. I specially remember Your Highness' late mother, whom I and my wife so deeply honoured — a woman whose unshakeable faith was and remains a pattern to me. Only with such faith as hers can we look out over these stormy times with quiet peace.

My friend of many years' standing, Professor Gustav von Schmoller, wrote:

I am convinced that it is a great misfortune for the Fatherland that you are leaving us. The German Empire has need of just such a helmsman as it has had in you for half a generation, to the greater good of Prussia and Germany. Your policy has had two characteristics: a sure and successful attitude towards other countries, which most skilfully avoided war, and, at home, moderate conservatism, which did everything that to-day is indispensable in the way of social reform and liberalism, if sudden upheavals are to be avoided. It was natural that the Centre should oppose you, and easy enough to see why the Liberals did not always manoeuvre skilfully, but the Conservatives cannot plead their electors' lack of intelligence as an excuse for having let you down as they did. I know no other instance of such ingratitude in a great political party. Though many single members of the party may declare that they were not accountable, since they had no means of forming a just estimate, its leaders must plead guilty to the grossest treachery and lack of vision. Millions of the best Germans are on your side, but how few will say so! Since I am one of those who feel they can write to you I could not bear not to tell you something of all this.

The National Party economist Adolf Wagner, a Franconian, born in Erlangen, who had been a professor in Berlin since 1870, and for many years the president of the Society for Political Sociology, was, to use the term current in those days, a "lecture-room Socialist." Thirty-four years previously I had been examined for the diplomatic service by him, and he had been kind enough to report most favourably on my thesis on Italian finances. Now he wrote:

May I beg Your Highness to accept from me also the assurance of my real regret at the news that you are retiring from those high offices which you have filled so brilliantly to the greater good of the nation. This party-constellation in the Reichstag which has led you to decide on such a step as that of requesting His Majesty to release you from your duties as Chancellor is one which every German patriot must deplore. That at least is the consensus of opinion on recent events in scientific circles. We shall all remain faithful to Your Highness.

Gerhart von Schulze-Gaevernitz was the descendant of an ancient family of scholars, whose sons for over a century have known how to combine theory with practice in a fashion which does honour to

the German professorial body. Friedrich Gottlob, a professor in
Jena in the first half of the nineteenth century — set agriculture on
a basis of political economy. Hermann, the Syndic for the Crown
in Bismarck's time, was a celebrated professor of Constitutional
Law. With his son, Gerhart, a professor of Political Economy at
Freiburg in Breisgau and at the same time a practical agricultural-
ist in Silesia, I had had many very interesting and, for me, informa-
tive conversations on economics and politics. Now he wrote:

I am afraid that not many contemporaries are really aware how rich
a future is contained, for those with eyes to see, in all that you have done
during your chancellorship. What ten years back appeared Utopian is
to-day — and this in great measure is due to Your Excellency — perhaps
still difficult of achievement, but no longer a hopeless undertaking. I
appeal to facts; *i.e.* ten years ago it seemed to us a wild impossibility to
dream of a time of naval parity in which Germany would have outgrown
her hopeless dependence on England in all overseas questions of commerce
and power. To-day we are quite conscious of our mission to assert our
power on sea as well as on land and make ourselves felt there. And we
may hope to induce our English cousins to awake from their seductive
dream of attacking us and so — without necessity for war — establish
the same recognition of our oversea interests as they accord to the United
States to-day. Your Highness was the powerful exponent, the eloquent
advocate of this "Germany strong for peace" as the idea is expressed
which little by little is finding its way into the popular consciousness.
Secondly: Ten years ago it was unthinkable that Social Democracy
would ever collaborate actively in the work of our monarchist state.
"Practical men" could see no salvation except in the forceful repression
of Socialism. If to-day the peaceful incorporation of Labour into the
body politic seems a possibility, though a remote one, our gratitude for
this must be in no small measure given to Your Highness, who has dealt
with this problem so adroitly. You have taken the sting out of Socialism
by the justice with which you handled it, which has become a general rule
throughout the Empire, and no less by the use of timely ridicule you have
managed to tear off that Socialist mask, so dear to the German philistine
who wished to terrify his contemporaries and so give himself an illusion
of power which rendered impossible the real task of the present — the
task of compromise — I mean, the mask of the "wild man." Thirdly:
Ten years ago we should never have dreamed it possible to extend within

the boundaries of our Empire that Agrarian foundation on which the German nation exists, since we have no proper outlets abroad. On the contrary, our whole Eastern territory, and with it our position in the world, seemed gravely threatened by the ever-advancing waves of Polish immigrants; hordes it was impossible to keep back. Your Highness has the credit of having handled the immigration question east of the Elbe as one of the most essential in our domestic policy. And to-day it is no longer Utopian, but a matter of practical politics, to colonize the menaced eastern frontier districts of our monarchy with German immigrants.

From the banking world Ernst von Mendelssohn-Bartholdy wrote:

Now that the dice are fallen, I am impelled to write and tell Your Highness how very deeply I deplore this last turn of events: that I consider it a real misfortune for Germany to have to forego the wise and skilful leadership of a man who seems to me more fitted than any other for the guidance of the ship of State. The nation owes Your Highness immeasurable thanks. If I, as *unus ex multis*, feel so impelled to express my very deep regret, it is because perhaps I have more right to do so than others, since so many important affairs brought me the honour of coming into touch with Your Highness. I shall never forget either our personal or our business relationship.

Arthur von Gwinner, the Director of the Deutsche Bank, and, incidentally, a son of the friend and biographer of my favourite philosopher, Schopenhauer, wrote:

Will Your Highness permit me to enclose the few words of painful regret which I had intended to say to you personally in a speech at the Lehrter Bahnhof? The police, however, were so scrupulously careful to keep order at your departure that I, like many others, found myself unable even to get a sight of Your Highness. You retire from the highest office in the Empire mourned, but unforgotten, by every intelligent man in the nation.

The cordons of police surrounding the Lehrter Bahnhof had, as I was afterwards told in confidence, received their orders straight from the Kaiser, who remarked to one of the equerries, "Ministerial changes should be made quietly. They are of very little importance and have nothing at all to do with the public."

Erstwhile Conservative adherents of long years' standing took pains to persuade me that the breach between us was my fault and not theirs. Count Waldemar Roon was one of the most stubborn Conservative leaders; the eldest son of the War Minister, Albrecht von Roon. The latter had been one of the most distinguished men whom the Prussian State has produced; a man whose name is ineffaceably written in German history. Albrecht von Roon had forged for us our glorious weapons for the victories of 1864, 1866, and 1870. In his deep patriotism and purity of sentiment, Count Waldemar was a true son of his father. But he was more uncompromising and not so gifted. He reproached me with having let myself be won over by the National Liberals whose political value I overrated, and whom he considered "so utterly undependable." I had behaved like the Pomeranian peasant who gives the good dog one bone and the bad one two. That is to say, I had favoured Liberals at the expense of Conservatives. Though I often differed from Waldemar Roon, I could never be seriously annoyed with him. When War broke out in 1914, he gave six sons to his country. Three of them sealed their faith to King and Fatherland with their blood. Their mother, a Blankenburg of the celebrated Pomeranian family with which Bismarck had been so friendly from his youth up, and in which he received impressions which were destined to last him all his life, especially in matters of religion, died of a broken heart. Roon himself was also destined to witness the terrible end of the War. Not long before his death in March, 1919, I received from him a letter which concluded in the following words:

"This is probably the last sign of life you will ever get from your old and true friend, Waldemar Roon, whose heart is sick unto death."

For such people as Count Waldemar Roon, I have always felt the deepest respect and sympathy, in spite of all our differences of opinion in matters of political tactics. A very different sort of person was the Reichstag deputy Georg Oertel, the editor of the Agrarian *Deutsche Tageszeitung*, the most popular leader of the Agrarian League. He was famous for his repartee and humour, displayed in every speech he made in the Reichstag, in his newspaper articles, and in conversation, — more famous still for his white waistcoat, a garment he invariably wore and which positively invited caricaturists, especially since it spanned an unusually massive corporation. Oertel was a thorough Saxon, and like many of his less distinguished countrymen concealed not a little cunning under the appearance of harmless *bonhomie*. But like Count Roon's, his friendship towards myself was genuine. He was quite sincere in writing to tell me that my resignation had been, since Bismarck's, the worst disappointment of his whole political career. Nevertheless, he considered that my death duties had made demands on the Agrarians which for practical reasons it would have been impossible to fulfill. Though I could not admit this point of view, I was ready enough to acknowledge the spirit in which Oertel had written to tell me that our personal relationship would always be one of his pleasantest memories, and that he would never cease to remember my kindness with gratitude. These were no mere empty phrases. In later years I often met Oertel again and was always on the best of terms with him.

It would take too long to reproduce the letters in which I answered in detail the objections of my Conservative friends. And, moreover, I wrote nothing so effective as the Liberal publicist Friedrich Dernburg, in an article on the effects of my chancellorship which appeared in the *Berliner Tageblatt*, two years after my retirement, at a time when from the Villa Malta windows I myself was gazing out on the Seven Hills. Friedrich Dernburg was a writer and publicist whose intellect and breadth of vision set him far above the political mêlée, and by political persuasion an Independent. He was the father of Bernhard Dernburg, the Colonial Secretary. He wrote as follows:

Whoever takes a clear unprejudiced view of Prince von Bülow's career as Imperial Chancellor must admit that this statesman who wished to have the words: Here lies an Agrarian Chancellor, inscribed on his tombstone, never failed to keep faith with himself. Prince Bülow wished to set the Conservative party on a new and more stable basis. He wanted to save Conservatives from themselves. In this attempt he displayed great breadth of vision, boldness, and resolve to act. Never has a statesman received less gratitude than did Prince Bülow from the members of his class and party. His plans were wrecked on their short-sighted egotism; the Prince was not even understood, and it is easy enough to appreciate the angry contempt with which Prince Bülow flung at them the words: "We shall meet at Philippi." That Philippi is almost upon us. And the Conservative Party, in its attitude at the time of Prince Bülow's fall, gave proof that parliamentary intrigue can set blinkers on the eyes of politicians, deprive them of any clear perception of the broad outlines of a political situation, set them clutching at petty advantages while they risk their whole existence as a party.

Doctor Mehnert, the strictly Conservative leader of the party in Saxony, and president of the Second Saxon Chamber, wrote:

Will Your Highness permit me also to say that I deeply regret your relinquishment of the conduct of affairs? For me it is inexpressibly painful to see a man whom I respect so deeply as yourself resign the post in which he achieved such great things for the glory, prestige, and well-being of our Empire. I am still unable to form any clear ideas of the probable future development and destiny of our great Fatherland. For me the person of Prince von Bülow is too intimately bound up with the conduct of German home and foreign policy for the successful development of either to seem to me possible without him. No statesman since Bismarck's day has done so much to promote German patriotism; no other statesman since Bismarck has caused the name of Germany to be so honoured in the world, or done so much to make it respected and keep it so. This was especially exemplified in the brilliant diplomatic campaign of last winter! May a beneficent fate decree that you are not leaving us for ever.

From the ranks of the Social Reformers I received the following written by Professor Doctor E. Francke:

Will Your Highness permit a man who has always striven to do his duty as unassumingly as possible, both as political economist and National and Liberal publicist, to tell you, in the name of many friends who share his opinions, how very deeply we all regret the retirement of an Imperial Chancellor who for twelve whole years has contributed with such marked and brilliant success to the wealth and prosperity of the Empire. Not for decades has Germany stood so powerful and honoured in the world as it does to-day. Never, both in town and country, has our people known such prosperity. Liberalism and independent thought had begun to take a new lease of life when Your Highness delivered us from the yoke imposed on us by the Centre and Socialism. We Social Reformers were well aware of this, and we rejoiced at the thought that our fourth Imperial Chancellor had a heart for the poor and downtrodden, an open hand for those who struggle and are oppressed. Your Highness' retirement from office is the end of many precious hopes.

Karl Rahardt, a member of the Chamber of Deputies, wrote:

Millions of good Germans will witness with regret and melancholy the retirement of their Imperial Chancellor, who rendered such long and meritorious service, and I, who write you this letter, am filled with bitterness and anger at the events of the last few weeks. I hate to have to admit that the members of my own party were mainly responsible for the wretched end of the business. If the middle classes are turning away from the Conservatives, this is not solely due to the fact that the proposed death duties are now replaced by a host of taxes aimed at commercial and middle-class well-being. Nor is our impatience with Conservative leadership merely caused by our mistrust of this unholy alliance with Poles and Centre. No — the real disgust in the middle classes has been caused by the deliberate plot to bring about the fall of a statesman who knew — as did our unforgettable Prince Bismarck — how to win for himself a place in the heart of every true German. May I assure Your Highness, as you set down your heavy responsibility, that the German middle class regarded you with unbounded love, trust, and reverence, acknowledging with a thankful heart that all which it seemed possible to do, with due regard for the interests of the State as a whole, has been done within the last ten years for those who have their living to get. I felt I had to say all this to Your Highness and should like moreover to assure you that, with the middle class as a whole, the skilled artisans in particular will remain ever faithful to the memory of the Fourth Imperial Chancellor who has done so much on their behalf.

The letter I received from Julius Kopsch, the Berlin President of the Party Organization of the People's Progressive Party, contained in it that trend of opinion which, three years later, was to lead on to the election results of 1912.

Will Your Highness permit a plain deputy of the Independent People's Party to send you this belated farewell, accompanied by the confident hope that, not long hence, we may see you in your old place in the Reichstag again? Herr von Heydebrand and his adherents will wish they had not been so victorious. The leadership in any majority always falls to that section of it which can dispose of the necessary skill and industry. This industry is lacking to the Conservatives, and they have not the necessary practical ability. Whatever they lack is abundantly possessed by the Centre Party, so that, in spite of all that Herr von Heydebrand may assert, the leadership will soon be in the hands of Messrs. Spahn and Erzberger. But whoever had to witness Herr Spahn's intrigues and the brutal pushfulness of Herr Erzberger at the sittings of the Budget Commission, can say, without claiming to be a prophet, that every decent Conservative will soon look back regretfully to the time when he could work side by side with honourable Liberals. Innumerable meetings have shown me what the German people really feels. Herr von Heydebrand's sense of power, which for long has been far too openly expressed not only in his dealings with the Government but even towards the Throne itself, will have done the Conservative cause no good. Your Highness, on the other hand, retires, as I hope only temporarily, accompanied by the thanks and gratitude of the greater, and certainly not the least estimable, part of the German nation.

The Union of Evangelical Workers' Associations elected me its honorary member, and so did the Union of Patriotic Workers' Societies. I was deeply grateful to them both.

More even than these political tributes did those received from soldiers rejoice my heart. My whole soul had been with the army, from that day when I first donned the king's coat, in that year of glory, 1870. Field Marshal General von Hahnke, for many years the head of the Military Cabinet, and the pattern of a true Prussian Foot Guardsman, wrote to me on July 14, 1909.

I should not like to be missing from those innumerable people who must be writing to let you know their deep esteem and respect on this ominous day when you relinquish your Commander's baton as Imperial Chancellor. Any one with the slightest inkling of how much will power, courage, insight, and experience — what knowledge and self-sacrificing ability — are required for an Imperial Chancellor's struggle on behalf of the power, honour, and well-being of his Fatherland, must acknowledge quite openly to-day that Your Highness has been a true Chancellor, a true fighter. These qualities needed for your office require at the same time that you should serve the monarch devotedly in the most difficult of conceivable circumstances. Valiantly as Your Highness has fought, you have resigned your command with equal pride and dignity and have earned a thousand times the freedom and rest which now await you.

This old Field Marshal knew, better than anybody, how hard it had been to defend for twelve years the lasting interests of the country, the dynasty, and the monarch, often against that monarch himself.

Field Marshal General Karl von Bülow, at that time an Infantry General, wrote on July 15, 1909:

As your cousin, and a representative of all the Bülows, I want to shake hands with you most cordially, after these last days, so rich in decisions. I think I may say that I speak on behalf of every member of the family when I tell you how sorry we all are that circumstances should have forced Your Highness to retire from the highest office in the State, though we all hope that this may not be the end of your successful work for the Fatherland. I know that if ever in future it is required of you by Emperor and Fatherland — and be assured that later they will have need of you — that you use your great strength again to shoulder the burden of the chancellorship, Your Highness will do so joyfully. But even to-day it is, and will ever remain, another laurel in the Bülow crown that Your Highness should have been such a Chancellor. The Bülows are all proud of such a member.

Count Hermann Wartensleben, the Cavalry General, once Quarter-master General of the German Southern Army when, under the command of General von Manteuffel, in the famous battle among the snow and ice, it forced the Bourbaki Corps to take refuge in Switzerland, wrote:

"Since here in the country I am naturally cut off from full information, and so cannot judge of the motives which impelled you to so ominous a step, I can only say: 'A great loss to the Fatherland — and who in the world can ever replace Your Highness!'"

The widow of my never forgotten colonel of 1870, Field Marshal von Loë, the Baroness Franziska Loë (née Countess Hatzfeld-Trachenberg), wired me as follows: "I congratulate you and the Princess, and pity the rest of us."

From a place which cherished ideals other than those of military glory Frau Daniela Thode, the eldest daughter of the nearly seventy-year-old Frau Cosima Wagner, wrote to my wife on her mother's behalf and on her own :

DEAR AND EVER-HONOURED PRINCESS MARIE,

We think, and have been thinking, so much about you and the Prince that we cannot refrain from sending you our most respectful greetings. Mamma, who, alas, is not so well again, and needs rest and careful looking after, has been able to follow all these momentous (and unpleasant !) recent political developments with the keenest interest, and begs me to send you her best love. The whole of Wahnfried sends you messages.

Three other letters of sympathy from women moved me. The widow of Von Bötticher, the late Minister of State, who had died two years previously, wrote :

Your Highness I am sure, will not take it amiss, if I say to you and to the Princess, who have both been so indescribably good to me, that I pray to God to grant you His very special blessing, at the moment of your retirement from your difficult and responsible office. I know so well how hard it is for a man to turn away from his life's work. I went through it all with my own dear husband, in July, 1897. Though endless love, sympathy, and friendship accompany you from the whole German people, I hope you will not mind counting me also among those who think of you with gratitude in their hearts.

My successor's aunt, Frau Freda von Bethmann-Hollweg, wrote to me :

You, my dear Prince, have always struggled in a spirit of devoted self-sacrifice. Such a spirit is its own most perfect recompense, though in your case it will ever be remembered in the annals of our German Fatherland ! Those fights are certainly worst of all in which we cannot show our wounds. You can imagine how much it has moved, and still pre-occupies me, to see my nephew assume your burden of office. May God be with him !

Finally I received a letter from the mother of my faithful colleague Loebell, an old lady of eighty-four, who wrote :

I shall never forget that moment, nine years ago, at which I and my dear late husband welcomed Your Highness' appointment to the chancellorship, for which we had both of us hoped so much, with such high expectations for Kaiser and Empire.   My husband went to his reward in the knowledge that all these hopes had been fulfilled.   But I have had to remain, as the sorrowful witness of your retirement, and my old heart, which loves my country, has been deeply grieved at the motives of those who have impelled you to it.

As soon as I was quite certain I should retire I had written to request our representatives in every important foreign post to thank on my behalf the sovereigns to whose courts they were accredited for the confidence I had always received from them in my conduct of foreign affairs.   The Russian Foreign Minister Alexander Petrovitch Isvolski answered me in a long personal letter :

Le chargé d'affaires d'Allemagne, le Comte de Mirbach, m'a fait part de Votre désir qu'au moment où Vous quittez le poste élevé que Vous avez occupé avec tant d'éclat, je fasse parvenir à mon Auguste Maître les sentiments d'attachement et de reconnaissance que Vous portez à Sa Majesté.   Je n'ai pas manqué de m'acquitter auprès de Sa Majesté de ce message, et je suis heureux de Vous transmettre les sincères remercîments de l'Empereur qui m'a ordonné en même temps de Vous exprimer combien Il a toujours apprécié Votre brillante et féconde activité et Vos efforts en faveur des bonnes relations entre la Russie et l'Allemagne.   Le Comte de Mirbach m'a également transmis ce dont Vous avez bien voulu le charger personnellement à mon adresse.   J'en ai été éxtremement touché, et je tiens à Vous dire, a mon tour, que je garderai toujours un souvenir inéffaçable de mes relations personnelles avec Vous, relations qui datent de si loin et qui j'espère vont se continuer pendant de longues années encore.   J'ai la certitude que ces relations ont apporté leur part de grande utilité à la bonne entente entre nos deux pays. C'est de tout mon cœur que je partage Votre contentement de ce qui a été fait en dernier lieu pour raffermir cette bonne entente et pour donner aux rapports entre la Russie et l'Allemagne un caractère d'entière confiance si conforme aux meilleurs traditions de leur histoire.   Vous savez combien je suis désireux de travailler dans ce sens et combien je suis persuadé qu'il n'existe, ni ne peut exister, aucune cause directe de malentendus entre nos Gouvernements.   Dieu veuille que les causes indirectes qui ont produit tant d'alarmes l'hiver dernier ne se reproduisent plus.   Laissez moi, mon cher Prince,

Vous assurer que mes sentiments de profonde admiration et de vraie amitié Vous accompagneront dans la nouvelle phase de Votre belle existence, dans laquelle je Vous souhaite de tout cœur de trouver repos et santé. Veuillez, je Vous prie, me mettre aux pieds de la Princesse de Bülow et agreez pour Vous même l'hommage de mon dévouement le plus sincère.

What caught my attention in this letter was the sentence: "*Dieu veuille que les causes indirectes qui ont produit tant d'alarmes l'hiver dernier ne se reproduisent plus.*" This sentence strengthened my conviction that friendly relationships between Germany and Russia had every chance of being preserved, and, along with them, the peace of the whole world. We, however, must be on our guard to avoid crossing the Russian path in the Dardanelles; nor must we allow Austria to oppose Russia in the Balkan Peninsula in a fashion which neither Tsar nor Tsardom could accept, without imperilling the dynasty, because it ran counter to century-old Russian tradition. At my last meeting with Bethmann-Hollweg on the eve of my departure from Berlin, I copied in a clear round hand on my visiting card these words of Alexander Isvolski and left them as a final admonition to prudence and circumspection with my successor. More than once had I warned both William II and Bethmann-Hollweg against clumsy attempts to repeat the policy by which I had managed to resolve the Bosnian crisis. To both, though without affording either much satisfaction, I repeated that old tag from Roman law, *Ne bis in idem*, as well as the neat little epigram from Terence, *Duo cum faciunt idem, non est idem*.

Aloys Lexa von Aehrenthal, who became a count as a reward for his success in having come so well out of the Bosnian crisis, thanks to our good support, wrote to me:

Most honoured Prince, Szögyényi assures me that your decision to retire remains unalterable, and that very soon we may expect the Imperial endorsement. I have looked forward with trepidation to this moment, and now, since it approaches nearer and nearer, I am filled with sincere and deep regret. I refrain from going more fully into the reasons which have caused you to take such a step. These must certainly have been compelling to have brought the Emperor William to the point of parting with you after so long a time in office and so many successes in all departments. You can look back with pride, my dear Prince, on these years devoted to Kaiser and Fatherland, and lay down your high office in the assurance that you have furthered Germany's development in every branch of her activities, and strengthened her structure as a State. We in Austria-Hungary are sincerely sorry to see you go, since we saw in you a convinced and tried representative of those ideas that have inspired the alliance between the two Empires. In this connection I have a commission to discharge from my All Gracious Master. His Majesty, the Emperor Francis Joseph, having learnt from Szögyényi's memorandum the tenor of his last interview with Your Highness, has commanded me to tell you that he will always remember most gratefully both Prince Bülow and his fidelity to the Alliance.

Tommasso Tittoni, the Italian Foreign Minister, sent me a long letter which I here reproduce in translation.

DEAR PRINCE AND FRIEND:

I have just received Your Highness' letter. Many thanks for all the charming things contained in it. I hope you will forgive my answering you in Italian, a language that Your Highness knows and loves. Your Highness was so good as to express all the kindness which has ever characterized our personal relationships as well as the sympathy you invariably have shown my country, ever since you first came to live in it. As Ambassador in Rome, Minister for Foreign Affairs, and Imperial Chancellor, you have never failed to harmonize Italian interests with German. It is thanks to you that the alliance between our two countries has remained so firm through the whole of your time in office, and that we have always managed to steer our course amid the shoals of many delicate situations. In observing the treaties Your Highness has ever shown the same good-will and loyalty to Italy which you yourself had every right to expect from her, and these sentiments we have reciprocated no less spontaneously and trustfully. Though Your Highness has seen fit to retire from your responsible post, accompanied by the esteem of your Sovereign and surrounded by universal respect and admiration, you still remain the leading personality in German politics. My political egotism therefore impels me to regard you still as a valued colleague to whom I, or whoever else may hold my post in future, can turn in the full assurance that our good-will towards you will be answered. Your Highness' letter makes me hope that your intention to seek repose in Rome will not entail a mere temporary residence there. Here you will not merely be able to resume the habits of the past and, with all your splendid talents, renew old friendships, but you will grow to understand our mentality and appreciate the impressions you receive from us. Your Highness has shown yourself not merely an admirer of our history; you are also firmly convinced both of our present and future significance to Germany. Now since you will be living among us, you will be able to witness our efforts to continue in an honourable peace and assure yourself of the moderation of our international policy and the justice of Italian aspirations; since these are not only apparent in the official acts of our Government but in the attitude of the whole Italian nation. I am certain that the esteem and sympathy with which Your Highness has ever honoured us will only increase in Rome. I shall hasten to give Their Majesties the King and Queen and Her Majesty the Queen Mother, the assurance of esteem and good-will you wished me to transmit to them. I will also give your very friendly message to the Onoreveole Giolitti and all our other mutual friends. As a Minister, an Italian, and a friend I greet you cordially.

Two days later, Tittoni wired:

Leurs Majestés le Roi et la Reine me telegraphient: Nous sommes très sensibles aux expressions contenues dans la lettre du Prince de Bülow. Nous vous prions de lui exprimer nos vifs remercîments. Sa Majesté la Reine mère me telegraphie: Je vous prie d'envoyer mes salutations des plus amicales et affectueuses au Prince de Bülow pour lequel j'ai toujours eu une estime profonde.

When the party constellations in the Reichstag began to be of such a sort that my retirement became a possibility, while at the same time I felt every day less certain of the Kaiser, I had written a long memorandum to our Ambassador in London, Count Metternich, to put him *au courant* of the situation in Berlin. At the end of my letter I had said: "I regret that I may have to retire before I have achieved an understanding with England on the question of naval construction." Not only was I in favour of such an agreement but, provided it were made under conditions with which Metternich was familiar, it seemed to me essential to both countries. I also believed, I said, that had I remained longer in office, I should have been able to bring it about; just as, after many ups and downs, I had reached such an understanding on the Morocco question as had placed our relationships with France on a sounder basis. Nevertheless, I concluded, I am sure that Schön, who is full of the best intentions, will not deviate from the policy laid down by me, and I am handing it over to him in perfect order. The supposition that other motives or factors besides that of an unfavourable party constellation in the Reichstag had impelled me to resign was beside the point. I had to the very end of my chancellorship enjoyed the full confidence of His Majesty, who saw my departure with regret. I had advised both Schön and His Majesty most urgently to keep Count Metternich at his post, in the interests of our relationship with England.

My reason for suggesting in this letter that my resignation was solely due to the Reichstag, and in no way to the attitude of the Emperor, was my unwillingness to expose the Gracious Person of my Sovereign, more especially in the eyes of this German Ambassador, to England. My favourable report on Schön was, alas, not justified by his further political activities. As soon as my retirement was accomplished I begged Metternich to present my thanks to the King and Queen of England for all the friendship they had both graciously shown me for many years. To Metternich himself I added that, personally, I did not mind in the least resigning after twelve years in office, to pass the evening of my days by the Elbe and the historic Tiber, as a free man. Only one Chancellor, our great and unforgettable Bismarck, had remained any longer in office; Manteuffel had not remained so long and Hardenberg's time had been the same.

Metternich answered my letter on July 19, 1909:

In obedience to instructions received in your letter of the 9th inst. I took occasion, a few days ago, to assure Their Majesties of your gratitude for Their good-will and friendship towards you, which has persisted for so many years. Both Sovereigns spoke most cordially of the long personal friendship they had enjoyed with you. The King remarked that Her Majesty had even known you as a boy. Both enquired with lively interest as to your plans for the future, and I explained and described your intention, and that of the Princess, to establish your future residence on the banks of the Elbe, in Norderney, and in your Villa Malta, which you purchased some years ago, in Rome. Our conversation ended by my receiving special instructions from His Majesty to present you with his very best wishes for your future health and well-being. I was to say that he hopes that you will enjoy your new freedom to the full.

Mr. Hill, the American Ambassador in Berlin, who, for some trivial reason, on his appointment had been most ungraciously received by William II, but whom I, in the interests of Germany, had been careful always to treat with friendship, if only because in his own country he had a strong position, and many friends, wrote to me:

My dear Prince von Bülow,

Your very kind personal note of farewell written at the moment of your departure from Berlin was forwarded to me and received at Geneva. I beg Your Serene Highness to accept from me my thanks for our official relations, which have been to me a source of the greatest satisfaction and are not interrupted without a sense of loss and sincere regret. I shall never cease to remember with gratitude the cordial reception I received from you upon my arrival in Berlin and I hope I have some occasion to demonstrate the sincere affection I feel for the great Empire which you have so long and faithfully served. Please remember me most kindly to Her Serene Highness Princess von Bülow and believe me faithfully yours,

David S. Hill.

From the Austrian side the Ambassador, Count Szögyényi, was instructed to present me with the warmest thanks of the Imperial and Royal Government for my never-failing loyalty to the Alliance and no less for my generally "enlightened" policy. The good Count discharged his commission with much emphasis. The semi-official *Wiener Fremdenblatt* devoted to me a rhetorical article, containing the following:

Prince Bülow always knew how to live in his age. Through his foreign, as through his domestic policy, there ran the same unerring thread of logic, perceptible under every apparent twist and turn. Germany knows how much she is losing in von Bülow, but we too are most unwilling to say farewell to him.

The Clerico-Feudal "Black-Yellow" Vienna *Vaterland* wrote:

With Prince Bülow there retires from public life a statesman of marked individuality, who knew how to invest even his policy with his characteristics as a man. We can only hope that it may also be granted his successor to remain on such pleasant terms with Austria-Hungary, since the guarantee of European peace is a reasonable German attitude in foreign affairs.

It was fairly evident, however, that in spite of all these outward tributes, my retirement had, in reality, caused Vienna to rejoice rather than grieve. This was not merely the feeling of such firebrands as General Conrad von Hötzendorf, who resented the fact that I had always energetically discouraged their longing for "a bright, brisk little war", — to-day against Russia or Italy, to-morrow against Serbia or Roumania; it was also the consensus of opinion with Austrian ministers, politicians, and diplomats, and this in spite of the many services I had rendered the Habsburg Monarchy.

But reasons were not far to seek. In my dealings with the Dual Monarchy, I had never forgotten my favourite axiom of Prince Talleyrand, — that the relationship in every alliance is that of a horse and rider. I had always considered it important to be the rider in my dealings with Austrian ministers and had understood how to remain so. As rider, therefore, I would permit no misplaced curvettings and prancings and, more especially during the Bosnian crisis, had always sharply discouraged the bellicose whimsys of Vienna and Budapest. I had so guided our policy in this crisis that, while strengthening and supporting Austria, I refused to allow Germany to be estranged from, or perhaps even driven to war with, Russia solely on Austria's behalf. The Austrian historian Friedjung who, in spite of all his feeling for Germany, and his German culture, was at heart a Conservative Austrian, sums up in the following bittersweet remarks the results of the Bosnian crisis, in his book on the Age of Imperialism. "Whereas Austria-Hungary did not emerge unscathed from the Bosnian crisis, Germany was left in the full enjoyment of her hard-won triumph in 1909. Bülow even managed to remain on almost friendly terms with Isvolski."

Finally I had never tolerated Austrian attempts to sabotage our policy in the Eastern Marches. Such attempts were always being made, partly by Prince Max Furstenberg, in direct contact with William II; partly through social channels, by Szögyényi.

This lack of any real affection for me in the breasts of the younger members of the Austrian *corps diplomatique* found almost grotesque expression in a banquet given by the more aristocratic members of the Centre Party, in a big Berlin hotel, to celebrate my retirement from the chancellorship, and to which the secretaries and attachés of the Austro-Hungarian Embassy all accepted invitations. Count Hans Oppersdorff presided at this feast of victory and rejoicing. He was eminently qualified to do so since, at that time a Centre deputy, he went over, in after years, to the party of the Poles and traitors to Germany. Count Szögyényi called on me at once, as soon as he heard of this celebration, to assure me how deeply he regretted it. The culprits had been severely reprimanded, etc. But it is clear enough, from the Viennese archives, published in 1918 on the fall of the Monarchy, that at the time of Prince Bismarck's fall, Count Emmerich Széchényi, then Austro-Hungarian Ambassador in Berlin, was not ill pleased by the event. I am therefore in excellent company, as far as the emotions aroused by me in many Austrian breasts are concerned.

From Vienna I received a letter from the writer Alfred von Berger, at one time director of the Deutsches Schauspielhaus in Hamburg, and at that time of the Vienna Hofburgtheater. He wrote:

Innumerable expressions of opinion have shown me how much admiration and confidence go with you into private life from all sections of the German people, other than those whose vision is distorted by Reichstag intrigues and party feeling. Many will rejoice at the thought that you can rest at the zenith of your powers, since this gives them the hope that Germany will not lack a wise and experienced leader in those stormy days ahead, of which they already feel the sick presentiment.

From Blankenese I heard from my neighbour and near compatriot, Gustav Frenssen, the poet and author of "Jörn Uhl" and "Drei Getruen": "I whose delight it is to ponder and relate the lives of sterling people must be one of those who write to thank you for all that you have done for the country.   In the devotion and esteem of many years, I remain your, Gustav Frenssen."

Another poet-friend, Adolf Wildbrandt, wrote as follows:

My dear, and very honoured Friend,

For many days I have been wondering whether to write to you.   Few things have been more difficult to decide !   What a fate for Germany — that you will soon have ceased to be her chancellor !   And for me ! Since few people can have felt more deeply than I what you were, and how very much you meant to us !   What sort of Conservatives have we got !   Or rather — how are they being led !   I am dismayed !   Something inside me keeps repeating : "He 'll come back !   Within four, or at most five years, we shall see him back in the Wilhelmstrasse !"   And I hope we shall.

Gerhart Hauptmann, too, in cordial terms, expressed his regret at my retirement, his friendship and sympathy.   The Librarian of the Wartburg, the poet, Richard Voss, wired to my wife : "Deeply, and with the whole nation, I mourn this misfortune to Germany, who has lost both you and her chancellor."

From Switzerland, where he had gone on sick leave, I heard from Ernst von Dryander, the Chief Court Chaplain, and Superintendent General of the Electoral March who, in spite of his many years of intimacy with William II, wrote as follows:

Your Highness will not, I hope, think me presumptuous if I write here from the mountains, where news always reaches a few days late, to tell you how very deeply, and at the same time painfully, I sympathize with you in all these recent happenings in politics.   I am really impelled to express my fullest agreement with Your Highness in the matter of this quite unintelligible and, in my opinion, unwarranted attitude of the Conservative Party, whose Chaplain I am in the Upper House, — and also to thank you most heartily for your brilliant and resolute guidance of the Fatherland.   I can merely regret that these bold and admirable schemes for the reform of Imperial finances should merely end as they have done, in our loss (apart from any other we may sustain) of the strong, clearsighted guidance of Your Highness.

Adolf von Harnack, now that the Imperial sun of favour, in whose rays he delighted to bask, no longer shone on me, had begun, by cau-

tious degrees, to seem less cordial. He wrote me the following pleasant little letter, — but merely in reply to my wife's invitation to
stay with us next year at the Villa Malta, when his pastoral duties
led him to Rome:

MOST HONOURED PRINCE AND EQUALLY HONOURED VON BÜLOW!

Allow me to thank you for all your kindness, for all your trust and
friendship which have made me so happy. Let me thank you too for
having infused the spirit of freedom and humanity into our State, in
spite of its cast-iron bureaucracy; — that patient and joyous freedom
inspired to do so much good and bear with so much ill, as love is inspired.
It is just this freedom which will enable you, and the dear and deeply
honoured Princess, ever to triumph over fate. *Debellantes inimicos ab
amicis prodimur.* (As we fight down our enemies our friends betray us.)
Such is the traditional fate of heroes. But what you have done cannot be
destroyed, it must remain. Some of it is already effective, some is a
presage of the future. In deepest devotion and friendship,

Ever Your Highness',
VON HARNACK.

Malvida von Meysenbug, the life-long friend of both myself and
my wife, who had died six years previously, on April 26, 1903, had,
as every reader of her "Memoiren einer Idealistin" knows, adopted
a daughter, Olga Herzen, whose father had been a Russian Left Wing
journalist and agitator, Alexander Ivanovitch Herzen. He was
the son of a Russian Prince Jakovleff, and of a Swabian girl, Luis-
chen Haag of Stuttgart. Herzen had been sent to Siberia by the
Tsar Nicholas I, for having read Hegel. Alexander II reprieved him,
but only to intern him in Novgorod. From there he managed to
fly to London, where he published his monthly review *Kolokol* (*The
Bell*): — the first review to raise a storm against Tsarism (which
till then had only been opposed by palace revolutions and nobles'
conspiracies) in the name of the great principles of the French Revolution. Malvida had married her adopted daughter to a very distinguished French *savant* and historian, Gabriel Monod, the editor
of the *Revue Historique*, and head of the École Normale in Paris.
Though a patriotic Frenchman, Monod, on humanitarian grounds,
and those of logic, was an outspoken pacifist. He wrote to my wife:

Nous avons suivi les événements de la dernière semaine avec une vive sympathie, sympathie qui n'était pas seulement dictée par notre amitié pour Monsieur de Bülow et pour Vous, mais aussi par la conviction que la politique de M. de Bülow était aussi utile aux intérêts généraux de la civilisation qu'aux intérêts spéciaux de l'Allemagne. Beaucoup de mes compatriotes en jugent autrement que moi et croient que la politique du Chancelier était étroitement nationale et inspirée par des sentiments hostiles à la France et à l'Angleterre. J'ai toujours soutenu vis-à-vis des amis qui pensaient ainsi que si M. de Bülow, comme c'était son devoir, mettait les intérêts permanents de l'Allemagne au premier rang de ses préoccupations, il regardait le maintien de la paix comme le premier de ses intérêts, et considérait les bons rapports de la France avec l'Allemagne comme nécessaires au maintien de la paix. Bien loin qu'il ait jamais cherché à troubler ces rapports, je suis persuadé que son action personnelle a toujours tendu à éviter les imprudences qui pouvait la compromettre. Mais toute politique à part, car chaque pays et chaque Ministre a le droit d'entendre ses devoirs à sa manière, nous avons constamment pensé à vous pendant cette crise, souffrant pour Vous de ce qu'elle a pu avoir de pénible, et nous nous sommes aussi réjouis que M. de Bülow puisse après ces années de dur et utile labeur jouir d'un repos bien mérité.

At the request of the Voluntary Association for the Promotion of Jewish Interests to which, in a wider sphere of activities, I had always been as well disposed as was my dear father before me in the little Grand Duchy of Mecklenburg-Strelitz, the Rabbi, Doctor Breuer, sent me the following telegram:

In this moment in which Your Highness is about to retire from public life after ten years of unflagging activities for the good of the Fatherland, may I offer you from the bottom of my heart, in the name of all Jewish Conservative and orthodox bodies throughout Germany, our deepest thanks for the good-will that you have shown towards our religious interests. In particular do we wish to thank you heartily for the kind way in which, last year in Norderney, you listened to the case laid before you by our Vice President for the necessity of Sabbath rest, which means so much to us. We have commissioned this same Vice President, now in Norderney, to thank you personally and at the same time to convey to you the blessings of all law-abiding Jews, and their best wishes for Your Highness' future well-being.

The editor in chief of the *Frankfurter Zeitung*, Theodor Curti, wrote:

I cannot refrain from telling you how much I deplore your resignation. For a long time it has been apparent in many sections of the German nation that there was the will and strong desire to bridge the abyss between the parties and reach some new understanding which might lead to another régime. This great hope, now unfulfilled, was linked to the authority of your name. I shared it and ever rejoiced to think that a man of such distinguished attainments, devoted to the service of the State, had made his name a national possession. I think therefore that I may join my voice to those many powerful voices now raised to deplore your resignation. I remain in full esteem,

Your very devoted
CURTI.

The *Frankfurter Zeitung* had attacked me sharply on occasion, during my chancellorship, and particularly my economic policy. Its editor at the time was by birth a Swiss. That is perhaps the reason why he judged me and my activities with an absence of prejudice, unusual towards one's party opponents in Germany.

I have already mentioned a Swiss friend who lived in Paris, and who even there had remained true to his pacifist ideals. He had many political connections, not only in France. He had already written on July 1, 1909:

I am all the more depressed and disturbed by what is happening in Berlin since I can trace every hidden thread, and know what is going on behind the scenes. Nor am I ignorant of a determination long since reached by one of the most powerful factors — indeed at present an all-powerful factor — in Germany. Nobody can usefully replace Prince Bülow; especially at a time like this, pregnant with the gravest decisions for the whole future of the world. In Germany there are many *dii minorum gentium*, but no politician like Prince Bülow! This should be realized in a certain quarter.

The "most powerful factor" was naturally William II.

These verses from an unknown hand reached me on the day I left Berlin:

Fürst Bülow

Er scheidet aus dem Amt, des er gewaltet
Mit kluger Kraft und einer feinen Kunst.
Was er geschaut, gewollt hat und gestaltet,
Hoch ragt es über Launenspiel und Gunst.
Ein ganzer Mensch! Sein Name wird nicht schwinden
Vom Meilenstein der ruhelosen Zeit.
Er, dem selbstmörderisch die blöden Blinden
Den Lorbeer flochten der Undankbarkeit.
Ein Mann des Glücks für seiner Heimat Ehre,
Des Glücks für seines eignen Wesens Art,
So ghet er fort in Waffenschmuck und Wehre,
Die Sonne leuchtet seiner Lebenfahrt.[1]

My resignation sent a wind of opinion rustling through the leaves of the German Press. It is not given to Germans, as it is to French, Italians, and Englishmen, to judge any statesman who has merited something of his country, and played some part in public life, more by his good points than his defects, more by his successes than his failures, and class him according to the former in the national Pantheon. In Germany we love destructive criticism, very often petty and narrow-minded, more often still of a philistine, lower-middle-class character. The *Kreuzzeitung*, however, while deploring my difference of opinion with the Conservative party, added:

In foreign policy the fourth Chancellor found himself faced with a formidable task of maintaining our continental position in face of all the difficulties with which Bismarck had already had to struggle. But to

[1] To Prince von Bülow.
He turns from those high matters that obeyed
His penetrating skill and subtle art.
What he had seen, defined, informed, and swayed
Untouched by fear or favour, stands apart.
He was a man! His name shall ever be
A milestone in the weary stretch of time;
He whom base fools in malice, from the tree
Of self-destroying, blind ingratitude,
Have crowned with evil laurels; — who has stood
With honour for his country's happiness; —
A man who brought good fortune to his kind,
Who goes his way in panoplied success,
And lighted by the sun of his own mind.

these in his case there was added the task, now a very delicate one, of maintaining good relationships with England, Japan, and America, in spite of the development of our overseas interests, our export industry, and increased foreign commerce. Prince Bülow succeeded magnificently. No intelligent opponent of this Chancellor has ever tried to contest these services. The Pan-Germans often made it very difficult for him to remain on good terms with England. In the Morocco affair with equal zeal and clumsiness, the Independents strove to upset his plans. But this Chancellor's quiet caution nearly always set aside these obstacles, so that his guidance of our foreign policy, even at the stormiest moments, produced at home a feeling of absolute security and evoked more astonished tributes to his success in other countries than in Germany. Much has been said of Prince von Bülow's "aesthetism", of his skill as an orator, his gestures. But he was a better artist when he said nothing and proceeded to act in silence. The results of such occasions could dumbfound the most carping and pedantic of critics.

Though I had of course to be thankful for such recognition as I received from my countrymen in the German Press, the pregnant remarks of several foreign and in particular of several great English newspapers, afforded me more satisfaction from the standpoint of the *argumentum e contrario*. That organ of the English Foreign Office, the *Morning Post*, wrote of my retirement as follows:

"It is unpleasant for any opponent of Prince Bülow to have to admit, as he must admit, that it is many years since Germany has been so powerful and influential as at present."

The *London Daily Telegraph* opined:

"Prince von Bülow goes out of office having done more than any other man to guide the German State successfully through a period of unusual difficulty."

In its leader this great English newspaper added:

"To-day German power is relatively as preponderant in Europe as it was throughout the strongest phases of Bismarckian government. It is above all a fact that at the moment the German Empire is in every way more splendid, stronger, and more prosperous than it was when Prince von Bülow took office."

In English eyes, the London newspaper continued, the most note-worthy thing about Prince von Bülow was that he, a statesman without parliamentary experience, had at once revealed himself, with the sole exception of Clemenceau, the best parliamentary speaker on the Continent. But besides his gifts as an orator, he had shown himself possessed of a fund of sound human understanding in the conduct of practical affairs. The article ended with regrets that, now Prince Bülow was retired, the personal initiative of the Kaiser would most likely become, more than formerly, the preponderant influence in the State. The Chancellor's personal relationship to his Sovereign had grown every day more strained. This, in the interests of peace, was to be deplored, since the temporary activities and expert statecraft of Prince Bülow might well be revealed as having been of the highest value.

I was very much amused by the following sketch in the Paris *Figaro*:

"A perfect acrobat, Pied Piper and tight-rope dancer, — brilliant at improvisations — unprejudiced, but utterly unscrupulous. By nature inclined to be indolent, but with a will kept always alert by the instinct of self-preservation; amazingly adroit at twists and turns. Certainly never the man to be thrown into despair by changes of opinion or contradictions."

The very anti-German *Temps*, the most influential of French newspapers, ended its article, acknowledging the many personal qualities of Prince von Bülow, with the following remark on his foreign policy:

"Even those, and France is among them, who did not always derive satisfaction from him, cannot shut their eyes to his achievements. At least they remember that he always was sufficiently pliable to avoid the acutest crises into which trifles might always have thrown France and Germany."

I had never concealed the fact that I considered the Eastern Marches question the most important question of Prussian policy; that I saw it as a matter of life or death to the German people and intended to handle it as such. From no quarter of the Fatherland did I receive so many hearty regrets at my retirement as from the Eastern frontiers of the Monarchy. Among them there were certainly many letters in which an undertone of anxiety for the future of the Eastern Marches was unmistakable. The German Eastern Marches Association wired:

"In the history of the century-old struggle for the Eastern Marches, Prince von Bülow's name will ever receive first place as the true champion of Germanization."

Particularly hearty were those messages I received from the city of Bromberg, which years ago had presented me with its freedom. Since then, weighed down with the cares and sorrows of the present, I have remembered these Bromberg citizens and their greeting. *Nessun maggior dolore che ricordarsi del tempo felice nella miseria.* The then flourishing, and in the vast majority of its citizens, German city of Bromberg, rejoices to-day in the name of Bydgocz. The German schools there are suppressed, the German shops and businesses closed down. Hundreds of German officials, teachers, shopkeepers, and skilled artisans have been driven out. These true representatives of all that is best in the German middle classes were forced to leave their once so prosperous city, — a city which in 1772 the great King had released from Polish misery and enslavement.

In contrast to the Landowners' Association, solely devoted to stirring up discontent, and which had put up so stubborn an opposition to my death duties, I enjoyed to the very end the help and support of the German Agrarian Council, whose invaluable president the Reichstag — and Landtag — deputy Count Hans von Schwerin-Löwitz, assured me on retirement of the "unalterable and undivided" gratitude of all German landowners. The following telegram from Albert Ballin, the Director in Chief of the Hamburg-America Line, shows that at least I had not failed in my attempt to foster the interests of German foreign commerce, overseas trade, and industry:

The period of Your Highness' chancellorship has witnessed the greatest development, the richest harvest ever reaped in Germany by industry, trade and overseas traffic. Every representative of industrial and commercial progress will be ever grateful to Your Highness for the care you have shown for Germany's economic interests. As a tribute to what you have done, I intend to propose to the Hamburg-America Line that our next great steamer be christened the "*Fürst von Bülow.*"

The Alma Mater Berolinensis sent its "true friend and unprejudiced disciple of science" its most cordial farewell messages, together with "thousands of wishes for a long and happy evening of your life enhanced by the gratitude of all Germans."

The Academy of Posen begged me to accept its honorary membership. It had always esteemed me as an active co-founder and supporter.

The Bench of Magistrates of Berlin decided to re-christen the Babelsberger Platz which henceforth should be called Fürst Bülow Platz.

INDEX

INDEX

ADALBERT, PRINCE, son of William II, leaves Kiel at the revolution, 335

Adrianople, taken by Bulgarians, 127

Aehrenthal, Count Aloys Lexa von, Austro-Hungarian Minister of Foreign Affairs, and Isvolski, 144; on von Bülow's retirement, 397

Agadir, 98–100, 125, 126, 201, 202

Albanians, 364

Albedyll, Emil von, 30, 180

Albert, King of Bavaria, 337

Alexander I, Tsar, 157, 196

Alexander II, Tsar, 405

Alexandra, Queen of England, her answer to von Bülow's telegram of condolence, 98

Alizé, M., French Minister in Munich, 200

Alma Mater Berolinensis, on von Bülow's retirement, 412

Almereyda, editor of *Bonnet Rouge*, 288

Alsace-Lorraine, 295, 305, 310

Altenstein, Baron von, 342

Amelia, Duchess, 78

Americans, in the war, 311

Amerongen, 329, 330

Amphill, Lord, English Ambassador in Berlin, 276

Anglo-German Club, 149

Anglo-German relations, 17, 18, 59, 138, 139, 141, 152

Arenberg, Prince Franz, 6

Armistice of Compiègne, 348–351

Arndt, Ernst Moritz, 112, 228

Auer, Ignaz, 336

Augusta, Empress, 111

Augusta Victoria, Empress, at Potsdam, 71; birthday soirée, 72; her telegram that "the situation was very serious", 159; telegram of Emperor to, 194; receives Jagow, 219; her anger at England, 221; entertains the von Bülows at luncheon, 267; eager for reinstatement of von Bülow, 293; keeps

Emperor in dark as to true situation, 314; at Amerongen, 325, 326

Austria-Hungary, check on policy of, needed, 96; policy in Balkans, 128; danger in German alliance, 129; planned anti-Serbian *coup* in 1913, 144; ultimatum to Serbia, 158, 172, 173, 183, 187–189, 200–202, 211, 220, 221, 236, 250, 254, 259; given *carte blanche* by Germany, 175, 183, 200, 201, 236; intends to settle with Serbia, 176; breaks off relations with Serbia, 184; partially mobilizes against Serbia, 187; Italian policy of, 210–212, 257–259; makes effort for separate peace, 298, 309, 310; women in Vienna Court, 298

Austrian pride, 128

Avarna, Duke of, 212

BAGDAD RAILWAY, 290

Balkan League, 128

Balkans, war in, 126, 127; Austrian policy in, 128

Ballin, Albert, 139; meets von Bülow at Hamburg, 6; suggests conference between Tirpitz and Lord Fisher, 7; interview with Emperor, 7; accompanies von Bülow to Cuxhaven, 8; tells anecdote of Rathenau, 47; at Empress's birthday soirée, 72; his efforts to reconcile Emperor with von Bülow, 130; shaken by the war, 159; his description of scene in Chancellor's palace, 187; his advice not asked, 198; on the ultimatum, 199, 200; advises von Bülow not to send letter to Bethmann, 218; letter of von Bülow to, on Italian mission, 220, 221; letters to von Bülow on war situation, 221, 237, 238; on Erzberger, 233; on Berlin rulers, 272; on Bethmann, 288; on submarine warfare, 292; visits von Bülow at Flottbek, 313; at Head-

Redwood Library

SELECTIONS FROM THE RULES

Three volumes may be taken at a time
and three on one share. Two unbound
num of a monthly and three numbers of a
wee lication are counted as a volume.

other than 7-day and 14-day ones
ma out 28 days. **Books cannot be
re transferred.**

overdue are subject to a fine of one
y for fourteen days, **and five cents a
each day thereafter.**

glect to pay the fine will debar from
the Library.

book is to be lent out of the house of
to whom it is charged.

person who shall soil (deface) or
lose a book belonging to the Library
able to such fine as the Directors may
shall pay the value of the book or of
t be a part of a set, as the Directors
All scribbling or any marking or
atever, folding or turning down the
vell as cutting or tearing any matter
belonging to the Library, will be con-
cement and damage.